Managing
Industrial Development
Projects

VNR PROJECT MANAGEMENT

Series

PROJECT LEADERSHIP by Briner, Geddes, and Hastings

PROJECT MANAGEMENT DICTIONARY by Clelend and Kerzner

PROJECT MANAGEMENT HANDBOOK, 2E by Cleland and King

MANAGING PEOPLE FOR PROJECT SUCCESS by Culp and Smith

GETTING ORGANIZED WITH MACPROJECT II by Day

PROJECT MANAGEMENT: SUCCESSFUL SCHEDULING by Dreger

GUIDE TO COMPUTERIZED SCHEDULING by East and Kirby

PROJECT MANAGEMENT, 4E by Kerzner

MANAGING PROJECTS WITH MICROSOFT PROJECT FOR WINDOWS by Lowery

MANAGING PROJECTS WITH MICROSOFT PROJECTS 3.0 by Lowery

PROJECT MANAGEMENT FOR ENGINEERS by Rosenau

SUCCESSFUL PROJECT MANAGEMENT, 2E by Rosenau

MANAGING NEW PRODUCT DEVELOPMENT PROJECTS by Rosenau and Moran

MANAGING INDUSTRIAL DEVELOPMENT PROJECTS by Badiru

Managing Industrial Development Projects

A Project Management Approach

Adedeji Bodunde Badiru
School of Industrial Engineering,
University of Oklahoma

VNR PROJECT MANAGEMENT

Series

VNR VAN NOSTRAND REINHOLD
New York

I(T)P Van Nostrand Reinhold is a division of International Thomson Publishing. ITP logo is a trademark under license.

Printed in the United States of America.

Van Nostrand Reinhold
115 Fifth Avenue
New York, NY 10003

International Thomson Publishing
Berkshire House
168-173 High Holborn
London WC1V7AA, England

Thomas Nelson Australia
102 Dodds Street
South Melbourne 3205
Victoria, Australia

Nelson Canada
1120 Birchmount Road
Scarborough, Ontario
M1K 5G4, Canada

16 15 14 13 12 11 10 9 8 7 6 5 4 3 2 1

Library of Congress Cataloging-in-Publication Data

Badiru, Adedeji Bodunde, 1952-
    Managing industrial development projects : project management
approach / Adedeji Bodunde Badiru.
        p.   cm.
    Includes bibliographical references and index.
    ISBN 0-442-01087-7
    1. Industrial development projects.   2. Industrial project
management.   I. Title.
HD2329.B33   1993
338.9'0068—dc20   93-68
                                                                   CIP

To Iswat,
Mojirade Sikiratu Abidemi,
Kolawole Ibrahim Adetokunboh,
Omotunji Adedayo Taofiq, and
Late Hidayatu Omolade Bisola

Contents

Preface

Interest in project management has been growing steadily over the past several years. Business, industry, and academic institutions have been committing more and more resources to project-management efforts. Many professional organizations now offer regular project-management training workshops. The success of project-management techniques in traditional areas such as construction management has paved the way for innovative applications of the techniques in other problem areas such as quality improvement, manufacturing management, and industrial development. In the public sector, more and more communities are turning to project management for their public projects. Industrial development projects particularly need project-management techniques because of the complexity of the interactions required to implement the projects.

Industrial development is a problem that is faced by many nations and communities around the world. Even in developed countries such as the United States, there are pockets of local communities where industrial development is a primary goal. Despite the heightened interest in industrial development, there are few formal guidelines for public administrators and other professionals for managing industrial development projects. Industrial development has traditionally been managed within the framework of conventional public management philosophy. Unfortunately, such philosophies often have a limited and localized focus. The result is that the community or country pursuing industrial development finds itself unable to respond or adapt to the dynamism of modern and global markets. In today's integrated and international developments, no community can implement industrial development projects with complete disregard for the changing environment.

This book provides the necessary reference and guidelines for those involved (directly or indirectly) with industrial development projects. The nature of industrial development projects does require a proven model that practitioners can follow when confronted with complex industrial development problems. The techniques of project management, if properly packaged, can provide a powerful tool for managing industrial development projects. For example, the systems approach to project management, if applied to industrial development projects, can ensure that critical interfaces with other communities or countries are not neglected.

The wind of change that is currently blowing all over the world now calls for a book of this nature. From Africa to Asia, countries around the world are struggling to achieve or maintain industrial development. Project management can help bring the benefits of industrial development to the various segments of a nation.

Chapter 1 presents an overview of industrial development. The complexity of industrial development projects is discussed. A guideline is presented for strategic planning for industrial development projects. The various factors that influence industrial development efforts are outlined. Chapter 2 presents a general introduction to project management. The recommended steps for project management are presented. A project-implementation model is also presented. Chapter 3 presents project-planning approaches. The desired components of a project plan are described. The required forms of project feasibility studies are also described.

Chapter 4 presents project-organization models. Guidelines are presented for selecting the project manager and staffing the project. The importance of communication in project organization is emphasized. Suggestions are offered for securing the services of experts for the various functions required in project organization. The chapter concludes with a case study of the organization of a multinational project. Chapter 5 presents the basic techniques for scheduling industrial development projects. The Critical Path Method and Program Evaluation and Review Technique are used with illustrative examples. Resource allocation to project schedules is also discussed.

Chapter 6 presents project control strategies. The steps for effecting the control of a project are presented. Basic learning-curve analysis is introduced as a tool for performance evaluation for project control. Chapter 7 presents the techniques of economic analysis for project management. Several examples are used to illustrate project cash flow analysis. Chapter 8 discusses the important issue of technology transfer to support industrial development efforts. Chapter 9 discusses the cultural and human resource issues in industrial development projects. Chapter 10 presents general guidelines for managing multinational projects and case studies to illustrate successful industrial development efforts in certain countries. Appendices on factors that may be of interest in industrial development projects are offered. An extensive bibliography concludes the book for the reader's further reference.

The development of a good project plan is one thing; the successful implementation of the plan is another thing. Readers are urged to follow the project-management guidelines in this book to ensure that good project plans are implemented effectively to provide a better quality of life due to industrial development.

ACKNOWLEDGMENTS

I thank my friends and colleagues in the School of Industrial Engineering, University of Oklahoma, for their continuing support. Particular thanks go to Dr. Simin Pulat and Dr. Bob Foote for their ardent encouragement for this book project. I thank Dr. Mustafa Pulat, Mr. Agboola Akande, and Professor Prateeb Chuntaketa for providing information for some of the case studies used in this book. I also thank the entire staff of Van Nostrand Reinhold for their prompt and efficient handling of the manuscript. Special thanks go to Geraldine Albert, Chris Grisonich, Betty Sheehan, Bob Argentieri, Bob Esposito, and the copy editor, Marie-Josée A. Schorp. I thank my wife, Iswat, for picking up the slack on the home front while I devoted most of my time to writing this book.

Adedeji Bodunde Badiru

1

The Path to Industrial Development

There is no limit to development.

Industrial development is one of the primary means of improving the standard of living in a nation. History indicates the profound effect that the industrial revolution had on world development. Industrial development will continue to play an active role in the economic strategies of rational nations as they strive to cater to the basic needs of their peoples. Nations that continue to seek international aid for one thing or another should begin now to lay a solid foundation for industrial development so that they will be ready for the twenty-first century. A nation that cannot institute and sustain industrial development will be politically delinquent and economically retarded. A good industrial foundation can positively drive the political and economic processes in any nation.

To achieve and sustain industrial development, both the technical and managerial aspects must come into play. This book addresses the managerial processes necessary to facilitate industrial development. Specifically, a project-management approach is presented as a viable means of achieving industrial development. The concepts, strategies, tools, and techniques of project management are outlined in concise formats to facilitate ease of use by the practitioner. Some of the sections are very brief by design so as to avoid overburdening the reader with unnecessary details. This chapter covers general perspectives of industrial development. Subsequent chapters address specific guidelines for project-management techniques relevant to industrial development. Project management facilitates a totally integrated development approach. This permits us to tackle a variety of related problems at the fundamental levels.

1

1.1 COMPLEXITY OF INDUSTRIAL DEVELOPMENT PROJECTS

The economic and social problems facing many nations in the present technological age are very challenging. The gloomy trends have been characterized by the stagnant state of established industries, decline in productivity, closure of poorly managed corporations, globalization of markets, increased dependency on physical technology, increased apathy toward social issues, proliferation of organized and sophisticated illegal financial deals, requirement for expensive capital investments, and neglect of economic diversification endeavors.

Above all, we witness a gradual erosion of the developed countries to the Third World and the decline of the Third World to Fourth World. The gloomy statistics can be found in reports published by the World Bank and the United Nations Industrial Development Organization (UNIDO). To stem the declines, industrial development or improvement projects must be critically analyzed.

An industrial development project is a complex undertaking that crosses several fields of endeavors. The diverse political, social, cultural, technical, organizational, and economic issues that intermingle in industrial development compound the development efforts. Sophisticated managerial approaches are needed to control the interaction effects of these issues. Financial power is a necessary but not sufficient requirement for industrial development. A common mistake by a developing economy is simply to dump scarce financial resources at a development problem without making adequate improvement in the management processes needed to support the development goal. Focusing on the technical aspects of a development project to the detriment of the managerial aspects will only create the potential for failure. A project-management approach can facilitate an integrated understanding of the complex issues involved in industrial development and, thus, pave the way for success.

Figure 1-1 illustrates the global nature of industrial development efforts. Contrary to general belief, industrial development problems are not limited to the developing nations alone. Even in developed and industrialized nations, large pockets of industrially neglected communities can be found. Residents of these communities live in abject poverty despite the ambient affluence of the overall nation. The countries that are most blessed with natural resources are often those that suffer most from industrial neglect. The problem is typically that they do not know how to initiate and implement the projects that are needed to exploit the available resources.

The industrial development strategies presented in this book can be applied at various levels within the hierarchy of a society. For example, a

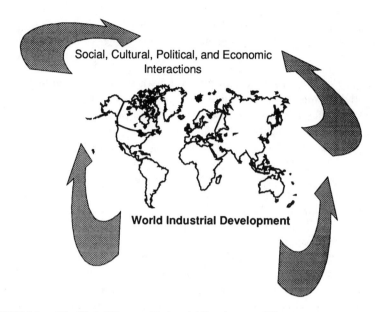

FIGURE 1-1.   The Global Nature of Industrial Development Efforts.

community, settlement, village, township, borough, state, region, or a nation can all benefit identically by instituting proper industrial development plans and strategies.

As a good example, the Arkansas Industrial Development Commission set up by then Governor Bill Clinton (now U.S. president) has been quite successful. It is reported that between 1989 and 1991, the state attracted more new and expanded plant investment per citizen than any of the neighboring states (U.S. News & World Report, Sept. 14, 1992, page 66). Responsiveness to the needs of prospective industry has been a major factor in the success of the industrial development effort. Project management techniques can facilitate further responsiveness and pave the way for bigger industrial gains.

1.2 STRATEGIC PLANNING FOR INDUSTRIAL DEVELOPMENT

A plan is the map of the wise. Industrial planning determines the nature of actions and responsibilities required to achieve industrial development goals. Strategic planning involves the long-range aspects of development efforts.

Planning forms the basis for all actions. Strategic planning for industrial development can be addressed at three distinct levels:

Supralevel Planning. Planning at this level deals with the big picture of how industrial development fits the overall and long-range needs of the society. Questions faced at this level may concern the potential contributions of industrial development to the standard of living in the society, the development of resources needed to provide basic amenities in the society, the required interfaces between development projects within and outside the society, the government support for industrial development, responsiveness of the local culture, and political stability.

Macro-Level Planning. Planning at this level may address the overall planning within a defined industrial boundary. The scope of the development effort and its operational interfaces should be addressed at the macro level planning. Questions addressed at the this level may include industry identification, product definition, project scope, availability of technical manpower, availability of supporting resources, import/export procedures, development policies, effects on residential neighborhoods, project funding and finances, and project-coordination strategies.

Micro-Level Planning. This deals with detailed operational plans at the task levels of industrial development. Definite and explicit tactics for accomplishing specific development objectives should be developed at the micro level. Factors to be considered at the micro level planning may include scheduled time, training requirement, tools required, task procedures, reporting requirements, and quality requirements.

Industrial development projects are capital intensive. If not planned properly, industrial development may prove to be uneconomic.

1.3 INDUSTRIAL DEVELOPMENT AND ECONOMIC DEVELOPMENT

Industrialization is one side of the economic coin. Industrial development can directly translate to economic development if proper management practices are followed. Industrial development can be formulated as a basic foundation for economic vitality and national productivity improvement. Some of the major factors that can positively impact interactions of industrial and economic processes include:

- Unification of national priorities.
- Diversification of the economic strategy.
- Strong strategy for development of rural areas.
- Adequate investment in research and development.
- Stable infrastructure to support development effort.
- Political stability that prevents economic disruption.
- Social and cultural standards that improve productivity.

Industrial development plays different types of roles in economic development. The structure of certain economies are such that the economic and industrial systems are on different development tracks. For example, in the former Soviet Union, production systems were established mostly to support the military system to the detriment of the economic system. This is why the Soviet Union was hardly ever able to attain significant economic power despite the formidable military power it possessed. To facilitate the interaction of industrial and economic endeavors, plans must be made to allow the industrial system to coexist symbiotically with other production forces. This can be done in any capitalist, communist, developing, or undeveloped nations.

1.3.1 Stages of National Development

The various stages of national development can be defined in terms of *First World, Second World, Third World,* and *Fourth World.* If the ongoing declines in some nations are not stemmed, we may soon see the emergence of a *Fifth World.* The prevailing stages are described as follow:

First World. This refers to industrialized nations with market-oriented economies. These are mostly capitalist or western nations. The United States, Canada, Britain, and Japan are prime examples of the First World. The First World is also sometimes referred to as the free world.
Second World. This refers to centrally planned communist-oriented economies. The large productive power of these nations are typically not channeled

toward broad national economic development. The former Soviet Union, Eastern Europe, China, Cuba, and North Korea are examples of countries that may be said to belong to the Second World.

Third World. This refers to poor, underdeveloped economies that prefer to refer to themselves as "developing" economies. Many of the countries in the Third World were formerly under colonial powers. Examples of Third World nations can be found in Asia, Latin America, and some developing nations of Africa.

Fourth World. This refers to the nations that are hopelessly confined to widespread, abject poverty. In addition to their economic misfortunes, these nations are also typically under political tumult. The political instability makes any development plan largely unachievable. It is unfortunate that nations that need stability more than others often suffer most from political commotion. The frequency of change of government, for example, in many African countries, precludes the consistency of development goals.

The Third World is the most commonly used of the four stages of classification. The concept of a Third World originated as a political description for nations that were not aligned with either the communist or the free world. The term later took on an economic connotation. The Second World has been shrinking rapidly in recent years with the increasing collapse of the communist system. Unfortunately, the independent nations that are emerging from former communist enclaves are degenerating into the third and lower levels of development. Now is the time for these nations to lay a solid foundation for their industrial development so that they can move to higher levels of national development.

1.3.2 The Need for Technological Change

Technological change is needed to spur industrial development. Technological progress calls for the use of technology. Technology, in the form of information, equipment, and knowledge, can be used productively and effectively to reduce production costs, improve service, improve product quality, and generate higher output levels. The information and knowledge involved in technological progress include those that improve the performance of management, labor, and raw materials.

Technological progress plays a vital role in improving total productivity. Statistics on developed countries, such as in the United States, show that in the period 1870–1957, 90 percent of the rise in real output per man-hour can be attributed to technical progress. It has been shown that industrial or economic growth is dependent on improvements in technical capabilities as well as on increases in the amount of the conventional factors of capital and labor. Technological change is not necessarily defined by a move toward the most modern capital equipment. Rather, technological changes should be designed to occur through improvements in the efficiency in the use of existing equipment. The challenge to developing countries is to find ways to develop an infrastructure that promotes and uses available technological resources.

1.3.3 The Need for Social Change

Change is the root of advancement. Industrial development requires change. A society must be prepared for change. Efforts that support industrial development must be instituted into every aspect of the society. If the society is better prepared for change, then positive changes can be achieved. The "pain but no gain" aspects of industrial development can be avoided if proper preparations have been made for industrial changes. Industrial development requires an increasingly larger domestic market. The social systems that make up such markets must be carefully coordinated. The socioeconomic impact on industrialization cannot be overlooked.

Social changes are necessary to support industrial development efforts. Social discipline and dedication must be instilled in the society to make industrial changes possible. The roles of the members of a society in terms of being responsible consumers and producers of industrial products must be outlined. People must be convinced of the importance of the contribution of each individual whether that individual is acting as a consumer or as a producer. Industrial consumers have become so choosy that they no longer will simply accept whatever is offered in the marketplace. In cases where social dictum directs consumers to behave in ways not conducive to industrial development, changes must be instituted. If necessary, acquired taste must be developed so people like and accept the products of local industry.

To facilitate consumer acceptance, the quality of industrial products must be improved to competitive standards. In the past, consumers were expected to make do with the inherent characteristics of industrial products regardless of potential quality and functional limitations. This has changed drastically in recent years. To satisfy the sophisticated taste of the modern consumer, products must exhibit a high level of quality and of responsiveness to the needs of the consumer. Only high-quality industrial products and services can survive the prevailing market competition and, thus, fuel the enthusiasm for further development efforts. Some of the approaches for preparing a society for industrial development changes are as follows:

- Make industrial changes in small increments.
- Highlight the benefits of industrial development.
- Keep citizens informed of the impending changes.
- Get citizen groups involved in the decision process.
- Promote industrial change as a transition to a better society.
- Allay the fears about potential loss of jobs due to industrial automation.
- Emphasize the job opportunities to be created by industrial development.

Stipulation for the use of local raw materials is one policy that may necessitate a change in social attitudes. The society (consumers and producers) must understand the importance of local raw materials in industrial development. When backed against the wall of production, producers must develop the necessary indigenous technology or processes for using local materials.

1.3.4 Producer, Retailer, and Consumer Education

Inflation can adversely affect industrial development projects. Inflation is a disease that feeds on itself, but not without the help of people. The basic attitude of citizens toward consumption and wealth greatly determines the trend of inflation. Everyone wants to buy and sell consumer products without paying attention to the production efforts needed to generate them. Sellers want to sell at whatever exorbitant prices they can get. Naive buyers do not help the situation either, willing as they are to buy whatever they want at whatever the asking price even if it means sacrificing their economic soul—and the soul of the whole nation along with it.

Producers, encouraged by the high demand, shrewdly cuts production and, thus, reduce market supply, which then elevates consumer prices even further. The fact that a product is in short supply makes the consumer yearn for more of it. The product quickly becomes a status symbol. The few who can get it claim to be the "class" of the society; and they are willing to pay whatever price to maintain that status quo. For example, a Mercedes Benz car is one of the ultimate status symbols in most emerging economies. Those in the "upper class" are willing to acquire at least one at any cost; even if it means starving their families in the acquisition process.

Each consumptive individual is unaware of the economic misery he or she is contributing to national development efforts. If we try and convince the citizens to scale down their purchase of nonessential products to help combat inflation, they will probably claim that their neighbors have the same items; so why shouldn't they? As far as they are concerned, the economy can falter all it wants; all they want is their own "fair" share of the national pie. We don't really blame them. It is not that they are unpatriotic, it is just that they don't know any better.

This is why educating the public is an important aspect of combating inflation and paving the way for industrial development. The producer, the retailer, and the buyer all need to know the real causes of inflation, its boomerang effects, and its potential remedies. Those who perpetrate inflation by asking or paying higher prices should know that they only hurt themselves more.

The government should play a very active role in the education process. The indoctrination process needs to start right at the grassroots. Children should be exposed to the concepts of battling inflation so that they can grow up to become responsible producers, retailers, or consumers. The early instillation of these concepts to the nation's youth will even have the beneficial side effect of imbibed national pride, which should serve the social and political interests of the nation in later years. Most of the leadership problems in many countries can be traced to a lack of deep-rooted pride and interest in the national welfare.

Nothing is more discouraging than to hear people proclaim how they have given up on their nation. They claim that nothing works, that no improvements are forthcoming, and that the government is unresponsive to the society's needs. How do we expect people who talk like that to perform when they themselves reach a position of authority? Certainly, their attitudes will not change overnight. They carry the negative impressions up to the higher offices, and all they will do there is just watch the afflictions and assert their views by saying, "Didn't I say nothing works in this country?" Obviously, such people have not had any early exposure to knowledge that would instill national pride in them.

Government programs cannot succeed without the people's cooperation in the implementation process. Herein lies the irony of governing and being governed. We blame the government for not instituting corrective programs, and we turn right around to take actions that innocently sabotage the prevailing programs, thereby compounding the burden of the government. People must be educated about the implications of their actions.

When a consumer product is in short supply, everyone complains and blames the system. No one reflects on the contribution he or she could make toward the production and supply of the products. We may consider the case of a factory worker who buys a locally made product and complains of its inferior quality compared to imported brands. He forgets that he himself is in a unique position to contribute significantly to the quality of local products through his on-the-job activities. There have been reports of American auto industry workers buying Japanese cars because those imported cars are more reliable. This is like sending a signal that says "I build this car, I know about it, please don't buy it!" What a fallacy of production dedication. The worker bites the hand that feeds him.

To illustrate further the above problem, let us consider the following hypothetical scenario of an American auto industry employee: as the demand for Japanese cars increases, so do the prices of the cars. So, the employee asks his employer for higher wages so that he can buy his dream Japanese car. In order to pay those higher prices, his employer raises the prices of his own cars to make more money. When the prices of the local cars go up without a comparable increase in quality (thanks to the employee's work delinquency), the public buys even less of the cars. So, the employer sells fewer cars and makes less money. In the end, the employee is laid off. His education is incomplete. His sense of economic awareness needs to be broadened.

Another example involves recent political arguments over the "right-to-work" law in the State of Oklahoma. The law was to assure workers of their rights to work without joining unions. Proponents of the law were mostly those at administrative levels. Grassroot opposition to the law came from workers themselves. They would rather have unions that would lobby for higher wages, among other things, for them. But the real issue of the impact of unions on the industrial system was never quite understood by the workers. Those who were fortunate enough to be properly exposed knew exactly what they were supporting or opposing. Others, unfortunately, never saw the light. As can be seen from the examples above, the economic system needed to support industrial development can be very complex. Individual actions, as innocent and minor as they may appear, can go a long way in the gradual destruction of the overall economy. We should be convinced that the education of the public is a key factor in solving many economic problems before industrial development can take place.

1.4 POLITICAL STABILITY AND INDUSTRIAL DEVELOPMENT

Politics determines the crux of economics; economics determines the crux of politics. With the changing political environments in developing nations, it is difficult to stabilize government policies. It seems that some governments are perpetually in transient states. Just when policies are beginning to take a firm hold, a new administration comes in and, as a show of authority, overturns all previous achievements. Billions of dollars have been wasted by succeeding governments through the absurd practice of abandoning projects started by preceding administrations regardless of merit.

For the sake of national progress, governments should make a commitment to carry on worthwhile projects irrespective of who started them. Foresight should also be exercised when embarking on new industrial projects to ensure that subsequent government officials can find the merit of their continuation. Laying a solid foundation for an industrial development project can facilitate a lasting coexistence of political, economic, and industrial activities. The major role of government in industrial development must be that of a facilitator. This can be particularly important in intergovernment

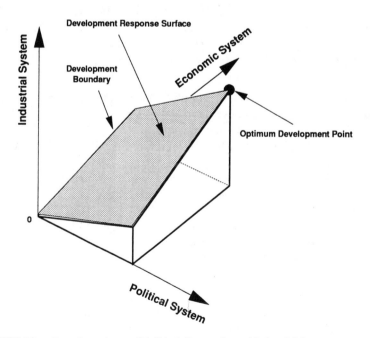

FIGURE 1-2.   Interdependence of Political, Economic, and Industrial Systems.

negotiations for mutual development. The interdependence of the political, economic, and industrial systems is depicted in Figure 1-2.

The performance of the industrial system is shown to be dependent on the states of the economic and political systems. If the economic and political processes are at low levels, no significant industrial development can be expected. As the economy picks up and the political atmosphere improves, the level of industrial development will begin to increase. To maximize industrial output, the political and economic systems must operate at conducively high levels. This is why a developing nation must recognize that chaotic political situations will adversely affect overall national development efforts.

1.5 GLOBAL INFLUENCES ON INDUSTRIAL DEVELOPMENT

New world economic order calls for new approaches to development. The recent changes around the world will have profound effects on international trade. The changes in Eastern Europe, the advancements in Western Europe, the reunification of Germany, the breakup of the former Soviet Union, and the emergence of Africa as a viable market will all affect international trade in the coming years. The quality of industrial products will be one common basis for trade communication. Companies and countries must recognize the trend and refocus their efforts. Some of the key aspects of globalization that will impact industrial development efforts include:

- Transition of some countries from trade partners to trade competitors.
- Reduction of production-cycle time to keep up with the multilateral introduction of products around the world.
- Increased efforts to cope with the reduction in product life cycle from years to months.
- Increased responsiveness to the needs of a mixed workforce.
- Need to eradicate cultural barriers.
- Relaxation and expansion of trade boundaries.
- Integration of operations and services and consolidation of efforts.
- More effective and responsive communication media.
- Increased pressure for multinational cooperation.
- Need for multicompany and multiproduct coordination.

The interdependence of world projects in modern times makes it imperative that global development efforts be pursued. Political, industrial, economic, and social disasters in one nation can easily spill over to other nations and create adverse chain reactions. Refugee problems now plaguing many nations are cruel reminders that nations can no longer exist in isolation. For example, because the U.S. economy dominates one-fourth of total world output, economic events in the United States can directly affect other nations' economies.

1.5.1 Japanese Influence

The emergence of Japan as an economic leader has had a profound effect on the modern industrial revolution. The Japanese approaches, as evidenced by products around the world, have provided the impetus for new approaches to industrialization. Japanese quality-improvement and management models are now widely adopted all over the world. The key to the success of Japan in the world market is the multilateral approaches used for product development and manufacturing. In a Japanese production environment, industrial product quality is viewed as a bottom-up, top-down, and lateral integration of functions. The Japanese approach to product quality is simple and effective. It is the simplicity of the approach that makes it workable in many organizations. Despite its simplicity, it has been effective in capturing market segments all over the world. The quality of Japanese products has helped attract potential buyers and provide impetus for further industrial development investments. The Japanese approach to product-quality improvement includes the following components:

- Significant emphasis is placed on training.
- Attitude of pride in workmanship is encouraged.
- Employees are given the necessary tools for performing their jobs.
- Avenues for identifying, analyzing, and correcting problems are put in place.
- Each employee exhibits a sense of responsibility for the products and services.

Most of the basic tools that the Japanese use to study and improve industrial processes originated from Western organizations. But the Japanese have found an effective way to make practical uses of these tools even while the developers are still debating the merits of the tools. The drive and motivation for industrial development is one of Japan's major exports to the rest of the world. The success story of Japan has been a source of inspiration as several developing nations look inward for their own technological developments. Overdependency on other nations for industrial development creates trade imbalances that stymie development efforts. Japan's example encourages developing nations to start with internal efforts rather than depending on supposedly developed nations. Japan has demonstrated that a nation's economic power can nowadays be more important than its military strength. But, as has been demonstrated by the case of the Kuwait-Iraq conflict, the economic power must be supported by cooperative political and administrative processes.

1.5.2 New European Influence

The new European influence on industrialization has become more acclaimed with the advent of the European Economic Community (EEC). The EEC has brought on the adoption of national and international industrial quality standards. The 1957 Treaty of Rome established four areas of European cooperation: continental trade, regional research and technology development, economic and monetary union, and working conditions and environment. Twelve countries make up the EEC: Britain, France, Germany, Italy, Ireland, Belgium, Holland, Luxembourg, Spain, Portugal, Denmark, and Greece. The Single European Act of February of 1986 amended the Treaty of Rome to facilitate progress with the unification program.

The Single Europe Act (SEA) of 1992 unified over 350 million Europeans into a single market. In the EEC, labor, capital, goods, and services may cross borders freely. The main purpose of unification is to ensure that products manufactured in one country will be admitted to the markets of all other member countries. The unified Europe will be one of the largest and fastest growing markets for the next several decades. Every government and every individual in the EEC member countries, as well as those outside the EEC, will be affected by widespread changes in many economic domains, including regulations on industrial standards.

The goals of EEC are achieved by establishing and adhering to standards. Standards that are written by different European countries that pertain to the same area will be unified into one integrated standard. The EEC has agreements with the European Free Trade Association (EFTA; members: Austria, Finland, Iceland, Norway, Sweden, and Switzerland) for the adoption of standards. Many European companies are now requiring their suppliers, both within and outside the EEC, to comply with European quality standards. Because of the removal of trade barriers in Europe, companies want to be assured that their suppliers will deliver high-quality products and services.

Instead of negotiating quality requirements with each customer, companies will be required to submit to auditing by licensed quality-system auditors in order to be registered as complying suppliers. Most companies that expect to export their products to Europe are now planning to conform to the quality standards. These standards are now being required for doing business in the international marketplace. Thus, the European quality requirements has fueled the race for better industrial practices all over the world. In terms of share numbers, the European influence cannot be ignored. Statistics attest to this fact:

- A combined population of 355 million.
- A combined GNP of $5 trillion.
- The creation of 1.8 million new jobs.
- An estimated increase of $260 billion in goods and services.
- The potential for attracting technical manpower away from developing and developed countries.

1.5.3 North American Alliance

The trend toward economic integration is growing rapidly. In addition to the widely publicized EEC, other national alliances are emerging around the world for industrial and economic development purposes. One example is the North American Free Trade Agreement (NAFTA) between the United States of America, Canada, and Mexico. The NAFTA will create the largest trading zone in the world. It will eliminate barriers that have previously limited the flow of industrial goods between the three countries. Although it is presently opposed by several U.S. labor groups, it is expected that it will eventually become operational to the benefit of all three countries. The agreement would eliminate all duties, tariffs, and other trade barriers within the United States of America, Canada, and Mexico over a period of fifteen years. The new trade, economic, and industrial opportunities to be created by the NAFTA will have a telling effect on the industrial development efforts of other countries in terms of new market horizons.

1.5.4 Other National Alliances

Keeping to the worldwide trend, an economic group of fifteen developing nations has been formed to pursue economic and industrial development programs that have joint benefits to the members. The group, known as the G-15 Economic Council, is currently being chaired by Nigeria. The objectives of the group include promoting trade among developing countries through the exchange of information between government, business, and individual entrepreneurs. When fully operational, G-15 would provide synergistic economic assistance to industrialists in the member nations. Economic unification by several developing countries can help them pool their resources into a significant industrial development asset. Furthermore, economic integration can help induce peace not only in the developing nations but throughout the world.

A good example of economic integration can be found in the activities of the multinational Organization for Economic Cooperation and Development (OECD) and of the Economic Community of West African States (ECOWAS). Similarly, the governments of the seven leading industrial nations, the United States of America, Britain, Japan, Canada, Germany, Italy, and France, have been cooperating to determine how best to advance their mutual economic interests. The development of uniform mutually beneficial industrial and economic strategies has been the group's primary goal.

1.5.5 Benchmarking for Industrial Development

With good examples to follow, any nation can improve. Metrics based on a nation's most critical development needs should be developed. The objective is to equal or surpass the best example in terms of industrialization. *Benchmarking* is a process whereby target standards are established based on the best examples available. In its simplest term, benchmarking implies learning from the best. The premise of benchmarking is that if a nation can replicate the best examples, it will become one of the best. A major objective of benchmarking is to identify negative gaps, as shown in Figure 1-3, where other nations surpass a subject nation in terms of industrial development. An attempt can then be made to close the gaps by pursuing appropriate development efforts.

Benchmarking requires a continuous comparison with the best. Updates must be obtained from nations already benchmarked, and new nations to be benchmarked must be selected on a periodic basis. Measurement, analysis, feedback, and modification should be incorporated into the development program. A benchmark-feedback approach can be useful for establishing a continuous drive toward industrial development benchmarks. Such a model is shown in Figure 1-4.

The figure shows the block diagram representation of input–output relationships of the components in a benchmarking environment. In the model, $I(t)$ represents the set of benchmark inputs to the subject nation. The inputs may be in terms of data, information, raw material, technical skill, or other basic resources. The index t denotes a time reference. $A(t)$ represents the feedback loop actuator. The actuator facilitates the flow of inputs to various segments of the subject. $G(t)$ represents the forward transfer that coordi-

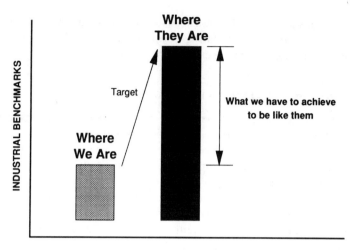

FIGURE 1-3.   Benchmark Gaps for Industrial Development.

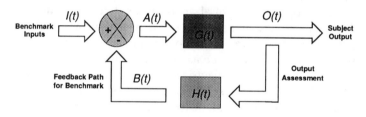

FIGURE 1-4.   Development Benchmark-Feedback Model.

nates input information and resources to produce the desired output, $O(t)$. $H(t)$ represents the control process that monitors the status of development and generates the appropriate feedback information, $B(t)$, that is sent to the input-transfer junction. The feedback information is necessary to determine what control actions should be taken at the next development stage. The primary responsibility of a development team should involve ensuring the proper forward and backward flow of information and knowledge concerning the level of industrial development with respect to the benchmarked inputs.

1.6 UNIQUE FACTORS IN INDUSTRIAL DEVELOPMENT

Although technology continues to push the limit of perfection in developed nations, people in underdeveloped nations continue to be relegated to antiquated production tools. Industrial development has unique aspects that must be considered in formulating development strategies. Some of these aspects are discussed in the sections that follow.

1.6.1 Rural Area Development for Industrialization

Because of their underdeveloped state, rural areas offer significant potentials for industrial development. Ironically, it is that same underdevelopment that makes them susceptible to neglect. Productive members of rural areas move to urban areas in large numbers in search of better life. The more the technological advancement in a nation, the more the rural residents migrate to urban areas. Consequently, the manpower needed to support the development of a rural area is often not available. The key to keeping the manpower in the localities is the development of the localities and the creation of employment opportunities. Rural neglect has created highly uneven distribution of population in most countries. Urbanization without industrialization is doomed to economic failure.

The sparse population in rural areas means that large land areas with potential for industrial setups are available at relatively low cost. This makes them particularly attractive for the location of new plants. But investors often shy away from the rural areas because of the limited availability of supporting resources such as electrical power, water, communication, raw materials, and transportation services. If power, water, transportation, and communication are guaranteed, the development of the rural areas will, no doubt, be effected successfully. In addition to ensuring these services, a nation should offer incentives (e.g., tax cuts) to rural investors. Some key elements of rural area development include:

- Improvement of basic infrastructure.
- Creation of investment incentives for local businesses.
- Establishment of academic institutions geared to local educational needs.
- Establishment of technology extension services through academic institutions.
- Creation of a local clearinghouse for technology information.

- Government assistance for local product development.
- Provision of adequate rural health care services.

1.6.2 Cultural Barriers to Industrialization

Cultural barriers can inhibit industrial development. Most industrialization programs are fueled by foreign ideas, technologies, and approaches. In many cultures, veils have been developed to protect the society against foreign influences. The greatest fear often involves the potential moral decadence that may accompany industrial development as people migrate from one nation to another in response to the development process. Cultural barriers may also prohibit certain segments of a society from participating fully in the development process. Such cultural barriers must be eradicated to pave the way for industrial development.

Some cultures have evolved to a level of indifference to fraudulent and corrupt practices that are detrimental to development efforts. In some cases, corruption is viewed as an accepted way of doing business. Cultural permissive attitudes to corruption must be altered before general development can take hold. Loyalty to overall development goals rather than individual pursuits are required as a part of cultural changes for industrial development.

1.6.3 Role of Education in Industrial Development

He who owns the knowledge controls the power. Education should play a vital role in industrial development. In the modern day of high technology, adequate education is needed to succeed in any workplace, whether it is a hamburger stand, an administrative office, or a manufacturing plant. Even in some industrialized nations, a large percentage of the adult population in neglected communities is functionally illiterate. It used to be that the children of these poverty-stricken communities were needed to drive the wheels of manual labor in local factories. But the industries of the 1990s and beyond, with increasing push for automation, will not need much of the services of the low-grade workers. Education geared toward the new industrial direction will, thus, be needed to participate actively in industrial development. Poor parents always proclaim that they don't want their children to end up where they did. Yet, no viable educational efforts are made to ensure that they don't.

University-Industry Interaction Model
Knowledge is an everlasting capital. There must be intellectual freedom that permits the transition of theory into practice. The establishment of a formal process for the interface of institutions of higher learning and industry can be one of the capitals for industrial development. Universities have unique capabilities that can be aligned with industry capabilities to produce symbiotic working relationships. Private industrial research projects must complement public industrial research ventures.

University Capability and Industrial Capability
Academic institutions have a unique capability to generate, learn, and transfer technology to industry. The quest for knowledge in academia can fuel the search for innovative solutions to specific industrial problems. Cooperating industry is a fertile ground for developing prototypes of new academic ideas. Industrial settings are good avenues for practical implementation of technology. Industry-based implementation of university-developed technology can serve as the impetus for further efforts to develop new technology. Technologies that are developed within the academic community mainly for research purposes often fade into oblivion because of the lack of a formal and coordinated mechanism for industrial implementation. The potentials of these technologies go untapped for the several following reasons:

- The developer does not know which industry may need the technology.
- Industry is not aware of the technology available in academic institutions.
- There is no coordinated mechanism for technical interface between industry and university groups.

Universities interested in technology development are often hampered by the lack of adequate resources for research and training activities. Industry can help in this regard by providing direct support for industrial groups to address specific industrial problems. The universities also need real problems to work on as projects or case studies. Industry can provide these under a cooperative arrangement.

Integration of Needs and Capabilities
The respective needs and capabilities of universities and industrial establishments can be integrated symbiotically to provide benefits for each group. University courses offered at convenient times for industry employees can create opportunity for university–industry interaction. Class projects for industry employees can be designed to address real-life industrial problems. This will help industry employees to have focused and rewarding projects. Class projects developed in the academic environment can be successfully

implemented in actual work environments to provide tangible benefits. With a mutually cooperative interaction, new developments in industry can be brought to the attention of academia, and new academic research developments can be tested in industrial settings. Figure 1-5 shows a potential model for university-industry interface. The model provides a feedback loop process that facilitates continuing interaction between university and industry. Such a model creates a conducive environment for professional exchanges. The exchanges can involve multilateral linking of students, faculty, technical experts, managers, administrators, educators, scholars, and even clerical staff.

Technology Clearinghouse
Academic institutions can serve as convenient locations for technology clearinghouses. Such clearinghouses can be organized to provide up-to-date information for industrial development activities. Specific industrial problems can be studied at the clearinghouse. The clearinghouse can serve as a repository for information on various technology tools. Industry would participate in the clearinghouse through the donation of equipment, funds,

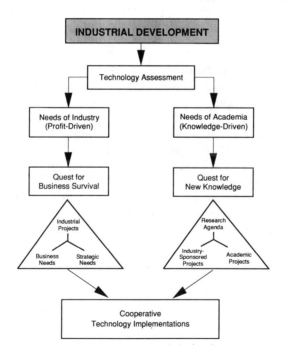

FIGURE 1-5.   University-Industry Interaction Model.

and personnel time. The services provided by a clearinghouse could include a combination of the following:

- Provide consulting services on technology to industry.
- Conduct on-site short courses with practical projects for industry.
- Serve as a technology library for general information.
- Facilitate technology transfer by helping industry identify which technology is appropriate for which problems.
- Provide technology-management guidelines that will enable industry to implement successfully new technology in existing operations.
- Expand training opportunities for engineering students and working engineers.

Center of Excellence for Industrial Development

The government can sponsor cooperative interactions between academia and industry by providing broad-based funding mechanisms. For example, the U.S. National Science Foundation (NSF) has a program to provide funds for industry/university cooperative research centers. The leaders of a nation pursuing industrial development should actively support cooperative efforts between universities and industry. The establishment of centers of excellence for pursuing industrial development-related research is one approach to creating a conducive atmosphere for industry-university interaction. Several states in the United States of America have used this approach to address specific development needs.

1.6.4 Role of Women in Industrial Development

Women can and are beginning to play important roles in national development. Women have significant potentials in terms of political, economic, and industrial roles in a nation. In developing nations particularly, women have played important economic roles as traders for a long time. The economic power garnered from their entrepreneurial activities should be transformed to decision-making power for industrial development. In very democratic nations, the political power of women has been more pronounced primarily through voting rights. These rights should be directed at policymaking endeavors that can facilitate industrial development.

Women groups have emerged in some developing nations to use their collective powers better. Many of the efforts of these groups have been directed at development. For example, the National Council for Women Development has been very active politically in Ghana. In Nigeria, the Rural Women Development program, spearheaded by the First Lady of the nation, is directed at improving the economic impact of rural women. Small-scale industries owned by women have been one of the tangible outputs of these women's movements.

1.6.5 Role of Agriculture in Industrial Development

A hungry society cannot be an industrially productive society. It is generally believed that an underdeveloped economy is characterized by an agricultural base. Based on this erroneous belief, several developing nations have abandoned their previously solid agricultural base in favor of industrialization. The fact is that a strong agricultural base is needed to complement industrialization efforts. Many developing nations have learned this lesson in a very hard way. If industrialization does not yield immediate benefits, the society will be exposed to the double jeopardy of hunger and material deprivation. Once abandoned, agriculture is a difficult process to recoup. Since agricultural processes take several decades to perfect, revitalization of abandoned agriculture may require several decades. Agriculture should play a major role in the foundation for industrial development. The agricultural sector can serve as a viable market for a developed industry.

It is interesting to note how the *agricultural revolution* led to the *industrial revolution.* Human history indicates that humans started out as nomad hunters and gatherers, drifting to wherever food could be found. About 12,000 years ago, humans learned to domesticate both plants and animals. This agricultural breakthrough allowed humans to become settlers and thereby to spend less time in search of food. More time was, thus, available for pursuing innovative activities, which led to discoveries of better ways of planting and raising animals for food. That initial agricultural discovery eventually paved the way for the agricultural revolution.

During the agricultural revolution, mechanical devices, techniques, and storage mechanisms were developed to aid the process of agriculture. These inventions made it possible for more food to be produced by fewer people. The abundance of food meant that more members of the community could spend that time for other pursuits rather than the customary labor-intensive agriculture. Naturally, these other pursuits involved the development and improvement of the tools of agriculture. The extra free time brought on by more efficient agriculture was, thus, used to bring about minor technological improvements in agricultural implements. These more advanced agricultural tools led to even more efficient agriculture. The transformation from the *digging stick* to the *metal hoe* is a good example of the raw technological innovation of that time.

With each technological advance, less time was required for agriculture, thereby permitting more time for further technological advancements. The advancements in agriculture slowly led to more stable settlement patterns. These patterns led to the emergence of towns and cities. With central settlements away from farmlands, there developed a need for transforming agricultural technology to domicile technology that would support the new city life. The transformed technology was later turned to other productive uses that eventually led to the emergence of the industrial revolution. To this day, the entwined relationships between agriculture and industry can still be seen, although one would have to look harder and closer to see them. Figure 1-6 shows a modern representation of the intersection of agricultural economy, industrial economy, and other economic processes.

1.6.6 Manpower Supply for Industrial Development

Technical, administrative, and service manpower will be needed to support industrial development. People make development possible. No matter how

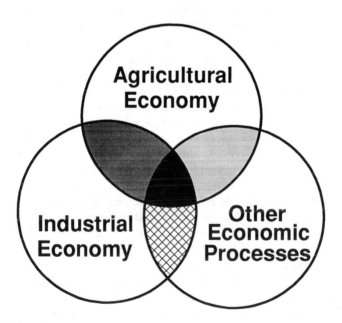

FIGURE 1-6.   Intersection of Agricultural and Industrial Economic Processes.

technically capable a machine may be, people will still be required to operate or maintain it. Soon after World War II, it was generally believed that physical capital formation was a sufficient basis for development. That view was probably justified at that time because of the role that machinery had played during the war. It was not obvious then that machines without a trained and skillful work force did not constitute a solid basis for development. It has now been realized that human capital is as crucial to development as physical capital. The investment in manpower development must be given a high priority in the development plan. Some of the important aspects of manpower-supply analysis for industrial development include:

- Level of skills required.
- Mobility of the manpower.
- The nature and type of skills required.
- Retention strategies to reduce brain drain.
- Potential for coexistence of people and technology.
- Continuing education to facilitate adaptability to technology changes.

1.6.7 Role of Technology in Industrial Development

Technology can facilitate industrial development. But technology must be managed properly to play an effective role. A multitude of new technologies has emerged in recent years. Hard and soft technologies, such as desktop computers, cellular manufacturing, and artificial intelligence, have received much attention in the literature. But much more remains to be done in actual implementation. It is important to consider the peculiar characteristics of a new technology before establishing adoption and implementation strategies for industrial development. The justification for the adoption of a new technology should be a combination of several factors rather than a single characteristic of the technology. The important characteristics to consider include productivity improvement, improved product quality, reduction in production cost, flexibility, reliability, and safety.

An integrated evaluation must be performed to ensure that a proposed technology is justified both economically and technically. The scope and goals of the proposed technology must be established right from the beginning of an industrialization project. This entails the comparison of industry objectives with overall national goals in the following areas:

1. *Market Target.* This should identify the customers of the proposed technology. It should also address items such as market cost of proposed product, assessment of competition, and market share.
2. *Growth Potential.* This should address short-range expectations, long-range expectations, future competitiveness, future capability, and prevailing size and strength of the competition.

3. *Contributions to National Goals.* Any prospective technology must be evaluated in terms of direct and indirect benefits to be generated by the technology. These may include product price versus value, increase in international trade, improved standard of living, cleaner environment, safer workplace, and improved productivity.

4. *Profitability.* An analysis of how the technology will contribute to profitability should consider past performance of the technology, incremental benefits of the new technology versus conventional technology, and value added by the new technology.

5. *Capital Investment.* Comprehensive economic analysis should play a significant role in the technology-assessment process. This may cover an evaluation of fixed and sunk costs, cost of obsolescence, maintenance requirements, recurring costs, installation cost, space-requirement cost, capital-substitution potentials, return on investment, tax implications, cost of capital, and other concurrent projects.

6. *Skill and Resource Requirements.* The utilization of resources (manpower and equipment) in the pretechnology and posttechnology phases of industrialization should be assessed. This may be based on material input/output flows, high value of equipment versus productivity improvement, required inputs for the technology, expected output of the technology, and utilization of technical and nontechnical personnel.

7. *Risk Exposure.* Uncertainty is a reality in technology-adoption efforts. Uncertainty will need to be assessed for the initial investment, return on investment, payback period, public reactions, environmental impact, and volatility of the technology.

8. *National Productivity Improvement.* An analysis of how the technology may contribute to national productivity may be verified by studying industry throughput, efficiency of production processes, utilization of raw materials, equipment maintenance, absenteeism, learning rate, and design-to-production cycle. Chapter 8 presents further details about the importance of technology to industrial development.

1.7 A FOUR-LEGGED TOWER MODEL FOR INDUSTRIALIZATION

Industrialization built on a solid foundation can hardly fail. The major infrastructural ingredients for durable industrial, economic, and technological developments are electrical power, water, transportation, and communication facilities. These items should have priority in major industrial development projects. Of course, accommodation is another basic need that must be accounted for in an industrial development strategy. A four-legged

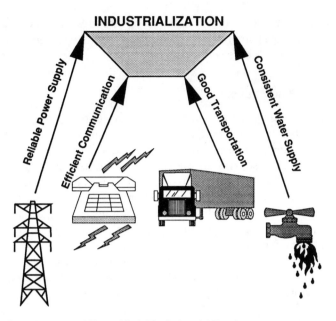

FIGURE 1-7.   Four-Legged Tower Model for Industrial Development.

tower model to provide a foundation for industrial development is presented in Figure 1-7. Such development seeks to ensure the following amenities:

Primary Amenities

- Reliable power supply.
- Consistent water supply.
- Good transportation system.
- Efficient communication system.

Supporting Amenities

- Housing.
- Education.
- Health care.

The provision of adequate health care facilities is particularly essential to building a strong industrial base. A healthy society is a productive society, a sick society will be a destitute society. Diseases that often ravage impoverished nations can curtail the productive capabilities of the citizens. The destructive effects of many of these diseases can be stemmed by prompt access to basic health care services.

1.7.1 Reliable Power Supply

Electricity is the major source of power for production facilities. This fact has been realized by developing countries for a long time. Yet, not enough effort has been directed at adequate generation and reliable distribution of this very important resource. Where electricity has been generated in abundant quantities, reliable distribution has been miserably lacking. Plants have been shortsightedly constructed without planning for adequate power supply. No wonder then that most industries in developing economies are running only at a fraction of their capacities. The problems plaguing power-supply companies should be critically studied so that a lasting solution can be found. A large portion of the initial development efforts should be directed at ensuring adequate power supply. Once supply is found to be reliable and stable, major production endeavors can then be pursued.

1.7.2 Consistent Water Supply

In today's technology, chemicals play a significant role in product development. Water is an indispensable component of the use of chemicals in industrial operations. Water is needed not only to sustain life but also to support the many products that make life livable. Water facility development should be addressed in two categories: *industrial water needs* and *potable water needs*. Because of its huge demand, industry should not compete with households for water supply. As with electricity, reliable water supply should be ensured before urging investment in production facilities. There are cases where a new industry opens, has water supply for a few weeks, and then is stunned by the reality of empty pipes. This is nothing more than an arrant display of lack of industrial foresight.

1.7.3 Good Transportation System

It is a fact that nothing moves without transportation. In the ancient days of geographically limited commerce, speedy transportation was less of a concern. But in the modern society, the global market has necessitated interactions with faraway locations. Developed economies appreciate the necessity of these interactions and they develop transportation systems to meet the needs. Developing economies are "still developing" because their transportation systems, in many respects, are yet to catch up with the rest of the world.

Progress in modern commerce depends on the facilities for conveying products from one location to another efficiently.

After power and water, transportation should have the third priority in the strategic development plan. Good roads should be constructed and maintained to provide a lasting support for the development efforts. Industrial access roads, as well as personnel access roads, should be constructed. The economic loss can be enormous if the transportation system is neglected even in a developed economy. For example, the U.S. Transportation Department estimates that Americans waste over $30 billion a year in lost time on travel roads. The impact of such huge losses can be devastating for a developing economy.

It should be understood that the development of a good transportation system can take a very long time at a very high cost. As an example, the U. S. interstate system has been going on for over thirty-five years, and it is yet to be completed. Expected to be completed in 1998, the interstate system would cover over 44,000 miles of four-lane, limited access, high-speed, coast-to-coast, divided highway. It will have cost almost $130 billion by the time it is completed. Covering only about 1 percent of the U.S. road mileage, the interstate system is to carry over 20 percent of the nation's traffic. Because of its accessibility, the U.S. interstate system has fueled development in several communities.

1.7.4 Efficient Communication System

Communication propels commerce. Telephone and postal services constitute alternate means of conducting business. The lack of reliable telephone service forces business people to make physical appearances when conducting even the most minor of transactions. This, of course, necessitates the increased use of roads, thereby, overloading the already inadequate transportation system. In an underdeveloped community, business that can be conveniently conducted over the telephone is normally conducted by physical presence. The requirement for physical mobility directly takes a person from productive activities, consequently creating adverse effects on national productivity.

In addition, frequent road transportation increases the exposure of the traveller to the hazards of the precarious transportation system. The more the people need to be on the roads, the more the congestion, and the higher the risks of road mishaps, which have been known to rob a nation of some of its productive citizens. The reliability of electric power, water, transportation, and communication services is essential for a sound industrial development. Nations with well-developed communication systems have used them to further their development programs. On the other hand, those who have not paid proper attention to their communication systems will continute to struggle with dormant or regressing economies.

1.8 DEVELOPMENT OF INDIGENOUS ECONOMIC MODEL

The formulation of an indigenous economic model is relevant for industrial development. The unique aspects of a developing economy that will necessitate indigenous models are discussed in this section. The reasons why the imported economic principles and models may not work in a developing nation are presented. The success of indigenous economic models in an underdeveloped area can serve as a useful paradigm for industrial development endeavors in nations with similar economic plights. A synergistic implementation of indigenous economic models will have a positive impact on the overall world economy. Both the economic and noneconomic aspects of industrial development must be accounted for in developing an indigenous model.

The depressed state of the economy in many parts of the world has reached such an agonizing and complex point that a long-lasting solution may not be easily identifiable. Well-founded laws and principles of economics have been used in the process of formulating existing economic policies. Unfortunately, none of the policies has yielded totally satisfactory results in underdeveloped nations. There has been no short-term success, and there is no guarantee of long-term success. Restrictions on importation, barter agreements, structural adjustment of currency value, and other economic policies are just a few examples of the concerted efforts being made by some developing countries. The fact that some of these efforts have been or may be unsuccessful indicates that there are certain aspects of the peculiar economic situation that are being overlooked, oversimplified, or unrecognized in a developing nation.

1.8.1 Imported Economic Models

The standard economic models that are widely employed throughout the world were developed based on societal behaviors. Many emerging economies, with their peculiarities, simply don't fit the formulation of those models. That, perhaps, is why the economies in those societies have not responded positively to the traditional economic policies. Let us consider the laws of supply and demand for example. The laws are based on the assumption that consumers and producers will respond to certain inputs in some rational fashion. The downward-sloping demand curve, shown in Figure 1-8, indi-

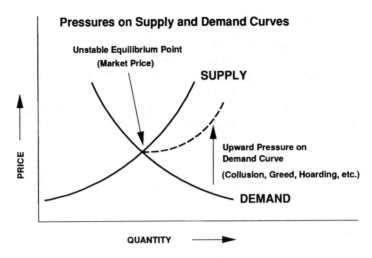

FIGURE 1-8.   Conventional Supply and Demand Curves.

cates that consumers will buy less of a product as the price increases. By analogy, the upward-sloping supply curve indicates that suppliers will supply more of a product as the price increases. Quite logical!

Contradictorily, in many developing societies, the basic supply and demand laws may not be directly applicable. This is because people are expected to behave in manners foreign to their social, cultural, political, and economic structures and attitudes. Rather than try to mold a developing nation to fit existing economic models, attempts should be made to modify the models to fit the unique situations of the nations. Only then can we have models that accurately explain and predict the actions of "developing" consumers and, thus, provide reliable guidelines for effective national economic policies. Atta (1981) constructed a macroeconomic model of the Ghanian economy. The model emphasized the supply side of a small open economy. This presents a good example of an economic view tailored to an indigenous scenario.

The indigenous banking system that has been established in India is another excellent example of an economic strategy tailored to a unique national need. The indigenous banking system is based on the strength of personal relations, which is a strong social link in India. The personal relations are used to vouch for creditworthiness instead of the conventional collateral approach. This indigenous banking system has worked very well and has made it possible for rural people, who would have otherwise not gone to the western-style banks, to actively engage in banking transactions.

1.8.2 Indigenous Scenarios

In a developing nation, the familiar curves of supply and demand may be mangled by several factors. Some of these factors are quite obvious. Some, on the other hand, are very subtle and can only be fully identified, understood, and quantified through dedicated economic research. Economic research must be directed specifically at formulating indigenous economic models. Some important factors that should be considered in such a research effort include:

1. The level of propensity to consume in a developing nation (consumption orientation rather than production orientation).
2. The inferiority complex that prompts some societies to prefer imported goods and services.
3. The lack of self-pride in the products of local labor.
4. The affinity for black-market transactions.

These factors, in addition to others to be determined through appropriate research, should form the nucleus of an economic model for a developing country.

As far back as 1975, the United Nations (UN) initiated a program to ensure that adequate quantitative information is available for the planning of economic and social development in Africa. An indigenous economic model could be a significant component of such quantitative information. It should be recognized that many developing nations are capable of generating their own economic precedents. They typically have the number (in population) and the capability to support indigenous models. Through the practice of hoarding, "developing" retailers already know how to create artificial scarcity. They already know how to mount a social assault on the equilibrium point of the standard supply and demand curves. So, there in no such thing as a "market price" in many developing nations. Some suppliers have already customized the principles of fair competition to accommodate collusion. Through the forces of collusion, the suppliers can collectively dictate their harsh terms to hapless consumers.

In order to lay a serious foundation for industrial development, indigenous economists should be charged with the responsibility of conducting the appropriate research to study the feasibility of indigenous economic models for a nation that is aspiring to be industrialized. This may be effectively accomplished through postgraduate thesis research at the nation's institutions of higher learning. The research may be accomplished under the universitiy-industry cooperative model suggested earlier.

In an in-depth analysis of national development planning, Gharajedaghi (1986) stressed the fact that a plan of action must not be shortsighted by descriptive adjectives that tell us nothing about the nature of the problem being solved. In government functions, there is a tendency to place responsibility for dealing with a problem in that part of government where a relevant functional adjective can be found. For example, if a problem is found in transportation, the blames are directed at the transportation department. The responsibility for dealing with the problem is automatically assumed to be that of the department even though the root of the problem may be a lack of public discipline. Adjectives and nouns used to describe problems (e.g., health, finance, social, economic, political, etc.) often tell us nothing about the real problem being faced. The adjectives simply indicate the point of view of the person looking at the problem. This pitfall must be avoided if a workable indigenous economic model is to be found. All aspects of a nation's economic system (e.g., social, education, information, etc.) must be assessed in the development of the model.

1.8.3 Chaotic Economic System

The prevailing economic system in many developing countries can, at best, be characterized as unstructured. Various cultural, social, regional, economic, and tribal factors intermingle to produce a nebulous and unstable system. This volatile system may be portrayed schematically as shown in Figure 1-9.

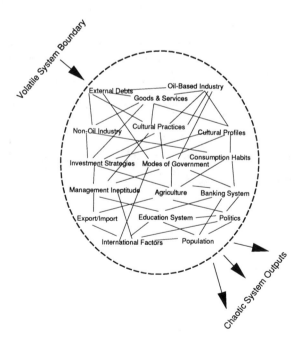

FIGURE 1-9.   Unstructured Economic System.

In the figure, several factors interact in undefined manners to produce uncontrollable outputs. In such a chaotic atmosphere, it is impossible to implement successfully any worthwhile industrial development policy. To have a chance for economic and industrial success, the intrinsic relationships among the several factors must be studied, understood, and combined in a structured format to generate reasonably predictable outputs. In this case, economic success is not defined merely in terms of favorable cash reserves or temporary trade fortunes. As certain situations of the past have shown, such precarious fortunes without solid foundations can quickly evaporate. Rather, economic success should be defined in terms of the ability of the national economy to sustain itself over long periods of time. Self-sustenance can be achieved by understanding and strategically controlling local economic factors. This will pave the way for steadfast industrial development.

1.8.4 Structured Economic System

An indigenous economic model will entail a careful analysis of each of the local economic factors discussed earlier. The specific ways in which each factor interacts with others can then be identified. Subsequently, synergistic integration of all the factors can be developed in order to achieve a formal indigenous model. The structural modeling may be depicted as shown in

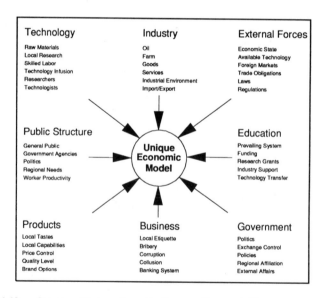

FIGURE 1-10.   Structured Integration of Indigenous Economic Factors.

Figure 1-10. In the figure, some selected factors are used to illustrate how categories of economic inputs may interact to define an indigenous economic profile. Within each category, relevant factors are identified and studied based on their interrelationships. The microanalysis of each economic category can then be used to determine how the diverse factors interact at the macro level. Thus, the output of the national economy can be predicted more accurately for a given set of inputs. Consequently, more reliable economic policies, conducive to industrial development, can be formulated.

1.8.5 Benefits of Indigenous Economic Model

The benefits of having an indigenous economic model are numerous. If successful, the model can encourage the country to undertake other self-help projects that might otherwise be left to external forces. It can serve as an incentive for citizens to believe in their own economic system. It can force people to exhibit more responsibility in their actions. The nation can exude pride for taking her own destiny in her own hands. The implementation of the model can serve as an example and guideline for other countries in similar economic plights.

The economic model can be presented to the citizens as an accurate description of their behaviors. That may compel them to reflect and become more conscious of the way they approach consumption of goods and services; thereby providing avenues for controlling inflation. The model can be an educational tool by making each sector of the economy more appreciative of the rationale behind the actions of other sectors. The idea of an indigenous economic model should provide the directions in which to look for solutions to pervasive development problems, and it is hoped that those qualified would pursue the appropriate economic research.

1.9 PRODUCT STANDARDIZATION FOR INDUSTRIAL DEVELOPMENT

Product standardization is another factor that can facilitate industrial development. If a standard is available, product interchangeability will be possible. Thus, the market for an industrial product can expand. With an expanded market, better levels of industrialization can be achieved. Units of measure have been one area where standardization has been pursued in many nations. For example, conversion to the metric system has been pursued by several nations as a means to facilitate product compatibility and to increase world trade. As more and more countries are switching to metric, a standard system of measurements will simplify international trade. The process of standardization is complicated. But once the initial difficulties of adopting a standard have been overcome, industrial exchanges will become easier.

One of the major problems in industrial development is the lack of product integration. We may be effective in making good individual products. But when it comes to fitting the products together to arrive at an overall assembled system, we may have difficulties if there are no prevailing standards. Products should be designed with consideration for how they support one another to achieve an overall workable system.

1.10 INDUSTRIAL QUALITY STANDARD

Product quality can be the ultimate industrial weapon. Higher product quality is required for a company to become more competitive both locally and in international trade. Higher quality is the basis for achieving the competitive edge needed to fuel industrial development. Important decisions must be made regarding the quality of products and services. With the increasing global pressures of quality requirements, the traditional concept of quality control must be expanded to the concept of total quality management. Traditional quality control attempts to meet a specified quality standard typically through product inspection. By contrast, quality management addresses the broader issues of eliminating quality problems and improving product quality through all facets of production.

The overall quality-management effort should address both the quality-assurance functions and the quality-control functions. Quality assurance is concerned with the functions of anticipating and preventing quality problems. Quality assurance encompasses all the actions necessary to ensure that the product or service generated will conform to quality requirements. Quality-assurance personnel serve as the liaison between the customer and the product. They evaluate and outline quality specifications with respect to customer requirements. Quality control is concerned with the operational techniques for detecting, recording, and taking actions to eliminate quality problems. Quality management involves an integrated management of all the functions that can have an impact on the quality of a product.

Under the notion of quality management, quality-control inspection serves only as an aid in detecting quality problems and providing signals for needed improvement. Quality inspections will not necessarily lead to better quality of products. In fact, strict quality-inspection policies take a pessimistic view at a production process in which products with poor quality characteristics are expected. Thus, inspections are performed to locate those defective products. In competitive industrial markets, efforts must be made to prevent quality problems rather than designing mechanisms to detect problems. Proper attention must be given to all the crucial factors in a process.

1.10.1 International Quality Standards

The strive for better quality worldwide has led to the need for unified international quality standards. Responding to this need, the International Organization for Standardization (ISO) in Geneva, Switzerland, has prepared the quality standard known as ISO 9000. The ISO is a special international agency for standardization composed of the national standards bodies of ninety-one countries.

ISO 9000 Standard

ISO 9000 is a set of five individual but related international standards on quality management and quality assurance. The standards were developed to help companies effectively document the quality-system elements required to maintain an efficient quality system. The standards were originally published in 1987. They are not specific to any particular industry, product, or service. The five individual standards that make up the ISO 9000 series are explained below:

ISO 9000: Title: *Quality management and quality assurance standards: Guidelines for use.*

This is the road map that provides guidelines for selecting and using 9001, 9002, 9003, and 9004. A supplementary publication, ISO 8402, provides quality-related definitions.

ISO 9001: Title: *Quality Systems: Model for quality assurance in design/development, production, installation, and servicing.*

This is the most comprehensive standard. It presents a model for quality assurance for design, manufacturing, installation, and servicing systems.

ISO 9002: Title: *Quality Systems: Model for quality assurance in production and installation.*

This presents a model for quality assurance in production and installation.

ISO 9003: Title: *Quality Systems: Model for quality assurance in final inspection and test.*

This presents a model for quality assurance in final inspection and test.

ISO 9004: Title: *Quality Management and Quality Systems Elements: Guidelines.*

This provides guidelines to users in the process of developing in-house quality systems.

Importance of ISO 9000 to Industrialization

The ISO 9000 standards help in determining capable suppliers with effective quality-assurance systems. The standards help reduce buyers' quality costs through confidence and assurance in suppliers' quality practices. Compliance with an ISO 9000 standard provides a means for contractual agreement between the buyer and the supplier. Companies that are certified and registered as meeting the ISO standards are perceived as viable suppliers to their customers. Those that are not are viewed as providing less-desirable products and services. The high-quality perception encouraged by ISO 9000 can help motivate efforts for industrialization.

ISO standards are designed to address a variety of quality-management scenarios. For example, if a supplier has only a manufacturing facility with no design or development function, then ISO 9002 would be used to evaluate the quality system. Each country has her own quality-system standards that relate to the ISO 9000 standards. Each individual company is encouraged to register formally for compliance with the standards. In fact, ISO 9000 registration has become an important factor considered when companies select their suppliers.

The ISO 9000 series standards define the minimum requirements a supplier must meet to assure its customers that they are receiving high-quality products. This has had a major impact on companies around the world. Through the ISO standards, suppliers can now be evaluated consistently and uniformly. The ISO 9000 series has been adopted in the United States by the American National Standards Institute (ANSI) and the American Society

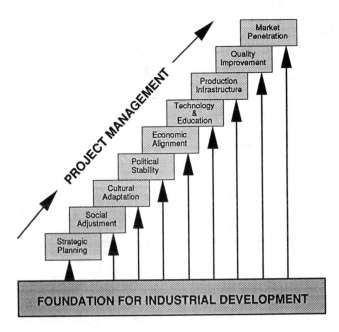

FIGURE 1-11.   The Path of Industrial Development.

for Quality Control (ASQC) as ANSI/ASQC Q90 standards. The European equivalent of ISO 9000, named EN 290000 series, is also now having global impact.

Good quality standards can help an industrial enterprise to know exactly what is expected with respect to the quality of industrial products and services. This awareness can positively affect morale and provide the impetus for further commitment to quality and industrial development. Figure 1-11 summarizes the path to industrial development. The chapters that follow present specific guidelines for using project approaches in the industrialization effort.

1.11 ENVIRONMENTAL IMPACT OF INDUSTRIALIZATION

Environmental concerns are a major issue in industrial development programs. Environmental prudence must be exercised in all industrial development projects. New manufacturing processes and technologies have unleashed unprecedented levels of environmental waste. The disposal of unfamiliar industrial wastes would need to be taken into consideration in the overall development project. Activities designed to preserve environmental quality should be included in the task list of any industrial development project right from the planning stages. Industrial health hazards and industrial toxic waste disposal must be included in the overall management approach to industrial development.

Nations around the world are now confronted with increasing deterioration of environmental health. There is a wide range of developing environmental crises. A few of the recent concerns involve the following:

- The release of chemical chlorofluorocarbons (CFCs) is diminishing the ozone layer that protects the earth from ultraviolet radiation.
- Maritime plastic wastes create widespread devastation of sea life.
- Emissions of sulfur dioxide and other compounds from industrial and automotive exhaust pipes create an "acid rain" effect that harms forests and causes an imbalance in the chemistry of lakes.
- Raw sewage, garbage, and medical wastes wash up on beaches along several coastlines, creating maritime problems of immense proportions.
- Huge piles of municipal garbage and hidden masses of hazardous industrial wastes create serious environmental concerns for local government authorities.
- Decades of stockpiling nuclear weapons have left tons of radioactive wastes around federal facilities. These wastes carry potential dangers whose full environmental impacts are yet to be assessed.

- Oil tanker accidents that spill millions of gallons of crude oil in biologically sensitive waters create big cleanup and recovery problems.
- The continued combustion of fossil fuels, combined with deforestation around the world, contribute to a potential "greenhouse effect" of global warming.
- Overefficient insulation of private dwellings create an encapsulation of polluted indoor air that seriously threaten the health of the inhabitants.

These environmental problems have been developing for years. Lack of proper management of projects that affect the environment continue to compound the problems. Unfortunately, the actions necessary to abate the problems have not kept pace with the level of destruction. The resources that are supposed to sustain our existence (the air we breathe, the water we drink, and the land we live on) now pose serious dangers to our health. Spending by U.S. industry for pollution-control equipment and services is now approaching $100 billion annually. Through the activities of the Environmental Protection Agency (EPA), the U.S. government has intensified its commitment to improving the environment. President Bush campaigned on an "environmentalist" platform. Several laws addressing environmental issues are now pending in the U.S. Congress. In summer of 1989 President Bush proposed a revision of the Clean Air Act that would add an estimated $14 to $18 billion to the nation's environmental construction bill.

On March 17, 1989, the "Indoor Air Quality Act of 1989" was introduced in the U.S. Congress. This Act authorized $48.5 million each year for 1990 through 1994 for a federal indoor air pollution-control program. In addition to authorizing grants for developing indoor air management strategies and response programs, the Act required the EPA to do the following:

1. Establish a research and development program in cooperation with federal, state, and local agencies.
2. Publish and revise, at least biennially, a list of known indoor air contaminants.
3. Provide "Contaminant Health Advisories."
4. Issue a National Indoor Air Quality Response Plan.
5. Establish an Office of Indoor Air Quality.
6. Create a National Indoor Air Quality Information Clearinghouse to collect and disseminate information related to indoor air pollution.

The above environmental concerns and control actions will directly affect industrial development efforts, not only in a single nation but across the world. The integrated approach of project management will facilitate a global view of how a proposed project may affect the environment and how to mitigate the effects.

2

Introduction to Project Management

Good management is the root of business survival.

Project management can play a crucial role as nations all over the world strive to improve or sustain their industrialization levels. Project management can facilitate on-time and within-budget industrialization programs. Project-management techniques are widely used in many enterprises, including construction, banking, manufacturing, marketing, health care services, transportation, R&D, and public services. Development programs represent another fertile area for the application of project-management techniques.

The basic benefits include:

- Increase in the awareness of prevailing goals and objectives.

- Coordination and integration of the efforts of functional teams and groups.

- Clear definition of responsibilities and accountability.

- Clarification of project priorities.

- Increase in scheduling effectiveness and timeliness of projects.

- Better allocation and utilization of resources.

- Improved multiproject communication, cooperation, and coordination.

These benefits are consistent with the objectives of industrial development. Consequently, effort must be directed at the application of project management to industrial development. Typically, much money is invested in industrial development efforts, with little attention given to the project-management process. This shortcoming often leads to project failures. If a project-management approach is used early, it can help reduce project time and cost while improving performance.

2.1 PROJECT MANAGEMENT APPROACH

Project management is the process of managing, allocating, and timing resources to achieve a given goal in an efficient and expedient manner. The objectives that constitute the specified goal may be in terms of time, costs, or technical results. A project can be quite simple or very complex. An example of a simple project is painting a small vacant room. An example of a complex project is building a new industrial complex. Industrial development project is difficult because of the number and complexity of the interactions required to make it successful. Getting the job done is the primary purpose of project management. The wide applicability of project management has been extensively recognized in business and industry. For example, in the application of project management to quality-improvement projects, Juran (1988) states that: "The project approach is important. When it comes to quality, there is no such thing as improvement in general. Any improvement in quality is going to come about project-by-project and no other way." (p. 45)

Management-by-Project (MBP) is a concept we highly recommended. It is applicable to all types of endeavors, including forecast formulation and implementation, establishment of new industry, launching a new product, construction of public facilities, conversion to new technology, and so on. Project management can facilitate the manufacture of industrial products and make them cheaper and faster to reach the market ahead of the competition. The standard hierarchy of the elements of project management consists of system, program, project, task, and activity.

System. A project system consists of interrelated elements organized for the purpose of achieving a common goal. The elements are expected to work synergistically to generate a unified output that is greater than the sum of the individual outputs of the components.

Program. Program commonly denotes very large and prolonged undertakings. It is a term that is typically applied to project endeavors that span several years. Large-scale industrial development efforts may be referred to as development programs. Programs are usually associated with particular systems. For example, an industrial development program within a national development system.

Project. Project is the term generally applied to time-phased efforts of much

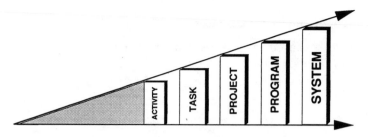

FIGURE 2-1.   Progression from Activity to Program.

smaller scope and duration than programs. Programs are sometimes viewed as consisting of a set of projects. Government projects are often referred to as programs because of their broad and comprehensive natures. The industrial sector tends to use the term *project* because of the focused nature of most industrial efforts.

Task. A task is a functional element of a project. A project is normally composed of contiguous arrays of tasks that jointly contribute to the overall project goal.

Activity. An activity can be defined as a single element of a project. Activities are generally smaller in scope than tasks. In a detailed analysis of a project, an activity may be viewed as the smallest, practically indivisible work element of the project. As an example, we can consider a manufacturing plant as a system. A plantwide endeavor to improve productivity can be viewed as a program. The installation of a flexible manufacturing system is a project within the productivity-improvement program. The process of identifying and selecting equipment vendors is a task, and the actual process of placing an order with a preferred vendor is an activity. Figure 2-1 presents the functional and hierarchical relationships among the components of a project.

The techniques of project management can help accomplish goals relating to better product quality, improved resource utilization, better customer relations, higher productivity, and fulfillment of due dates. These can generally be expressed in terms of the following project constraints:

- Performance specifications.
- Schedule requirements.
- Cost limitations.

2.1.1 Steps of Project Management

The project-management process is often summarized into the following four major functions:

> • Project planning.
>
> • Project organization.
>
> • Project scheduling.
>
> • Project control.

Each phase may be further broken down to show details of its components. In practice, the specific contents of each phase and breakdown of the phases may be dictated by the prevailing situation and organizational requirements. The phases are not necessarily implemented in a strict order. Events that occur during the scheduling phase, for example, may necessitate revising the project plan. In that case, replanning may involve several of the elements included in the initial planning phase.

During project implementation, the project-management phases should

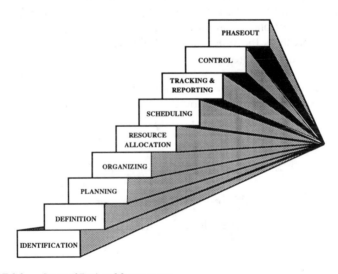

FIGURE 2-2.   Steps of Project Management.

be broken down into specific steps. Figure 2-2 presents the major steps in project management. The life cycle of a project typically consists of several steps going from problem identification, definition, specifications, project formulation, organizing, resource allocation, scheduling, tracking and reporting, and control to project termination. The steps are typically performed strategically in accordance with the specified project goal. Some of the steps are discussed briefly below, and some are discussed further in subsequent sections.

Problem Identification
Problem identification is the stage where a need for a proposed project is identified, defined, and justified. A project may be concerned with the development of new products, implementation of new processes, or improvement of existing facilities.

Project Definition
Project definition is the phase at which the purpose of the project is clarified. A *mission statement* is the major output of this stage. For example, a prevailing low level of productivity may prompt a need for a new manufacturing technology. In general, the definition should specify how project management may be used to avoid missed deadlines, poor scheduling, inadequate resource allocation, lack of coordination, poor quality, and conflicting priorities.

Project Planning
Project planning determines how to initiate and execute the objectives of a project. Because of the need for complete coverage, a separate chapter is devoted to further details on project planning.

Project Organizing
Project organization specifies how to integrate the functions of the personnel involved in a project. Organizing is normally done concurrently with project planning. Directing is an important aspect of project organization. Directing involves guiding and supervising project personnel. It is a crucial aspect in the management function. Directing requires skillful managers who can interact with subordinates effectively through good communication and motivation techniques. A successful manager improves the performance of subordinates by directing them, through proper task assignments, toward the project goal.

Workers perform better when there are clearly defined expectations. They need to know how their job functions contribute to the overall goals of the project. Workers should be given some flexibility for self-direction in the process of performing their functions. Individual worker needs and limitations should be recognized by the project manager when directing project functions. Project directing consists of the following elements:

Supervising. Monitoring, guiding, and reviewing the day-to-day activities of subordinates with respect to project goals. Empathy should be a basic consideration when supervising subordinates.

Delegating. Assignment of responsibility or secondary authority to subordinates for the execution of certain functions so as to enhance the utilization of manpower resources.

Motivating. Boosting the morale and interest of subordinates in performing their jobs. This requires understanding the needs, motives, and feelings of subordinates and an appreciation for the nature of their responses to certain directives.

Resource Allocation
Project goals and objectives are accomplished by applying resources to functional requirements. Resources are generally made up of people and equipment, which are typically in short supply. For example, the people needed for a particular task may be committed to other ongoing projects. A crucial piece of equipment may be under the control of an uncooperative department.

Project Scheduling
Scheduling is often recognized as the major function in project management. The main purpose of scheduling is to allocate resources so that the overall project objectives are achieved within a reasonable time span. In general, scheduling involves the assignment of time periods to specific tasks within the work schedule. Resource availability, time limitations, urgency level, required performance level, precedence requirements, work priorities, technical constraints, and other factors complicate the scheduling process. Thus, the assignment of a time slot to a task does not necessarily ensure that the task will be performed satisfactorily in accordance with the schedule. Consequently, careful control must be developed and maintained throughout the project-scheduling process. A separate chapter is devoted to further discussion of this topic.

Project Tracking and Reporting
This phase involves the process of checking whether or not project results conform to plans and specifications. Tracking and reporting are prerequisites for project control. A properly organized report of project status will quickly identify the deficiencies in the progress of the project and help pinpoint necessary corrective actions.

Project Control
With project control, necessary actions are taken to correct unacceptable deviations from expected performance. Control is effected by measurement, evaluation, and corrective action. Measurement is the process of measuring the relationship between planned performance and actual performance with respect to project objectives. The variable to be measured, the measurement scale, and measuring approach should be clearly specified during the planning stage.

Project Phaseout
Phaseout is the last stage of a project. The phaseout of a project is as important as its initiation. There should be as much commitment to the termination of a project at the appropriate time as the commitment to initiating it. A project should not be allowed to drag on needlessly after the expected completion time. A terminal activity should be defined for a project during the project-planning phase. An example of a terminal activity may be the submission of a final report, the "power-on" of new equipment, or the signing of a release order. The conclusion of such an activity should be viewed as the completion of the project.

To prevent a project from dragging on needlessly, definite arrangements should be made about when the project should end. However, provisions should be made for follow-up activities or projects that may further improve the results of the initial project. These follow-up or spin-off projects should be managed as totally separate projects but with proper input–output relationships between the sequence of projects. If a project is not terminated when appropriate, the motivation for it will wane, and subsequent activities may become counterproductive. This is particularly true for technology-based projects where the "fear of the unknown" and "resistance to change" are already major obstacles.

2.2 PROJECT-IMPLEMENTATION MODEL

It is helpful to have a model that can be adopted for project-implementation purposes. The comprehensive model presented below is recommended for the essential tasks in project planning, scheduling, and control.

1. Planning
  I. Specify project background
     a. Define current situation and process
        1. Understand the process
        2. Identify important variables
        3. Quantify variables

    b. Identify areas for improvement
      1. List and explain areas
      2. Study potential strategy for solution
  II. Define unique terminologies relevant to the project
      1. Industry-specific terminologies
      2. Company-specific terminologies
      3. Project-specific terminologies
 III. Define project goal and objectives
    a. Write mission statement
    b. Solicit inputs and ideas from personnel
 IV. Establish performance standards
    a. Schedule
    b. Performance
    c. Cost
  V. Conduct formal project feasibility
    a. Determine impact on cost
    b. Determine impact on organization
    c. Determine project deliverables
 VI. Secure management support

2. Organizing

  I. Identify project-management team
    a. Specify project-organization structure
      1. Matrix structure
      2. Formal and informal structures
      3. Justify structure
    b. Specify departments involved and key personnel
      1. Purchasing
      2. Materials management
      3. Engineering, design, manufacturing, etc.
    c. Define project-management responsibilities
      1. Select project manager
      2. Write project charter
      3. Establish project policies and procedures
  II. Implement Triple C model
    a. *Communication*
      1. Determine communication interfaces
      2. Develop communication matrix
    b. *Cooperation*
      1. Outline cooperation requirements
    c. *Coordination*
      1. Develop work-breakdown structure

      2. Assign task responsibilities
      3. Develop responsibility chart

3. Scheduling and Resource Allocation

  I. Develop master schedule
    a. Estimate task duration
    b. Identify task-precedence requirements
      1. Technical precedence
      2. Resource-imposed precedence
      3. Procedural precedence
    c. Use analytical models
      1. CPM
      2. PERT
      3. Gantt chart
      4. Optimization models

4. Tracking, Reporting, and Control

  I. Establish guidelines for tracking, reporting, and control
    a. Define data requirements
      1. Data categories
      2. Data characterization
      3. Measurement scales
    b. Develop data documentation
      1. Data-update requirements
      2. Data-quality control
      3. Establish data-security measures
 II. Categorize control points
    a. Schedule audit
      1. Activity network and Gantt charts
      2. Milestones
      3. Delivery schedule
    b. Performance audit
      1. Employee performance
      2. Product quality
    c. Cost audit
      1. Cost-containment measures
      2. Percent completion versus budget depletion
III. Identify implementation process
IV. Phaseout the project
    a. Performance review
    b. Strategy for follow-up projects
    c. Personnel retention and releases
 V. Document project and submit final report

The model above gives a general guideline for project planning, scheduling, and control. The skeleton of the model can be adopted for specific implementation as required for specific projects. Not all projects will need to address all the contents of the model. Customization will always be necessary when implementing the model. For an industrial development project, the unique aspects of the project, as discussed in Chapter 1, should be taken into consideration when customizing the model. The functions and activities encompassed by the project-implementation model do not have to be carried out in a sequential order. Some functions may overlap as illustrated by the bar chart in Figure 2-3.

2.2.1 Selling the Project Plan

The project plan must be sold throughout an organization. For an industrial development project, selling the project plan may involve dealing with various community groups. For some projects, the plan may need to be sold at the national level. Different levels of detail will be needed when presenting the project to various groups. The higher the level of management, the lower the level of detail. Top-level management will be more interested in the

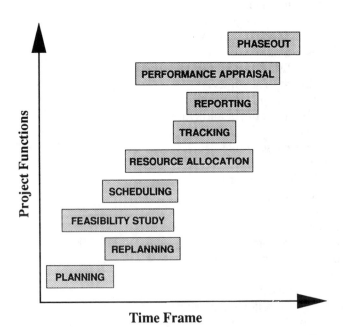

FIGURE 2-3.   Bar Chart of Project-Implementation Functions.

global aspects of the project. For example, when presenting the project to management, it is necessary to specify how the overall organization will be affected by the project. When presenting the project to the supervisory-level staff, the most important aspect of the project will be the operational level of detail.

At the worker or operator level, the individual will be more concerned about how the project requirements will affect his or her job. The project manager or analyst must be able to accommodate these various levels of detail when presenting the plan to both participants and customers of the project. Regardless of the group being addressed, the project presentation, at a minimum, should cover the essential elements below at the appropriate levels of detail:

Project Background.
Project Description.
    Goals and objective.
    Expected outcome.
Performance Measure.
Conclusions.
Recommendations.

2.3 THE TRIPLE C APPROACH

The Triple C model presented by Badiru (1987) is an effective project management approach. The model states that project management can be enhanced by implementing it within the integrated functions of:

- Communication
- Cooperation
- Coordination

The model facilitates a systematic approach to project planning, organizing, scheduling, and control. The Triple C model is distinguished from the 3C approach commonly used in military operations. The military approach emphasizes personnel management in the hierarchy of command, control, and communication. This places communication as the last function. The

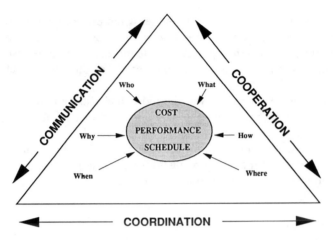

FIGURE 2-4.   Implementation of Triple C Model for Control.

Triple C, by contrast, suggests communication as the first and foremost function. It can be implemented for project planning and control purposes. In Figure 2-4, the model shows the important interfaces between communication, cooperation, coordination, performance, cost, and schedule control. The Triple C model highlights what must be done and when. It also helps to identify the resources (manpower, equipment, facilities, etc.) required for each effort.

2.3.1 Communication

The communication function of project management involves making all those concerned aware of project requirements and progress. Those who will be affected by the project directly or indirectly, as direct participants or as beneficiaries, should be informed as appropriate regarding the following:

- The scope of the project.
- The personnel contribution required.
- The expected cost and merits of the project.
- The project-organization and implementation plan.
- The potential adverse effects if the project should fail.

- The alternatives, if any, for achieving the project goal.
- The potential direct and indirect benefits of the project.

The communication channel must be kept open throughout the project life cycle. In addition to internal communication, appropriate external sources should also be consulted. The project manager must:

- Exude commitment to the project.
- Utilize a communication responsibility matrix.
- Facilitate multichannel communication interfaces.
- Identify internal and external communication needs.
- Resolve organizational and communication hierarchies.
- Encourage both formal and informal communication links.

2.3.2 Cooperation

The cooperation of the project personnel must be explicitly elicited. Merely voicing a consent for a project is not enough assurance of full cooperation. The participants and beneficiaries of the project must be convinced of the merits of the project. Some of the factors that influence cooperation in a project environment include manpower and resource requirements, budget limitations, past experiences, conflicting priorities, and lack of uniform organizational support. A structured approach to seeking cooperation should clarify the following:

- The cooperative efforts required.
- The precedents for future projects.

- The implication of lack of cooperation.
- The criticality of cooperation to project success.
- The organizational impact of cooperation.
- The organizational impact of cooperation.
- The time frame involved in the project.
- The rewards of good cooperation.

Cooperation is a basic virtue of human interaction. More projects fail due to a lack of cooperation and commitment than any other project factors. To secure and retain the cooperation of project participants, one must elicit a positive first reaction to the project. The most positive aspects of a project should be the first items of project communication. For project management, there are different types of cooperation that should be understood:

Functional Cooperation. Cooperation induced by the nature of the functional relationship between two groups. The two groups may be required to perform related functions that can only be accomplished through mutual cooperation.

Social Cooperation. Type of cooperation achieved by the social relationship between two groups. The prevailing social relationship motivates cooperation that may be useful in getting project work done.

Legal Cooperation. Type of cooperation that is imposed through some authoritative requirement. In this case, the participants may have no choice other than to cooperate.

Administrative Cooperation. Cooperation brought on by administrative requirements that make it imperative that two groups work together on a common goal.

Associative Cooperation. Cooperation that may also be referred to as collegiality. The level of cooperation is determined by the association that exists between two groups.

Proximity Cooperation. Cooperation due to the fact that two groups are geographically close is referred to as proximity cooperation. Being close makes it imperative that the two groups work together.

Dependency Cooperation. Cooperation caused by the fact that one group depends on another group for some important aspect. Such dependency is usually of a mutual two-way nature. One group depends on the other for one thing, and the latter group depends on the former for some other thing.

Imposed Cooperations. Type of cooperation in which external agents must be employed to induce cooperation between two groups. This is applicable for cases where the two groups have no natural reason to cooperate. This is where the approaches presented earlier for seeking cooperation can become very useful.

Lateral Cooperation. Cooperation with peers and immediate associates. Lateral cooperation is often easy to achieve because existing lateral relationships create a conducive environment for project cooperation.

Vertical Cooperation. Cooperation that is implied by the hierarchical structure of the project. For example, subordinates are expected to cooperate with their vertical superiors.

Whichever type of cooperation is available in a project environment, the cooperative forces should be channeled toward achieving project goals. A documentation of prevailing level of cooperation is useful for winning further support for a project. Clarification of project priorities will facilitate personnel cooperation. Relative priorities of multiple projects should be specified so that a project that is of high priority to one segment of an organization is also of high priority to all groups within the organization. Some guidelines for securing cooperation for industrial development projects are presented below:

- Establish achievable goals for the project.
- Clearly outline individual commitments required.
- Integrate project priorities with existing priorities.
- Eliminate the fear of job loss due to industrialization.
- Anticipate and eliminate potential sources of conflict.
- Use an open-door policy to address project grievances.
- Remove skepticism by documenting the merits of the project.

2.3.3 Coordination

After successfully initiating the communication and cooperation functions, the efforts of the project personnel must be coordinated. Coordination facilitates harmonious organization of project efforts. The development of a responsibility chart can be very helpful at this stage. A responsibility chart is a matrix consisting of columns of individual or functional departments and rows of required actions. Cells within the matrix are filled with relationship codes that indicate who is responsible for what. The responsibility chart helps avoid neglecting crucial communication requirements and obligations. It can help resolve questions such as:

- Who is to do what?
- How long will it take?
- Who is to inform whom of what?
- Whose approval is needed for what?
- Who is responsible for which results?
- What personnel interfaces are required?
- What support is needed from whom and when?

2.3.4 Resolving Project Conflicts with Triple C

When implemented as an integrated process, the Triple C model can help avoid conflicts in a project. When conflicts do develop, it can help in resolving the conflicts. Several sources of conflicts can exist in industrial development projects. Some of these are:

Schedule Conflict. Conflicts can develop because of improper timing or sequencing of project tasks. This is particularly common in large multiple projects. Procrastination can lead to having too much to do at once, thereby creating a clash of project functions and discord between project team members. Inaccurate estimates of time requirements may lead to infeasible activity schedules. Project coordination can help avoid schedule conflicts.

Cost Conflict. Project cost may not be generally acceptable to the clients of a project. This will lead to project conflict. Even if the initial cost of the project is acceptable, a lack of cost control during project implementation can lead to conflicts. Poor budget-allocation approaches and a lack of financial feasibility study will cause cost conflicts later on in a project. Communication and coordination can help prevent most of the adverse effects of cost conflicts.

Performance Conflict. If clear performance requirements are not established, performance conflicts will develop. Lack of clearly defined performance standards can lead each person to evaluate his or her own performance based on personal value judgments. In order uniformly to evaluate quality of work and monitor project progress, performance standards should be established by using the Triple C approach.

Management Conflict. There must be a two-way alliance between management and the project team. The views of management should be understood by the team. The views of the team should be appreciated by management. If this does not happen, management conflicts will develop. A lack of a two-way interaction can lead to strikes and industrial actions can be detrimental to project objectives. The Triple C approach can help create a conducive dialog environment between management and the project team.

Technical Conflict. If the technical basis of a project is not sound, technical conflicts will develop. Industrial development projects are particularly prone to technical conflicts because of their significant dependence on technology. Lack of a comprehensive technical feasibility study will lead to technical conflicts. Performance requirements and systems specifications can be integrated through the Triple C approach to avoid technical conflicts.

Priority Conflict. Priority conflicts can develop if project objectives are not defined properly and applied uniformly across a project. Lack of direction in project definition can lead each project member to define his or her own goals, which may be in conflict with the intended goal of a project. Lack of consistency of project mission is another potential source of priority conflicts. Overassignment of responsibilities with no guidelines for relative significance levels can also lead to priority conflicts. Communication can help defuse priority conflicts.

Resource Conflict. Resource-allocation problems are a major source of conflicts in project management. Competition for resources, including personnel, tools, hardware, software, and so on, can lead to disruptive clashes among project members. The Triple C approach can help secure resource cooperation.

Power Conflict. Project politics lead to power play that can adversely affect the progress of a project. Project authority and project power should be clearly delineated. Project authority is the control that a person has by virtue of his or her functional post. Project power relates to the clout and influence that a person can exercise due to connections within the administrative structure. People with popular personalities can often wield a lot of project power in spite of low or nonexistent project authority. The Triple C model can facilitate a positive marriage of project authority and power to the benefit of project goals. This will help define clear leadership for a project.

Personality Conflict. Personality conflict is a common problem in projects involving a large group of people. The larger a project, the larger the size of the management team needed to keep things running. Unfortunately, a large management team creates an opportunity for personality conflicts. Communication and cooperation can help defuse personality conflicts.

In summary, conflict resolution through Triple C can be achieved by observing the following rules:

- Confront the conflict and identify the underlying causes.
- Be cooperative and receptive to negotiation as a mechanism for resolving conflicts.
- Distinguish between proactive, inactive, and reactive behaviors in a conflict situation.
- Use communication to defuse internal strife and competition.
- Recognize that short-term compromise can lead to long-term gains.
- Use coordination to work toward a unified goal.

It is the little, often neglected, aspects of a project that lead to project failures. Several factors may constrain the project implementation. All the relevant factors can be evaluated under the Triple C model right from the project-planning stage. The adaptation of the nursery rhyme below illustrates the importance of little factors for project success.

Fall of the Kingdom

- For the want of a nail, the horse shoe was lost;
- For the loss of the horse show, the horse was lost;
- For the loss of the horse, the rider was lost;
- For the loss of the rider, the message was lost;
- For the loss of the message, the battle was lost;
- For the loss of the battle, the war was lost;
- For the loss of the war, the Kingdom was lost;
- All for the want of a nail!

Failure of the Project

- For the want of communication, the data was lost;
- For the lack of the data, the information was lost;
- For the lack of the information, the decision was lost;
- For the lack of the decision, the cooperation was lost;
- For the lack of the cooperation, the planning was lost;
- For the lack of the planning, the coordination was lost;
- For the lack of the coordination, the project failed.
- All for the want of communication!

2.4 PROJECT-DECISION PROCESS

The decision process for project management consists of a series of steps. The steps facilitate a proper consideration of the essential elements of decisions in a project environment. These essential elements include problem statement, information, performance measure, decision model, and an implementation of the decision. A recommended project-decision process is outlined:

Step 1. Problem Statement
A problem involves choosing between competing, and probably conflicting, alternatives. The components of problem solving in project management include:

> - Describing the problem.
>
> - Defining a model to represent the problem.
>
> - Solving the model.
>
> - Testing the solution.
>
> - Implementing and maintaining the solution.

Problem definition is very crucial. In many cases, *symptoms* of a problem are recognized more readily than its *cause* and *location*. Even after the problem is accurately identified and defined, a benefit/cost analysis may be needed to determine if the cost of solving the problem is justified.

Step 2. Data and Information Requirements
Information is the driving force of the project-decision process. Information clarifies the relative states of past, present, and future events. The collection, storage, retrieval, organization, and processing of raw data are important components for generating information. Without data, there can be no information. Without good information, there cannot be a valid decision. The essential requirements for generating information are:

> - To ensure that an effective data-collection procedure is followed.
>
> - To determine the type and the appropriate amount of data to collect.

- To evaluate the data collected with respect to information potential.
- To evaluate the cost of collecting the required data.

For example, suppose that a manager is presented with a recorded fact that says, "sales for the last quarter are 10,000 units." This constitutes ordinary data. There are many ways of using this piece of data to make a decision depending on the manager's value system. An analyst, however, can ensure the proper use of the piece of data by transforming it into information such as, "sales of 10,000 units for last quarter are low." This type of information is more useful for the manager for decision-making purposes.

Step 3. Performance Measure

A performance measure for the competing alternatives should be specified. The decision maker assigns a perceived worth or value to the available alternatives. Setting a measure of performance is crucial to the process of defining and selecting alternatives.

Step 4. Decision Model

A decision model provides the basis for the analysis and synthesis of information and is the platform over which competing alternatives are compared. To be effective, a decision model must be based on a systematic and logical framework for guiding project decisions. A decision model can be a verbal, graphical, or mathematical representation of the ideas in the decision-making process. A project-decision model should have the following characteristics:

- It should be a simplified representation of the actual situation.
- It should explain and predict the actual situation.
- It should be valid and be appropriate for the intended analysis.
- It should be applicable to similar problems.

There are five basic types of decision models for project management.

Descriptive Models. These are directed at describing a decision scenario and identifying the associated problem. For example, a project analyst might use an activity network model to identify bottleneck tasks in a project.

Prescriptive Models. These furnish procedural guidelines for implementing actions. The Triple C model, for example, is a model that prescribes the procedures for achieving communication, cooperation, and coordination in a project environment.

Predictive Models. These models are used to predict future events in a problem environment. They are typically based on historical data about the problem situation. For example, a regression model based on past data may be used to predict future productivity gains associated with expected levels of resource allocation.

Satisficing Models. These are models that provide trade-off strategies for achieving a satisfactory solution to a problem within given constraints. Goal programming and other multicriteria techniques provide good satisficing solutions. As an example, these models are helpful for cases when time limitation, resource shortage, and performance requirements constrain the implementation of a project.

Optimizing Models. These models are designed to find the best available solution to a problem subject to a certain set of constraints. For example, a linear programming model can be used to determine the optimum product mix in a production environment.

In many situations, two or more of the above models may be involved in the solution of a problem. For example, a descriptive model might provide insights into the nature of the problem; an optimizing model might provide the optimal set of actions to take in solving the problem; a satisficing model might modify the optimal solution by incorporating practicality; a prescriptive model might suggest the procedures for implementing the selected solution; and a predictive model might predict the expected outcome of implementing the solution.

Step 5. Decision Making

Using the available data, information, and the decision model, the decision maker will determine the real-world actions that are needed to solve the stated problem. A sensitivity analysis may be useful for determining what changes in parameter values might cause a change in the decision.

Step 6. Decision Implementation

A decision represents the selection of an alternative that satisfies the objective stated in the problem statement. A good decision is useless until it is implemented. An important aspect of a decision is to specify how it is to be implemented. Selling the decision and the project plan to management requires a well-organized, persuasive presentation. The way a decision is presented can directly influence whether or not it will be adopted. The presentation of a decision should include at least the following: an executive summary, technical aspects, managerial aspects, resources required, cost, and time frame for implementing the decision.

2.5 GROUP DECISION MAKING

Many decision situations are complex and poorly understood. No one person has all the information to make all decisions accurately. As a result, crucial decisions are normally made by a group of people. Some organizations use outside consultants with appropriate expertise to make recommendations for important decisions. Other organizations set up their own internal consulting groups that attend to decision problems without having to go outside the organization. American Airlines, 3M, and IBM are examples of organizations that use various levels of internal consulting groups. Decisions can be made through linear responsibility, in which case one person makes the final decision based on inputs from other people. Alternately, decisions can be made through shared responsibility, in which case a group of people share the responsibility for making joint decisions. The major advantages of group decision making are:

1. *The ability to Share Experience, Knowledge, and Resources.* Many heads are better than one. A group will possess greater collective ability to solve a given decision problem.
2. *Increased Credibility.* Decisions made by a group of people often carry more weight in an organization.
3. *Improved Morale.* Personnel morale can be positively influenced because many people have the opportunity to participate in the decision-making process.
4. *Better Rationalization.* The opportunity to observe other people's views can lead to an improvement in an individual's reasoning process.

2.5.1 Approaches to Group Decision Making

Group decision making is done by a number of different approaches. Some of the approaches are discussed in the sections that follow.

Brainstorming
Brainstorming is a way of generating many new ideas. In brainstorming, the decision group comes together to discuss alternate ways of solving a decision problem. The members of the brainstorming group may be from different

departments, may have different backgrounds and training, and may not even know one another. The diversity of the constituents helps to create a stimulating environment for generating many different ideas. The technique encourages free outward expression of new ideas no matter how far-fetched the ideas might appear. No criticism of any new idea is permitted during the brainstorming session. A major concern in brainstorming is that extroverts may take control of the discussions. For this reason, an experienced and respected leader is needed to manage the brainstorming discussions. The group leader establishes the procedure for proposing ideas, keeps the discussions in line with the group's mission, discourages disruptive statements, and encourages the participation of all members.

After the group runs out of more ideas, open discussions are held to weed out the unsuitable ones. Is it expected that even the rejected ideas may stimulate the generation of other ideas that may eventually lead to other favored ideas. Some guidelines for improving the brainstorming session are:

- Focus on a specific decision problem.
- Keep ideas relevant to the intended decision.
- Be receptive to all new ideas.
- Evaluate the ideas on a relative basis after exhausting new ideas.
- Maintain an atmosphere conducive to cooperative discussions.
- Maintain a record of the ideas generated.

Delphi Method

The traditional approach to group decision making is to obtain the opinion of experienced participants through open discussions. An attempt is then made to reach a consensus among the participants. However, open group discussions are often biased because of the influence or even subtle intimidation from dominant individuals. Even when the threat of a dominant individual is not present, opinions may still be swayed by group pressure. This is often called the "bandwagon effect" of group decision making.

The Delphi method, developed by Gordon and Helmer (1964), attempts to overcome these difficulties by requiring individuals to present their opinions anonymously through an intermediary. The method differs from the other interactive group methods because it eliminates face-to-face confrontations. It was originally developed for forecasting applications. But it has been modified in various ways for application to different types of decision making. The method can be quite useful for project-management decisions. It is particularly effective when decisions must be based on a broad set of factors. The Delphi method is normally implemented as follows:

1. *Problem Definition.* A decision problem that is considered significant to the organization or project is identified and clearly described.

2. *Group Selection.* An appropriate group of experts or experienced individuals is formed to address the particular decision problem. Both internal and external experts may be involved in the Delphi process. A leading individual is appointed to serve as the administrator of the decision process. The group may operate through the mail or gather together in a room. In either case, all opinions are expressed anonymously on paper. If the group meets in the same room, care should be taken to provide enough room so that members do not have the feeling that someone may accidentally or deliberately spy on their responses.

3. *Initial Opinion Poll.* The technique is initiated by describing the problem to be addressed in unambiguous terms. The group members are requested to submit a list of major areas of concern in their specialty areas as they relate to the decision problem.

4. *Questionnaire Design and Distribution.* Questionnaires are prepared to address the areas of concern related to the decision problem. The written responses to the questionnaires are collected and organized by the administrator. The administrator aggregates the responses in a statistical format. For example, the average, mode, and median of the responses may by computed. This analysis is distributed to the decision group. Each member can then see how his or her responses compare with the anonymous views of the other members.

5. *Iterative Balloting.* Additional questionnaires based on the previous responses are passed to the members. The members submit their responses again. They may choose to alter or not alter their previous responses.

6. *Silent Discussions and Consensus.* The iterative balloting may involve anonymous written discussions of why some responses are correct or incorrect. The process is continued until a consensus is reached. A consensus may be declared after five or six iterations of the balloting or when a specified percentage (e.g., 80 percent) of the group agrees on the questionnaires. If a consensus cannot be declared on a particular point, it may be displayed to the whole group with a note that it does not represent a consensus.

In addition to its use in technological forecasting, the Delphi method has been widely used in other general decision making. Its major characteristics of anonymity of responses, statistical summary of responses, and controlled procedure make it a reliable mechanism for obtaining numeric data from subjective opinion. The major limitations of the Delphi method are:

1. Its effectiveness may be limited in cultures where strict hierarchy, seniority, and age influence decision-making processes.

2. Some experts may not readily accept the contribution of nonexperts to the group decision-making process.
3. Because opinions are expressed anonymously, some members may take the liberty to make ludicrous statements. However, if the group composition is carefully reviewed, this problem may be avoided.

Nominal Group Technique

Nominal group technique is a silent version of brainstorming. Rather than asking people to state their ideas aloud, the team leader asks each member to jot down a minimum number of ideas, for example, five or six. A single list of ideas is then composed on a chalkboard for the whole group to see. The group then discusses the ideas and weeds out some iteratively until a final decision is made. The nominal group technique is easier to control. Unlike brainstorming, where members may get into shouting matches, it permits members to silently present their views. In addition, it allows introversive members to contribute to the decision without the pressure of having to speak out too often.

In all of the group decision-making techniques, an important aspect that can enhance and expedite the decision-making process is to require that members review all pertinent data before coming to the group meeting. This will ensure that the decision process is not impeded by trivial preliminary discussions. Some disadvantages of group decision making are:

1. Peer pressure in a group situation may influence a member's opinion or discussions.
2. In a large group, some members may not get to participate effectively in the discussions.
3. A member's relative reputation in the group may influence how well his or her opinion is rated.
4. A member with a dominant personality may overwhelm the other members in the discussions.
5. The limited time available to the group may create a time pressure that forces some members to present their opinions without fully evaluating the ramifications of the available data.
6. It is often difficult to get all members of a decision group together at the same time.

Despite the noted disadvantages, group decision making definitely has many advantages that may nullify the shortcomings. The advantages as presented earlier will have varying levels of effect from one organization to another. The Triple C principle presented in Chapter 1 many also be used to improve the success of decision teams. Team work can be enhanced in group decision making by following the guidelines below:

1. Get a willing group of people together.
2. Set an achievable goal for the group.
3. Determine the limitations of the group.
4. Develop a set of guiding rules for the group.
5. Create an atmosphere conducive to group synergism.
6. For major decisions and long-term group activities, arrange for team training that allows the group to learn the decision rules and responsibilities together.

2.6 PROJECT LEADERSHIP

Good leadership is the guiding light for the future. Good leaders lead by demonstrating good examples. Others pretend to lead by dictating. It is well-known that people learn and act best when good examples are available to emulate. Even the examples learned in babyhood or childhood can stay with an individual throughout a lifetime. A leader should have a spirit of performance that stimulates his or her subordinates to perform at their own best. Rather than dictate what needs to be done, a good leader would show what needs to be done. Showing, in this case, does not necessarily imply actual physical demonstration of what is to be done. Rather, it implies projecting a commitment to the function at hand and a readiness to participate as appropriate.

Good leadership is an essential component of project management. Project leadership involves dealing with managers and supporting personnel across the functional lines of the project. It is a misconception to think that a leader leads only his or her own subordinates. Leadership responsibilities can cover functions vertically up or down. A good project leader can lead not only his or her subordinates but also the entire project organization including the highest superiors. Leadership involves recognizing an opportunity to make improvement in a project and taking the initiative to implement the improvement. In addition to inherent personal qualities, leadership style can be influenced by training, experience, and dedication. Some pitfalls to avoid in project leadership are:

Politics and Egotism
- Forget personal ego.
- Don't glamorize personality.
- Focus on the big picture of project goals.

- Build up credibility with successful leadership actions.
- Cut out the politics and develop a spirit of cooperation.

Preaching versus Implementing
- Back up words with action.
- Adopt a "do as I do" attitude.
- Avoid a "do as I say" attitude.
- Participate in joint problem solving.
- Develop and implement workable ideas.

A good leader must pay attention to details. Former U.S. President Richard Nixon, recalling his management of the events leading to the Watergate scandal (Nixon, 1990), said, "I should have known that leaders who do big things well must be on guard against stumbling on the little things." This is a good lesson for project leaders, who should pay attention to even the little details of project management.

2.7 SYSTEMS APPROACH TO INDUSTRIAL PROJECT MANAGEMENT

The emergence of systems development has had an extensive effect on project management in recent years. A system can be defined as a collection of interrelated elements brought together to achieve a specified objective. In a management context, the purposes of a system are to develop and manage operational procedures and to facilitate effective decision-making process. A systems approach is particularly essential for industrial development projects because of the various factors that are expected to interact. Four of the major desired characteristics of an industrial project system include:

- Possession of a definite objective.
- Ability to interact with the environment.
- Ability to invoke self-regulation.
- Ability to carry out self-adjustment.

Project-management practitioners should serve as systems integrators. One of their primary responsibilities should involve ensuring the proper flow of information to control project efforts. The classical approach to the decision process follows rigid lines of organizational charts. By contrast, the system approach considers all the interactions necessary between the various elements of a project system in the decision process.

The various elements (or subsystems) of the project system act concurrently in a separate but interrelated fashion to achieve a common goal. This synergism helps to expedite the decision process and to enhance the effectiveness of project decisions. The supporting commitments from other subsystems of the organization serve to counterbalance the weaknesses of a given subsystem. Thus, the overall effectiveness of the system will be greater than the sum of the individual results from the subsystems.

The increasing complexity of organizations and projects makes the systems approach essential in today's management environment. As the number of complex projects increase, there will be an increasing need for project-management professionals who can function as systems integrators. Figure 2-5 shows an example of a production system in an industrial environment. Inputs from the environment are capital, labor, and raw material. The synergistic components of the overall system are the production operations, personnel functions, and facilities. These components interact under managerial guidance to produce products, services, and profit. Any industrial project will operate in a similar manner. It will get inputs from the environment, and it will produce outputs to satisfy the needs of the society.

Any project can be formulated as a system. Project-management techniques should play a role at all the stages of implementing any system. Ten

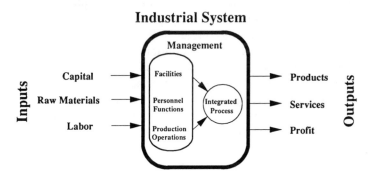

FIGURE 2-5.   Production System in an Industrial Environment.

major steps for successfully implementing a new industrial system are presented below. The system may be of a hardware nature, software nature, or both. The guidelines may be followed in the order and context presented or modified to suit specific project scenarios.

1. *Definition of Problem.* Define the problem using keywords that signify the importance of the problem to the overall organization. Locate experts in this area who are willing to contribute to the effort. Prepare and announce the development plan.

2. *Personnel Assignment.* The project group and the respective tasks should be announced. A qualified project manager should be appointed and a solid line of command and project control should be established.

3. *Project Initiation.* Arrange organizational meeting, during which a general approach to the problem should be discussed. Prepare specific development plan and arrange for the installation of needed hardware and tools.

4. *System Prototype.* Develop a prototype system, test it, and learn more about the problem from the test results.

5. *Full-System Development.* Expand the prototype to a full system, evaluate the user interface structure, and incorporate user training facilities and documentation.

6. *System Verification.* Get experts and potential users involved, ensure that the system performs as designed, and debug the system as needed.

7. *System Validation.* Ensure that the system yields expected outputs. Validate the system by evaluating performance level, such as percentage of success in so many trials, measuring the level of deviation from expected outputs, and measuring the effectiveness of the system output in solving the problem being addressed.

8. *System Integration.* Implement the full system as planned, ensure the system can coexist with systems already in operation, and arrange for technology transfer to other projects.

9. *System Maintenance.* Arrange for continuing maintenance of the system. Update solution procedures as new pieces of information become available. Retain responsibility for system performance or delegate to a well-trained and authorized personnel

10. *Documentation.* Prepare full documentation of a system, prepare a user's guide, and appoint a user consultant.

2.7.1 Systems Integration for Industrial Development

No industrial system can survive as an individual entity. With the increasing shortages of resources, more emphasis will need to be placed on the sharing of resources. No longer will an organization be able to operate as a self-sufficient island. Resource sharing may involve physical equipment, conceptual items, information, ideas, and so on. The integration of industrial systems facilitates the sharing of resources. Systems integration should be a major focus in industrial development projects. Industrial competition will force several enterprises to begin to appreciate the value of integrating their operations. For these reasons, systems integration has emerged as one of the crucial functions in project management. Integration can help link the design and manufacturing groups in order to achieve product coordination. System integration may involve physical integration of technical components, objective integration of operations, conceptual integration of management processes, or a combination of any of these.

Systems integration involves the linking of components to form subsystems and the linking of subsystems to form composite systems within a single organization or across several organizations. It facilitates the coordination of diverse technical and managerial efforts to enhance organizational functions, reduce cost, save energy, improve productivity, and increase the utilization of resources. Systems integration emphasizes the identification and coordination of the interface requirements between the components in an integrated system. The components and subsystems operate synergistically to optimize the performance of the total system. Systems integration ensures that all performance goals are satisfied with a minimum of expenditure of time and resources. Some important aspects of systems integration in an industrial environment are:

1. *Multiuser Integration.* This involves the use of a single component by separate subsystems to reduce both the initial cost and the operating cost during the project life cycle.
2. *Resource Coordination.* This involves integrating the resource flows of two normally separate subsystems so that the resource flow from one subsystem to the other minimizes the total resource requirements in a project.
3. *Functional Integration.* This involves the restructuring of functions and reintegration of subsystems to optimize costs when a new subsystem is introduced into the project environment.

A systems approach to industrial development project will consider all the interactions necessary between the various elements of the project. This will include people and machines. The supporting cooperative actions of subsystems in the industrial project environment will serve to counterbalance the weaknesses at certain points in the project. The individual capabili-

FIGURE 2-6.   Industrial Systems Integration.

ties of the subsystems will complement each other. Figure 2-6 depicts an integrated industrial system.

The figure shows the integration of various subsystems with respect to production objectives. For multiple projects, a variety of systems and subsystems will need to interact productively. A representative list of such linked systems may include the following:

- Management system.
- Manufacturing system.
- Quality-information system.
- Financial information system.
- Marketing information system.
- Inventory-information system.
- Personnel-information system.

- Production-information system.
- Design and engineering system.
- Management-information system.

These systems and subsystems should not be allowed to have conflicting priorities within the same organization. In order to achieve industrial development goals, project analysts must ensure that the subsystems view development as a universal responsibility. Development objectives must be prioritized, integrated, and applied uniformly throughout the development project with a global systems objective. In a bureaucratic system, project information may be fragmented, consisting of stacks of papers buried under desks. The system is often ill-structured, made up of a multitude of unintegrated files located at several sites. When management information is needed, new studies must be undertaken because crucial data cannot be located. An integrated systems approach to industrial project management is a mechanism that can help overcome this information deficiency. The major benefits of an integrated industrial system are:

- Systematic solution of development problems.
- Interaction with other production environments.
- Specification of the interrelationships of organizations.
- Cooperative regulation and adjustment of functions.
- Uniformity of development of goal objectives.

With respect to industrial development, interaction with the environment may be defined in terms of what the market environment wants. The objective of the industrial system is to achieve an acceptable level of development. The self-regulation characteristic relates to the system's ability to maintain the stipulated development level once it is achieved. The self-adjustment characteristic relates to the system's ability to make amendment should the development level deviate significantly from the required level. The acceptable industrial performance level itself should not be stagnant. It should be revised periodically and upgraded as market desires or project scenarios change. Systems integration should involve the linking of all the functions in the life cycle of an industrial project including:

1. Design.
2. Planning.

3. Production.
4. Distribution.
5. Field operation.

Systems integration is particularly important when introducing new technology into an existing system. It involves coordinating new operations to coexist with existing operations. It may require the adjustment of functions to permit sharing of resources, development of new policies to accommodate product integration, or realignment of managerial responsibilities. It can affect both hardware and software components of an organization. Presented below are guidelines and important questions appropriate for industrial systems integration:

- What are the unique characteristics of each component in the integrated system?
- How do the characteristics complement one another?
- What physical interfaces exist between the components?
- What data/information interfaces exist between the components?
- What ideological differences exist between the components?
- What are the data-flow requirements for the components?
- Are there similar integrated systems operating elsewhere?
- What are the reporting requirements in the integrated system?
- Are there any hierarchical restrictions on the operations of the components of the integrated system?
- What are the internal and external factors expected to influence the integrated system?
- How can the performance of the integrated system be measured?
- What benefit/cost documentations are required for the integrated system?
- What is the cost of designing and implementing the integrated system?
- What are the relative priorities assigned to each component of the integrated system?
- What are the strengths and weaknesses of the integrated system?
- What resources are needed to keep the integrated system operating satisfactorily?
- Which section of the organization will have primary responsibility for the operation of the integrated system?
- What are the quality specifications and requirements for the integrated systems?

Asking the above questions will greatly increase the chances of success with the project-management efforts. These questions should be posed during the planning phase when modifications to the project plan are still possible. If the questions come up only when problems have developed, then the project-management effort may fail.

3

Project Planning

A plan is the map of the wise.

Project-planning procedures and guidelines for industrial development projects are presented in this chapter. The required components of a plan are discussed, as well as motivation, one of the factors that influence project plans. Important considerations in industrial development project feasibility studies, guidelines for issuing or responding to request for proposals, and budgeting as a planning tool for development efforts are presented. Industry conversion is suggested as a potential means of meeting industrial development goals. Work breakdown structure is discussed as it relates to getting more accurate work data for project plans. The need for legal considerations in industrial project plans and the pros and cons of contracting out are also covered.

3.1 PROJECT-PLANNING OBJECTIVES

Project planning provides the basis for the initiation, implementation, and termination of a project. It sets guidelines for specific project objectives, project structure, tasks, milestones, personnel, cost, equipment, performance, and problem resolutions. An analysis of what is needed and what is available should be conducted in the planning phase of industrial development projects. The availability of technical expertise within and outside the organization should be reviewed. If subcontracting is needed, the nature of the contract should undergo a thorough analysis. The question of whether the project is needed at all should be addressed. The "make," "buy," "lease," "subcontract," or "do nothing" alternatives should be given unbiased review opportunities.

   In the initial stage of project planning, internal and external factors

75

should be determined and given priority weights. Examples of internal influences on project plans include the following:

- Infrastructure.
- Project scope.
- Labor relations.
- Project location.
- Project leadership.
- Organizational goal.
- Management approach.
- Technical manpower supply.
- Resource and capital availability.

In addition to internal factors, project plans are often influenced by external factors. An external factor may be the sole instigator of a project, or it may manifest itself in combination with other external and internal factors. Such external factors include:

- Public needs.
- Market needs.
- National goals.
- Industry stability.
- State of technology.
- Industrial competition.
- Government regulations.

3.2 COMPONENTS OF A PLAN

Planning is an ongoing process that is conducted throughout the project life cycle. Initial planning may relate to overall organizational efforts. This is where specific projects to be undertaken are determined. Subsequent planning may relate to specific objectives of the selected project. In general, an industrial development project plan should consist of the following components:

1. *Summary of Project Plan.* This is a brief description of what is planned. Project scope and objectives should be enumerated. The critical constraints on the project should be outlined. The types of resources required and available should be specified. The summary should include a statement of how the project complements organizational and national goals, budget size, and milestones.
2. *Objectives.* The objectives should be very detailed in outlining what the project is expected to achieve and how the expected achievements will contribute to overall goals of development. The performance measures for evaluating the achievement of the objectives should be specified.
3. *Approach.* The managerial and technical methodologies of implementing the project should be specified. The managerial approach may relate to project organization, communication network, approval hierarchy, responsibility, and accountability. The technical approach may relate to company experience on previous projects and currently available technology.
4. *Contractual Requirements.* This portion of the project plan should outline reporting requirements, communication links, customer specifications, performance specifications, deadlines, review process, project deliverables, delivery schedules, internal and external contacts, data security, policies, and procedures. This section should be as detailed as practically possible. Any item that has the slightest potential of creating problems later should be documented.
5. *Project Schedule.* The project schedule signifies the commitment of resource against time in pursuit of project objectives. An industrial development project schedule should specify when the project will be initiated and when it is expected to be completed. The major phases of the project should be identified. The schedule should include reliable time estimates for project tasks. The estimates may come from knowledgeable personnel, past records, or forecasting. Task milestones should be generated on the basis of objective analysis rather than arbitrary stipulations. The schedule in this planning stage constitutes the master project schedule. Detailed activity schedules should be generated under specific project functions.
6. *Resource Requirements.* Project resources, budget, and costs are to be documented in this section of the project plan. Capital requirements

should be specified by tasks. Resources may include personnel, equipment, and information. Special personnel skills, hiring, and training should be explained. Personnel requirements should be aligned with schedule requirements so as to ensure their availability when needed. Budget size and source should be presented. The basis for estimating budget requirements should be justified, and the cost allocation and monitoring approach should be shown.

7. *Performance Measures.* Measures of evaluating project progress should be developed. The measures may be based on standard practices or customized needs. The method of monitoring, collecting, and analyzing the measures should also be specified. Corrective actions for specific undesirable events should be outlined.

8. *Contingency Plans.* Courses of actions to be taken in the case of undesirable events should be predetermined. Many projects have failed simply because no plans have been developed for emergency situations. In the excitement of getting a project under way, it is often easy to overlook the need for contingency plans.

3.3 PROJECT MOTIVATION

Motivation is an essential component of implementing project plans. National leaders, public employees, management staff, producers, and consumers may all need to be motivated about industrial development plans. Those who will play active direct roles in the project must be motivated to ensure productive participation. Direct beneficiaries of the project must be motivated to make good use of the outputs of the development project. Other groups must be motivated to play supporting roles to the project.

Motivation may take several forms. For projects that are of a short-term nature, motivation could either be impaired or enhanced by the strategy employed. Impairment may occur if a participant views the project as a mere disruption of regular activities or as a job without long-term benefits. Long-term projects have the advantage of giving participants enough time to readjust to the project efforts.

3.3.1 Motivation Concepts

Frederick Taylor (1911) stated that "management was knowing exactly what you wanted men to do, and seeing to it that it was done in the best and cheapest way." Koontz and O'Donnel (1959) defined management as the function of getting things done through people. McGregor (1960) states that successful management depends significantly on the ability to predict and control human behavior. Whatever definition is used, management ultimately involves some human elements with behavioral and motivational implications. In order to get a worker to work effectively, he or she must be motivated. Some workers are inherently self-motivating. There are workers for whom motivation is an external force that must be managerially instilled. McGregor (1960) viewed worker performance under two basic concepts of Theory X and Theory Y.

The Axiom of Theory X

Theory X assumes that the worker is essentially uninterested and unmotivated to perform his or her work. Motivation must be instilled into the worker by the adoption of external motivating agents. A Theory X worker is inherently indolent and requires constant supervision and prodding to perform. To motivate a Theory X worker, a mixture of managerial actions may be needed. The actions must be used judiciously based on the prevailing circumstances. Examples of motivation approaches under Theory X are:

- Rewards to recognize improved effort.
- Strict rules to constrain worker behavior.
- Incentives to encourage better performance.
- Threats to job security associated with performance failure.

The Axiom of Theory Y

Theory Y, assumes that the worker is naturally interested and motivated to perform his or her job. The worker views his or her job function positively and uses self-control and self-direction to pursue project goals. Under Theory Y, management has the task of taking advantage of the worker's positive intuition so that the worker's actions coincide with the objectives of the project. Thus, a Theory Y manager attempts to use the worker's self-direction as the principal instrument for accomplishing work. In general, Theory Y facilitates the following:

- Worker-designed job methodology.
- Worker participation in decision making.

- Cordial management or worker relationship.
- Worker individualism within acceptable company limits.

There are proponents of both Theory X and Theory Y, and managers that operate under each or both can be found in any organization. The important thing to note is that whatever theory one subscribes to, the approach to worker motivation should be conducive to the achievement of the overall goal of the project.

Hierarchy of Needs

The needs of project participants must be taken into consideration in any industrial development project planning. Maslow (1943) presented what is usually known as Maslow's Hierarchy of Needs. He stresses that a person's needs are ordered in an hierarchical fashion consisting of five categories as listed below:

1. *Physiological Needs.* The needs for the basic things of life, such as food, water, housing, and clothing. This is the level where access to money is most critical. The basic needs are of immense concern in industrial development environments.
2. *Safety Needs.* The needs for security, stability, and freedom from threat of physical harm. In industrial development projects, the fear of environmental damage due to industrialization may mitigate project efforts.
3. *Social Needs.* The needs for social approval, friends, love, affection, and association. Industrialization may bring about better economic outlook that may enable each individual to be in a better position to meet his or her social needs.
4. *Esteem Needs.* The needs for accomplishment, respect, recognition, attention, and appreciation. These needs are important not only at the individual level, but also at the national level.
5. *Self-actualization Needs.* These are the needs for self-fulfillment and self-improvement. They also involve the stage of opportunity to grow professionally. Industrial development projects may lead to self-actualization opportunities for individuals to assert themselves socially and economically.

Hierarchical motivation implies that the particular motivation technique used for a given person should depend on where the person stands in the hierarchy of needs. For example, the needs for esteem take precedence over the physiological needs when the latter are relatively well satisfied. Money, for example, cannot be expected to be a very successful motivational factor for an individual who is already on the fourth level of the hierarchy of needs. The hierarchy of needs emphasizes the fact that things that are highly craved in youth tend to assume less importance later in life.

Hygiene Factors and Motivators

Herzberg (1960) presents a motivation concept that takes a look at the characteristics of work itself. He claims that there are two motivational factors classified as the *hygiene factors* and *motivators*. He states that the hygiene factors are necessary but not sufficient conditions for a contented worker. The negative aspects of the factors may lead to a disgruntled worker, whereas their positive aspects do not necessarily enhance the satisfaction of the worker. Examples include:

1. *Administrative Policies.* Bad policies can lead to the discontent of workers while good policies are viewed as routine with no specific contribution to improving worker satisfaction.
2. *Supervision.* A bad supervisor can make a worker unhappy and less productive, but a good supervisor cannot necessarily improve worker performance.
3. *Working Condition.* Bad working conditions can enrage workers, but good working conditions do not automatically generate improved productivity.
4. *Salary.* Low salaries can make workers unhappy, disruptive, and uncooperative, but a raise will not necessarily provoke them to perform better.
5. *Personal Life.* Miserable personal life can adversely affect worker performance, but a happy life does not imply that that person will be a better worker.
6. *Interpersonal Relationships.* Good peer, superior, and subordinate relationships are important to keep a worker happy and productive, but extraordinarily good relations do not guarantee that a worker will be more productive.
7. *Social and Professional Status.* Low status can force workers to perform at their "level," whereas high status does not imply that they will perform at a higher level.
8. *Security.* A safe environment may not motivate a worker to perform better, but an unsafe condition will certainly impede productivity.

Motivators should be inherent in the work itself. If necessary, work should be redesigned to include inherent motivating factors. Some job motivators are:

1. *Achievement.* The job design should give consideration to opportunity for worker achievement and avenues to set personal goals to excel.

2. *Recognition.* A mechanism for recognizing superior performance and innovation should be built into the job.
3. *Work Content.* The work content should be interesting enough to motivate and stimulate the creativity of the worker. The amount and the organization of the work should be designed to fit a worker's needs.
4. *Responsibility.* The worker should have some measure of responsibility for how the job is performed. Personal responsibility leads to accountability, which invariably yields better work performance.
5. *Professional Growth.* The work should offer an opportunity for advancement so that the worker can set his or her own achievement level for professional growth within a project plan.

These examples may be described as job-enrichment approaches with the basic philosophy that work can be made more interesting in order to induce an individual to perform better. Normally, work is regarded as an unpleasant necessity (a necessary evil). A proper design of work will encourage workers to become anxious to go to work to perform their jobs.

Management by Objective
Management by objective (MBO) is a concept whereby a worker is allowed to take responsibility for the design and performance of a task under controlled conditions. It gives each worker a chance to set objectives in achieving project goals. The worker can monitor progress and take corrective actions when needed without management intervention. Workers under the concept of Theory Y appear to be the best suited for the MBO concept. Management by objective has some disadvantages, including the possible abuse of the freedom to self-direct and disruption of overall project coordination. The advantages of MBO include the following aspects:

1. It encourages each worker to find better ways of performing the job.
2. It avoids oversupervision of professionals.
3. It helps workers in become better aware of what is expected of them.
4. It permits timely feedback on worker performance.

Management by Exception
Management by exception (MBE) is an after-the-fact management approach to control. Contingency plans are not made, and there is no rigid monitoring. Deviations from expectations are viewed as exceptions to normal courses of events. When intolerable deviations from plans occur, they are investigated, and only then is an action taken. The major advantage of MBE is that it lessens management workload and cost. However, it is a dangerous concept, especially for high-risk industrial development projects. Many of the problems that can develop in industrial development projects are such that

after-the-fact corrections are expensive or even impossible. As a result, MBE should be carefully evaluated before adopting it.

Motivational concepts can be implemented successfully for specific industrial development projects. They may be used as single approaches or in a combined strategy. The motivation approaches may be directed at individuals or groups of individuals, locally or at the national level.

3.4 PROJECT-FEASIBILITY STUDY

The feasibility of a project can be ascertained in terms of technical factors, economic factors, or both. A feasibility study is documented with a report showing all the ramifications of the project.

Technical Feasibility. Technical feasibility refers to the ability of the process to take advantage of the current state of the technology in pursuing further improvement. The technical capability of the personnel, as well as the capability of the available technology, should be considered.

Managerial Feasibility. Managerial feasibility involves the capability of the infrastructure to achieve and sustain process improvement. Management support, employee involvement, and commitment are key elements required to ascertain managerial feasibility.

Economic Feasibility. Economic feasibility involves the likeliness of the proposed project to generate economic benefits. A benefit cost analysis and a break-even analysis are important aspects of evaluating the economic feasibility of an industrial project. The tangible and intangible aspects of the project should be translated into economic terms to facilitate a consistent basis for evaluation.

Financial Feasibility. Financial feasibility should be distinguished from economic feasibility. Financial feasibility involves the capability to raise the appropriate funds needed to implement the proposed project. Project financing can be a major obstacle in industrial development projects because of the level of capital required. Loan availability, creditworthiness, equity, and loan schedules are important aspects of financial-feasibility analysis.

Cultural Feasibility. Cultural feasibility deals with the compatibility of the proposed project with the cultural setup of the project environment. In manual-labor-intensive communities, industrialization functions must be integrated with the local cultural practices and beliefs. For example, an industry that requires the services of females must take into consideration the cultural norms affecting the position of women in the workplace. In rural areas, industrialization efforts must not violate culturally sacred grounds that have religious implications.

Social Feasibility. Social feasibility addresses the influences that a proposed project may have on the social system in the project environment. The ambient social structure may be such that certain categories of workers may be in short supply or nonexistent. The effect of the project on the social status of the project participants must be assessed to ensure compatibility. It should be recognized that workers in certain industries may have certain status symbols within the society.

Safety Feasibility. Safety feasibility is another important aspect that should be considered in project planning. Safety feasibility refers to an analysis of whether the project is capable of being implemented and operated safely with minimal adverse effects on the environment. Unfortunately, environmental-impact assessment is often not adequately addressed in industrial development projects.

Political Feasibility. A politically feasible project may be referred to as a "politically correct project." Political considerations often dictate the direction for a proposed project. This is particularly true for industrial development projects that may have significant government inputs and political implications. For example, political necessity may be a source of support for a project regardless of the project's merits. On the other hand, worthy projects may face insurmountable opposition simply because of political factors. Political-feasibility analysis requires an evaluation of the compatibility of project goals with the prevailing goals of the political system.

3.4.1 Scope-of-Feasibility Analysis

In general terms, the elements of a feasibility analysis for an industrial development project should cover the following items:

1. *Need Analysis.* This indicates a recognition of a need for the project. The need may affect the organization itself, another organization, the public, or the government. A preliminary study is then conducted to confirm and evaluate the need, and a proposal of how it may be satisfied is then made. Pertinent questions that should be asked include:

> - Is the need significant enough to justify the proposed project?
> - Will the need still exist by the time the project is completed?

- What are the alternate means of satisfying the need?
- What is the economic impact of the need?

2. *Process Work.* This is the preliminary analysis done to determine what will be required to satisfy the need. The work may be performed by a consultant who is an expert in the project field. The preliminary study often involves system models or prototypes. For industrial projects, an artist's conception and scaled-down models may be used for illustrating the general characteristics of a process.

3. *Engineering and Design.* This involves a detailed technical study of the proposed project. Written quotations are obtained from suppliers and subcontractors and technology capabilities are evaluated as needed. Product design, if necessary, should be done at this stage.

4. *Cost Estimate.* This involves estimating project cost to an acceptable level of accuracy. Levels of around minus 5 percent to plus 15 percent are common at this level of a project plan. Both the initial and operating costs are included in the cost estimation. Estimates of capital investment, recurring, and nonrecurring costs should also be contained in the cost-estimate document.

5. *Financial Analysis.* This involves an analysis of the cash-flow profile of the project. The analysis should consider rates of return, inflation, sources of capital, payback periods, break-even point, residual values, and sensitivity. This is a critical analysis because it determines whether and when funds will be available to the project. The cash-flow profile helps support the economic and financial feasibility of the project.

6. *Project Impacts.* This portion of the feasibility study provides an assessment of the impact of the proposed project. Environmental, social, cultural, and economic impacts may be some of the factors that will determine how an industrial development project is perceived by the public. The value-added potential of the project should also be assessed. For example, a value-added tax may be assessed based on the price of a product and the cost of the raw material used in making the product. The tax so collected may be viewed as a contribution to government coffers.

7. *Conclusions and Recommendations.* The feasibility study should end with the overall outcome of the project analysis. This may indicate an endorsement or disapproval of the project. Recommendations on what should be done should be included in this section of the report.

3.4.2 Industry Conversion

The conversion of an existing industry to a new industry may be a possible approach to satisfy industrial development plans. Industries that are no longer meeting the needs of the society because of economic, social, cultural, or military (defense) requirements may have suitable alternate roles to play in the industrialization efforts. For example, economic and military reforms in the former Soviet Union have created opportunities for private industry in what used to be military-oriented production facilities. Recent changes in the international security environment have prompted several nations to start to investigate how military technology may be converted for industrial purposes. Proposed industrial development projects should consider the possibility of industry conversion to achieve project goals.

3.4.3 Assessment of Local Resources

The feasibility of an industrial development project should consider an assessment of the resources available locally to support the proposed production operations. Most developing countries are blessed with abundant natural resources. The sad fact is that these resources are often underdeveloped and underutilized. When the resources are fully developed, it is often through exploitation by foreign powers. Many countries that enjoyed oil discovery and boom in the 1970s are now suffering from the effects of the oil burst because they failed to diversify in the use of their natural resources.

Japan, with meagre natural resources, has been able to ascend the economic ladder to become a major economic and technological power. The success of Japan is due to the commitment and concerted efforts of her citizens. Japan is less of a consuming nation, the Japanese conserve earnings while at the same time concentrating on production for export. While the rest of the world wallowed in consumption, Japan shrewdly manipulated market forces. If Japan can do it with little or no help from nature, why can't a country with huge natural resources do it? The answer may lie partly in the fact that poor project-management approaches are used. Thus, there is a low degree of commitment to excellence in managing production facilities to produce competitive goods and services.

The blame is often placed on the lack of technical expertise. But when the expertise is available, it is frequently underused or misappropriated. It is true that local experts working individually accomplish nothing in the overwhelming bureaucracy that engulfs their expertise. For local experts to have an impact, there must be a coalition. A strong professional coalition is the only means of bringing about a meaningful change.

Task forces should be set up to document the availability of domestic resources and their respective potentials for derivative products. The products should be prioritized based on pressing society needs and international market demands. The development of the resources and products should then be pursued with unflinching national commitment devoid of political tendencies. Need-oriented research for the development of local products from local resources should be funded by the government.

3.5 PROJECT PROPOSALS

Once a project is shown to be feasible, the next step is to issue a request for proposal (RFP) depending on the funding sources involved. Proposals are classified as either "solicited" or "unsolicited." Solicited proposals are those written in response to a request for proposal, whereas unsolicited ones are those written without a formal invitation from the funding source. Many companies prepare proposals in response to inquiries received from potential clients. Many proposals are written under competitive bids. If an RFP is issued, it should include statements about project scope, funding level, performance criteria, and deadlines.

The purpose of the RFP is to identify companies that are qualified successfully to conduct the project in a cost-effective manner. Formal RFPs are sometimes issued to only a selected list of bidders who have been preliminarily evaluated as being qualified. These may be referred to as *targeted RFPs*. In some cases, general or open RFPs are issued and whoever is interested may bid for the project. This, however, has been found to be inefficient in many respects. Ambitious, but unqualified, organizations waste valuable time preparing losing proposals. The receiving agency, on the other hand, spends much time reviewing and rejecting worthless proposals. Open proposals do have proponents who praise their "equal opportunity" approach.

In industry, each organization has its own RFP format, content, and procedures. The request is called by different names including PI (procurement invitation), PR (procurement request), RFB (request for bid), or IFB (invitation for bids). In some countries, it is sometimes referred to as request for tender (RFT). Irrespective of the format used, a RFP should sollicit information on bidder's costs, technical capability, management, and other characteristics. It should, in turn, furnish sufficient information on the expected work. A typical detailed RFP should include:

1. *Project Background.* Need, scope, preliminary studies, and results.
2. *Project Deliverables and Deadlines.* What products are expected from the project, when the products are expected, and how the products will be delivered should be contained in this document.
3. *Project Performance Specifications.* Sometimes, it may be more advisable to specify system requirements rather than rigid specifications. This gives the systems or project analysts the flexibility to use the most

updated and most cost-effective technology in meeting the requirements. If rigid specifications are given, what is specified is what will be provided regardless of cost and level of efficiency.

4. *Funding Level.* This is sometimes not specified because of nondisclosure policies or because of budget uncertainties. However, whenever possible, the funding level should be indicated in the RFP.

5. *Reporting requirements.* Project reviews, format, number and frequency of written reports, oral communication, financial disclosure, and other requirements should be specified.

6. *Contract Administration.* Guidelines for data management, proprietary work, progress monitoring, proposal-evaluation procedure, requirements for inventions, trade secrets, copyrights, and so on should be included in the RFP.

7. *Special Requirements (as applicable).* Facility-access restrictions, equal opportunity/affirmative action, small-business support, access facilities for the handicap, false-statement penalties, cost sharing, compliance with government regulations, and so on should be included if applicable.

8. *Boilerplates (as applicable).* These are special requirements that specify the specific ways in which certain project items are handled. Boilerplates are usually written based on organizational policy and are not normally subject to conditional changes. For example, an organization may have a policy that requires that no more than 50 percent of a contract award will be paid prior to the completion of the contract. Boilerplates are quite common in government-related projects. Thus, industrial development projects may need boilerplates for environmental impacts, social contribution, and financial requirements.

3.5.1 Proposal Preparation

Whether responding to an RFP or preparing an unsolicited proposal, care must be taken to provide enough detail to permit an accurate assessment of a project proposal. The proposing organization will need to find out the following:

- Project time frame.
- Level of competition.
- The agency's available budget.

- The organization of the agency.
- The person to contact within the agency.
- Previous contracts awarded by the agency.
- Exact procedures used in awarding contracts.
- Nature of the work done by the funding agency.

The proposal should present the detailed plan for executing the proposed project. The proposal may be directed to a management team within the same organization or to an external organization. However, the same level of professional preparation should be practised for both internal and external proposals. The proposal contents may be written in two parts: technical section and management section:

1. Technical Section of Project Proposal
a. *Project Background*
   Previous developments.
   Primary objectives.
   Secondary objectives.
   Project scope.
b. *Technical Approach*
   Technology required.
   Technology available.
   Problems and their resolutions.
   Work-breakdown structure.
c. *Work Statement*
   Task definitions and list.
   Expectations.
d. *Schedule*
   Gantt charts.
   Milestones.
   Deadlines.

2. Management Section of Project Proposal
a. *Project Staff and Experience*
   Staff vita

b. *Organization*
   Task assignment.
   Project manager, liaison, assistants, consultants, etc.
c. *Cost Analysis*
   Personnel cost.
   Equipment and materials.
   Computing cost.
   Travel.
   Documentation preparation.
   Cost sharing.
   Facilities cost.
d. *Delivery Dates*
   Specified deliverables.
e. *Quality-Control Measures*
   Rework policy.
f. *Progress and Performance Monitoring*
   Productivity measurement.
g. *Cost-control measures*

An executive summary or cover letter may accompany the proposal. The summary should briefly state the capability of the proposing organization in terms of previous experience on similar projects; unique qualification of the project personnel; advantages of the organization over other potential bidders; and reasons why the project should be awarded to the bidder.

3.5.2 Proposal Incentives

In some cases, it may be possible to include an incentive clause in a proposal in an attempt to entice the funding organization. An example is the use of cost-sharing arrangements. Other frequently used project proposal incentives include bonus and penalty clauses, employment of minorities, public service, and contribution to charity. If incentives are allowed in project proposals, their nature should be critically reviewed. If not controlled, a project-incentive arrangement may turn out to be an opportunity for an organization to buy itself into a project contract.

3.6 BUDGET PLANNING

After the planning for a project has been completed, the next step is the allocation of the resources required to implement the project plan. This is referred to as budgeting or capital rationing. Budgeting is the process of allocating scarce resources to the various endeavors of an organization. It involves the selection of a preferred subset of a set of acceptable projects due to overall budget constraints. Budget constraints may result from restrictions on capital expenditures, shortage of skilled manpower, shortage of materials, or mutually exclusive projects. The budgeting approach can be used to express the overall organizational policy. The budget serves many useful purposes including the following:

- Performance measure.
- Incentive for efficiency.
- Project-selection criterion.
- Expression of organizational policy.
- Plan of how resources are expended.
- Catalyst for productivity improvement.
- Control basis for managers and administrators.
- Standardization of operations within a given horizon.

The preliminary effort in the preparation of a budget is the collection and proper organization of relevant data. The preparation of a budget for a project is more difficult than the preparation of budgets for regular and permanent organizational endeavors. Recurring endeavors usually generate historical data that serve as inputs to subsequent estimating functions. Projects, on the other hand, are often one-time undertakings without the benefits of prior data. The input data for the budgeting process may include inflationary trends, cost of capital, standard-cost guides, past records, and forecast projections. Budget-data collection may be accomplished by one of several available approaches including top-down budgeting and bottom-up budgeting.

3.6.1 Top-Down Budgeting

Top-down budgeting involves collecting data from upper-level sources such as top and middle managers. The cost estimates supplied by the managers may come from their judgments, past experiences, or past data on similar project activities. The cost estimates are passed to lower-level managers, who then break the estimates down into specific work components within the project. These estimates may, in turn, be given to line managers, supervisors, and so on to continue the process. At the end, individual activity costs are developed. Figure 3-1 shows the hierarchical structure of a top-down budgeting strategy. The top management issues the global budget while the line worker generates specific-activity budget requirements.

One advantage of the top-down budgeting approach is that individual work elements need not be identified prior to approving the overall project

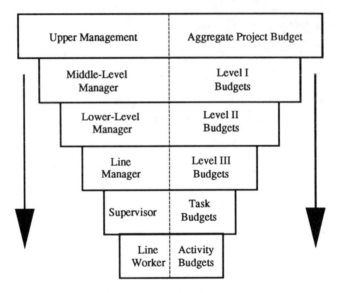

FIGURE 3-1.   Top-Down Budgeting Approach.

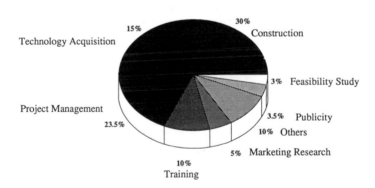

FIGURE 3-2.   Industrial Development Budget-Distribution Pie.

budget. Another advantage of the approach is that the aggregate or overall project budget can be reasonably accurate even though specific activity costs may contain substantial errors. There is, consequently, a keen competition among lower-level managers to get the biggest slice of the budget pie. An example of a budget-distribution pie is shown in Figure 3-2.

3.6.2 Bottom-Up Budgeting

This approach is the reverse of the top-down budgeting. In this method, elemental activities, their schedules, descriptions, and labor skill-requirements are used to construct detailed budget requests. The line workers who are actually performing the activities are requested to furnish cost estimates. Estimates are made for each activity in terms of labor time, materials, and machine time. The estimates are then converted to dollar values. The dollar estimates are combined into composite budgets at each successive level up the budgeting hierarchy. If estimate discrepancies develop, they can be resolved through the intervention of senior management, junior management, functional managers, project managers, accountants, or financial consultants. Analytical tools such as learning-curve analysis, work sampling, and statistical estimation may be used in the budgeting process as appropriate to improve the quality of cost estimates.

All component costs and departmental budgets are combined into an overall budget and sent to top management for approval. A common problem with bottom-up budgeting is that individuals tend to overstate their needs with the notion that top management may cut the budget by some percentage. It should be noted, however, that sending erroneous and misleading estimates will only lead to a loss of credibility. Properly documented and justified budget requests are often spared the budget axe. Honesty and accuracy are invariably the best policies for budgeting.

3.6.3 Zero-Base Budgeting

This is a budgeting approach that bases the level of project funding on previous performance. It is normally applicable to recurring programs, especially in the public sector. Accomplishments in past funding cycles are weighed against the level of resource expenditure. Programs that are stagnant in terms of their accomplishments relative to budget size do not receive additional budgets. Programs that have suffered decreasing yields are subjected to budget cuts or even elimination. On the other hand, programs that experience increments in accomplishments are rewarded with larger budgets.

A major problem with zero-base budgeting is that it puts participants under tremendous data-collection, organization, and program-justification pressures. Too much time may be spent documenting program accomplishments to the extent that productivity improvement on current projects may be sacrificed. For this reason, the approach has received only limited use in practice. However, proponents believe it is a good means of making managers and administrators more conscious of their management responsibilities. In a project-management context, the zero-base budgeting approach may be used to eliminate specific activities that have not contributed to project goals in the past.

3.7 PROJECT-BREAKDOWN STRUCTURE

Project-breakdown structure (PBS) refers to the breakdown of a project for planning, scheduling, and control purposes. The breakdown is often referred to as a work breakdown structure (WBS). This represents a family-tree hierarchy of project operations required to accomplish project objectives. Tasks that are contained in the WBS collectively describe the overall project. The tasks may involve physical products (e.g., steam generators), services (e.g., testing), and data (e.g., reports, sales data). The WBS serves to describe the link between the end objective and the operations required to reach that objective. It shows work elements in the conceptual framework for planning and controlling. The objective of developing a WBS is to study the elemental

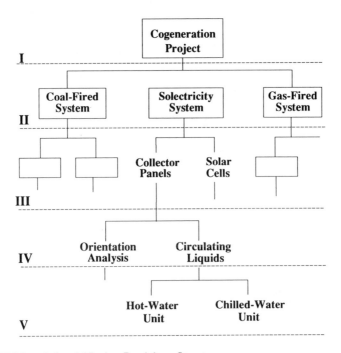

FIGURE 3-3.   Industrial Project Breakdown Structure.

components of a project in detail. It permits the implementation of the "divide and conquer" concepts. Overall project planning and control can be improved by using a WBS approach. A large project may be broken down into smaller subprojects that may, in turn, be systematically broken down into task groups.

Individual components in a WBS are referred to as WBS elements, and the hierarchy of each is designated by a level identifier. Elements at the same level of subdivision are said to be of the same WBS level. Descending levels provide increasingly detailed definition of project tasks. The complexity of a project and the degree of control desired determine the number of levels in the WBS. An example of a WBS for an industrial cogeneration plant is shown in Figure 3-3.

The three major components of the plant are at level 2: solectricity system (i.e., electricity from solar energy), coal-fired system, and gas-fired system. Each component is successively broken down into smaller details at lower levels. The process may continue until specific project activities are reached. The basic approach for preparing a WBS is as follows:

Level 1: Level 1 contains only the final project purpose. This item should be identifiable directly as an organizational budget item.
Level 2: Level 2 contains the major subsections of the project. These subsections are usually identified by their contiguous location or by their related purposes.
Level 3: level 3 contains definable components of the level-2 subsections.

Subsequent levels are constructed in more specific details depending on the level of control desired. If a complete WBS becomes too crowded, separate WBSs may be drawn for the level-2 components. A specification of work (SOW) or WBS summary should normally accompany the WBS. A SOW is a narrative of the work to be done. It should include the objectives of the work, its nature, resource requirements, and tentative schedule. Each WBS element is assigned a code that is used for its identification throughout the project life cycle. Alphanumeric codes may be used to indicate element level as well as component group. For example the solectricity system in Figure 3-3 may have a code of A2, whereas the gas line construction may be C3.

3.8 LEGAL CONSIDERATIONS IN PROJECT PLANNING

Managing has always been a tough job. Today, that job is even tougher. The work force is more volatile, technology is more dynamic, and the society is less predictable. The number of legal issues that arise is increasing at an alarming rate. The job of project management has, consequently, become more strenuous. Today any prudent manager should give serious considerations to the legal implications of project operations. Many organizations that have failed to recognize legal consequences have paid dearly for their mistakes.

There are several examples of project errors and legal problems. Some of the families of the astronauts killed in the space shuttle *Challenger* sued NASA for millions of dollars. Some of the managerial staff involved in the Chernobyl accident in the Soviet Union lost their jobs and were legally convicted for dereliction of duty and criminal negligence. Several of the managerial staff at Chernobyl were sentenced to stiff jail terms. The Love Canal incident near Niagara Falls is still haunting residents and those responsible. The U.S. Justice Department filed a law suit against Hooker Chemical Company, the company responsible for dumping the Love Canal industrial waste. In 1980, New York State sued the same company for $635 million for negligence. The Three Mile Island accident of 28 March, 1979, in Pennsylvania caused the loss of $2 billion and an erosion of public confidence in the nuclear industry. The Bhopal disaster in India on December 3, 1984, left over 3,000 dead, some 250,000 disabled, and is still costing the Union Carbide Company a great deal of legal problems. The oil spill in Alaska will have legal repercussions for many years to come.

With the emergence of new technology and complex systems (e.g., genetic engineering), it is only prudent to anticipate dangerous and unmanageable events. The key to preventing disasters is thoughtful planning and cautious preparation. Industrial development projects are particularly prone to legal problems, the most pronounced of which are related to environmental damage. Industrial project planning should include a comprehensive evaluation of the potential legal aspects of the project.

3.9 INFORMATION FLOW
FOR PROJECT PLANNING

Information flow is very crucial in industrial development project planning. Information is the driving force for project decisions. The value of information is measured in terms of the quality of the decisions that can be generated from the information. What appears to be valuable information to one user may be useless to another. Similarly, the timing of information can significantly affect its decision-making value. The same information that is useful in one instant may be useless in another. Some of the crucial factors affecting the value of information include accuracy, timeliness, relevance, reliability, validity, completeness, clearness, and comprehensibility.

Proper information flow in project management ensures that tasks are accomplished when, where, and how they are needed. Figure 3-4 presents a model of the flow and use of information in a project environment. The information-flow model is presented as an input–output–feedback loop.

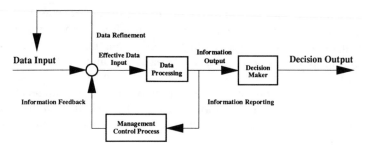

FIGURE   3-4. Project Information-Flow Model.

Information starts with raw data (e.g., numbers, facts, specifications). The data may pertain to raw material, technical skills, or other factors relevant to the project goal. The data are processed to generate information in the desired form. The information-feedback model acts as a management-control process that monitors project status and generates appropriate control actions. The contribution of the information to the project goal is fed back through an information-feedback loop. The feedback information is used to enhance future processing of input data to generate additional information. The final information output provides the basis for improved management decisions. The key questions to ask when requesting, generating, or evaluating information for project management are:

- What data are needed to generate the information?
- Where are the data going to come from?
- When will the data be available?
- Is the data source reliable?
- Are there enough data?
- Who needs the information?
- When is the information needed?
- In what form is the information needed?
- Is the information relevant to project goals?
- Is the information accurate, clear, and timely?

As an example, the information-flow model described may be implemented to facilitate the inflow and outflow of information linking several functional areas of an organization, such as design, manufacturing, marketing, and customer relations departments. The lack of communication between functional departments has been blamed for much of the organizational problems in industry. The use of a standard information-flow model can help alleviate many of the communication problems. The information-flow model can be expanded to take into account the uncertainties that may occur in project environments.

3.9.1 Cost of Information

As desirable as information is, too much information can be detrimental to the progress of a project. The marginal benefit of information decreases as its size increases. However, the marginal cost of obtaining additional information may increase as the size of the information increases. Figure 3-5 presents a comparison of cost and benefit of information.

The optimum size of information is determined by the point that represents the widest positive difference between information benefits and costs. The costs associated with information can often be measured accurately. However, the benefits may be more difficult to document. The size of

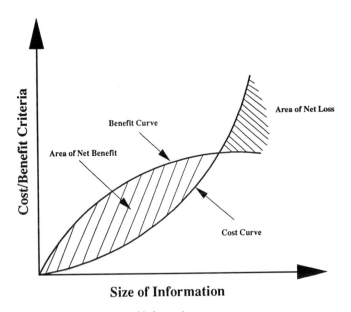

FIGURE 3-5.   Cost versus Value of Information.

information may be measured in terms of a number of variables including number of pages of documentation, number of lines of code, size of computer-storage requirement. In any case, the amount of information presented for project-management purposes should be carefully condensed to cover only what is needed to make effective decision. Information condensation may involve pruning the information that is already available or limiting what needs to be acquired.

The cost of information is composed of the cost of the resources required to generate the information. The required resources may include computer time, personnel man-hours, software cost, and so on. Unlike the value of information, which may be difficult to evaluate, the cost of information is somewhat more tractable. However, the development of accurate cost estimates prior to actual project execution is not trivial. The degree of accuracy required in estimating the cost of information depends on the intended uses of the estimates. Cost estimates may be used as general information for control purposes. Cost estimates may also be used as general guides for planning purposes or for developing standards. The bottom-up cost-estimation approach is a popular method used in practice. This method proceeds by breaking the cost structure down into its component parts. The cost of each element is then established. The sum of these individual cost elements gives an estimate of the total cost of the information.

3.9.2 Value of Information

It is important to assess the value of project information relative to its cost before deciding to acquire it. Investments for information acquisition should be evaluated just like any other capital investment. The value of information is determined by how the information is used. In project management, information has two major uses. The first relates to the need for information on running the daily operations of a project. Resource allocation, material procurement, replanning, rescheduling, hiring, and training are just a few of the daily functions for which information is needed. The second major use of information in project management relates to the need for information to make long-range project decisions. The value of information for such long-range decision making is even more difficult to estimate because the future cost of not having the information today is not known.

The classical approach to determining the value of information is based on the value of perfect information. The expected value of perfect information is the maximum expected loss due to imperfect information. Using probability analysis or other appropriate quantitative methods, the project analyst can predict what a project outcome might be if certain information is available or not available. For example, if it is known for sure that it will rain on a certain day, a project manager might decide to alter the project schedule so that only non-weather-sensitive tasks are planned on that particular day. The value of the perfect information about the weather would then be measured in terms of what loss could have been incurred if that information was not available. The loss may be in terms of lateness penalty, labor idle time, equipment damage, or ruined work.

Without resorting to any complex probability analysis, an experienced project manager can accurately estimate the expected losses; and hence, the value of the perfect information about the weather. The cost of the same information may be estimated in terms what it would cost to consult with a weather forecaster or the cost of buying a subscription to a special weather-forecast channel on cable television.

Industrial development project planning may include an evaluation of the possibility of subcontracting part of the project work. Subcontracting may be needed for various reasons including lower cost, higher efficiency, or logistical convenience. The following section presents the various aspects and concerns of subcontracting as they may affect industrial development projects.

3.10 THE PROS AND CONS OF CONTRACTING OUT[1]

In the past decade, the idea that local governments could be made more efficient by contracting the delivery of services to private firms has received considerable attention. Contracting out public services is not a new idea. The growth of big, all-providing government is a recent phenomenon that dates back no further than the late nineteenth century; and in most cases, it is even more recent than that.

Described by the International City Management Association (ICMA) in 1984 as the most widely accepted and frequently used alternative service-delivery approach, private contracting was first proposed by the English economist Edwin Chadwick in 1859. The concept soon was adopted by several French cities for the supply and delivery of water and sewerage services. By 1900, Boston, Philadelphia, and Washington were contracting private resource-recovery services, with contractors paid a per-ton fee for collection and disposal of solid waste.

In 1948 Scottsdale, Arizona, contracted for private protection; in 1953

---

[1]Akande, Agboola, "Potential Problems in Introducing the Concept of 'Contracting Out' (Privatization) in Developing Nations," working paper, Department of Public Administration, University of Oklahoma, 1987. (Reproduced by permission).

Lakewood, California, started franchising virtually all public services to private firms. In the last few years, local-government privatization has made significant progress in several capital-intensive service areas. For example, 33 percent of municipal waste currently is disposed of privately. Since 1981 more than seventy resource-recovery plants have been built and privatized, and now more than 50 percent of the drinking water is supplied and treated by privately owned facilities.

The idea of "contracting out" or privatization has been a major debate in many developing countries in recent times. Both native and foreign scholars have contributed to the possibilities of introducing this idea on a large scale. This case study examines what problems might develop from the introduction of such a concept in a developing nation.

The general concept of "contracting out" in the American sense is examined, highlighting the advantages and disadvantages, as well as historical and current trends in privatization. After examining what the potential problems of "exporting" the American model to developing countries might be, comments and recommendations are offered. This case study suggests the steps that might be taken to solve most of the problems associated with the adaptation of the American model of "contracting out" for the purpose of industrial development.

3.10.1 General Assessment of Contracting Out

During the eighteenth and most of nineteenth centuries, when refuse collection was generally not mandatory, that is, households did not have to subscribe to and were not given regular service, most American cities had private collection. Many cities had competitive systems. Old but still hotly controversial, the idea of letting private industry do more of government's work became very important in the 1980s. Pressed by tax revolts and spending limits, federal and local officials have been buying more and more services from corporations.

Privatization (contracting out) has been defined in many ways by different scholars. Privatization can be defined as a process by which some of the functions of the public sector are transferred to privately owned companies. Alternately, it can be defined as the private development, ownership, management, and operation of facilities for public use that traditionally are owned and operated by local government. Savas (1982, p. 61) explains that in contract service, government is the service arranger, and a private organization is the service producer.

According to Fisk, Kiesling, and Muller (1978, p. 1), the basic concept of private delivery is that it serves as an analog to the private market, where if competition between buyers and sellers exists, the market price may be taken as a measure of the benefit received. In "contracting out," a local government contracts with private firms (profit or non-profit) to provide goods or delivery services. The contract may be to have all or a portion of the service provided by the private firms. Cost reduction and improved efficiency are the major reasons for contracting with the private sector, the assumption being that private firms can deliver the service at a lower cost than a government agency. The rationale for this is that private firms have more incentives to keep costs down, especially if there is competition for the contracts among potential suppliers.

There are variations as to how governments contract out services to the private sector. In order to stimulate competition, a government may split the jurisdiction into districts with firms competing for each district. This allows smaller organizations to compete. Another variation is where the local government divides the work into segments, with some work allocated to the public agency and other work distributed to private contractors. Some governments also encourage direct competition between local government agencies and private firms.

3.10.2 Advantages of Contracting Out

The competition that occurs as a result of contracting should lead to a lower cost for equivalent service or to better performance at a similar cost. Wesemann (1981, p. 15) argues in terms of overhead cost. He contends that private firms would have fewer employees, which translates into reduction in personnel, payroll, and supervising costs. Fewer employees also means that less equipment, equipment maintenance, and building space are needed.

Another advantage of contracting out is that it produces better management and management information. Through contracting, government managers can devote their attention to planning and monitoring rather than managing day-to-day operations. This allows the contractor to devote his full attention to routine operating problems. This kind of specialization may lead to better municipal management. Because it demands explicit statements regarding the work to be done, contracting may generate information that may otherwise not be available to local government. Contracting out also permits greater flexibility in adjusting program size (Hatry, 1983, p. 15). This deals with either increasing or reducing program operations without lengthy negotiations with municipal employees. This fact looms larger when one considers that private firms do not have to go through the rigors of political maneuvers.

Yet another advantage of contracting out is that it can check the growth of government, an issue that has been the cause of complaints by the opponents of big government. Contracting offers a way out of this dilemma because it restricts the number of government employees. However, caution should be exercised when considering this factor because restricting the number of government employees by contracting out some services does not necessarily lower total public expenditure.

Privatization is also advantageous in that it helps during government cut-back processes. If a government has to cut back on services because of a special financial situation, contracted services can be reduced without having to lay off employees. Government also does not have to worry about paying unemployment compensation and the problem of idle equipment. Furthermore, in case of a necessary mid-year cutback as a result of a financial emergency, the quantity of services to be purchased can be cut back if the contract is well written. This will not be the case if the service is being provided by the municipal government because municipal employees would still have to be paid, even if the service is reduced.

Finally, contracting provides specialized skills that may not be available in the public sector. In contracting, employees are provided with specialized skills that could not be justified in full-time employees because of limited need. These specialized skills are used infrequently and, therefore, it would be economically unwise for a municipality to hire a full-time employee for these kinds of services. However, privatization, despite its several advantages, also has some weaknesses.

3.10.3 Disadvantages of Contracting Out

The most common disadvantage of contracting out is corruption. Contracting is often associated with bribery, kickbacks, and collusive biddings. Also, contracts frequently have been used as a tool for political patronage. The desire of private firms to obtain contracts and increase profits has put great pressures on them to engage in such acts as bribery and payoff. Whenever a municipality is involved in awarding a large contract, it is open to charges of corruption. This is the main argument presented against contracting out by public employee unions.

Although there have been various arguments by supporters of subcontracting that local governments are capable of monitoring contracts and, therefore, able to cut the incidents of corruption, evidence suggests otherwise. For example, the theme of two of Hanrahan's books—*Government for Sale* (1977) and *Government by Contract* (1983)—is corruption. In *Government by Contract* (p. 1), he cites a case in which Senator David Pryor overheard two contractors inflate a bid they were about to submit to the Department of Health from $25,000 to $50,000. In *Government for Sale* (p. 38), he gives an account of Browning Ferries Industries, Inc., admitting to making about $100,000 in payments to unnamed public officials between 1972 and 1976.

These cases show that it will be deceiving to argue that corruption in contracting does not exist.

A second disadvantage of contracting out is that employees get displaced as a result of this concept, and this in turn may cause serious opposition from unions. Contracting current government services may imply that the number of employees be reduced, either by lay off or by attrition. Whichever way this happens, the local unions may react with costly legal challenges that will adversely affect the economic welfare and productivity of the municipal government.

Opponents of privatization have also argued that there is little or no accountability whenever a government engages in contracting. When citizens complain about a contracted service, government often can do little more than complain in turn to the contractor or enter into costly negotiations or termination proceedings. At a time when many citizens feel government is too removed from the people, contracting out—at least in this sense—pushes the level of accountability and responsiveness to citizens' complaints one more step away.

A potential weakness of contracting out is that it may result in poorer services for citizens. Because the objective of private firms is the maximization of profits, a firm may skimp on its service whenever possible in order to increase its profits. Private firms can "cut corners" by hiring inexperienced, transient personnel at low wages, ignoring contract requirements, or providing inadequate supervision.

Another case against privatization is that whenever a government engages in contracting, it loses full control over the final service. Because of the difficulty of writing and enforcing performance contracts, particularly when they deal with the quantity and quality of final products and services, a government often loses some degree of control over these products and services. This loss of control is one of the principal reasons why bureaucrats resist the idea of privatization. Apart from the fear of losing their jobs, they also lose some of their status whenever the amount of control they exercise over certain services diminishes.

One last problem with contracting out is the fear that private contractors may not complete operations. Unlike the government, contractors may go bankrupt or cease operations. If the local government has no alternate plan, the result can be a serious deprivation of service to the public. Take for example a city that contracts out sewerage treatment and has no back-up plan. What will such a city do in case the private firm goes bankrupt or its employees go on strike? The results could be devastating for the city government because it would be a difficult task for the public officials to explain satisfactorily to the tax-paying citizens. This is a serious problem for public officials, and it may mitigate against a city contracting out certain services even when it could cut costs. Contracting out, like any other concepts, though having many strong points, also has its weaknesses.

3.10.4 Potential Problems of Contracting Out in Developing Nations

Privatization has been seriously considered in many developing nations. First on the list of problems is the country's history, a problem that is often ignored whenever a system or concept is about to be 'imported' into a country. Most developing nations share a similar colonial history. During the colonial period, Britain, which was in control of some of the developing countries, introduced a system in which a great amount of government participation was required. Just like in Britain, all the utility services, including water, electricity, health, and education, were all put under direct government control.

In the wake of independence, these state-owned services were automatically retained by the indigenous public sector. Government participation is all that many developing nations have known since their inception. This has spanned several years of colonization and a few years of self-rule. It, therefore, should not be a surprise that privatization poses significant problems. These government institutions are very deep-rooted, and their influence is of tremendous proportions. The institution rests on tradition, and it will, therefore, require a total commitment and unity of efforts by all concerned to undo what history has installed. It is an uphill task.

A second potential problem would be politics of the country. There is the fear of the loss of political control and influence that some leaders have enjoyed for so long. Government participation in all sectors of the country provides a fertile ground for political meddling in management decisions, recruitment, promotion, retention of redundant staff, and prostitution of disciplinary procedures by ethnocentric considerations. All these factors give unimaginable power and influence to their politicians who, naturally would resist the introduction of privatization as this would result in the erosion of these powers and influence.

Corruption, which also has been advanced as one of the chief weaknesses of privatization in developed countries is perhaps the biggest problem that will face an attempt to privatize in developing countries. It is a fact that corruption was the principal factor upon which the military rode back into the political affairs of some developing nations by toppling the civilian regimes. The 10-percent concept could be used here to illustrate how deep-rooted corruption has been in some countries, in which it is common practice to give 10 percent of the dollar value of any contract awarded to the public official responsible for awarding the contract. This gave a new meaning to the process of contracting out. However, it should be noted that this problem is prevalent in most countries, not just in developing nations. As a result of this flagrant practice, corruption would pose a formidable problem if a country is to adopt the concept of contracting out for industrial development.

Another potential problem to privatization is that posed by the intellectuals in developing countries. This problem is ideological in nature. They have put forward the argument that privatization is a betrayal of the country's political sovereignty. They call the adoption of contracting out a sellout to imperialism or to local capitalism. Their reason for opposing this concept rests on technology. They argue that to contract out public services, a high degree of technological capability is required, something that most developing nations lack. This in turn means that to implement privatization successfully, there must be some foreign participation. Local entrepreneurs also lack adequate capital and managerial staff. Therefore, foreign contractors have to be involved in order to fill the gaps created by these inadequacies. Consequently, there is the fear of ideological invasion and economic denial due to the use of foreign experts.

The fifth factor which has an enormous potential for becoming a stumbling block is labor unions. A government is the single largest employer in a developing country, and every civil servant, both state and federal is statutorily a member of some labor union. The union leadership has seen attempts to privatize as a ploy to get rid of thousands of public employees. The union often threatens a nationwide civil strike. They fear that privatization will only benefit the wealthy few, further skewing income and wealth distribution in favor of the wealthy. Bureaucratic rules and regulations may have an even stronger impact. For example, it is against the civil service codes in many nations for government to terminate any employee except on accusations of inefficiency, corruption, or abuse of office.

In some countries, military governments look to the higher civil service for political legitimacy, and the politicians rely on their votes and administrative support. Any strains in relationship may translate into the withdrawal of this support, usually, the beginning of the end for any government. This situation is not peculiar to developing countries. Even in the developed countries, though to a lesser extent, the unions have some powers.

A final problem worthy of discussion is that of ethnic and regional differences and the issue of national character in some of the developing countries. The concept of national character simply means that for anything to be successfully implemented in the country it must have a semblance of the national makeup of the country. The adoption of privatization, if it happens, would have to be done on a national basis, taking off in all sectors simultaneously. But when one thinks of the deep-rooted differences that exist between two factions in a country, one is tempted to conclude that privatization is doomed in many nations. Already, while one faction is in total support of contracting out the western way, another faction may only want commercialization, a strategy that would emphasize only the reform of existing government agencies with the hope that they will work better. So, for privatization to be successfully introduced, a compromise needs to be developed between ethnic and regional groups. These, essentially are the issues that need to be addressed if any meaningful attempt is to be made at privatizing the delivery of public services in a developing country.

3.10.5 Recommendations for Contracting Out

A set of recommendations for contracting out are presented here. The first recommendation deals with timing. The timing of the introduction of this concept must be perfect. The proponents of this idea must recognize that the prevailing political leadership's support is very important to the successful implementation of contracting out. A leader that is dedicated to the idea is required. Educational campaign is another strategy that could help ensure a successful privatization. Seminars, lectures, and debates should be organized. The advantages of contracting out should be the theme of such exercises. Also, evidence of successful practice of privatization should be made available to the public at large.

Examples of successful service contracting can be found in several developed nations. Canada contracts out her solid waste collection. Of all the cities with over 2,500 population in the United States, 37 percent had municipal collection, 21 percent had contract collection, 7 percent had franchise, and 38 percent had private collection (Savas, 1979, p. 3). Most of the cities in Denmark contract with a single private firm for fire and ambulance service, and that about two-thirds of the people in Sweden get their fire-protection services from private enterprises. In pursuing this effort benefits, such as cost savings gained through contracting out these services should be highlighted. Successful past experiments are bound to help the cause of privatization in a developing nation.

In introducing privatization to a developing country, competition must be a cornerstone in the planning. Mechanisms that would ensure competition among private firms must be developed. When there is competition, the citizens are assured of low project costs. Ensuring competition allows the consumer to shop around for the cheapest and most efficient service. The citizens should have a free choice of deciding from whom they buy services. If this is the case, the fear of labor unions about concentrating wealth in the hands of a few people will be allayed. On the cautionary side, government should make sure not to replace a government monopoly with another private monopoly. Gradual introduction and disaggregation of service (breaking up of service into pieces) is a worthwhile approach. This allows changes to occur on a gradual basis. If the changes are gradual or incremental, the political pain and economic risk in service redesigning will be reduced. If the introduction is gradual, government will have time to evaluate the system to see if it works or not.

Finally, the adoption or nonadoption of privatization should be non-political. It should not be made an election or a political issue. Private firms should be insulated from all sorts of political maneuverings that pervade a developing nation. When this is done, the problem of equity distortion will be reduced. This is on the assumption that a private firm would sell services to anybody who is ready to buy what it has to offer, regardless of the person's political views.

3.10.6 Importance of Subcontracting in Industrial Development

In many nations industrial development is still largely the responsibility of the government. Consequently, an ineffective government can imply low industrial development. Appropriate areas for contracting out should be critically evaluated during the planning stages for industrial development projects. However, effective contract management and corruption-control measures should be put in place before industrial development subcontracts are issued.

4

Project Organization

Good organization is the foundation for fruition.

This chapter presents topics in organization approaches for industrial development projects. Some organizational models are discussed with respect to the specific needs of development projects. Guidelines are presented for the selection of a project manager and for staffing the project office. Suggestions on how to conduct more effective project meetings and guidelines for project communication within the organizational structures are offered. The complexity of organizing multinational projects is addressed. A checklist of the factors to consider when organizing international projects is presented. The chapter ends with a case study that illustrates the maze of national networks involved in coordinating a large multinational high-tech project.

4.1 ORGANIZATION STRUCTURES

Once the initial plans for a project have been finalized, the next step is the development of the operational structure of the project. This involves the selection of an organizational structure that shows the management line and the responsibilities of the project personnel. Any of the numerous approaches available may be used. The structure may be defined in terms of functional specializations, departmental proximity, standard management boundaries, operational relationships, or product requirements.

Industrial development projects should be based on well-designed structures that permit effective information and decision processes. Traditional organization models consist of the decision-making, bureaucracy, social, and systems structures. The decision-making structure handles the policies and general directions of the overall organization. The bureaucracy is concerned with the administrative processes. Some of the administrative functions may not be directly relevant to the main goal of the organization, but they are, nonetheless, deemed necessary. Bureaucratic processes are potential sources of delays for development projects because of government involvement. The social structure facilitates amiable interactions among the personnel. Such interpersonal relationships are essential for the group effort needed to achieve company objectives. The systems structure can better be described as the link between the various synergistic segments of the organization.

4.1.1 Formal and Informal Organization Structures

The formal organization structure represents the officially sanctioned structure of a functional area. The informal organization on the other hand, develops when people organize themselves in an unofficial way to accomplish an objective that is in line with the overall project goals. The informal organization is often very subtle in that not everyone in the organization is aware of its existence. Both formal and informal organizations are practiced in every project environment. Even organizations with strict hierarchical structures, such as the military, still have some elements of informal organization.

Span of Control

The functional organization calls attention to the form and span of management that is suitable for company goals. The span of management (also known as the span of control) can be wide or narrow. In a narrow span, the functional relationships are streamlined with fewer subordinate units reporting to a single manager. An example of a narrow span of control is shown in Figure 4-1. The wide span of management, as shown in Figure 4-2, permits several subordinate units to report to the same boss. The span of control required for a project is influenced by a combination of the following:

- The level of planning required.
- The level of communication desired.
- The effectiveness of delegating authority.
- The dynamism and nature of the subordinate's job.
- The competence of the subordinate in performing on the job.

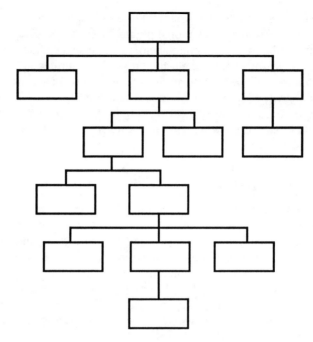

FIGURE 4-1.   Narrow Span of Control.

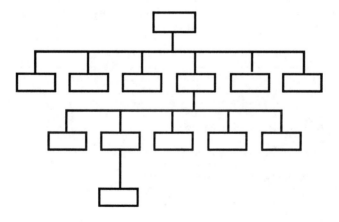

FIGURE 4-2.   Wide Span of Control.

Given a favorable project environment, the wide span of management can be very effective. From a motivational point of view, workers tend to have a better identification with upper management because there are fewer hierarchical steps to go through to reach the "top." More professional growth is possible because workers assume more responsibilities. In addition, the wide span of management is more economical because of the absence of extra layers of supervision. However, the narrow span of management does have its own appeals in situations where there are several mutually exclusive skill levels in the organization.

4.1.2 Functional Organization

The most common type of formal organization is known as the functional organization, whereby people are organized into groups dedicated to particular functions. Depending on the size and the type of auxiliary activities involved in a project, several minor, but supporting, functional units can be developed for an industrial development project.

Projects that are organized along functional lines are normally resident in a specific department or area of specialization. The project home office or headquarters are located in the specific functional department. For example, projects that involve manufacturing operations may be under the control of the vice-president of manufacturing, whereas a project involving new technology may be assigned to the vice-president for advanced systems. Figure 4-3 shows examples of projects that are functionally organized. The advantages and disadvantages of a functional organization structure are:

Advantages of Functional Organization Structure

- Improved accountability.
- Discernible line of control.
- Flexibility in manpower utilization.
- Enhanced comradeship of technical staff.
- Improved productivity of specially skilled personnel.
- Potential for staff advancement.
- Home office can serve as a refuge for project problems.

Disadvantages of Functional Organization Structure

- Divided attention between project goals and regular functions.

- Conflict between project objectives and regular functions.

- Poor coordination of similar project responsibilities.

- Unreceptive attitude by the surrogate department.

- Multiple layers of management.

- Lack of concentrated effort.

4.1.3 Product Organization

Another approach to organizing a project is to use the end product or goal of the project as the determining factor for personnel structure. This is often referred to as the pure project organization or, simply, project organization. The project is set up as a unique entity within the parent organization. It has

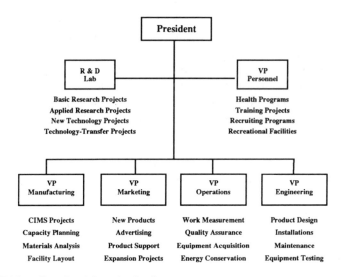

FIGURE 4-3.   Functional Organization Structure.

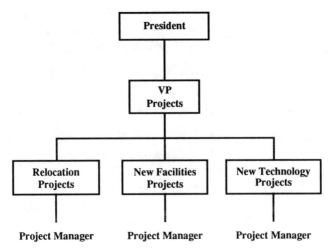

FIGURE 4-4.   Product Organization Structure.

its own dedicated technical staff and administration. It is linked to the rest of the system through progress reports, organizational policies, procedures, and funding. The interface between product-organized projects and other elements of the organization may be strict or liberal depending on the organization. An example of a pure project organization is shown in Figure 4-4. The project staff is assembled by assigning personnel from different functional areas.

Product organization is common in large, project-oriented organizations. Unlike functional organization, product organization decentralizes functions. It creates a unit consisting of specialized skills around a given project or product. Sometimes referred to as team, task force, or product group, product organization is common in public, research, and manufacturing organizations where specially organized and designated groups are assigned specific functions. A major advantage of product organization is that it gives the project members a feeling of dedication to and identification with a particular goal.

A possible shortcoming of product organization is the requirement that the product group be sufficiently funded to be able to stand alone without sharing resources or personnel with other functional groups or programs. Product group may be viewed as an ad hoc unit that is formed for the purpose of a specific goal. The personnel involved in the project are dedicated to the particular mission at hand. At the conclusion of the mission, they may be reassigned to other projects. Product organization can facilitate the most diverse and flexible grouping of project participants and permits highly dedicated attention to the project at hand. The advantages and disadvantages of the product organization structure are:

Advantages of Product Organization Structure

- Simplicity of structure.

- Unity of project purpose.

- Condensation of communication lines.

- Full authority given to the project manager.

- Quicker decisions due to centralized authority.

- Skill development due to project specialization.

- Improved motivation, commitment, and concentration.

- Project teams reporting directly to the project manager (one boss).

Disadvantages of Product Organization Structure

- Narrow view of project personnel (as opposed to global organization view).

- Mutually exclusive allocation of resources (one man to one project).

- Duplication of efforts on different but similar projects.

- Monopoly of organizational resources.

- Concern about life after the project.

- Reduced skill diversification.

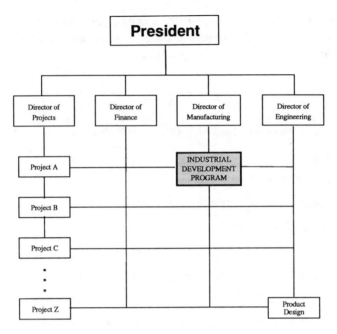

FIGURE 4-5.   Matrix Organization Structure.

4.1.4 Matrix Organization Structure

The matrix organization is a popular choice of management professionals'. A matrix organization exists where there is multiple managerial accountability and responsibility for a job function. There are usually two chains of command: horizontal and vertical. The horizontal line deals with the functional line of responsibility, and the vertical line deals with the project line of responsibility. An example of a project organized under the matrix model is given in Figure 4-5.

The project that is organized under a matrix structure may relate to specific industrial problems, marketing issues, product-quality improvement, and so on. The project line in the matrix is usually of a temporary nature, whereas the functional line is more permanent. Matrix organization is dynamic. Its actual structure is determined by the prevailing activities of the project. Matrix organization has several advantages and some disadvantages as outlined:

Advantages of Matrix Organization Structure

- Consolidation of objectives.
- Multilateral flow of information.
- Improved morale of project team.
- Lateral mobility for job advancement.
- Efficient sharing and utilization of resources.
- Continuity of functions after project completion.
- Stimulating interactions with other functional teams.

Disadvantages of Matrix Organization Structure

- Higher overhead cost due to additional lines of command.
- Potential conflict among project priorities.
- Problems of having multiple bosses.
- Complexity of the structure.

Despite its disadvantages, matrix organization is widely used in practice. Its numerous advantages seem to outweigh the disadvantages. In addition, its problems can be overcome with good project planning, which can set the tone for a smooth organization structure.

Matrix organization is a collaborative effort between product and functional organization structures. It permits both vertical and horizontal flows of information. The matrix model is sometimes called a "multiple-boss" organization. It is a model that is becoming increasingly popular as the need for information sharing increases. For example, industrial development projects require the integration of specialties from different functional areas.

Under matrix organization, projects are permitted to share critical resources and management expertise.

Traditionally, industrial projects are conducted in serial functional implementations such as R&D, engineering, manufacturing, and marketing. At each stage, unique specifications and work patterns may be used without consulting the preceding and succeeding phases. The consequence is that the end product may not possess the originally intended characteristics. For example, the first project in the series might involve the production of one component, whereas the subsequent projects might involve the production of other components. The composite product may not achieve the desired performance because the components were not designed and produced from a unified point of view. In today's interdependent industrial projects, such lack of a unified design will lead to overall project failure.

4.1.5 Mixed Organization Structure

Another approach for organizing an industrial development project is to adopt a combined implementation of functional, product, and matrix structures. This permits the different structures to coexist simultaneously in the same project. In an industrial project, for example, the project of designing a new product may be organized using matrix while the subproject of designing the production line may be organized along functional lines. The mixed model facilitates flexibility in meeting special problem situations. The structure can adapt to the prevailing needs of the project or the needs of the overall organization. However, a disadvantage is the difficulty in identifying the lines of responsibility within a given project.

4.2 SELECTING THE PROJECT MANAGER

The project manager is the individual who has the primary responsibility of ensuring that a project is implemented according to the project plan. The project manager will have a wide span of interaction within and outside the project environment and has to be very versatile and effective in handling different types of project situations whether positive or negative.

The process of selecting a project manager for an industrial development project requires very careful consideration because it is one of the most critical project decisions. In the simplest of terms, the project manager should be someone who can get the project job done promptly and satisfactorily; who should possess both technical and administrative credibility; who must be perceived as having the necessary technical knowledge to direct the project; who must be up-to-date with the technologies pertinent to the project requirements; who must be conversant with the industry's terminologies; and who must be a good record keeper. Because the project manager is the vital link between the project and upper management, he or she must be able to convey information at various levels of detail. A project manager's leadership qualities should be outstanding. Because leadership is difficult to predict, judgment should be based on previous performances. Leadership is an after-the-fact attribute. Therefore, caution should be exercised in extrapolating prior observations to future expectations when evaluating candidates for the post.

The selection process should be as formal as a regular recruiting process. A pool of candidates may be developed through nominations, applications, eligibility records, shortlisted group, or management suggestions. The candidates should be made aware of the nature of the project and what they would be expected to do. Formal interviews may be required in some cases, particularly those involving large projects. In a few cases, the selection may have to be made by default if there are no other suitably qualified candidates. Default appointment of a project manager implies that no formal evaluation process is carried out. Political considerations and quota requirements often lead to default selection of project managers. As soon as a selection is made, an announcement should be issued to inform the project team of the management hierarchy and leadership. The desirable attributes of a project manager are:

Attributes of a Good Project Manager

- Inquisitiveness.
- Good labor relations.
- Good motivational skills.
- Availability and accessibility.
- Good analytical and technical background.
- Versatility with company operations.
- Good rapport with senior executives.
- Perseverance toward project goals.

- Excellent communication skills.
- Receptive ears for suggestions.
- Technical and administrative credibility.
- Good leadership qualities.
- Good diplomatic skills.
- Congenial personality.

4.3 STAFFING THE PROJECT

One of a project manager's first tasks is the selection of personnel for the project. In some cases, the project manager simply inherits a project team that has been formed beforehand. In that case, the project manager's initial responsibility will be to ensure that a good project team has been formed. The project team should be chosen on the basis of skills relevant to the project requirements and personal reliability. The personnel required may be obtained either from within the organization or from outside sources. If outside sources are used, a clear statement should be made about the duration of the project assignment. If opportunities for permanent absorption into the organization exist, the project manager may use that fact as an incentive both in recruiting for the project and in running the project. An incentive for internal personnel may be the opportunity for advancement within the organization.

Job descriptions should be prepared in unambiguous terms. Formal employment announcements may be issued or direct contacts through functional departments may be utilized. The objective is to avoid having a pool of applicants that is either too large or too small. If job descriptions are overly broad, many unqualified people will apply. Yet, if the descriptions are too restrictive, very few of those qualified will apply. Some skill tolerance or allowance should be established. Since it is nearly impossible to obtain the perfect candidate for each position, some preparation should be made for in-house specialized skill development to suit the project objectives. Typical job classifications in a project environment include the following:

- Project administrator.
- Project director.
- Project coordinator.

- Program manager.
- Project manager.
- Project engineer.
- Project assistant.
- Project specialist.
- Task manager.
- Project auditor.

4.3.1 Staff-Selection Criteria

When evaluating applicants, especially those from outside sources, the following factors should be to considered:

- Recommendations.
- Salary requirements.
- Geographical preference.
- Education and experience.
- Past project performance.
- Time frame of availability.
- Frequency of previous job changes.
- Versatility for project requirements.
- Completeness and directness of responses.
- Special project requirements (quotas, politics, etc.).
- Overqualification. Overqualified workers tend to be unhappy at lower job levels.
- Applicant's carefulness in filling out application materials. This is important because most project environments are report-intensive and accurate reporting is essential.

An initial screening of the applicants on the basis of the factors above may help reduce the applicant pool to a manageable level. If company policy permits, direct contact over the telephone or in person may then be used to prune the pool of applicants further. A direct conversation usually brings out more accurate information about applicants. In many cases, people fill out applications by writing what they feel the employer wants to read rather than what they want to say. Direct confrontation can often help to find out if the applicant is really interested in the job, whether he will be available when needed, or whether he possesses vital communication skills. However, direct contacts should be carefully executed. If not properly conducted, the applicant may develop the wrong notion of being the leading candidate or having the job wrapped up.

Confidentiality of applications should be maintained particularly for applicants who do not want a disclosure to their current employers. References should be checked out, and the information obtained should be used with utmost discretion. Interviews should then be arranged for the prime candidates. Final selection should be based on the merits of the applicants rather than on mere personality appeal. Both the successful and the unsuccessful candidates should be informed of the outcome as soon as administrative policies permit. There is nothing more unsettling than keeping hopeful applicants in limbo waiting for interview results. Inform them early, and let them get on with their other functions.

In many industrial fields, manpower shortage is a serious problem. The problem of recruiting in such circumstances becomes that of expanding the pool of applicants, rather than that of pruning the pool. It is a big battle among employers to entice highly qualified technical personnel away from one another. Some recruiters have even been known to resort to unethical means in the attempt to lure prospective employees. Some approaches that may be considered for alleviating the severity of skilled manpower shortage are:

- Employee-exchange programs.
- Transfer for other projects.
- In-house training for new employees.
- Use of temporary project consultants.
- Diversification of in-house job skills.
- Cooperative arrangements between employers.
- Continuing education for present employees (sponsored by the employer).

Committees may be set up to guide the project effort from the recruitment stage to the final implementation stage. Figure 4-6 shows a generic organizational chart for the project office and the role of a project committee. The primary role of a committee should be to provide supporting consultations to the project manager. Such a committee might use the steering-committee model, which is formed by including representatives from different functional areas. The steering committee should serve as an advisory board for

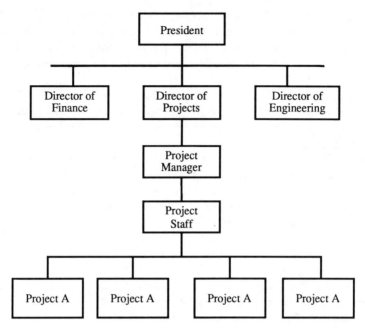

FIGURE 4-6.   Organization of the Project Office.

the project. A committee may be set up under one of the following two structures:

1. *Ad Hoc Committee.* This is set up for more immediate and specific purpose (e.g., project-feasibility study).
2. *Standing Committee.* This is set up on a more permanent basis to oversee ongoing project activities.

4.4 CONDUCTING ORGANIZATIONAL MEETINGS

Effective management of meetings is an important skill for any managerial staff. It is well-known that most employees feel that most meetings waste time and impede productivity. This is because most meetings are poorly organized, improperly managed, called at the wrong time, or even unnecessary. In some organizations, meetings are conducted as a matter of routine requirement rather than by necessity. Meetings are essential for communication and decision making. Unfortunately, many meetings accomplish ing and waste everyone's time. A meeting of thirty people wasting only thirty minutes in effect wastes fifteen full hours (30 times 30 minutes)! That much time, in a corporate setting, may amount to thousands of dollars in lost time. Badiru (1988) presents a list of observations about project meetings:

Observation 1. Most of the information passed out at meetings can be more effectively disseminated through ordinary memo. The proliferation of desktop computers and electronic mail should be fully exploited to replace most meetings.

Observation 2. The point of diminishing returns for any meeting is equal to the number of people who are actually needed for the meeting. The more people at a meeting, the lower the meeting's productivity. The extra attendees only serve to generate unconstructive and conflicting ideas that impede the meeting's progress.

Observation 3. Not being invited to a meeting could be viewed as an indication of the high value placed on your time within the organization. They cannot afford to have you away from your job.

Observation 4. Regularly scheduled meetings with specific time slots complete their evolutionary cycle by becoming social assemblies.

Observation 5. The optimal adjourn time of a meeting is equal to the scheduled start time plus five times the number of agenda items minus the start-up time. Mathematically, this is expressed as:

$$L = (T + 5N) - S,$$

Where
L = optimal length
T = scheduled time
N = number of agenda items
S = meeting start-up time (i.e., time taken to actually call the meeting to order).

Since it is difficult to do away with meetings, both the necessary and the unnecessary ones, we just have to learn to live with them and make the most of them. Presented below are some guidelines for running meetings more effectively:

1. Do pre-meeting homework.
   List topics to be discussed (agenda).
   Establish the desired outcome for each topic.
   Determine how the outcome will be verified.
   Determine who really needs to be there.

Evaluate the suitability of meeting time and venue.

Categorize meeting topics (e.g., announcements, important, urgent).

Assign time duration to each topic.

Convince yourself that the meeting is really needed.

Consider alternatives to the meeting (e.g., memo, telephone, electronic mail).

2. Circulate written agenda prior to the meeting.
3. Start meeting on time.
4. Review agenda at the beginning.
5. Get everyone involved; if necessary employ direct questions and eye contacts.
6. Keep to the agenda; do not add new items unless they are absolutely essential.
7. Be a facilitator for meeting discussions.
8. Avoid group conflicts.
9. Redirect wayward discussions back to meeting topics.
10. Retain leadership and control of the meeting.
11. Recap the accomplishments of each topic before going to the next. Let those who have made commitments (e.g., follow-up actions) know what is expected of them.
12. End meeting on time.
13. Prepare and distribute minutes. Evaluate meeting success relative to established goals.

4.5 ROLE OF GENDER IN PROJECT ORGANIZATION

The role of gender in project organization is something that is rarely discussed in project-management publications. Gender considerations particularly relates to the role of women in project organizations. The sensitivity of the topic may be what causes some authors to shy away from it. Yet, it should be addressed in the light of the increasing number of women in the work force. Technical and managerial jobs that have traditionally been viewed as male occupations are now equally pursued by both sexes.

The U.S. Bureau of Labor statistics reported that more than 14 percent of women workers (20 million) in 1987 were employed as professionals. Not only are women entering these occupations, but they are also doing a fine job at them. Women tend to be resourceful, dedicated, emphatic, and empathic in their work habits. These are precisely the qualities that facilitate successful project management. However, the road to the top is not always smooth. The traditional obstacles still abound. Project organizers should be receptive,

appreciative, and open-minded to the potentials of women in project-management environments. Both males and females must be educated on how to coexist professionally for the benefit of project goals.

The increasing numbers of women who are executives at big companies are faced with new situations that, though rarely acknowledged publicly, are causing discomfort among both men and women in corporate settings. Some potential areas of concern in project organization involving women are:

1. Concerns about out-of-town travels for project-management purposes.
2. Concerns about female professionals not getting honest job-performance feedbacks from male supervisors, even though the feedbacks are needed to improve their professional skills.
3. Concerns about the different emotional reactions that may develop in a project environment.
4. Concerns about discomfort arising from a male-female project team traveling together.
5. Concerns about potential areas of miscommunication and misconceptions when male and females interact at work.

4.5.1 Guidelines for Personnel Interactions

There is a need to open communication lines on the above concerns, particularly in industrial development project environments. Some companies have been hiring consultants to run "gender-awareness" training sessions. In order to enhance project efforts, the following guidelines—for both males and females—are offered for personnel interactions in a project environment:

1. *Leadership Style.*
   Dissociate yourself from the male/female stereotypes.
   Display a personality of self-confidence.
   Feel comfortable at closed-door meetings.
   Establish self-concept of your job functions.
   Engage in professional networking without being pushy.
   Be cautious of personal discussions that may be misconstrued.
   Perform a self-assessment of your professional strengths.
   Dress professionally without being flashy.
   Avoid the role of "godmother" to female employees.
   Be assertive without being autocratic.
   Keep up with the developments in your technical field.
   Do your best without overexerting yourself.
   Take positive initiative where others procrastinate.

2. *Supervision.*
   Delegate when appropriate without stereotypical considerations.
   Motivate subordinates with your vigor and objective approach.
   Set goals and prioritize them.
   Develop objective performance-appraisal mechanisms.
   Discipline as required promptly.
   Find time to relate to former peers.
   Don't overmanage women.
   Don't be bashful of mentoring or being mentored.
   Establish your credibility and decisiveness.
   Don't be intimidated by difficult employees.
   Use empathy in your decision-making process.
3. *Communication.*
   Be professional in your communication approach.
   Do your homework about the communication needs.
   Contribute constructively to meaningful discussions.
   Flaunt your knowledge without being patronizing.
   Convey your ideas effectively to gain respect.
   Demonstrate that you have earned your position.
   Cultivate good listening habits.
   Incorporate charisma into your communication approach.
4. *Handling Conflicts.*
   Learn the politics and policies of your organization.
   Align your goals with organizational goals.
   Conquer your fear of confrontation.
   Form a mediating liaison between peers, subordinates, and superiors.
   Control your emotions in tense situations.
   Find out your organizations policies on sexual harassment.
   Be conversant with the law regarding sexual harassment.
   Never take work conflicts home and vice versa.
   Avoid power struggle but claim your functional rights.
   Handle mistakes honestly without being condescending.

4.6 PROJECT COMMUNICATION MODES

When clear communication is maintained between management and employees and among peers, many project problems can be averted. Project communication may be in the form of:

- One to many.
- One to one.
- Many to one.

- Written and formal.
- Written and informal.
- Oral and formal.
- Oral and informal.
- Nonverbal gesture.

Good communication is effected when what is implied is perceived as intended. Effective communications are vital to the success of any project. Despite the awareness that proper communications form the blueprint for project success, many organizations still fail woefully in the communication functions. The study of communication is complex. Factors that influence the effectiveness of communication within a project organization structure include the following:

1. *Personal Perception.* Each person perceives events on the basis of personal psychological, social, cultural, and experiential background. As a result, no two people can interpret a given event the same way. The nature of events is not always the critical aspect of a problem situation. Rather, the problem is often the different perceptions of the various people involved.
2. *Psychological Profile.* The psychological makeup of each person determines personal reactions to events or words. Thus, individual needs and level of thinking will dictate how a message is interpreted.
3. *Social Environment.* Communication problems sometimes arise because people have been conditioned by their prevailing social environment to interpret certain things in unique ways. Vocabulary, idioms, organizational status social stereotypes, and economic situation are among the social factors that can thwart effective communication.
4. *Cultural Background.* Cultural differences are among the most pervasive barriers to project communications especially in today's multinational organizations. Language and cultural idiosyncrasies often determine how communication is approached and interpreted.
5. *Semantic and Syntactic Factors.* Semantic and syntactic barriers to communication usually occur in written documents. Semantic factors are those that relate to the intrinsic knowledge of the subject of the communication. Syntactic factors are those that relate to the form in which the communication is presented. The problems created by these factors become acute in situations in which response, feedback, or reaction to the communication cannot be observed.
6. *Organizational Structure.* Frequently, the organization structure in which a project is conducted has a direct influence on the flow of information and, consequently, on the effectiveness of communication. Organization

hierarchy may determine how different personnel levels perceive a given communication.

7. *Communication Media.* The method of transmitting a message may also affect the value ascribed to the message and, consequently, how it is interpreted or used. The common barriers to project communications are:
- Inattentiveness.
- Lack of organization.
- Outstanding grudges.
- Preconceived notions.
- Ambiguous presentation.
- Emotions and sentiments.
- Lack of communication feedback.
- Sloppy and unprofessional presentation.
- Lack of confidence in the communicator.
- Lack of confidence by the communicator.
- Low credibility of communicator.
- Unnecessary technical jargon.
- Too many people involved.
- Untimely communication.
- Arrogance or imposition.
- Lack of focus.

Some suggestions on improving the effectiveness of communication are presented below. The recommendations may be implemented as appropriate for any of the forms of communication listed earlier. The recommendations are for both the communicator and the audience.

1. Never assume that the integrity of the information sent will be preserved as the information passes through several communication channels. Information is generally filtered, condensed, or expanded by the receivers before being relayed to the next destination. When preparing communication that needs to pass through several organization structures, one safeguard is to compose the original information in a concise form to minimize the need for recomposition.
2. Give the audience a central role in the discussion. A leading role can help make a person feel as a part of the project effort and responsible for the project's success. He or she can then have a more constructive view of project communication.
3. Do homework and think through the intended accomplishment of the communication. This helps eliminate trivial and inconsequential communication efforts.

4. Carefully plan the organization of the ideas embodied in the communication. Use indexing or points of reference whenever possible. Grouping ideas into related chunks of information can be particularly effective. Present the short messages first. Short messages help create focus, maintain interest, and prepare the mind for the longer messages to follow.

5. Highlight why the communication is of interest and how it is intended to be used. Full attention should be given to the content of the message with regard to the prevailing project situation.

6. Elicit the support of those around you by integrating their ideas into the communication. The more people feel they have contributed to the issue, the more expeditious they are in soliciting the cooperation of others. The effect of the multiplicative rule can quickly garner support for the communication purpose.

7. Be responsive to the feelings of others. It takes two to communicate. Anticipate and appreciate the reactions of members of the audience. Recognize their operational circumstances, and present your message in a form they can relate to.

8. Accept constructive criticism. Nobody is infallible. Use criticism as a springboard to higher communication performance.

9. Exhibit interest in the issue in order to arouse the interest of your audience. Avoid delivering your messages as a matter of routine organizational requirement.

10. Obtain and furnish feedback promptly. Clarify vague points with examples.

11. Communicate at the appropriate time, at the right place, to the right people.

12. Reinforce words with positive action. Never promise what cannot be delivered. Value your credibility.

13. Maintain eye contact in oral communication and read the facial expressions of your audience to obtain real-time feedback.

14. Concentrate on listening as much as on speaking. Evaluate both the implicit and explicit meanings of statements.

15. Document communication transactions for future references.

16. Avoid asking questions that can be answered "yes" or "no." Use relevant questions to focus the attention of the audience. Use questions that make people reflect on their words. For example, ask "How do you think this will work?" instead of "Do you think this will work?"

17. Avoid patronizing the audience. Respect their judgment and knowledge.

18. Speak and write in a controlled tempo. Avoid emotionally charged voice inflections.

19. Create atmosphere for formal and informal exchange of ideas.

20. Summarize the objectives of the communication and how they will be achieved.

4.7 ORGANIZING INTERNATIONAL PROJECTS

Projects that cross national boundaries either in concept or in implementation have unique characteristics that create project-management problems. In multinational projects, individual organizational policies are not enough to govern operations. Factors that normally influence these projects include:

- Territorial laws and regulations.
- Geographical segregation and restricted access.
- Time differences.
- Different scientific standards of measure.
- Trade agreements.
- Different government and political ideologies.
- Different social, cultural, and labor practices.
- Different stages of industrialization.
- National security concerns.
- Protection of proprietary technology information.
- Strategic military implications.
- Traditional national allies and adversaries.
- Taxes, duties, and other import/export charges.
- Foreign-currency exchange rates.
- National extradition/protection agreements.
- Paperwork, permits, and restrictions.
- Health, weather, and environmental considerations.
- Poor, slow, or incompatible communication links.

International communication is perhaps one of the most difficult factors to deal with. The task of international transfer of technology and mutual project support takes on critical dimensions because of differences in the structures, objectives, and interests of the different countries involved. One common communication problem is that information destined for another country may have to pass through several levels of approval before reaching the point of use. The information is subject to all types of distortions and perils in its arduous journey. The integrity of the information may not be preserved as it is passed from one point to another. When implementing international projects, the following considerations should be reviewed:

1. *Product.*
    Type of product expected.
    Portability of the product.
    Product maintenance.
    Required training.
    Availability of spare parts.
    Feasibility for intended use.
    Local-versus-overseas productions.

2. *Technology.*
   Local availability of required technology.
   Import/export restrictions on the technology.
   Implementation requirements.
   Supporting technologies.
   Adaptation to local situations.
   Lag between development and applications.
   Operational approvals required.
3. *Political and Social Environment.*
   Leadership and consistency of national policies.
   Political and social stability.
   Management views.
   Cultural adaptations.
   Bureaucracies.
   Structures of formal and informal organizations.
   Acceptance of foreigners and formation of relationships.
   Immigration laws.
   Ethnicity.
   General economic situation.
   Religious situations.
   Population pressures.
   Local development plans.
   Decision-making bureaucracies.
4. *Labor.*
   Union regulations.
   Wage structures.
   Personnel dedication loyalty, and motivation.
   Educational background and opportunities.
   Previous experience.
   Management relationships.
   Economic condition and level of contentment.
   Interests, attitudes, personalities, and leisure activities.
   Taxation policies.
   Logistics of employee relocation.
   Productivity consciousness.
   Demarcation of private and business activities.
   Local communication practices and facilities.
   Local customs.
5. *Market.*
   Market needs.
   Inflation.
   Stability.

Variety and availability of products.
Cash, credit, and billing requirements.
Exchange rates.
National budget and Gross National Product.
Competition and size of market.
Transportation facilities.

6. *Plant and Residential Amenities.*
Location.
Structural condition.
Accessibility.
Facilities available.
Proximity to business centers.
Topography.
Basic amenities (water, light, sewage, etc.).

7. *Financial Services.*
Banking.
International money transfer.
Currency strength and stability.
Local sources of capital.
Interest rates.
Efficiency in conducting transactions.
Investment laws.

With all these various factors, international project managers must undergo more extensive training than the conventional training. A foreign manager in an international project must be open-minded, flexible, adaptive, and able to learn quickly. Since he or she will be working in an unfamiliar combination of social, cultural, political, and religious settings, the manager must have a keen sense of awareness and should be unassuming and responsive to local practices. An evaluation of the factors presented above in the context of the specific countries involved should help the international project manager to be better prepared for this expanded role. The role of expertise transfer and professional nationals should also be considered in international project organization. The section that follows addresses this issue.

4.7.1 Expertise Transfer to Combat Brain Drain

For industrial development projects, the project organizers (preferably the government) should make sure that there is access to qualified nationals who are recognized professionals in their fields. The skilled professionals can be invited as needed to contribute to certain aspects of the industrial development project. As the development takes shape, the professionals will take more and more pride in their own contributions and they will find it encouraging to contribute even more. Eventually, they will feel comfortable enough to return home on a permanent basis. The fact is that a patriotic citizen does not have to be physically based in his or her own homeland to contribute to the land's development. Frequent professional exchanges will greatly facilitate the contribution of foreign-based professionals. Suggested below are some strategies for transferring expertise for industrial development projects.

1. Develop a technical database of locally based and foreign-based qualified nationals. Give these professionals the first chance to tackle development projects in their home countries. For the foreign-based professionals, the existing citizen-registration programs at many national embassies can be expanded to accommodate the information on technical expertise.

2. Encourage professional and technical interactions of locally based and foreign-based nationals.

3. Recognize that expatriates are not necessarily the best experts for local projects since many of these expatriates might even have been trained by nationals that are stationed abroad. The irony of development projects in developing nations is that when companies abroad need experts, their nationals are among the technical professionals they rely on. But when these nations need experts, they look for foreign experts.

4. Invite professional nationals stationed abroad to conduct seminars, workshops, and short courses on specific economic and industrial development topics in their home countries.

5. Recognize the importance of maintaining a pool of professional nationals abroad. These professionals provide access to the latest technological developments and information around the world.

6. Develop avenues for the foreign-based nationals to transfer their expertise to their home countries. The foremost avenues are through training programs and joint projects.

7. Encourage and support the efforts of nationals who have formed professional groups abroad.

8. Organize an annual government-sponsored conference on "World Technological Interface." This should be an application-oriented conference that will bring qualified nationals together.

9. Establish a national industrial productivity center. Provide adequate funding, international visibility, and autonomy for the center. The center can be the foundation for implementing local economic and industrial development strategies.

10. Formulate the economic/industrial development and expertise-transfer strategies into a long-term commitment that will last for generations rather than the traditional quick-fix schemes.

4.8 CASE STUDY OF MULTINATIONAL PROJECT COORDINATION[1]

This case study involves a large-scale international project comprised of the engineering, procurement, and construction of seven liquid gas tanks together with their ancillary system and control building in a Middle East country. The use and capacity of the tanks are as follow:

1. Three LNG tanks of 80,000 cubic meters each.
2. Two LPG Propane tanks of 50,000 cubic meter each.
3. Two LPG Butane tanks of 50,000 cubic meters each.

The ancillary systems that are part of the project include:

1. A Propane and Butane vapor-recovery systems.
2. A low-pressure flare system.
3. An off-site control room.

Project Setting

The construction is to be done on Dax Island in the Persian Gulf (Middle East), approximately 300 miles from the city of Abu Dhabi (the capital of the United Arab Emirates). Dax is a small island of two square miles and has a population of 5,000, all of whom work in the only two plants on the island. Because the project is large, the island will have an additional 3,000 people working and living on it during the construction phase, a considerable increase in population. The island has a salty ground and cannot grow any vegetation. Also, there isn't any source for fresh water except for the desalinated sea water. Desalination is a very slow process and can be the cause of considerable delays when it comes to concrete pouring.

Technical Requirements

Each of the seven tanks will consist of two separate and structurally independent liquid containers: a primary inner metallic container, and a secondary outer concrete container. Each of the containers will be constructed out of material suitable for the low-temperature liquid.

Each container should be capable of holding the required volume of the stored liquid for an indefinite period without any deterioration of the container or its surroundings. The secondary concrete container should be

---

[1]Based on personal, first-hand project account by Dr. Saba Bahouth, University of Central Oklahoma, Edmond, Oklahoma.

capable of withstanding the effect of fire exposure from the adjacent tanks and an external impact of 21 tons traveling at high speed without loss of structural integrity. Adequate insulation should be provided between the primary and secondary tanks to limit heat-in leaks. All the tanks should be provided with the necessary pumping and piping systems for the receipt, storage, and loading of the LNG and PLG from the nearby plant to the different tankers. A blast-proof off-site control room should be provided. All storage and loading operations should be controlled from this control room. The project's total cost is estimated at U.S. $600,000,000. The detailed project network consists of around 48,000 activities.

Organizational Relationships

GASC company is the owner of the above project. Their main offices are located in Abu Dhabi city. GASC is an operating company that had never managed any engineering or construction project. GASC turned to its mother company, NOCC, for help and signed an agreement with them for the management of this project.

NOCC is the national oil company of the Emirate of Abu Dhabi with main offices in Abu Dhabi city. It is completely owned by the government of Abu Dhabi and plays an extremely important role in the national economy. It is headed by a general manager responsible for the eight different directorates, one of which is the Projects Directorate. One of the divisions of the Projects Directorate is the Gas Projects Division, headed by a manager. The Gas Projects Division is selected to manage the above project.

GASC is one of several operating companies whose majority of shares are owned by NOCC. NOCC's share in GASC is 60 percent, and the remaining shares are owned by TOTAC of France, SHELC of Holland, PBC of Great Britain, and MITSC of Japan. Although it is considered convenient to have the major owning company manage the project for GASC, such an arrangement has its own drawbacks, mainly the fact that the client company (who should have the final say in its own project) is a subsidiary of the hired management company.

The Gas Projects Division is staffed with a skeleton staff. Although very capable, this staff can only oversee the management of the project but cannot perform all the actual engineering, procurement, and construction management. The Houston-based KELLC was selected to provide the services under the direct supervision of the Gas Projects Division. KELLC's scope of work includes the basic design of the tanks, the detailed design of all the piping and ancillary systems, the procurement of all free-issue materials, and the management of construction. All the engineering and procurement activities are to be performed out of KELLC's regional office in London.

KELLC, a well-known process engineering firm, has limited experience with concrete tanks. Their selection was conditional on their acceptance to hire the Belgian civil-engineering firm TRACT as a consultant to help them in the critical civil-engineering problems. NOCC will also hire the American-based consulting firm DMRC to do the soil-investigation and -testing work.

The construction work is packaged into fifteen small contracts and one large (75 percent of the total construction work) contract. All the small contracts were awarded to local construction companies, whereas the main large contract, which included the tanks, piping, and ancillary systems, was awarded to the Chicago-based CBAIC company. CBAIC will have to open three new offices. One office will be located in London, next to KELLC's regional office, during the engineering phase. Another office will be in Abu Dhabi city for the construction management. A third office will be on Dax island for the construction operations. CBAIC is a reputable tanking contractor. However, its experience in concrete tanks is quite limited. They will have to hire the French civil-engineering firm SBC as subcontractors. SBC's experience in low temperature concrete is limited. They will have to hire the specialized Belgian firm CBC as a consultant.

Safety and Environmental Considerations

The project's safety requirements are very high. The safety of those living on such a small island in case of any accident is of a major concern to the owning company. To ensure that the required quality and safety standards are achieved, NOCC will hire the French "Third Party Inspection" company BVC as a consultant.

Since the engineering office is in London, the French and the Belgian engineers are to commute to London as necessary to provide their inputs to the project. This will continue for the whole engineering phase, which is expected to last two years.

Procurement activities will be handled out of KELLC's London office. Materials and equipment are to be delivered to the construction site. Supplies will be purchased in the open market at the most competitive prices. Steel will be purchased from Japan and Belgium; pipes from Germany, France, and Japan; valves from Sweden and France; pumps from the United States of America; compressors from Switzerland and Japan; and vessels from Italy. A total of around 600 purchase orders will be issued.

Analysis of Project Scenario

The organizational setup has to be quite flexible and capable of changing in accordance with the project requirements. Because it is expected to b fast-track project, the most active period will be the second half of the engineering phase, which corresponds to the first half of the construction phase. The organizational setup for the project stretches across national boundaries, practices, and regulations. It is thus very important that efforts of the project staff be closely coordinated.

The existing scenario suggests that all the planning, organizing, and staffing functions are fixed. However, the existing organizational setup and overall project plan pose some possible problems. The possible problems associated with the existing setup are discussed along with suggestions on how they could have been alleviated by applying sound management principles to the planning, organizing, and staffing functions. Management should have especially considered and forecasted possible future problems and made provisions for handling them.

Understanding the scope and limitations of the project is vital because of the fact that it is a multinational high-tech project and of such a large size. Special management practices suitable for high-tech and multinational projects should be applied.

Sources of Possible Problems and Solutions

The core of possible problems associated with this project lies in the complex organizational structure and the fact that it is a large, multinational high-tech project. The problem sources, associated possible problems that could arise, and recommended solutions or alternatives to alleviate the problems are listed in the next sections.

Subcontracting to Mother Company
GASC turned to its mother company, NOCC, for help and contracted with NOCC for management of the project. There could be several drawbacks associated with this situation. NOCC may become overcontrolling as GASC is its subsidiary and begin to generate and implement decisions without contacting GASC for approval. For example, NOCC may overlook the performance standards specified in the blueprints and set new performance standards that are lower than those specified by GASC. NOCC may feel that their way of accomplishing jobs is best and that, because GASC had to come to them for help, making their own changes can only benefit the project. However, this will only create a poor final product.

GASC knows the expectations of the project and has planned for that in the blueprints and specifications. However, GASC is playing no part in the internal decision making as the project evolves. This is going to produce conflicts that will slow the project down and create many more scheduling problems, financial problems, and other problems that were not planned for initially. If GASC had carefully covered the planning function, they would have foreseen the potential problems and realized that their participation in decisions is of utmost importance for the project to be streamlined and for the final system to perform its intended function efficiently. Thus, GASC could have either hired a more qualified staff internally with more expertise in management, or they could have taken a team of their top managers to coordinate with NOCC on the project to ensure things were going as planned.

Too Many Companies Involved

Too many companies involved can result in several levels of responsibility. The situation is compounded by the fact that the companies are so globally widespread. Too many levels of responsibility creates unnecessary red tape and could cause much delay in the project's phases, along with employee frustration and disinterest. First, NOCC was not equipped to handle such a large-scale project and, thus, should be eliminated from the organizational setup. This decision should have been made in the planning stages as mentioned previously. However, in considering the organizing stage, NOCC would also be eliminated because of its poor managing abilities clearly shown in the poorly planned organizational setup.

The organizational structure does not give a logical design of the interfaces needed among personnel in order to ensure a dedicated pursuit of the common goals in association with the project, nor was it approached carefully so as to facilitate coordination. Although this is a large project that requires much expertise in various fields, a better approach would have been to simplify the levels of responsibilities by contracting with fewer companies that are more specialized. The benefits of this approach outweigh the costs. If the foundation of responsibility level and organizational hierarchy is not set up adequately from the start, then the directing and controlling functions will be limited, and project success may not be possible.

Potential Communication Problems

Several communication problems could arise due to the fact that the project is high tech and multinational.

The difference in cultural backgrounds and the complex organizational structure of this project would influence how communication is approached and how it will be perceived by different levels of personnel. The management should form an environment in which formal and informal exchange of ideas can take place. Due to the numerous levels of responsibility and cultural and language differences between countries, any form of communication that must pass through these several levels should be concisely formatted. This will ensure that the original information is clearly communicated and not altered as it passes through the various levels. Clear communication is very important in preventing project problems.

The difference in times zones presents several communication obstacles to overcome. Thus, to help resolve these problems, a global time frame has to be determined during which all the project offices in the following cities or countries can communicate on any given day (twenty-four hours) by teleconference: London, Rome, Chicago, Abu Dhabi, Dax, Tokyo, Geneva, Bonn, Paris, Sweden, and Belgium. In approaching the problem of determining the time window, the two locations with the greatest time difference (Japan and Chicago) and the major project offices (London, Abu Dhabi, and Dax) were jointly considered. The optimal time window is one hour each day in which Chicago will communicate from 6:00 A.M. to 7:00 A.M. and Japan from 9:00 P.M. to 10:00 P.M. Thus, this time frame gives the major project offices a practical communication time during their daily business hours. This is important since most project interactions will originate from these offices.

Another problem in communication is the language barriers between the various countries. To ensure that information is streamlined and correctly perceived, interpreters that are fluent in these various foreign languages should be employed at the various project offices. Effective communication ensures that coordination will be increased within all the units, thus enhancing cooperation and creating satisfaction among the members of the project.

Increases in Island Population
A considerable increase in island population during the construction phase will have to be planned for. An added 3,000 people to Dax increases the island's population by 60 percent. It is known that the island is currently starved of natural resources. Thus, high priority should be given to conserve these resources. Upper management should ensure that sufficient facilities be provided for the employees without polluting or destroying the natural environment.

Delivery of Supplies
Ordering supplies from so many different countries creates problems in logistics.

Due to geographical diversity of the incoming supplies, delays and backlogs are likely to occur. A sound inventory system should be implemented to minimize any logistic problems or delays so that the project deadlines are accomplished.

Suggestions for Managing a Global High-Tech Project

In dealing with high-tech projects, the management must be more versatile. Several factors must be considered, including how to control the uncertain high-tech operations and how to streamline information among the various personnel. Multinational projects require management practices designed specifically for their operations. Several factors to consider and specific suggestions for this project are listed:

Strategic Planning. Because a frequent problem with technology is the extension of useful life well beyond the period of obsolescence, it is vital that NOCC define the long-range purpose and useful life of the project so that replacement of the system can be planned for financially.

Cost/Benefit Analysis. The bottom line in most operations is combined profit/benefit and performance. NOCC should analyze the cost of the high technology required versus the benefits to see if this project could be profitable.

Technology Assessment. The technology itself should be assessed in detail. GASC should determine whether there are alternative technologies that can perform the required objective of the project.

Acquisition. In the planning stage, NOCC should evaluate the policy of procuring and implementing the high-tech system. NOCC should evaluate the hardware and software components of the project, communications-site selection and installation, and development and implementation, along with training and post-implementation evaluation of the project.

Trade Agreements. Several contracts on procurement of supplies will need to be closely regulated to ensure all governmental policies of the various countries are strictly followed.

Different Labor Practices. Labor practices vary from country to country in terms of the number of hours of work per day, the number of days to work per week, unions, relationships between personnel, payment practices, and so on. A compromise should be developed among the various workers and contracting companies to address these various factors.

Different Governmental and Political Ideologies. Differences among countries on politics could create several conflicts especially if top management allows political ambitions to influence their actions toward work on the project. Thus, these differences in governments must be discussed and accounted for in the initial planning stage of the project.

Information Management. Information is a critical resource in managing high-tech operations. The organizational efficiency of the project will be affected by the quality of information generated and how the information is used. A multinational project manager may be bogged down with the problems of receiving too much information. Sophisticated data-processing and information-handling mechanisms will be needed to govern the mass of information that may be associated with a project.

In coordinating the activities of each phase of the project, a central division should be set up to monitor all the activities that go on and keep all the members of the project informed of the current situation. The organizational structure should also be streamlined to make use of the systems approach, in which project teams interact both horizontally and vertically.

Undertaking such a vast multinational high-tech project requires a management with special expertise and capabilities. The project manager should have broad authority over all elements of the project and engage in all necessary managerial and technical actions required to complete the project successfully. Also, the project manager should have appropriate authority in making technical and design decisions and should be able to control funds, schedule, and quality of product.

Due to the large size of this international project, a team of managers is recommended in order successfully to control and direct the project. Cooperation, communication, and coordination are vital to the interactions among the managers. The management team should be experienced and well educated in management principles as applied to high-tech and multinational projects to ensure harmony throughout the decision-making processes. The case study presented here gives insight to a real-world situation in which documented management principles can be applied for optimal project outcome.

A conducive organization structure must be formulated. Since there are interdependencies and subsidiary relationships among many of the companies involved in the project, the conventional organization structures may not be adequate. A sophisticated form of the mixed organization structure will, thus, be required. In summary, the potential problems that may adversely affect the project organization are:

- Shortage of food supply.
- Security concern (high-tension zone).
- Potential cost overruns.
- Potential for catastrophic accidents.
- Foreign rules and regulations.
- Trade restrictions.
- Communication delays.

- Language barriers.
- Lack of fresh water.

Recommendations

The following recommendations for the case study are offered:

- Simplify the levels of responsibilities by contracting with fewer companies.
- Minimize the interdependencies of companies by using nonsubsidiary companies.
- Predetermine communication time zones that are compatible with the timing of project decisions.
- Reevaluate the level of technology required for the project.
- Arrange for special favorable trade exceptions to facilitate movement of personnel and materials.

5

Project Scheduling

Timeliness is the essence of development.

This chapter presents the basic approaches to scheduling a network of activities that make up a project. A network of development-oriented activities provide the basis for scheduling an industrial development project. The critical path method (CPM) and the program evaluation and review technique (PERT) are the two most popular techniques for project scheduling. Another technique, the precedence diagramming method (PDM), provides an approach to compressing a project schedule. A CPM, PERT, or PDM network graphically represents the contents and objectives of the project. Because industrial development projects can span a period of several years, the activity networks are often subject to significant schedule delays. Careful planning and proper scheduling approaches can help alleviate the potential delays in these projects. The basic project-network analysis is typically implemented in three phases: network planning phase, network scheduling phase, and network control phase.

5.1 PROJECT NETWORK PLANNING

Network planning is sometimes referred to as activity planning. This involves the identification of the relevant activities for the project and their precedence relationships. Precedence requirements may be determined on the basis of technological, procedural, or imposed constraints. The activities are then represented in the form of a network diagram. The two popular models for network drawing are the activity-on-arrow (AOA) and the activity-on-node (AON) conventions. In the AOA approach, arrows are used to represent activities, and nodes represent starting and ending points of activities. In the AON approach, nodes represent activities, and arrows represent precedence relationships. Time-, cost-, and resource-requirement estimates are developed for each activity during the network planning phase. The estimates may be based on historical records, time standards, forecasting, regression functions, or other quantitative models.

5.2 PROJECT NETWORK SCHEDULING

Network scheduling is performed by using forward-pass and backward-pass computational procedures. These computations give the earliest and latest starting and finishing times for each activity. The amount of slack or float associated with each activity is determined. The activity path with the minimum slack in the network is used to define the critical activities and the duration of the project. Resource allocation and timecost trade-offs are other functions performed during network scheduling.

5.3 PROJECT NETWORK CONTROL

Project network control involves tracking the progress of a project on the basis of the network schedule and taking corrective actions when needed. An evaluation of actual performance versus expected performance deter-mines deficiencies in the project progress. The advantages of project net-work analysis are the fact that:

Advantages for Communication

- It clarifies project objectives.

- It serves as a visual communication tool.

- It presents a documentation of the project plan.

- It establishes the specifications for project performance.

- It provides a starting point for more detailed task analysis.

Advantages for Control

- It encourages team interactions.

- It gives a clear message of what is expected.

- It helps determine what corrective actions are needed.
- It presents a measure for evaluating project performance.

Advantages for Team Interactions
- It clarifies personnel roles.
- It facilitates ease of applications.
- It specifies functional interfaces on the project.
- It offers a mechanism for a quick introduction to the project.

5.4 CRITICAL PATH METHOD TECHNIQUE

The critical path method (CPM) was originally developed for the du Pont company in 1957. The technique has enjoyed extensive application in construction and in various types of projects. The activity-precedence relationships in a CPM network fall into the three major categories listed below:

Activity-Precedence Restrictions
- Technical restrictions.
- Procedural restrictions.
- Imposed restrictions.

Technical-precedence requirements are caused by the technical relationships among activities in a project. For example, in conventional construction, walls must be erected before the roof can be installed. Procedural-precedence requirements are determined by policies and procedures, which are often subjective with no concrete justification. Imposed-precedence requirements can be classified as resource imposed, state imposed, or environment imposed. For example, resource shortages may require that one task be done before another. The current status of a project (e.g., percent completion) may determine that one activity be performed before another. The environment of a project, for example, weather changes and the effects of concurrent projects, may determine the precedence relationships of the activities in a project.

The primary goal of the CPM analysis of a project is the determination of the "critical path." The critical path determines the minimum completion time for a project. The computational analysis involves forward-pass and backward-pass procedures. The forward pass determines the earliest start time and the earliest completion time for each activity in the network. The backward pass determines the latest start time and the latest completion time. The notations used to designate an activity in a project network are presented below:

A: activity identification.
ES: earliest starting time.
EC: earliest completion time.
LS: latest starting time.
LC: latest completion time.
t: activity duration.

During the forward-pass analysis of the network, it is assumed that each activity will begin at its earliest starting time. An activity can begin as soon as the last of its predecessors is finished. The completion of the forward pass determines the earliest completion time of the project. The backward-pass analysis is a reverse of the forward pass. It begins at the latest project completion time and ends at the latest starting time of the first activity in the project network. The rules for the forward-pass and backward-pass analyses in CPM are presented below. These rules are implemented iteratively until the ES, EC, LS, and LC have been calculated for all nodes in the activity network.

Rule 1. Unless otherwise stated, the starting time of a project is set equal to zero. That is, the first node in the network diagram has an ES of zero. Thus,

$$\text{ES of First Activity} = 0.$$

If a desired starting time is specified, then

$$\text{ES of First Activity} = \text{Specified Starting Time}.$$

Rule 2. The ES for any activity is equal to the maximum of the EC's of the immediate predecessors of the activity. That is,

$$ES = \text{Maximum \{Immediately Preceding EC's\}}.$$

Rule 3. The EC of an activity is the activity's ES plus its estimated time. That is,

$$EC = ES + \text{\{Activity Time\}}.$$

Rule 4. The EC time of a project is equal to the of the very last node in the project network. That is,

$$EC \text{ of Project} = EC \text{ of Last Activity}.$$

Rule 5. Unless the LC of a project is explicitly specified, it is set equal to the EC of the project. This is called the *zero project slack convention.* That is,

$$LC \text{ of Project} = EC \text{ of Project}.$$

Rule 6. If a desired deadline is specified for the project, then

$$LC \text{ of Project} = \text{Specified Deadline}.$$

It should be noted that an LC or deadline may sometimes be specified for a project based on contractual agreements.

Rule 7. The LC for an activity is the smallest of the LS's of the activity's immediate successors. That is,

$$LC = \text{Minimum \{Immediate Succeeding LS's\}}.$$

Rule 8. The LS for an activity is the LC minus the activity time. That is,

$$LS = LC - \text{(Activity Time)}.$$

5.4.1 Scheduling Example

Table 5-1 presents a sample data set for the seven major phases of a large project. The network representation for the example is given in Figure 5-1.

TABLE 5-1.   Data on Phases of a Large Project

Activity	Predecessor	Duration (months)
A	—	2
B	—	6
C	—	4
D	A	3
E	C	5
F	A	4
G	B, D, E	2

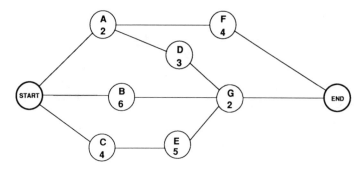

FIGURE 5-1.   Example of Activity Network.

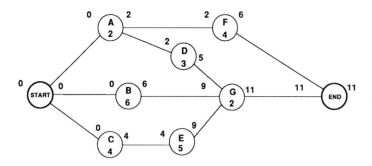

FIGURE 5-2.   Forward-Pass Analysis for CPM Example.

Starting and ending nodes are included in the network to designate single starting and ending points for the network.

Forward Pass
The forward-pass calculations are shown in Figure 5-2. Zero is entered as the ES for the initial node. Since the initial node for the example is a dummy node, its duration is zero. Thus, the EC for the starting node is equal to its ES. The ES values for the immediate successors of the starting node are set equal to the EC of the Start node, and the resulting EC values are computed. Each node is treated as the "start" node for its successor or successors. However, if an activity has more than one predecessor, the maximum of the EC's of the preceding activities is used as the activity's starting time. This happens in the case of activity G, whose ES is determined as Max {6, 5, 9} = 9. The EC time for the example is eleven months. Note that this is the maximum of the immediate preceding earliest completion times: Max {6, 11} = 11. Because the dummy ending node has no duration, its earliest completion time is set equal to its earliest start time of eleven months.

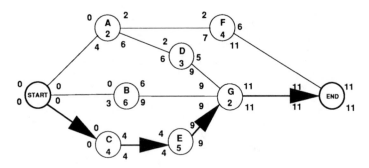

FIGURE 5-3.   Backward-Pass Analysis for CPM Example.

Backward Pass

The backward-pass computations establish the LS and LC for each node in the network. The results of the backward-pass computations are shown in Figure 5-3. Because no deadline is specified, the LC of the project is set equal to the EC. By backtracking and using the network-analysis rules presented earlier, the LC's and LS's are determined for each node. Note that in the case of activity A with two successors, the LC is determined as the minimum of the immediate succeeding LS's. That is, Min {6, 7} = 6. A similar situation occurs for the dummy starting node. In that case, the LC of the dummy start node is Min {0, 3, 4} = 0. As this dummy node has no duration, the LS of the project is set equal to the node's LC. Thus, the project starts at time 0 and is expected to be completed by time 11.

Within a project network, there are usually several possible paths, a number of activities must be performed sequentially, and some activities may be performed concurrently. If an activity has ES and EC times that are not equal, then the actual start and completion times of that activity may be flexible. The amount of flexibility an activity possesses is called a slack time. The slack time is used to determine the critical activities in the network, discussed in the next section.

5.4.2 Control of Critical Activities

The critical path is defined as the path with the least slack in the network diagram. All the activities on the critical path are said to be critical activities. These activities can create bottlenecks in the network if they are delayed. The critical path is also the longest path in the network diagram. In some networks, particularly large ones, it is possible to have multiple critical paths. If there is a large number of paths in the network, it may be very difficult to identify visually all the critical paths. The slack time of an activity is also referred to as its *float*. There are four basic types of activity slack:

1. *Total Slack (TS)*. Total slack is defined as the amount of time for which an activity may be delayed from its ES without delaying the LC of the project. The total slack of an activity is the difference between the LC and the EC of the activity, or the difference between the LS and the EC of the activity.

$$TS = LC - EC \text{ or } TS = LS - ES.$$

   Total slack is the measure that is used to determine the critical activities in a project network. The critical activities are identified as those having the minimum total slack in the network diagram. If there is only one critical path in the network, then all the critical activities will be on that one path.
2. *Free Slack (FS)*. Free slack is the amount of time for which an activity may be delayed from its ES without delaying the starting time of any of its immediate successors. Activity free slack is calculated as the difference between the minimum ES of the activity's successors and the EC of the activity.

$$FS = \text{Min \{Succeeding ES's\}} - EC.$$

3. *Interfering Slack (IS)*. Interfering slack or interfering float is the amount of time by which an activity interferes with (or obstructs) its successors when its total slack is fully used. This is rarely used in practice. The interfering float is computed as the difference between the total slack and the free slack.

$$IS = TS - FS.$$

4. *Independent Float (IF)*. Independent float or independent slack is the amount of float that an activity will always have regardless of the completion times of its predecessors or the starting times of its successors. Independent float is computed as:

$$\text{Independent Float} = \text{Max } \{0, (ES_j - LC_i - t)\},$$

where ES_j is the earliest starting time of the preceding activity, LC_i is the latest completion time of the succeeding activity, and t is the duration of the activity whose independent float is being calculated. Independent float takes a pessimistic view of the situation of an activity. It evaluates the situation whereby the activity is pressured from either side. That is, when its predecessors are delayed as late as possible while its successors are to be started as early as possible. Independent float is useful for conservative planning purposes, but it is not used much in practice. Despite its low level of use, independent float does have practical implications for better project management. Activities can be buffered with independent floats as a way to handle contingencies.

Referring to Figure 5-3, the total slack and the free slack for activity A are calculated, respectively, as:

$$TS = 6 - 2 = 4 \text{ months}$$
$$FS = \text{Min} \{2, 2\} - 2 = 2 - 2 = 0.$$

Similarly, the total slack and the free slack for activity F are:

$$TS = 11 - 6 = 5 \text{ months}$$
$$FS = \text{Min} \{11\} - 6 = 11 - 6 = 5 \text{ months}.$$

Table 5-2 presents a tabulation of the results of the CPM example. The table contains the earliest and latest times for each activity as well as the total and free slacks. The results indicate that the minimum total slack in the network is zero. Thus, activities C, E, and G are identified as the critical activities. The critical path is highlighted in Figure 5-3 and consists of the following sequence of activities:

$$\text{START} \rightarrow C \rightarrow E \rightarrow G \rightarrow \text{END}.$$

The total slack for the overall project itself is equal to the total slack observed on the critical path. The minimum slack in most networks will be

TABLE 5-2.   Result of CPM Analysis for Sample Project

Activity	Duration	ES	EC	LS	LC	TS	FS	Classification
A	2	0	2	4	6	4	0	Noncritical
B	6	0	6	3	9	3	3	Noncritical
C	4	0	4	0	4	0	0	Critical
D	3	2	5	6	9	4	4	Noncritical
E	5	4	9	4	9	0	0	Critical
F	4	2	6	7	11	5	5	Noncritical
G	2	9	11	9	11	0	0	Critical

zero because the ending LC is set equal to the ending EC. If a deadline is specified for a project, then we would set the project's LC to the specified deadline. In that case, the minimum total slack in the network would be given by:

$$TS_{Min} = (Project\ Deadline) - EC\ of\ the\ last\ node.$$

This minimum total slack will then appear as the total slack for each activity on the critical path. If a specified deadline is lower than the EC at the finish node, then the project will start out with a negative slack. That means that it will be behind schedule before it even starts. It may then become necessary to expedite some activities (i.e., crashing) in order to overcome the negative slack.

5.4.3 Gantt Charts

When the results of a CPM analysis are fitted to a calendar time, the project plan becomes a schedule. The Gantt chart is one of the most used tools for presenting a project schedule. A Gantt chart can show planned and actual progress of activities. The time scale is indicated along the horizontal axis, and horizontal bars or lines representing activities are ordered along the vertical axis. As a project progresses, markers are made on the activity bars to indicate actual work accomplished. Gantt charts must be updated periodically to indicate project status.

Figure 5-4 presents the Gantt chart for our illustrative example by using the ES's calculated earlier. Figure 5-5 presents the Gantt chart for the example based on the ES's times. Critical activities are indicated by the shaded bars. Figure 5-4 shows that the starting time of activity F can be delayed from month 2 until month 7 (i.e., TS = 5) without delaying the overall project. Likewise, A, D, or both may be delayed by a combined total of four months (TS = 4) without delaying the overall project. If all the four months of slack are used up by A, then D cannot be delayed. If A is delayed by one month, then D can be delayed by up to three months without causing a delay of G, which determines project completion. The Gantt chart also indicates that activity B may be delayed by up to three months without affecting the project-completion time.

In Figure 5-5, the activities are scheduled by their LS's. This represents the extreme case in which activity slack times are fully used. No activity in this schedule can be delayed without delaying the project. In Figure 5-5, only one activity is scheduled over the first three months. This is compared to the schedule in Figure 5-4 that has three starting activities. The schedule in Figure 5-5 may be useful if there is a situation that permits only few activities

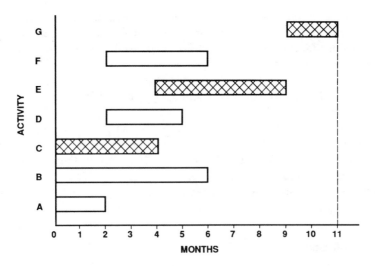

FIGURE 5-4.   Gantt Chart Based on Earliest Starting Times.

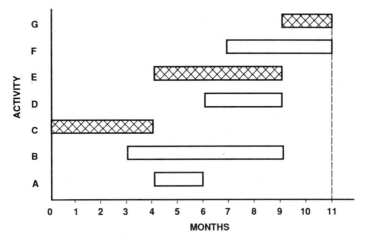

FIGURE 5-5.   Gantt Chart Based on Latest Starting Times.

to be scheduled in the early stages of the project. Such situations may involve shortage of project personnel, incomplete feasibility study, lack of initial budget, time for project initiation, time for personnel training, allowance for learning period, or general resource constraints. Scheduling of activities based on ES's indicates an optimistic view. Scheduling on the basis of LS's represents a pessimistic approach.

5.4.4 Variations of Gantt Chart

The basic Gantt chart does not explicitly show the precedence relationships among activities. However, the relationships can be shown by linking appropriate bars in the chart as shown in Figure 5-6. However, the linked bars become cluttered and confusing for large networks. Figure 5-7 shows a Gantt chart that presents a comparison of planned and actual schedule. Note that two tasks are in progress at the current time indicated in the figure. One of the ongoing tasks is an unplanned task. Figure 5-8 shows a Gantt chart on which important milestones have been indicated. Figure 5-9 shows a Gantt chart in which bars represent a combination of related tasks.

Tasks may be combined for scheduling purposes or for conveying functional relationships required on a project. Figure 5-10 presents a Gantt chart of project phases. Each phase is further divided into parts. Figure 5-11 shows a multiple-projects Gantt chart. Multiple-projects charts are useful for evaluating resource-allocation strategies. Resource loading over multiple projects may be needed for capital budgeting and cash-flow analysis decisions. Figure 5-12 shows a project-slippage chart that is useful for project tracking and control. Other variations of the basic Gantt chart may be developed for specific needs.

5.4.5 Schedule Compression

Schedule compression refers to reducing the length of a project network. This is often accomplished by crashing activities. Crashing or expediting reduce activity durations, thereby reducing project duration. Crashing is done as a trade-off between shorter task duration and higher task cost. It should be determined if the total cost savings realized from reducing the

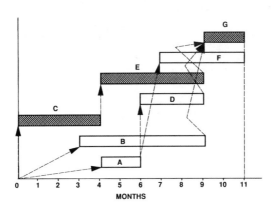

FIGURE 5-6.   Linked Bars in Gantt Chart.

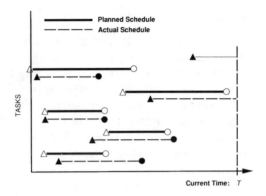

FIGURE 5-7.   Progress Monitoring Gantt Chart.

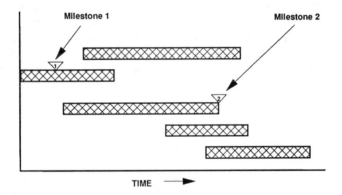

FIGURE 5-8.   Milestone Gantt Chart.

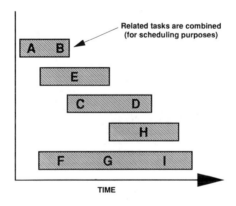

FIGURE 5-9.   Task-Combination Gantt Chart.

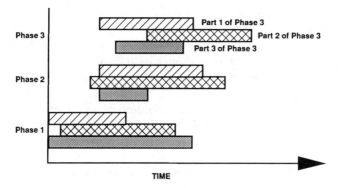

FIGURE 5-10.   Phase-Based Gantt Chart.

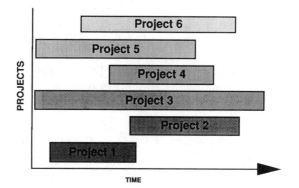

FIGURE 5-11.   Multiple-Projects Gantt Chart.

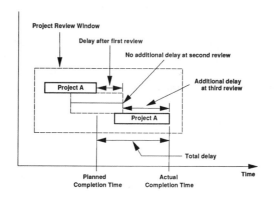

FIGURE 5-12.   Project Delay Tracking Gantt Chart.

project duration is enough to justify the higher costs associated with reducing individual task durations.

If there is a delay penalty associated with a project, it may be possible to reduce the total project cost, even though individual task costs are increased by crashing. If the cost saving on delay penalty is higher than the incremental cost of reducing the project duration, then crashing is justified. Under conventional crashing, the further the duration of a project is compressed, the higher the total cost of the project. The objective is to determine at what point to terminate further crashing in a network. Normal task duration refers to the time required to perform a task under normal circumstances. Crash task duration refers to the reduced time required to perform a task when additional resources are allocated to it.

If each activity is assigned a range of time and cost estimates, then several combinations of time and cost values will be associated with the overall project. Iterative procedures are used to determine the best time or cost combination for a project. Time/cost trade-off analysis may be conducted, for example, to determine the marginal cost of reducing the duration of the project by one time unit. Several approaches are available for determining which activities to crash in a project network. Two alternate approaches are presented below for computing the crashing criterion:

$$r = \text{Criticality Index}$$

$$r = \frac{\text{Crash Cost} - \text{Normal Cost}}{(\text{Normal Duration} - \text{Crash Duration})(\text{Criticality Index})}$$

The first approach gives crashing priority to the activity with the highest probability of being on the critical path. In deterministic networks, this refers to the critical activities. In probabilistic networks, an activity is expected to fall on the critical path only a percentage of the time. The second approach is a combination of cost consideration and of the critical-index approach. It relects the process of selecting the least cost expected value. The denominator of the expression represents the expected number of months by which the critical path can be shortened. For different project networks, different crashing approaches should be considered, and the one that best fits the nature of the network should be selected.

5.5 PROGRAM EVALUATION REVIEW TECHNIQUE

Program Evaluation Review Technique (PERT) is an extension of CPM that incorporates variabilities in activity durations into project network analysis. PERT has been used extensively and successfully in practice.

In real life, activities are often prone to uncertainties that determine the actual durations of the activities. In CPM, activity durations are assumed to be deterministic. In PERT, the potential uncertainties in activity durations are accounted for by using three time estimates for each activity. The three time estimates represent the spread of the estimated activity duration. The greater the uncertainty of an activity, the wider the range of the estimates.

5.5.1 PERT Calculations

PERT uses three time estimates and simple equations to compute the expected duration and variance for each activity. The PERT formulas are based on a simplification of the expressions for the mean and variance of a beta distribution. The approximation formula for the mean is a simple weighted average of the three time estimates, with the endpoints assumed to be equally likely and the mode four times as likely. The approximation formula for PERT is based on the recognition that most of the observations from a distribution will lie within plus or minus three standard deviations or a spread of six standard deviations. This leads to the simple method of setting the PERT formula for standard deviation equal to one-sixth of the estimated duration range. The PERT equations are presented below:

$$t_e = \frac{a + 4m + b}{6};$$

$$s^2 = \frac{(b - a)^2}{36},$$

Where
a = optimistic time estimate
m = most likely time estimate
b = pessimistic time estimate $(a < m < b)$
t_e = expected time for the activity
s^2 = variance of the duration of the activity.

After obtaining the estimate of the duration for each activity, the network analysis is carried out in the same manner previously illustrated for the CPM approach. The major steps in PERT analysis are as follows:

1. Obtain three time estimates a, m, and b for each activity.
2. Compute the expected duration for each activity by using the formula for t_e.
3. Compute the variance of the duration of each activity from the formula for s^2. It should be noted that CPM analysis cannot calculate variance of activity duration because it uses a single time estimate for each activity.
4. Compute the expected project duration, T_e. As in the case of the CPM,

the duration of a project in PERT analysis is the sum of the durations of the activities on the critical path.

5. Compute the variance of the project duration as the sum of the variances of the activities on the critical path. The variance of the project duration is denoted by S^2. It should be recalled that the CPM cannot compute the variance of the project duration because variances of activity durations are not computed.

6. If there are two or more critical paths in the network, choose the one with the largest variance to determine the project duration and the variance of the project duration. Thus, PERT is pessimistic with respect to the variance of project duration when there are multiple critical paths in the project network. For some networks, it may be necessary to perform a mean-variance analysis to determine the relative importance of the multiple paths by plotting the expected project duration versus the path-duration variance.

7. If desired, compute the probability of completing the project within a specified time period. This is not possible under the CPM.

In practice, a question often arises as to how to obtain good estimates of a, m, and b. Several approaches can be used in obtaining the required time estimates for the PERT. Some of the approaches are:

> - Estimates obtained from simple regression or forecasting.
> - Estimates furnished by an experienced person.
> - Estimates derived from heuristic assumptions.
> - Estimates dictated by customer requirements.
> - Estimates extracted from standard time data.
> - Estimates obtained from historical data.
> - Estimates generated by simulation.

The pitfall of using estimates furnished by an individual is that the estimates may be inconsistent based on the experience and personal bias of the person providing the estimates. Individuals responsible for furnishing time estimates are usually not experts in estimation and they generally have difficulty in providing accurate PERT time estimates. There is often a tendency to select values of a, m, and b that are optimistically skewed. This is because a conservatively large value is typically assigned to b by inexperienced individuals.

The use of time standards, on the other hand, may not reflect the changes occurring in the current operating environment because of new technology, work simplification, new personnel, and so on. The use of historical data and forecasting is very popular because estimates can be verified and validated by actual records. In the case of regression and forecasting, there is the danger of extrapolation beyond the data range used for fitting the regression and forecasting models. If the sample size in a historical data set is sufficient and the data can be assumed reasonably to represent prevailing operating conditions, the three PERT estimates can be estimated based on the historical data. In practice, probability distributions of activity times can be determined from historical data. The procedure involves three steps:

1. Appropriate organization of the historical data into histograms.
2. Determination of a distribution that reasonably fits the shape of the histogram.
3. Testing of the goodness of fit of the hypothesized distribution by using an appropriate statistical model. Most statistical texts present the details of how to carry out goodness-of-fit tests.

5.5.2 PERT Network Example

Suppose that we have the project data presented in Table 5-3. The expected activity durations and variances as calculated by the PERT formulas are shown in the last two columns of the table.

TABLE 5-3.   PERT Project Data

Activity	Predecessors	Time Estimates			t_e	s^2
		a	m	b		
A	—	1	2	4	2.17	0.2500
B	—	5	6	7	6.00	0.1111
C	—	2	4	5	3.83	0.2500
D	A	1	3	4	2.83	0.2500
E	C	4	5	7	5.17	0.2500
F	A	3	4	5	4.00	0.1111
G	B, D, E	1	2	3	2.00	0.1111

5.5.3 Probability Analysis of Project Duration

Since the project duration, T_e, can be assumed to be approximately normally distributed, the probability of meeting a specified deadline, T_d, can be computed by finding the area under the standard normal curve to the left of T_d. Figure 5-13 shows an example of a normal distribution describing the project duration.

Using the equation below, a relationship between the standard normal random variable, z, and the project duration variable can be obtained:

$$z = \frac{T_d - T_e}{S},$$

Where
T_d = specified deadline
T_e = expected project duration based on network analysis
S = standard deviation of the project duration.

The probability of completing a project by the deadline, T_d, is then computed as:

$$P(T \le T_d) = P\left(z \le \frac{T_d - T_e}{S}\right).$$

The probability is obtained from the normal table, which is widely available in statistics books.

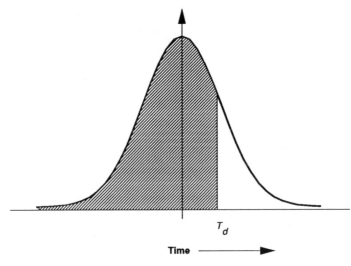

FIGURE 5-13.   Area under the Normal Curve.

In our PERT example, activities C, E, and G are found to be critical, and the project-completion time is eleven months. The probability of completing the project in ten months (i.e., $T_d = 10$) is calculated as shown below:

$$T_e = 11;$$

$$S^2 = V[C] + V[E] + V[G]$$
$$= 0.25 + 0.25 + 0.111$$
$$= 0.6111;$$

$$S = \sqrt{0.6111}$$
$$= 0.7817;$$

$$P(T \le T_d) = P(T \le 10)$$
$$= P\left(z \le \frac{10 - T_e}{S}\right)$$
$$= P\left(z \le \frac{10 - 11}{0.7817}\right)$$
$$= P(z \le -1.2793)$$
$$= 1 - P(z \le -1.2793)$$
$$= 1 - 0.8997$$
$$= 0.1003.$$

Thus, there is just over 10 percent chance of finishing the project within ten months. By contrast, the probability of finishing the project in thirteen months is calculated as:

$$P(T \le 13) = P\left(z \le \frac{13 - 11}{0.7817}\right)$$
$$= P(\le 2.5585)$$
$$= 0.9948.$$

Thus, there is an over 99-percent chance of finishing the project within thirteen months. If we desire the probability that the project can be completed within a certain lower limit (T_L) and a certain upper limit (T_U), the computation would proceed as follows: Let $T_L = 9$ and $T_U = 11.5$. Then,

$$P(T_L \le T \le T_U) = P(9 \le T \le 11.5)$$
$$= P(T \le 11.5) - P(T \le 9)$$
$$= P\left(z \le \frac{11.5 - 11}{0.7817}\right) - P\left(z \le \frac{9 - 11}{0.7817}\right)$$
$$= P(z \le 0.6396) - P(z \le -2.5585)$$
$$= P(z \le 0.6396) - [1 - P(z \le 2.5585)]$$
$$= 0.7389 - [1 - 0.9948]$$
$$= 0.7389 - 0.0052$$
$$= 0.7337.$$

5.6 PRECEDENCE DIAGRAMMING METHOD TECHNIQUE

Precedence diagramming method (PDM) was developed in the early 1960s as an extension of the basic PERT/CPM network analysis. It permits mutually dependent activities to be performed partially concurrently instead of serially. The usual finish-to-start dependencies between activities are relaxed to allow activities to be overlapped. This facilitates schedule compression. An example is the requirement that concrete should be allowed to dry for a number of days before drilling holes for hand rails. This is a finish-to-start constraint. The time between the finishing time of the first activity and the starting time of the second activity is called the *lead-lag* requirement between the two activities. Figure 5-14 shows the graphical representation of the basic lead-lags relationships between activity A and activity B.

SS_{AB} (Start-to-Start) Lead: This specifies that activity B cannot start until activity A has been in progress for at least SS time units.

FF_{AB} (Finish-to-Finish) Lead: This specifies that activity B cannot finish until at least FF time units after the completion of activity A.

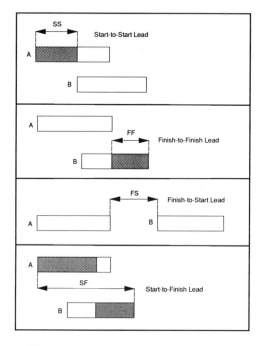

FIGURE 5-14.   Lead-Lag Relationships in PDM.

FS$_{AB}$ (Finish-to-Start) Lead: This specifies that activity B cannot start until at least FS time units after the completion of activity A. Note that PERT/CPM approaches use FS$_{AB}$ = 0 for network analysis.

SF$_{AB}$ (Start-to-Finish) Lead: This specifies that there must be at least SF time units between the start of activity A and the completion of activity B.

The leads or lags may, alternately, be expressed in percentages rather than in time units. For example, we may specify that 25 percent of the work content of activity A must be completed before activity B can start. If percentage of work completed is used for determining lead-lag constraints, then a reliable procedure must be used for estimating the percent completion. If the project work is broken up properly by using work-breakdown structure (WBS), it would be much easier to estimate percent completion by evaluating the work completed at the elementary task levels.

The lead-lag relationships may also be specified in terms of *at most* relationships instead of *at least* relationships. For example, we may have at most FF lag requirement between the finishing time of one activity and the finishing time of another activity. Splitting of activities often simplifies the implementation of PDM, as will be shown later with some examples. Some of the factors that will determine whether or not an activity can be split are technical limitations affecting splitting of a task, morale of the person working on the split task, setup times required to recommence split tasks, difficulty involved in managing resources for split tasks, loss of consistency of work, and management policy about splitting jobs.

5.7 RESOURCE ALLOCATION IN PROJECT NETWORKS

Basic CPM and PERT approaches assume unlimited resource availability in project network analysis. In a real project, both the time and resource requirements of activities are considered in developing network schedules. Projects are subject to three major constraints of time limitations, resource availability, and performance requirements. Because these constraints are difficult to satisfy simultaneously, trade-offs must be made. The smaller the resource base, the longer the project schedule and the lower the quality of work. Resource allocation facilitates the transition of a project from one state to another state.

Given that the progress of a project is in an initial state i, three possible changes can occur. Further progress may be achieved in moving to state $i + j$, the progress may be stagnant between state i and state $i + j$, or the progress may regress from state i to state $i + j$. Planning, scheduling, and control strategies must be developed to determine which is the next desired state of the project, when the next state is expected to be reached, and how to move toward it. Resource availability, as well as other internal and external factors, will determine the nature of the progress of a project from one state to another. Network diagrams, Gantt charts, progress charts, and resource-loading graphs constitute visual tools that can guide resource-allocation strategies.

5.7.1 Resource-Loading Graph

Resource loading refers to the allocation of resources to work elements in a project network. A resource-loading graph is a graphical representation of resource allocation over time. Figure 5-15 shows an example of a resource-loading graph, which may be drawn for the different resources types involved in a project.

The graph provides information useful for resource-planning and budgeting purposes. A resource loading graph gives an indication of the demand a project will place on an organization's resources. In addition to resource units committed to activities, the graph may also be drawn for other tangible and intangible resources of an organization. For example, a variation of the graph may be used to present information about the depletion rate of the budget available for a project. If drawn for multiple resources, it can help identify potential areas of resource conflicts. For situations in which a single resource unit is assigned to multiple tasks, a variation of the resource-loading graph can be developed to show the level of load (responsibilities) assigned to the resource over time.

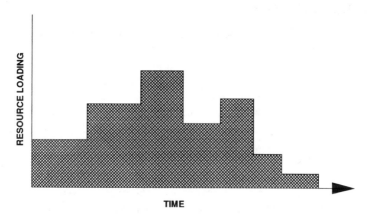

FIGURE 5-15.   Resource-Loading Graph.

5.7.2 Resource Leveling

Resource leveling refers to the process of reducing the period-to-period fluctuation in a resource-loading graph. If resource fluctuations are beyond acceptable limits, actions are taken to move activities or resources around in order to level out the resource-loading graph. For example, it is bad for employee morale and public relations when a company has to hire and lay people off indiscriminately. Proper resource planning will facilitate a reasonably stable level of the work force. Other advantages of resource leveling include simplified resource tracking and control, lower cost of resource management, and improved opportunity for learning. Acceptable resource leveling is typically achieved at the expense of longer project duration or higher project cost. Figure 5-16 shows a somewhat leveled resource loading.

When attempting to level resources, it should be noted that:

1. Not all of the resource fluctuations can be eliminated.
2. Resource leveling often leads to an increase in project duration.

Resource leveling attemps to minimize fluctuations in resource loading by shifting activities within their available slacks. For small networks, resource leveling can be attempted manually through trial-and-error procedures. For large networks, resource leveling is best handled by computer software techniques. Most of the available commercial project-management software packages have internal resource-leveling routines.

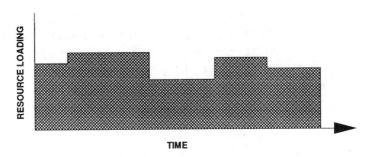

FIGURE 5-16.   Resource-Leveling Graph.

6

Project Control

Plan to control your project plan.

This chapter presents some approaches to project monitoring and control. The steps required to carry out project control, schedule control through progress review, guidelines for performance control, and the project information systems needed for control are discussed. An approach to terminating projects as a managerial control is outlined.

6.1 PROJECT-CONTROL PROCESS

The three factors (time, budget, and performance) that form the basis for the operating characteristics of a project also help determine the basis for project control. Project control is the process of reducing the deviation between actual performance and planned performance. To be able to control, we must be able to measure performance. Measurements are taken on each of the three components of project constraints: time, performance, and cost. Some of the factors involved in project control are:

1. *Time*
   Supply delays.
   Missed milestones.
   Delay of key tasks.
   Change of due dates.
   Unreliable time estimates.
   Increased need for expediting.
   Time-consuming technical problems.
   Impractical precedence relationships.
   New industry regulations that need time to implement.

2. *Performance*
   Poor quality.
   Poor training.
   Low reliability.
   Restricted access.
   Fragile components.
   Poor functionality.
   Maintenance problems.
   Technical difficulties.
   Change order from client.
   High-risk implementation.
   Conflict of functional objectives.
   Resources not available when needed.
   Adjustments needed because of new technology.
3. *Cost*
   Cost overruns.
   Price changes.
   Incorrect bids.
   High labor cost.
   Budget revisions.
   High overhead rates.
   Poor cost reporting.
   Inadequate resources.
   Increase in scope of work.
   Increased delay penalties.
   Insufficient project cash flows.

Project control may be handled in a hierarchical manner starting with the global view of a project and ending with the elementary level of unit performance. The hierarchy may be constructed as presented below:

$$\text{PROJECT} \rightarrow \text{PRODUCT} \rightarrow \text{PROCESS} \rightarrow \text{UNIT.}$$

A product is project dependent. A process is product dependent. The performance of a unit depends on the process from which the unit is made. Such a control hierarchy makes the control process more effective.

6.2 CONTROL STEPS

Parkinson's law states that a schedule will expand to fill available time and cost will increase to consume the available budget. Project control prevents a schedule from expanding beyond reason. It also ensures that a project can be completed within budget. A recommended project-control process is presented below:

Step 1. Determine the criterion for control. This means that the specific aspect to measure should be determined.

Step 2. Set performance standards. Standards may be based on industry practice, prevailing project agreements, work analysis, forecasting, and so on.

Step 3. Measure actual performance. The measurement scale should be predetermined. The measurement approach must be calibrated and verified for accuracy. Quantitative and nonquantitative factors may require different measurement approaches.

Step 4. Compare actual performance with the specified performance standard. The comparison should be done objectively and consistently based on the specified control criteria.

Step 5. Identify unacceptable variance from expectation.

Step 6. Determine the expected impact of the variance on overall project performance.

Step 7. Investigate the source of the poor performance.

Step 8. Determine the appropriate control actions needed to overcome (nullify) the variance observed.

Step 9. Implement the control actions with total dedication.

Step 10. Ensure that the poor performance does not recur elsewhere in the project.

6.2.1 Informal Control Process

Informal control refers to the process of using unscheduled or unplanned approaches to assess project performance and using informal control actions. Informal control requires unscheduled visits and impromptu queries to track progress. The advantages of informal control process are presented below:

Advantages of Informal Control Process

- It allows the project manager to learn more about project progress.

- It creates a surprise element that keeps workers on their toes.

- It precludes the temptation for "doctored" progress reports.
- It allows peers and subordinates to assume control roles.
- It facilitates prompt appraisal of latest results.
- It gives the project manager more visibility.

6.2.2 Formal Control Process

A formal control process deals with the process of achieving project control through formal and scheduled reports, consultations, or meetings. Formal control is typically more time-consuming.

Disadvantages of Formal Control Process

- It can be used by only a limited (designated) group of people.
- It reduces the direct visibility of the project manager.
- It encourages bureaucracy and "paper pushing."
- It requires a rigid structure.
- It is more time-consuming.

Despite its disadvantages, formal control can be effective for industrial development projects because of the size and complexity of such projects. With a formal control process, project responsibilities and accountability can be pursued in a structured manner. For example, standard audit questions may be posed in order to determine current status of a project and ro establish the strategy for future performance. Examples of such questions are:

- Where are we today?
- Where were we expected to be today?
- What are the prevailing problems?
- What problems are expected in the future?

- Where shall we be at the next reporting time?
- What are the major results since the last project review?
- What is the ratio of percent completion to budget depletion?
- Is the project plan still the same?
- What resources are needed for the next stage of the project?

A formal structured documentation of what questions to ask can guide the project auditor in carrying out project audits in a consistent manner. The availability of standard questions makes it unnecessary for the auditor to guess or ignore certain factors that may be crucial for project control.

6.3 MEASUREMENT SCALES FOR PROJECT CONTROL

Project control requires data collection, measurement, and analysis. In project management, the manager will encounter different types of measurement scales, depending on the particular items to be controlled. Data may need to be collected on project schedules, costs, performance levels, problems, and so on. The different types of data-measurement scales that are applicable are:

Norminal Scale of Measurement. A *nominal scale* is the lowest level of measurement scales. It classifies items into categories. The categories are mutually exclusive and collectively exhaustive. That is, the categories do not overlap, and they cover all possible categories of the characteristics being observed. For example, in the analysis of the critical path in a project network, each job is classified as either critical or not critical. Gender, type of industry, job classification, and color are some examples of measurements on a nominal scale.

Ordinal Scale of Measurement. An *ordinal scale* is distinguished from a nominal scale by the property of order among the categories. An example is the process of prioritizing project tasks for resource allocation. We know that first is above second, but we do not know how far above. Similarly, we know that better is preferred to good, but we do not know by how much. In quality control, classification of items into categories is an example of a measurement on an ordinal scale.

Interval Scale of Measurement. An *interval scale* is distinguished from an ordinal scale by having equal intervals between the units of measure. The assignment of priority ratings to project objectives on a scale of zero to 10 is an example of a measurement on an interval scale. Even though an objective may have a priority rating of zero, it does not mean that the objective has absolutely no significance to the project team. Similarly, the scoring of zero on an examination does not imply that a student knows absolutely nothing about the materials covered by the examination. Temperature is a good example of an item that is measured on an interval scale. Even though there is a zero point on the temperature scale, it is an arbitrary relative measure. Other examples of interval scale are IQ measurements and aptitude ratings.

Ratio Scale of Measurement. A *ratio scale* has the same properties as an interval scale, but with a true zero point. For example, an estimate of zero time unit for the duration of a task is a ratio-scale measurement. Other examples of items measured on a ratio scale are cost, time, volume, length, height, weight, and inventory level. Many of the items measured in a project-management environment will be on a ratio scale.

Another important aspect of data analysis for project control involves the classification scheme used. Most projects will have both *quantitative* and *qualitative* data. Quantitative data require that we describe the characteristics of the items being studied numerically. Qualitative data, on the other hand, are associated with object attributes that are not measured numerically. Most items measured on the nominal and ordinal scales will normally be classified into the qualitative-data category, whereas those measured on the interval and ratio scales will normally be classified into the quantitative-data category. The implication for project control is that qualitative data can lead to bias in the control mechanism because qualitative data are subject to the personal views and interpretations. As much as possible, data for project control should be based on a quantitative measurement.

6.4 DATA ANALYSIS FOR PROJECT CONTROL

Project data may be obtained from several sources. Some potential sources are:

- Formal reports.
- Interviews and surveys.
- Regular project meetings.
- Personnel time cards or work schedules.

The timing of data is also very important for project-control purposes. The contents, level of detail, and frequency of data can affect the control process. An important aspect of project management is the determination of the data required to generate the information needed for project control. The function of keeping track of the vast quantity of rapidly changing and interrelated data about project attributes can be very complicated. The fundamental steps involved in project data-requirement analysis are:

- Data collection.
- Data processing to generate information.

- Decision making.
- Implementation of action.

Data collection constitutes a crucial point in project control. Project decisions require information and information requires accurate data. Effective management requires proper information management. Information can be defined as the resource that facilitates effective project control. Data are processed to generate information. Information is analyzed by the decision maker to make the required decisions. Good decisions are based on appropriate information, which in turn is based on reliable data. Data analysis for project control may involve the following functions:

- Organizing and printing computer-generated information in a form usable by decision makers.
- Integrating diverse hardware and software to communicate in the same project environment.
- Using voice-activated computerized data analysis to expedite data processing and to reduce paperwork.
- Incorporating new technologies such as expert systems into data analysis.
- Preserving the integrity of data as they are transformed from one form to another to generate different types of information.
- Incorporating flexibility and sharing options into project communication networks.

A comprehensive documentation of project data requirements should be developed. If data are properly documented, the chances for misuse, misinterpretation, mismanagement, or mishandling will be minimized. Data are needed at every stage in the life cycle of a project from the problem-identification stage through the project phaseout stage. The various stages of data requirements in project management include the following:

1. Data related to problem identification.
2. Data resulting from an initial study of the problem.
3. Data on personnel and resource availability.
4. Data on project planning.
5. Data on project initiation.
6. Data on project schedule.
7. Data on project implementation.
8. Data on project tracking.
9. Data on performance measurement.
10. Data on project phaseout.

The components of the documentation of data requirements should address the following items:

- *Data Summary.* Data summary is a general summary of the information and decision for which the data are required, as well as the form in which the data should be prepared. The summary indicates the impact of the data requirements on the organizational goals.
- *Data-Processing Environment.* The processing environment identifies the project for which the data are required, the user personnel, and the computer system to be used in processing the data. It refers to the project request or authorization and relationship to other projects and specifies the expected data-communication needs and mode of transmission.
- *Data Policies and Procedures.* Data-handling policies and procedures describe policies governing data handling, storage, and modification and the specific procedures for changing the data. In addition, they provide instructions for data collection and organization.
- *Static Data.* Static-data description involves that portion of the data that is used mainly for reference purposes, and it is rarely updated.
- *Dynamic Data.* Dynamic-data description deals with that portion of the data that is frequently updated based on the prevailing circumstances in the organization.
- *Data Frequency.* Frequency of data update specifies the expected frequency of data change for the dynamic portion of the data; for example, quarterly. This data-change frequency should be described in relation to the frequency of processing.
- *Input Interface.* Data-input interface specifies the mechanism through which the data are entered. Data may be entered directly by the user through the computer keyboard, mouse, or light pen. Data may also be entered indirectly by retrieving them from an existing database.
- *Data Constraints.* Data constraints refer to the limitations on the data requirements. Constraints may be procedural, such as those based on corporate policy; technical, such as those based on computer limitations, or imposed, such as those based on conflicting project requirement.
- *Data Compatibility.* Data-compatibility analysis involves ensuring that data collected for present project needs will be compatible with future needs.
- *Data Contingency.* Data-contingency plans concern data-security measures in case of accidental or deliberate catastrophe affecting hardware, software, or people.

6.5 SCHEDULE CONTROL

The Gantt charts developed in the scheduling phase of a project can serve as the yardstick for measuring project progress. Project status should be monitored frequently. Symbols may be used to mark actual activity positions on the Gantt chart. A record should be maintained of the difference between the actual status of an activity and its expected status. This information should be conveyed to the appropriate personnel with a clear indication for the required control actions. The more milestones or control points there are in a project, the easier the control function. The larger number allows for more frequent and distinct avenues for monitoring the schedule. That way, problems can be identified and controlled before they accumulate and turn into more serious problems. However, more control points means higher control cost.

Schedule-variance magnitudes may be plotted on a time scale (e.g., on a daily basis). If the variance continues to get worse, drastic actions may be necessary. Temporary deviations without a lasting effect on the project may not be a cause for concern. Some control actions that may be needed for project-schedule delays are:

Schedule Control Actions

- Job redesign.
- Productivity improvement.
- Revision of project scope.
- Revision of project master plan.
- Expediting or activity crashing.
- Elimination of unnecessary activities.
- Reevaluation of milestones or due dates.
- Revision of time estimates for pending activities.

6.6 PERFORMANCE CONTROL

Many project-performance problems may not surface until after a project has been completed. This makes performance control very difficult. Effort should be made to measure all the interim factors that may influence final project performance. After-the-fact performance measurements are typically not effective for project control. Some of the performance problems may be indicated by time and cost deviations. So, when project time and cost show problems, an analysis of how the problems may affect performance should be made. Because project-performance requirements usually relate to the performance of the end products, controlling performance problems may necessitate altering product specifications. Performance analysis will involve checking key elements of the product such as these:

1. *Scope*
   Is the scope reasonable based on the project environment?
   Can the required output be achieved with the available resources?
2. *Documentation*
   Is the requirement specification accurate?
   Are statements clearly understood?
3. *Requirement*
   Is the technical basis for the specification sound?
   Are requirements properly organized?
   What are the interactions between specific requirements?
   How does the prototype perform?
   Is the raw material appropriate?
   What is a reasonable level of reliability?
   What is the durability of the product?
   What are the maintainability characteristics?
   Is the product compatible with other products?
   Are the physical characteristics satisfactory?
4. *Quality Assurance*
   Who is responsible for inspection?
   What are the inspection policies and methods?
   What actions are needed for nonconforming units?
5. *Function*
   Is the product usable as designed?
   Can the expected use be achieved by other means?
   Is there any potential for misusing the product?

Careful evaluation of performance on the basis of the above questions throughout the life cycle of a project should help identify problems early so that control actions may be initiated to forestall greater problems later.

6.6.1 Continuous Performance Improvement

Continuous performance improvement (CPI) is an approach to obtaining a steady flow of improvement in a project. The approach is based on the concept of continuous process improvement, which is used in quality-management functions. The iterative decision processes in project management can benefit quite well from the concept of CPI. It is a practical method of improving performance in business, management, or technical processes. The approach is based on the following key points:

- Early detection of problems.
- Incremental improvement steps.
- Projectwide adoption of CPI concept.
- Comprehensive evaluation of procedures.
- Prompt review of methods of improvement.
- Prioritization of improvement opportunities.
- Establishment of long-term improvement goals.
- Continuous implementation of improvement actions.

A steering committee is typically set up to guide the improvement efforts. The typical function of the steering committee with respect to performance improvement includes the following:

- Determination of organizational goals and objectives.
- Communication with the personnel.
- Team organization.
- Administration of the CPI procedures.
- Education and guidance for companywide involvement.
- Allocation or recommendation of resource requirements.

Figure 6-1 represents the conventional fluctuating approach to performance improvement. In the figure, the process starts with a certain level of performance. A certain performance level is specified as the target to be achieved by time T. Without proper control, the performance will gradually degrade until it falls below the lower control limit at time t_1. At that time, a drastic effort will be needed to raise the performance level. If neglected once again, the performance will go through another gradual decline until it again falls below the lower control limit at time t_2. Again, a costly drastic effort will be needed to improve the performance. This cycle of *degradation-innovation* may be repeated several times before time T is reached. At time T, a final

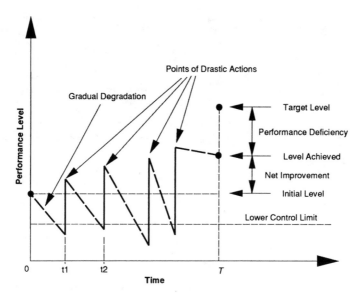

FIGURE 6-1.   Conventional Fluctuating Approach to Improvement.

attempt will be needed to raise suddenly the performance to the target level. But unfortunately, it may be too late to achieve the target performance.

There are many disadvantages of the conventional fluctuating approach to improvement. They are:

1. High cost of implementation.
2. Need for drastic control actions.
3. Potential loss of project support.
4. Adverse effect on personnel morale.
5. Frequent disruption of the project.
6. Too much focus on short-term benefits.
7. Need for frequent and strict monitoring.
8. Opportunity cost during the degradation phase.

Figure 6-2 represents the approach of continuous improvement. In the figure, the process starts with the same initial quality level and it is continuously improved in a gradual pursuit of the targeted performance level. As soon as they occur, opportunities to improve are implemented. The rate of improvement is not necessarily constant over the planning horizon. Hence, the path of improvement is shown as a curve rather than a straight line. The important aspect of CPI is that each subsequent performance level is at least as good as the one preceding it.

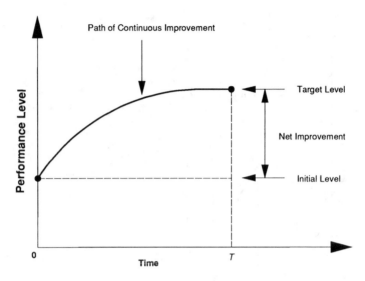

FIGURE 6-2.   Continuous Process Improvement Approach.

The major advantages of CPI include:

1. Better client satisfaction.
2. Clear expression of project expectations.
3. Consistent pace with available technology.
4. Lower cost of achieving project objectives.
5. Conducive environment for personnel involvement.
6. Dedication to higher quality products and services.

A concept similar to that of CPI is the continuous measurable improvement (CMI), a process through which employees are given the authority to determine how best their jobs can be performed and measured. Because employees are continually in contact with the job, they have the best view of the performance of the process. The employees can identify the most reliable criteria for measuring the improvements achieved in the project. Under CMI, employees are directly involved in designing the job functions. For example, instead of just bringing in external experts to design a new production line, CMI requires that management get the people (employees) who are going to be using the line involved in the design process. This provides valuable employee insights into the design mechanism and paves the way for the success of the design.

6.7 COST CONTROL

Several aspects of a project can contribute to the overall cost of the project. These must be carefully tracked to determine when control actions may be needed. Some of the important cost aspects of a project are below:

- Cost-estimation approach.
- Cost-accounting practices.
- Project cash-flow management.
- Company cash-flow status.
- Direct labor costs.
- Overhead rate costs.
- Incentives, penalties, and bonuses.
- Overtime payments.

The process of controlling project cost covers several key issues that management must address. These include:

1. Proper planning of the project to justify the basis for cost elements.
2. Reliable estimation of time, resources, and cost.
3. Clear communication of project requirements, constraints, and available resources.
4. Sustained cooperation of project personnel.
5. Good coordination of project functions.
6. Consistent policy for project expenditures.
7. Timely tracking and reporting of time, materials, and labor transactions.
8. Periodic review of project progress.
9. Revision of project schedule to adapt to prevailing project scenarios.
10. Evaluation of budget depletion versus project progress.

These items must be evaluated as an integrated control effort rather than as individual functions. The interactions between the various actions needed may be so unpredictable that the success achieved on one side may be masked by failure on another side. Such uncoordinated analysis makes cost control very difficult. Project managers must be alert and persistent in the cost-monitoring function.

Some government agencies have developed cost-control techniques aimed at managing large projects that are typical of government contracts. The cost and schedule control system (C/SCS) is based on WBS (work-breakdown structure), and it can quantitatively measure project performance at a particular point in a project. Another useful cost-control technique is the accomplishment cost procedure (ACP). This is a simple approach for relating resources allocated to actual work accomplished. It presents costs based on scheduled accomplishments rather than as a function of time. In order to determine the progress of an individual effort with respect to cost, the cost/progress relationship in the project plan is compared to the cost/progress relationship actually achieved. The major aspect of the ACP technique is that it is not biased against high costs. It gives proper credit to high costs as long as comparable project progress is maintained. The next chapter of this book presents more details on the cost aspects of a project.

6.8 INFORMATION FOR PROJECT CONTROL

As the complexity of systems increases, the information requirements increase. Project management has become very essential in many organizations because it offers a systematic approach to information exchange and use. Industrial development projects, in particular, require a well-coordinated communication system that can quickly reveal the status of each activity. Reports on individual project elements must be tied together in a logical manner to facilitate managerial control. The project manager must have prompt access to individual activity status as well as the status of the overall project. A critical aspect of this function is the prevailing level of communication, cooperation, and coordination in the project. The project-management information system (PMIS) has evolved as the solution to the problem of monitoring, organizing, storing, and disseminating project information. Many commercial computer programs have been developed for the implementation of PMIS. The basic reporting elements in a PMIS may include the following:

- Financial reports.
- Project deliverables.
- Current project plan.
- Project progress reports.
- Performance-requirements evaluation plots.
- Material-supply schedule.
- Subcontract work and schedule.

- Project conference schedule and records.

- Graphical project schedule (Gantt chart).

- Client delivery schedule.

- Time-performance plots (plan versus actual).

- Cost-performance plots (plan versus actual).

Many standard forms have been developed to facilitate the reporting process. With the availability of computerized systems, manual project-information systems are no longer used much in practice.

6.9 LEARNING CURVES AND PROJECT CONTROL

Learning and forgetting are natural phenomena that directly affect productivity and performance in a project. Industrial projects are particularly subject to the effects of learning and forgetting. Learning curve, also known as experience curve, represents the improved performance achieved through repeated performance of a specific function. Performance improvement due to the effect of learning has been extensively discussed in several publications in the past several decades.

Learning, in the context of project management, refers to the improved efficiency obtained from repetition of a task. Workers learn and improve by repeating operations. Learning is time dependent and externally controllable. Reductions in task times achieved through learning-curve effects can directly translate to schedule compression, project cost savings, and improved morale for the project team. Learning curves are essential for setting project goals, establishing schedules, and monitoring progress. The effect of learning is important for project planning and control.

Learning curves present the relationship between cost (or time) and level of activity. For example, an 80 percent learning effect indicates that a given operation is subject to a 20-percent productivity improvement each time the activity level or production volume doubles. A learning curve can serve as a predictive tool for obtaining time estimates for tasks that are repeated within a project life cycle. In practice, we can realize larger reductions in the early stages of learning than in the later stages when learning levels off.

A new learning curve does not necessarily commence each time a new operation is started because workers can sometimes transfer previous skills to new operations. The point at which the learning curve begins to flatten depends on the degree of similarity between the new operation and the previously performed operations. Typical learning rates that have been encountered in practice range from 70 percent to 95 percent. Learning curves are applicable to all aspects of project planning and control. Several terms have been used to describe the learning phenomenon over the years. Some of the terms synonymous with learning curve are progress function, cost-quantity relationship, cost curve, product-acceleration curve, improvement curve, performance curve, experience curve, and efficiency curve.

6.9.1 The Log-Linear Learning Curve

The log-linear model is often referred to as the conventional learning-curve model. This model states that the improvement in productivity is constant (constant slope) as output increases. There are two basic forms of the log-linear model: the average-cost function, and the unit-cost function.

6.9.2 Average-Cost Model

The average-cost model is more popular than the unit-cost model. It specifies the relationship between the cumulative average cost per unit and cumulative production. The relationship indicates that cumulative cost per unit will decrease by a constant percentage as the cumulative production volume doubles. The model is expressed as:

$$C_x = C_1 X^b$$

$$\log C_x = \log C_1 + b \log x,$$

Where
C_x = cumulative average cost of producing x units
C_1 = cost of the first unit
x = cumulative production count
b = the learning-curve exponent.

The relationship between the learning-curve exponent, b, and the learning-rate percentage, p, is given by:

$$b = \frac{\log p}{\log 2}$$

or

$$p = 2^b.$$

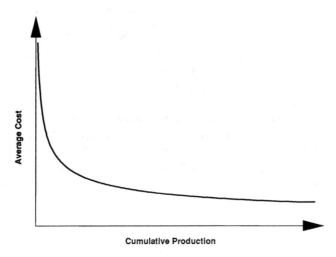

FIGURE 6-3.   Learning Curve for Performance Measurement.

Figure 6-3 shows the basic form of the log-linear learning curve. It is called a log-linear curve because it appears as a straight line when plotted on a log-log paper.

To illustrate learning-curve calculations, let us assume that 50 units of a product are produced at a cumulative average cost of $20 per unit. We want to compute the learning percentage when 100 units are produced at a cumulative average cost of $15 per unit. That is,

At first production level: units = 50; cost = $20.
At second production level: units = 100; cost = $15.

Using the log relationship, we obtain the following simultaneous equations:

$$\log 20 = \log C_1 + b \log 50$$

$$\log 15 = \log C_1 + b \log 100.$$

Subtracting the second equation from the first yields

$$\log 20 - \log 15 = b \log 50 - b \log 100.$$

That is,

$$b = \frac{\log 20 - \log 15}{\log 50 - \log 100}$$
$$= \frac{\log(20/15)}{\log(50/100)}$$
$$= -0.415.$$

Therefore,

$$p = 2^{-0.415}$$
$$= 0.75$$
$$= 75\% \text{ learning rate.}$$

Thus, this process is subject to a 75-percent learning effect. Let us consider another scenario. In a production run of a certain product, it was observed that the cumulative hours required to produce 100 units is 100,000 hours with a learning curve effect of 85 percent. For project-planning purposes, a project analyst needs to calculate the number of hours spent in producing the fiftieth unit.

Solution: Following the notation we used before, we have the following information:

p = 0.85
X = 100 units
C_x = 100,000 hours/100 units = 1,000 hours/unit.

Now,

$$0.85 = 2^b.$$

Therefore, $b = -0.2345$.
Also,

$$1,000 = C_1(100)^b.$$

Therefore, $C_1 = 2,944.42$ hours.
Thus,

$$C_{50} = C_1(50)^b$$
$$= 1,176.50 \text{ hours.}$$

That is, the cumulative average number of hours for 50 units is 1,176.50 hours. Therefore, cumulative total hours for 50 units = 58,824.91 hours.
Similarly,

$$C_{49} = C_1(49)^b$$
$$= 1,182.09 \text{ hours.}$$

That is, the cumulative average number of hours for 49 units is 1,182.09

hours. Therefore, cumulative total hours for 49 units = 57,922.17 hours. Consequently, the number of hours for the fiftieth unit is given by:

$$C_{50} - C_{49} = 58,824.91 \text{ hours} - 57,922.17 \text{ hours} = 902.74 \text{ hours}.$$

6.9.3 Unit-Cost Model

The unit-cost model is expressed in terms of the specific cost of producing the xth unit. The unit-cost formula specifies that the individual cost per unit will decrease by a constant percentage as cumulative production doubles. The functional form of the unit-cost model is the same as for the average-cost model except that the interpretations of the terms are different. It is expressed as:

$$UC_x = C_1 X^b,$$

Where
UC_x = cost of producing the xth unit
C_1 = cost of the first unit
x = cumulative production count
b = the learning-curve exponent
p = learning-rate percent.

From the unit-cost formula, we can derive expressions for the other cost basis. For the case of discrete product units, the total cost of producing x units is given by:

$$TC_x = \sum_{i=1}^{x} UC_i$$

$$= C_1 \sum_{i=1}^{x} (i)^b.$$

The cumulative average cost per unit is given by:

$$Y_x = \frac{TC_x}{x}$$

$$= \frac{1}{x} \sum_{i=1}^{x} UC_i$$

$$= \frac{C_1}{x} \sum_{i=1}^{x} (i)^b.$$

The marginal cost is found as follows:

$$MC_x = \frac{d[TC_x]}{dx}$$

$$= \frac{d\left[C_1 \sum\limits_{i=1}^{x} (i)^b\right]}{dx}.$$

For project operations, the effect of learning should be considered in developing activity time estimates. The formulas presented above may be evaluated in terms of time (or some other measure of worth) instead of cost. The analyst will simply replace each cost variable with the corresponding time variable.

6.9.4 Project Decisions Based on Learning-Curve Analysis

Results of learning-curve analysis are important for various types of economic analysis in project management. A reliable methodology for cost analysis for specific operations is essential to improving personnel productivity and enhancing product quality. The following sections present some examples of potential applications of learning curves in project planning and control.

Break-Even Analysis
The conventional break-even analysis assumes that variable cost per unit is constant. On the contrary, learning-curve analysis recognizes the potential reduction in variable cost per unit due to the effect of learning. Learning-curve models facilitate a study of the interactions of multiple factors present in large projects. These interactions are essential for break-even analysis and decision making.

Make-or-Buy Decisions
Make-or-buy decisions can be enhanced by considering the effect of learning on internal tasks within the project life cycle. Make-or-buy analysis involves a choice between the cost of producing an item and the cost of purchasing it or a choice between performing a task in-house and subcontracting it. Learning curves can provide the data for determining the accurate cost of performing a task in-house. A make-or-buy analysis can be coupled with break-even analysis to determine at which production level it will become cost-effective to make a product versus buying it.

Manpower Scheduling
A consideration of the effect of learning in the project-management environment can lead to a more accurate analysis of manpower requirements and of the accompanying schedules. In integrated multiple projects, where items move sequentially from one project level to another, the effect of learning curves can become even more applicable. The allocation of resources during project scheduling should be done with proper consideration for the effect of learning.

Production Planning
The overall production-planning process can benefit from learning-curve cost analysis. Preproduction planning analysis of the effect of learning curve can identify areas where better and more detailed planning may be needed. The more preproduction planning that is done, the higher the potential for lowering the production cost of the first unit, which has a significant effect on learning-curve analysis.

Labor Estimating
Learning curves have been used for years to estimate labor hour requirements. For manufacturing activities involving operations in different stations, several factors interact to determine the learning rate of workers. Multivariate curves can be of use in developing accurate labor standards in such cases. Learning-curve analysis can complement conventional work-measurement studies.

Budgeting and Resource Allocation
Budgeting or capital rationing is a significant effort in any operation. Learning-curve analysis can provide a management guide for allocating resources to operation components on a more equitable basis. The effects of learning can be particularly useful in "zero-base" budgeting policies. Other areas in which learning-curve analysis could be used for project control include product development, productivity analysis, goal setting, life-cycle costing, planning, resource-allocation decisions, operations planning, and lot sizing.

6.10 WORK RATE AND PROJECT CONTROL

Work rate and work time are essential components of estimating the cost of specific tasks in project management. Given a certain amount of work that must be done at a given work rate, the required time can be computed. Once the required time is known, the cost of the task can be computed on the basis of a specified cost per unit time. Work-rate analysis is important for resource-substitution decisions. The analysis can help identify where and when the same amount of work can be done with the same level of quality and within a reasonable time span by a less expensive resource. The results of learning-curve analysis can yield valuable information about expected work rate. The general relationship between work, work rate, and time is given by:

$$\text{Work Done} = (\text{Work Rate}) \times (\text{Time}).$$

This is expressed mathematically as:

$$w = rt,$$

Where

$w =$ amount of actual work done expressed in appropriate units. Example of work units are miles of road completed, lines of computer code typed, gallons of oil spill cleaned, units of widgets produced, and surface area painted.

$r =$ rate at which the work is accomplished

$t =$ total time required to perform the work excluding any embedded idle times.

It should be noted that work is defined as a physical measure of accomplishment with uniform density. That means, for example, that one line of computer code is as complex and desirable as any other line of computer code. Similarly, cleaning one gallon of oil spill is as good as cleaning any other gallon of oil spill within the same work environment. The production of one unit of a product is identical to the production of any other unit of the product. If uniform work density cannot be assumed for the particular work being analyzed, then the relationship presented above may lead to erroneous conclusions. Uniformity can be enhanced if the scope of the analysis is limited to a manageable size. The larger the scope of the analysis, the more the variability from one work unit to another, and the less uniform the overall work measurement will be. For example, in a project involving the construction of 50 miles of surface road, the work analysis may be done in increments of 10 miles rather than the total 50 miles at a time.

If the total amount of work to be analyzed is defined as one whole unit, then the relationship below can be developed for the case of a single resource performing the work:

Resource	Work Rate	Time	Work Done
Machine A	$\dfrac{1}{x}$	t	1.0

where $1/x$ is the amount of work accomplished per unit time. For a single resource to perform the whole unit of work, we must have the following:

$$\left(\frac{1}{x}\right)t = 1.0.$$

That means the magnitude of x must equal the magnitude of t. For example, if Machine A is to complete one work unit in thirty minutes, it must work at the rate of $1/30$ of work per unit time. If the absolute value of x is greater than the absolute value of t, then only a fraction of the required work will be performed. The information about the proportion of work completed may be useful for productivity-measurement purposes.

In the case of multiple resources performing the work simultaneously, the work relationship:

Resource, i	Work Rate, r_i	Time, t_i	Work Done, w
Machine A	r_1	t_1	$(r_1)(t_1)$
Machine B	r_2	t_2	$(r_2)(t_2)$
...	...	...	...
Machine n	r_n	t_n	$(r_n)(t_n)$
		Total	1.0

The relationship indicates that even though the multiple resources may work at different rates, the sum of the work they all performed must equal the required whole unit. In general, for multiple resources, we have the following relationship:

$$\sum_{i=1}^{n} r_i t_i = 1.0,$$

Where
n = number of different resource types
r_i = work rate of resource type i
t_i = work time of resource type i.

For partial completion of work, the relationship is:

$$\sum_{i=1}^{n} r_i t_i = p,$$

where p is the proportion of the required work actually completed.

Example. Machine A, working alone, can complete a given job in 50 minutes. After Machine A has been working on the job for 10 minutes, Machine B was brought in to work with Machine A in completing the job. Both machines working together finished the remaining work in 15 minutes. What is the work rate for Machine B?

Solution. The amount of work to be done is 1.0 whole unit.

The work rate of Machine A is 1/50.

The amount of work completed by Machine A in the 10 minutes it worked alone is $(1/50)(10) = 1/5$ of the required total work.

Therefore, the remaining amount of work to be done is 4/5 of the required total work. The two machines working together for 15 minutes yield the following results:

Resource, i	Work Rate, r_i	Time, t_i	Work Done, w
Machine A	1/50	15	15/50
Machine B	r_2	15	$15(r_2)$
		Total	4/5

$$\frac{15}{50} + 15(r_2) = \frac{4}{5},$$

which yields $r_2 = 1/30$. Thus, the work rate for Machine B is 1/30. That means Machine B, working alone, could perform the same job in 30 minutes. In this example, it is assumed that both machines produce identical quality of work. If quality levels are not identical, then the project analyst must figure in the potentials for quality/time trade-offs in performing the required work.

The relative costs of the different resource types needed to perform the required work may be incorporated into the analysis:

Resource, i	Work Rate, r_i	Time, t_i	Work Done, w	Pay rate, p_i	Pay, P_i
Machine A	r_1	t_1	$(r_1)(t_1)$	p_1	P_1
Machine B	r_2	t_2	$(r_2)(t_2)$	p_2	P_2
...	...	...	...	...	...
Machine n	r_n	t_n	$(r_n)(t_n)$	p_n	P_n
		Total	1.0		Budget

Using the above relationship for work rate and cost, the work crew can be analyzed to determine the best strategy for accomplishing the required work, within the required time, and within a specified budget. The results of the analysis can then help determine what control actions may be needed.

6.11 TERMINATING A PROJECT

Project termination is an important aspect of project control. Termination should be viewed as a control function since some projects can drag on unnecessarily if control is not instituted. There are several reasons for terminating projects. Some projects are terminated under cordial, arranged, and expected circumstances, whereas others are terminated under unpleasant circumstances that call for managerial control. If necessary, a project audit should be conducted to ascertain the need to terminate a project. Some of the common reasons include the following:

Reasons for Project Termination

- Cost overruns.
- New Technology.
- Missed deadline.
- Product obsolescence.
- Environmental concern.
- Government requirement.
- Excessive delay penalties.
- Technically impossible goals.
- Lack of project justification.
- Poor performance that is beyond remedy.
- Alternate objective to the initial plan.
- Project objective has been accomplished.
- Poor project plan that cannot be achieved.
- Lack of required manpower or other resources.

Even after the reasons for terminating the project have been identified, actual termination may not be easy to implement, especially for long-range and large projects that have spread their tentacles throughout an organization. Problems of morale may develop. Some workers may have grown accustomed to the extra attention, recognition, or advancement opportunities associated with the project. They may not see the wisdom of terminating it. The Triple C approach should be used in setting the stage for the termination of a project at the appropriate time. The termination process should cover the following items:

- Communicating with the personnel on the need for termination.
- Retraining workers for new functions.
- Reassignment of workers to other functions.
- Returning workers to their previous functions.
- Assuring the cooperation of those involved.
- Coordinating the required actions for termination.
- Withdrawing funding from the project (pulling the plug).

If the termination is handled properly, workers will be less agonized by the "loss," and there will be a smooth transition to other projects. Control charts may be used to track project performance before deciding what control actions are needed. Control limits are incorporated into the charts to indicate when control actions should be taken. Multiple control limits may be used to determine various levels of control points. Control charts may be developed for various aspects such as cost, schedule, resource utilization, performance, and other criteria for project evaluation.

Figure 6-4 represents a case of periodic monitoring of project progress. Cost is monitored and recorded on a monthly basis. If the cost is monitored on a more frequent basis (e.g., days), then we may be able to have a more rigid control structure. Of course, one will need to decide whether the

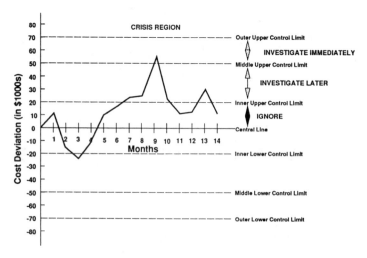

FIGURE 6-4.   Control Chart for Project Monitoring.

additional time needed for frequent monitoring is justified by the extra level of control provided. The control limits may be calculated with the same procedures used for average and range control charts in quality control, or they may be based on custom project requirements. In addition to drawing control charts for cost, we can also draw control charts for other measures of performance, such as task duration, quality, or resource utilization.

Figure 6-5 shows a control chart for cumulative cost. The control limits on the chart are indexed to the project percent complete. At each percent complete point, there is a control limit that the cumulative project cost is not expected to exceed. A review of the control chart shows that the cumulative cost is out of control at the 10-percent, 30-percent, 40-percent, 50-percent, 60-percent, and 80-percent completion points. Thus, the indication is that control actions should be instituted right from the 10-percent completion point. If no control action is taken, the cumulative cost may continue to be out of control and eventually exceed the budget limit by the time the project is finished.

The information obtained from the project-monitoring capabilities of project-management software can be transformed into meaningful charts that can quickly identify when control actions are needed. A control chart can provide information about resource overallocation as well as about unusually slow progress of work.

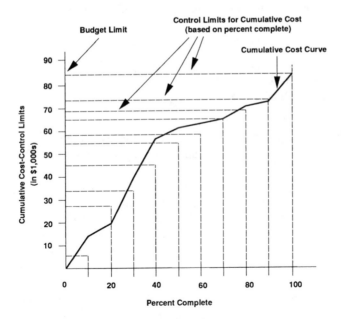

FIGURE 6-5.   Control Chart for Cumulative Cost.

7

Project Economic Analysis

Cut your project to fit your budget.

This chapter presents the basic techniques for performing economic analysis for project-management purposes. Large-scale projects must be evaluated on the basis of both technical and economic feasibility. A project must be gauged in terms of its capability to meet scheduled delivery of products, to achieve resource-utilization requests, and to meet performance requirements. In the assessment process, both quantitative and qualitative factors come into play. Some of the qualitative considerations were discussed in the preceding chapters. Economic feasibility is just one aspect of estimating the potential a project has to satisfy the required goals.

7.1 COST CONCEPTS FOR PROJECT MANAGEMENT

There are several cost concepts that influence the economic aspects of managing projects. Within a given scope of analysis, there may be a combination of different types of cost aspects to consider, such as:

Life-Cycle Cost. This is the sum of all costs, recurring and nonrecurring, associated with a project during its entire life cycle.

First Cost. This is the total initial investment required to initiate a project or the total initial cost of the equipment needed to start the project.

Operating Cost. This is a recurring cost needed to keep a project in operation during its life cycle. Operating costs may consist of such items as labor cost, material cost, and energy cost.

Maintenance Cost. This is a cost that occurs intermittently or periodically for the purpose of keeping project equipment in good operating condition.

196

Overhead Cost. This a cost incurred for activities performed in the operations of a project. The activities that generate over. support the project efforts rather than contributing directly to tl   ￼ject goal. The handling of overhead costs vary widely from company to company. Typical overhead items are electric power cost, insurance premiums, cost of security, and inventory-carrying cost.

Sunk Cost. This is a cost that occurred in the past and cannot be recovered under the present analysis. Sunk costs should have no bearing on the prevailing economic analysis and project decisions. Ignoring sunk costs is always a difficult task for analysts. For example, if $950,000 were spent four years ago to buy a piece of equipment for a technology-based project, a decision on whether or not to replace the equipment now should not consider that initial cost. But uncompromising analysts might find it difficult to ignore that much money. Similarly, an individual making a decision on selling a personal automobile would typically try to relate the asking price to what was paid for the automobile when it was acquired. This is wrong under the strict concept of sunk costs.

Opportunity Cost. This is the cost of forgoing the opportunity to invest in a venture that would have produced an economic advantage. Opportunity costs are usually incurred because of limited resources that make it impossible to take advantage of all investment opportunities. It is often defined as the cost of the best rejected opportunity. Opportunity costs can also be incurred because of a missed opportunity rather than an intentional rejection. In many cases, opportunity costs are hidden or implied because they typically relate to future events that cannot be accurately predicted.

Direct Cost. This is a cost directly associated with actual operations of a project. Typical sources of direct costs are direct material costs and direct labor costs. Direct costs are those that can be reasonably measured and allocated to a specific component of a project.

Indirect Cost. This is a cost that is indirectly associated with project operations. Indirect costs are those that are difficult to assign to specific components of a project. An example of an indirect cost is the cost of computer hardware and software needed to manage project operations. Indirect costs are usually calculated as a percentage of a component of direct costs. For example, the direct costs in an organization may be computed as 10 percent of direct labor costs.

Standard Cost. This is a cost that represents the normal or expected cost of a unit of the output of an operation. Standard costs are established in advance. They are developed as a composite of several component costs such as direct labor cost per unit, material cost per unit, and allowable overhead charge per unit.

Fixed Cost. This is a cost incurred irrespective of the level of operation of a project. Fixed costs do not vary in proportion to the quantity of output. Example of costs that make up the fixed cost of a project are administrative expenses, certain types of taxes, insurance cost, depreciation cost, and debt-servicing cost. These costs usually do not vary in proportion to quantity of output.

Variable Cost. This is a cost that varies in direct proportion to the level of operation or quantity of output. For example, the costs of material and labor required to make an item will be classified as variable costs since they vary with changes in level of output.

Total Cost. This is the sum of all the variable and fixed costs associated with a project.

Incremental Cost. This refers to the additional cost of changing the production output from one level to another. Incremental costs are normally variable costs.

Marginal Cost. This is the additional cost of increasing production output by one additional unit. The marginal cost is equal to the slope of the total cost curve or line at the current operating level.

Economies of Scale. This refers to a reduction of the relative weight of the fixed cost in total cost by increasing output quantity. This helps to reduce the final unit cost of a product. Economies of scale is often simply referred to as the savings due to *mass production.*

In a typical project, several cost elements intermingle. A project analyst must be careful to analyze all the relevant cost elements and include them as appropriate in the decision-making process.

7.2 BASIC CASH-FLOW ANALYSIS

Funds flow in and out throughout the life cycle of a project. It is important to evaluate the implications of cash flows and capital investments for project-management purposes. This section presents the basic techniques for analyzing cash-flow amounts located at discrete points in time. Subsequent sections explore specific scenarios for performing economic analysis in project management.

The time value of money is a crucial factor in the economic analysis of projects. This is particularly important for long-term projects that may be subject to changes in such things as interest rates, funds available, investment opportunities, and inflation. Students of engineering economic analysis are often taught that "a dollar today is worth more than a dollar tomorrow." How can this concept be implemented for project-management purposes?

The concept can be applied by looking at the equivalence of funds located at different points in time. The basic reason for performing economic analysis is to make a choice between mutually exclusive projects or alternatives that are competing for limited resources. The timing and amounts of expenditures and revenues will normally be different for each alternative. The techniques of computing cash-flow equivalence permits us to bring the competing cash flows to a common basis so that an informed choice can be made. The common basis often depends on the prevailing interest rate. Equivalence is dependent on interest rate. Two cash flows that are equivalent at a given interest rate will not be equivalent at a different interest rate.

7.2.1 Cash-Flow Conversion Factors

Cash-flow conversion involves the transfer of funds from one point in time to another. The following notations are used for the variables involved in the conversion process:

i = interest rate per period
n = number of interest periods
P = a present sum of money
F = a future sum of money
A = a uniform end-of-period cash receipt or disbursement
G = a uniform arithmetic gradient increase in period-by-period payments or disbursements.

In many cases, the interest rate used in performing economic analysis is set equal to the minimum attractive rate of return (MARR) of the decision maker. The MARR is also sometimes referred to as hurdle rate, required internal rate of return (IRR), return on investment (ROI), or discount rate. The value of the MARR should be chosen with the objective of maximizing the economic well-being of the organization. Setting this value is normally a policy issue that is affected by several factors within an organization.

Compound Amount Factor
The procedure for the single-payment compound-amount factor finds a future sum of money, F, that is equivalent to a present sum of money, P, at a specified interest rate, i, after n periods. This is calculated as:

$$F = P(1 + i)^n.$$

A graphic representation of the relationship between P and F follows:

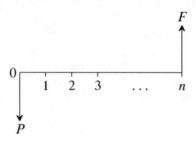

For example, a sum of $5,000 is deposited into a project account and left there to earn interest for fifteen years. If the interest rate per year is 12 percent, the compound amount after 15 years can be calculated as shown below:

$$F = \$5000(1 + 0.12)^{15}$$
$$= \$24,367.85.$$

Present-Worth Factor

The present-worth factor enables us to find P when F is given. The present-worth factor is obtained by solving for P in the equation for the compound-amount factor. That is,

$$P = F(1 + i)^{-n}.$$

Suppose it is estimated that $15,000 would be needed to complete the implementation of a project five years from now, how much should be deposited into a special project fund now so that the fund would accrue to the required $15,000 exactly five years from now? If the special project fund pays an interest of 9.2 percent per year, the required deposit would be:

$$P = \$15,000(1 + 0.092)^{-5}$$
$$= \$9,660.03.$$

Capital-Recovery Factor

The capital-recovery formula is used to calculate the uniform series of equal end-of-period payments, A, that are equivalent to a given present amount, P, as shown in the diagram:

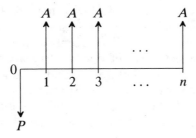

The capital-recovery amount is calculated as:

$$A = P\left[\frac{i(1 + i)^n}{(1 + i)^n - 1}\right].$$

Example: Suppose a piece of equipment needed to start a project must be bought. The first cost of the equipment is $50,000. The entire cost will have to be financed at 13.5 percent per year and repaid on a monthly installment schedule over four years. It is desired to calculate what the monthly loan payments will be. It is assumed that the first loan payment will be made exactly one month after the equipment is financed.

Solution: If the interest rate of 13.5 percent per year is compounded monthly, then the interest rate per month will be 13.5%/12 = 1.125 percent per month. The number of interest periods over which the loan will be repaid is 4(12) = 48 months. Consequently, the monthly loan payments are calculated to be:

$$A = \$50,000\left[\frac{0.01125(1 + 0.01125)^{48}}{(1 + 0.01125)^{48} - 1}\right]$$
$$= \$1,353.82.$$

Uniform Series Present-Worth Factor

The series present-worth factor is used to calculate the present worth equivalent, P, of a series of equal, end-of-period amounts, A. This is the converse of the capital-recovery factor. The equation for the series present worth factor is obtained by solving for P from the capital-recovery factor:

$$P = A\left[\frac{(1 = i)^n - 1}{i(1 + i)^n}\right].$$

As an example, suppose the sum of $12,000 must be withdrawn from an account to meet the annual operating expenses of a multiyear project. The project account pays an interest of 7.5 percent per year compounded on an annual basis. If the project is expected to last 10 years, how much must be deposited into the project account now so that the operating expenses of $12,000 can be withdrawn at the end of every year for ten years? The project fund is expected to be depleted to zero by the end of the last year of the project. The first withdrawal will be made one year after the project account is opened and no additional deposits will be made into the account during the project life cycle. The required deposit is calculated to be:

$$P = \$12,000 \left[\frac{(1 + 0.0725)^{10} - 1}{0.075(1 + 0.075)^{10}} \right]$$
$$= \$82,368.92.$$

Uniform Series Sinking-Fund Factor

The sinking-fund factor is used to calculate the uniform series of equal end-of-period amounts, A, that are equivalent to a single future amount, F. The graphic representation of the relationship between A and F is:

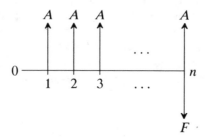

It should be noted that the future amount occurs at the same point in time as the last amount in the uniform series of payments. The equation relating A to F is:

$$A = F \left[\frac{I}{(1 + i)^n - 1} \right].$$

Example. How much end-of-year equal amounts must be deposited into a project account so that a balance of $75,000 will be available for withdrawal immediately after the twelfth annual deposit is made? The initial balance in the account is zero at the beginning of the first year. The account pays an interest of 10 percent per year.

Solution. Using the formula for the sinking-fund factor, the required annual deposits are:

$$A = \$75,000 \left[\frac{0.10}{(1 + 0.10)^{12} - 1} \right]$$
$$= \$3,507.25.$$

Uniform Series Compound-Amount Factor

The series compound amount factor is the converse of the series sinking-fund factor. The factor is used to calculate a single future amount that is equivalent to a uniform series of equal end-of-period payments. The factor is written as:

$$F = A \left[\frac{(1 + i)^n - 1}{i} \right].$$

For example, if equal end-of-year deposits of \$5,000 are made into a project fund paying 8 percent per year for ten years. How much can be expected to be available for withdrawal from the account for capital expenditure immediately after the last deposit is made?

$$F = \$5,000 \left[\frac{(1 + 0.08)^{10} - 1}{0.08} \right]$$
$$= \$72,432.50.$$

Capitalized Cost of a Project

Capitalized cost refers to the present value of a single amount that is equivalent to a perpetual series of equal end-of-period payments. This is an extension of the series present-worth factor with an infinitely large number of periods. This is shown graphically as:

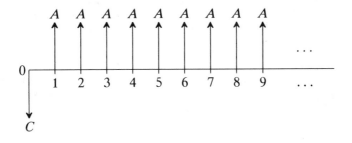

The capitalized-cost calculation is particularly useful for long-term public projects. The formula for calculating capitalized cost of a project is:

$$P = \frac{A}{i}.$$

Example. How much should be deposited into a general fund to provide a perpetual annual expense account of $6,000,000 for an industrial development project? Assume that the interest rate will remain constant at 8.5 percent per year.

Solution. Using the capitalized-cost formula, the required one-time deposit into the general fund is:

$$P = \frac{\$6,000,000}{0.085}$$
$$= \$70,588,235.29.$$

The formulas presented above represent the basic cash-flow conversion factors. The factors are widely tabulated, for convenience, in engineering economy books. Several variations and extensions of the factors are available. Such extensions include the arithmetic gradient series factor and the geometric series factor. Variations in the cash-flow profiles include situations in which payments are made at the beginning of each period rather than at the end and situations in which a series of payments contains unequal amounts. Conversion formulas can be derived mathematically for those special cases by using the basic factors presented.

7.2.2 Rule of 72

The "Rule of 72" is a simple rule used to estimate the length of time it will take a given amount of money to double at a given interest rate per period. The Rule of 72 gives the following formula for estimating the number of periods required for an investment to double:

$$n = \frac{72}{i},$$

where i is the interest rate expressed in percentage.

Referring to the single-payment compound-amount factor, we can set the future amount equal to twice the present amount and then solve for n, the number of periods. That is, $F = 2P$. Thus,

$$2P = P(1 - i)^n.$$

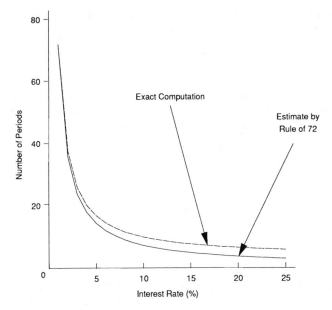

FIGURE 7-1.   Analysis of Rule of 72.

Solving for *n* in the equation yields an expression for calculating the exact number of periods required to double *P*:

$$n = \frac{ln(2)}{ln(1 + i)},$$

where *i* is the interest rate expressed in decimals. For example, at an interest rate of 5 percent per year, it will take any given amount 14.21 years to double in value. This, of course, assumes that the interest rate will remain constant throughout the planning horizon. A comparison of the Rule of 72 and of the exact formula indicates that both approaches yield very close results. Figure 7-1 shows a comparison of the approaches.

7.3 BREAK-EVEN AND MINIMUM-COST ANALYSIS

Once all the cost aspects are documented and properly organized, several types of economic analysis can be performed. Examples of the basic break-even analysis are presented in this section. The total cost of an operation may be expressed as the sum of the fixed and variable costs with respect to output quantity. That is,

$$TC(x) = FC + VC(x),$$

where x is the number of units produced, $TC(x)$ is the total cost of producing x units, FC is the total fixed cost, and $VC(x)$ is the total variable costs associated with producing x units. The total revenue resulting from the sale of x units is defined as:

$$TR(x) = px,$$

where p is the price per unit. The profit due to the production and sale of x units of the product is calculated as:

$$P(x) = TR(x) - TC(x).$$

The break-even point of an operation is defined as the value of a given parameter that will result in neither a profit nor a loss. The parameter of interest may be the number of units produced, the number of hours of operation, the number of units of a resource type allocated, or any other measure of interest. At the break-even point, we have the following relationship:

$$TR(x) = TC(x)$$

or

$$P(x) = 0.$$

In some cases, the relationship between cost and a parameter of interest can be expressed in a mathematical formula. For example, there may be a linear cost relationship between the total cost of a production project and the number of units produced. The cost expressions facilitate nice and simple analysis for project decision-making purposes. Figure 7-2 shows an example of a break-even point for a single project. Figure 7-3 shows examples of multiple break-even points that exist when multiple projects are compared.

When two project alternatives are compared, the break-even point refers to the point of indifference between the two alternatives. In Figure 7-3, $x1$ represents the point at which both Projects A and B are equally desirable, $x2$ that at which A and C are equally desirable, and $x3$ that at which B and C are equally desirable. The figure shows that if we are operating below a production level of $x2$ units, then Project C is the preferred project out of the three. If we are operating at a level more than $x2$ units, then project A is the best choice.

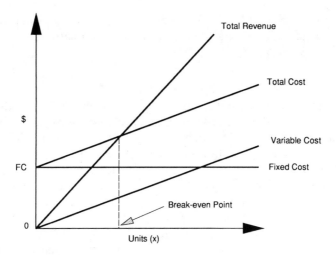

FIGURE 7-2.   Break-Even Point for Single Project.

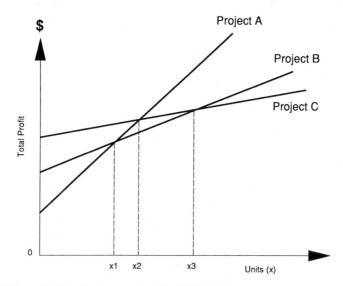

FIGURE 7-3.   Multiple Break-Even Points for Multiple Projects.

Example. Three project alternatives are being considered for producing a new product. The required analysis involves determining which alternative should be selected based on how many units of the product are produced per year. Based on past records, there is a known relationship between the number of units produced per year, x, and the net annual profit, $P(x)$, from each alternative. The level of production is expected to be between zero and 250 units per year. The net annual profits (in thousands of dollars) are given below for each alternative:

Project A: $P(x) = 3x - 200$
Project B: $P(x) = x$
Project C: $P(x) = (1/50)x^2 - 300$.

Solution. This problem can be solved mathematically by finding the intersection points of the profit functions and evaluating the respective profits over the given range of product units. However, it is much easier and visually helpful to solve it by a graphical approach. Figure 7-4 presents the simultaneous plot of the profit functions. Such a plot is called a break-even chart. The plot shows that Project B should be selected if between zero and 100 units are to be produced. Project A should be selected if between 100 and 178.1 units (178 actual units) are to be produced. Project C should be selected if more than 178 units are to be produced. It should be noted that if less than 66.7 units (66 actual units) are produced, Project A would generate net loss rather than net profit. Similarly, Project C would generate losses if less than 122.5 units (122 actual units) are produced.

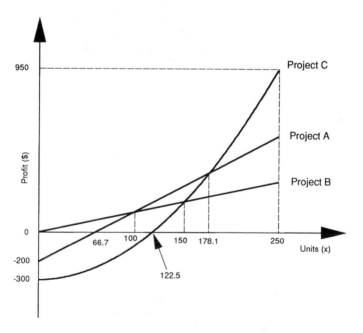

FIGURE 7-4.   Plot of Profit Functions.

7.3.1 Measurement of Profit Ratio

Break-even charts offer opportunities for several different types of analysis. In addition to determining the break-even points, it enables one to derive other measures of worth or criterion measure from the charts. A measure, called *profit ratio*, is introduced here for the purpose of obtaining a further comparative basis for competing projects.

Profit ratio is defined as the ratio of the profit area to the sum of the profit and loss areas in a break-even chart. That is,

$$\text{Profit Ratio} = \frac{\text{Area of Profit Region}}{\text{Area of Profit Region} + \text{Area of Loss Region}}.$$

For example, suppose the expected revenue and the expected total cost associated with a project are given, respectively, by the following expressions:

$$R(x) = 100 + 10x$$

$$TC(x) = 2.5x + 250,$$

where x is the number of units produced and sold from the project. Figure 7-5 shows the break-even chart for the project. The break-even point is shown to be twenty units. Net profits are realized from the project if more than twenty units are produced, whereas net losses are realized if less than twenty units are produced. It should be noted that the revenue function in Figure 7-5 represents an unusual case in which a revenue of $100 is realized when zero units are produced.

Let us calculate the profit ratio for this project if the number of units that can be produced is limited to between zero and 100 units. From Figure 7-5, the surface area of the profit region and the area of the loss region can be calculated by using the standard formula for finding the area of a triangle. That is, Area = (1/2)(Base)(Height). Using this formula, we have the following:

$$\text{Area of Profit Region} = \frac{1}{2}(\text{base})(\text{height})$$

$$= \frac{1}{2}(1,100 - 500)(100 - 20)$$

$$= 24,000 \text{ square units;}$$

$$\text{Area of Loss Region} = \frac{1}{2}(\text{base})(\text{height})$$

$$= \frac{1}{2}(250 - 100)(20)$$

$$= 1,500 \text{ square units.}$$

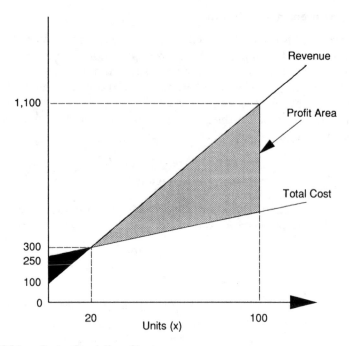

FIGURE 7-5.   Project Break-Even Chart.

Therefore, the profit ratio is computed as:

$$\text{Profit Ratio} = \frac{24,000}{24,000 + 1,500}$$
$$= 0.9411$$
$$= 94.11\%.$$

The profit ratio may be used as a criterion for selecting among project alternatives. If this is planned, the profit ratios for all the alternatives must be calculated over the same values of the independent variable. The project with the highest profit ratio will be selected as the desired project. For example, Figure 7-6 presents the break-even chart for an alternate project, say Project II. It is seen that both the revenue and cost functions for the project are nonlinear. The revenue and cost are defined as follows:

$$R(x) = 160x - x^2$$
$$TC(x) = 500 + x^2.$$

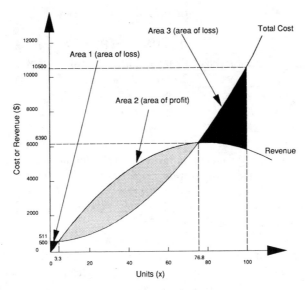

FIGURE 7-6. Break-Even Chart for Alternate Project.

If the cost and/or revenue functions for a project are not linear, the areas bounded by the functions may not be easily determined. For those cases, it may be necessary to use other methods of finding the bounded areas. An example of such a method is the use of definite integrals. Interested readers should consult any calculus book for the procedures for finding definite integrals. Figure 7-6 indicates that the project generates a loss if less than 3.3 units (3 actual units) or more than 76.8 units (76 actual units) are produced. The respective profit and loss areas on the chart are calculated as shown below:

$$\text{Area 1 (loss)} = \int_0^{3.3} [(500 + x^2) - (160x - x^2)]dx$$
$$= 802.8 \text{ unit} - \text{dollars};$$

$$\text{Area 2 (profit)} = \int_{76.8}^{76.8} [(160x - x^2) - (500 - x^2)]dx$$
$$= 132{,}272.08 \text{ unit} - \text{dollars};$$

$$\text{Area 3 (loss)} = \int_{76.8}^{100} [(500 + x^2) - (160x - x^2)]dx$$
$$= 48{,}135.98 \text{ unit} - \text{dollars}.$$

Consequently, the profit ratio for Project II is computed as:

$$
\begin{aligned}
\text{Profit Ratio} &= \frac{\text{Total Area of Profit Region}}{\text{Total Area of Profit Region} + \text{Total Area of Loss Region}} \\
&= \frac{132,272.08}{802.8 + 132,272.08 + 48,135.98} \\
&= 0.7299 \\
&= 72.99\%.
\end{aligned}
$$

The profit-ratio approach evaluates the performance of each alternative over a specified range of operating levels. Most of the existing evaluation methods use single-point analysis with the assumption that the operating condition is fixed at a given production level. The profit-ratio measure allows an analyst to evaluate the net yield of an alternative given that the production level may shift from one level to another. An alternative, for example, may operate at a loss for most of its early life, whereas it may generate large incomes to offset the losses in its later stages. The conventional methods cannot capture this type of transition from one performance level to another.

In addition to being used to compare alternate projects, profit ratio may also be used for evaluating the economic feasibility of a single project. In such a case, a decision rule will need to be developed. An example of a decision rule that may be used for this purpose is:

If profit ratio is greater than 75 percent, accept the project.
If profit ratio is less than or equal to 75 percent, reject the project.

7.4 DEVELOPING PROJECT BUDGET

Cost estimation and budgeting constitute a crucial aspect of project planning, monitoring, and control. Cost estimation and budgeting help establish the scheme for the allocation of the resources required to implement the project plan. Budgeting is often referred to as the process of allocating scarce resources to the various endeavors of an organization. It involves the selection of a preferred subset of a set of acceptable projects due to overall budget constraints. Budget constraints may result from restrictions on capital expenditures, shortage of skilled manpower, or shortage of materials. The budget analysis serves many useful purposes including the following:

- A plan of how resources are expended.
- A project-selection criterion.
- A projection of organizational policy.
- A basis for control by managers.

- A performance measure.
- A standardization of operations within a given time horizon.
- An incentive for improving productivity and efficiency.

The preliminary effort in the preparation of a budget is the collection and proper organization of the relevant cost data. A computer spreadsheet program can play a very important role in this aspect. The preparation of a budget for an industrial development project will be more difficult than the preparation of budgets for other types of projects. Recurring endeavors usually generate historical data that serve as inputs to subsequent estimating functions. Such estimation based on historical data can be performed by a spreadsheet program. Most projects are one-time undertakings without the benefits of prior data. In such cases, techniques such as forecasting and regression may be used in the cost-estimation process.

The input data for the budgeting process typically includes inflationary trends, cost of capital, standard cost guides, past records, and quantitative projections. All (or at least most) of the factors that can influence cost estimates should be considered in the budgeting process. These factors include job-improvement actions, impact of training, productivity enhancements, equipment upgrades, cost of absenteeism, technology changes, variations in resource base, and changes in cost of resources. Three major categories of cost estimation based on level of accuracy are normally used in project cost development. They are *order-of-magnitude estimates, preliminary cost estimates,* and *detailed cost estimates.*

Order-of-magnitude cost estimates are usually gross estimates based on the experience and judgment of the estimator. They are sometimes called "ballpark" figures. These estimates are typically made without a formal evaluation of the details involved in the project. The level of accuracy associated with order-of-magnitude estimates can range from −50 to +50 percent of the actual cost. These estimates provide a quick-and-dirty way of getting information for decision making at the initial stages of a project.

Preliminary cost estimates are also gross estimates with a higher level of accuracy. In developing preliminary cost estimates, more attention is paid to some selected details of the project. An example of preliminary cost estimate is the estimation of the labor cost before the project personnel is actually organized. Preliminary estimates are useful for evaluating project alternatives before final commitments are made. The level of accuracy associated with preliminary estimates can range from −20 to +20 percent of the actual cost.

Detailed cost estimates are developed after careful consideration is given to all the major details of a project. Considerable time is typically needed to obtain detailed cost estimates. Because of the amount of time and effort needed to develop detailed cost estimates, the estimates are usually developed after there is firm commitment that the project will take off. Detailed cost estimates are important for evaluating actual cost performance during the project. The level of accuracy associated with detailed estimates normally range from −5 to +5 percent of the actual cost.

There are two basic approaches to generating cost estimates. The first one is a variant approach, in which case cost estimates are based on variations of previous cost experiences. The other approach is the generative cost estimation, in which case cost estimates are developed from scratch without taking previous experiences into consideration. There are advantages and disadvantages of both approaches. The proper thing to do is to employ a mixture of both approaches depending on the prevailing project scenarios. Once cost estimates are obtained, they are used as inputs into the budgeting process.

7.4.1 Budgeting

Top-Down Budgeting
Top-down budgeting involves collecting data from upper-level sources such as top and middle managers. The figures supplied by the managers may come from their personal judgments, past experiences, or past data on similar project activities. The cost estimates are passed to lower-level managers, who then break the estimates down into specific work components within the project. These estimates may, in turn, be given to line managers, supervisors, and lead workers to continue the process until individual activity costs are obtained. Top management provides the global budget, and the functional-level employee provides specific budget requirements for project items.

Bottom-Up Budgeting
This approach is the reverse of the top-down budgeting. In this method, elemental activities, their schedules, descriptions, and labor skill requirements are used to construct detailed budget requests. Line workers familiar with specific activities are requested to furnish cost estimates. Estimates are made for each activity in terms of labor time, materials, and machine time. The estimates are then converted to appropriate cost basis. The dollar estimates are combined into composite budgets at each successive level up the budgeting hierarchy. If estimate discrepancies develop, they can be resolved through the intervention of senior management, mid-management, functional managers, project manager, accountants, or standard-cost consultants. Figure 7-7 shows the breakup of a project into phases and parts to facilitate bottom-up budgeting and improve both schedule and cost control.

Elemental budgets may be developed based on the timed progress of each part of the project. When all the individual estimates are gathered, we obtain a composite budget estimate. Figure 7-8 shows an example of the various

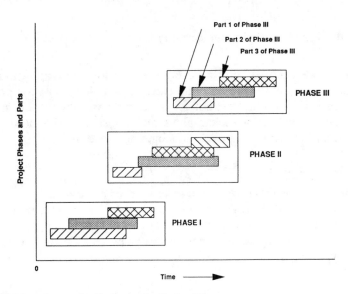

FIGURE 7-7. Bottom-Up Budgeting for Project Phases.

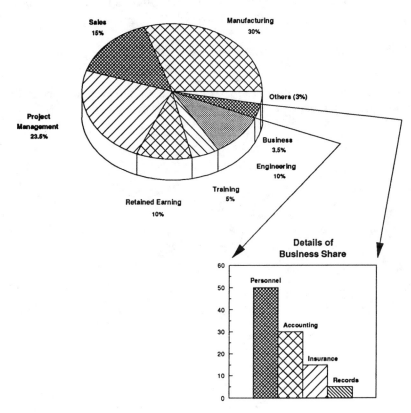

FIGURE 7-8. Components of Project Budget.

215

components that may go into an overall budget for an organization. The blown-up segment of the pie chart indicates the individual cost components making up that particular section of the chart. Analytical tools such as learning-curve analysis, work sampling, and statistical estimation may be employed in the cost-estimation and budgeting processes.

7.4.2 Cost Monitoring

As the project progresses, costs can be monitored and evaluated to identify areas of unacceptable cost performance. Figure 7-9 shows a plot of cost versus time for projected cost and actual cost. The plot permits a quick identification of when cost overruns occur in a project. Figure 7-10 presents another type of cost plot that may be used to evaluate cost performance in a project.

An approach similar to the profit ratio presented earlier may be used together with Figure 7-10 to evaluate the overall cost performance of a project over a specified planning horizon. Presented below is a corresponding formula for *cost performance index* (CPI):

$$CPI = \frac{\text{Area of Cost Benefit}}{\text{Area of Cost Benefit} + \text{Area of Cost Overrun}} .$$

As in the case of the profit ratio, CPI may be used to evaluate the relative performances of several project alternatives or to evaluate the feasibility and acceptability of an individual alternative.

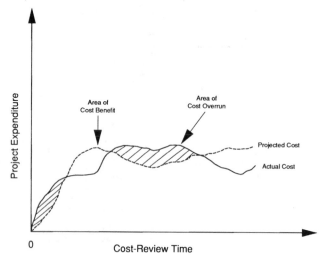

FIGURE 7-9.   Actual versus Planned Cost Monitoring.

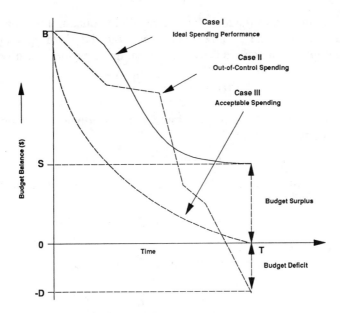

FIGURE 7-10.   Cost-Performance Monitoring.

7.5 PROJECT DEBT ANALYSIS

Industrial development projects may be funded by a combination of financing sources. For projects not funded by equity capital, it may be necessary to borrow funds. Many capital investment projects are financed with external funds. A careful analysis must be conducted to ensure that the repayment schedule and all its ramifications can be handled by the sponsoring organization. It may also be useful to calculate the project's equity break-even point. That point indicates the time when the unpaid balance on a loan is equal to the cumulative equity on the loan. With the approach presented here, the basic cost of servicing a project debt can be evaluated quickly.

7.5.1 Computational Procedure

The computational procedure for analyzing project debt follows the steps below:

1. Given a principal amount, P, a periodic interest rate, i (in decimals), and a discrete time span of n periods, the uniform series of equal end-of-period payments needed to amortize P is computed as:

$$A = \frac{P[i(1 + i)^n]}{(1 + i)^n - 1}.$$

It is assumed that the loan is to be repaid in equal monthly payments. Thus, $A(t) = A$, for each period t throughout the life of the loan.

2. The unpaid balance after making t installment payments is given by:

$$U(t) = \frac{A[1 - (1 + i)^{t - n}]}{i}.$$

3. The amount of equity or principal amount paid with installment payment number t is given by:

$$E(t) = A(1 + i)^{t - n - 1}$$

4. The amount of interest charge contained in installment payment number t is derived to be:

$$I(t) = A[1 - (1 + i)^{t - n - 1}],$$

where $A = E(t) + I(t)$.

5. The cumulative total payment made after t periods is denoted by:

$$C(t) = \sum_{k = 1}^{t} A(k)$$

$$= \sum_{k = 1}^{t} A$$

$$= A * t.$$

6. The cumulative interest payment after t periods is given by:

$$Q(t) = \sum_{x = 1}^{t} I(x).$$

7. The cumulative principal payment after t periods is computed as:

$$S(t) = \sum_{k = 1}^{t} E(k).$$

8. The percentage of interest charge contained in installment payment number t is:

$$f(t) = \frac{I(t)}{A} (100\%).$$

9. The percentage of cumulative interest charge contained in cumulative total payment up to and including payment number t is:

$$F(t) = \frac{Q(t)}{C(t)} (100\%).$$

10. The percentage of cumulative principal payment contained in the cumulative total payment up to and including payment number t is:

$$H(t) = \frac{S(t)}{C(t)} (100\%)$$
$$= 1 - F(t).$$

Example

Suppose an industrial project is to be financed by borrowing $500,000 from an industrial development bank. The annual nominal interest rate for the loan is 10 percent. The loan is to be repaid in equal monthly installments over a period of fifteen years. The first payment on the loan is to be made exactly one month after financing is approved. It is desired to perform a detailed analysis of the loan schedule. Table 7-1 presents a partial calculation of the loan-repayment schedule. The tabulated result shows a monthly payment of $5,373.04 on the loan.

Considering the situation after 10 months (i.e., $t = 10$), it is seen that:

$U(10)$ = $487,475.13 (unpaid balance)
$A(10)$ = $5,373.04 (monthly payment)
$E(10)$ = $1,299.91 (equity portion of the tenth payment)
$I(10)$ = $4,073.13 (interest charge contained in the tenth payment)
$C(10)$ = $53,730.40 (total payment to date)
$S(10)$ = $12,526.21 (total equity to date)
$f(10)$ = 75.81% (percentage of the tenth payment going into interest charge)
$F(10)$ = 76.69% (percentage of the total payment going into interest charge),
that is, over 76 percent of the sum of the first ten installment payments goes into interest charges.

At the end of the sample calculation, it is seen that by time $t = 180$, the unpaid balance has been reduced to zero. That is, $U(180) = 0.0$. The total payment made on the loan is $967,148.40. Thus, the total interest charge on the loan is $967,148.20 - $500,000 = $467,148.20. So, 48.30 percent of the total payment goes into interest charges. The information about interest charges might be very useful for tax purposes.

Looking at the tabulated values, it is seen that equity builds up slowly as unpaid balances decrease slowly. It is noted that very little equity is accumulated during the first three years of the loan schedule. This is shown graphically in Figure 7-11. The effects of inflation, depreciation, property appreciation, and other economic factors are not included in the analysis presented above. A project analyst should include such factors whenever they are relevant to the loan situation.

The point at which both curves intersect is referred to as the equity break-even point. It indicates when the unpaid balance is exactly equal to

TABLE 7-1.   Partial Result of Project-Loan Analysis

t	U(t)	A(t)	E(t)	I(t)	C(t)	S(t)	f(t)	F(t)
1	498,794.98	5,373.04	1,206.36	4,166.68	5,373.04	1,206.36	77.55	77.55
2	497,578.56	5,373.04	1,216.42	4,156.62	10,746.08	2,422.78	77.36	77.45
3	496,352.01	5,373.04	1,226.55	4,146.49	16,119.12	3,649.33	77.17	77.36
4	495,115.24	5,373.04	1,236.77	4,136.27	21,492.16	4,886.10	76.98	77.27
5	493,868.16	5,373.04	1,247.08	4,125.96	26,865.20	6,133.18	76.79	77.17
6	492,610.69	5,373.04	1,257.47	4,115.57	32,238.24	7,390.65	76.60	77.07
7	491,342.74	5,373.04	1,267.95	4,105.09	37,611.28	8,658.61	76.40	76.98
8	490,064.22	5,373.04	1,278.52	4,094.52	42,984.32	9,937.12	76.20	76.88
9	488,775.05	5,373.04	1,289.17	40,83.87	48,357.36	11,226.29	76.01	76.78
10	487,475.13	5,373.04	1,299.91	4,073.13	53,730.40	12,526.21	75.81	76.69
11	486,164.39	5,373.04	1,310.75	4,062.29	59,103.44	13,836.96	75.61	76.59
12	484,842.72	5,373.04	1,321.67	4,051.37	64,476.48	15,158.63	75.40	76.49
13	483,510.03	5,373.04	1,332.68	4,040.36	69,849.52	16,491.31	75.20	76.39
14	482,166.24	5,373.04	1,343.79	4,029.25	75,222.56	17,835.10	74.99	76.29
15	480,811.25	5,373.04	1,354.99	4,018.05	80,595.60	19,190.09	74.78	76.19
16	479,444.97	5,373.04	1,366.28	4,006.76	85,968.64	20,556.37	74.57	76.09
17	478,067.31	5,373.04	1,377.67	3,995.37	91,341.68	21,934.03	74.36	75.99
18	476,678.16	5,373.04	1,389.15	3,983.89	96,714.72	23,323.18	74.15	75.88
19	475,277.44	5,373.04	1,400.72	3,972.32	102,087.76	24,723.90	73.93	75.78
20	473,865.05	5,373.04	1,412.39	3,960.65	107,460.80	26,136.29	73.71	75.68
.	.	.	.	.	.	.	.	.
.	.	.	.	.	.	.	.	.
.	.	.	.	.	.	.	.	.
170	51,347.67	5,373.04	4,904.27	468.77	913,416.80	448,656.40	8.72	50.88
171	46,402.53	5,373.04	4,945.14	427.90	918,789.84	453,601.54	7.96	50.63
172	41,416.18	5,373.04	4,986.35	386.69	924,162.88	458,587.89	7.20	50.38
173	36,388.27	5,373.04	5,027.91	345.13	929,535.92	463,615.80	6.42	50.12
174	31,318.47	5,373.04	5,069.80	303.24	934,908.96	468,685.60	5.64	49.87
175	26,206.42	5,373.04	5,112.05	260.99	940,282.00	473,797.66	4.86	49.61
176	21,051.76	5,373.04	5,154.65	218.39	945,655.04	478,952.31	4.06	49.35
177	15,854.15	5,373.04	5,197.61	175.43	951,028.08	484,149.92	3.27	49.09
178	10,613.23	5,373.04	5,240.92	132.12	956,401.12	489,390.84	2.46	48.83
179	5,328.63	5,373.04	5,284.60	88.44	961,774.16	494,675.44	1.65	48.57
180	0.00	5,373.04	5,328.63	44.41	967,147.20	500,004.07	0.83	48.30

P = \$500,000; n = 15 years (180 months); i = 10% per year.

Table Legend
P = Principal amount
$U(t)$ = Unpaid balance after making t payments
$A(t)$ = Installment payment per year
$C(t)$ = Cumulative total payments after t years
$E(t)$ = Amount of principal paid with payment number t
$I(t)$ = Amount of interest charges paid with payment number t
$Q(t)$ = Cumulative interest charges paid after t years
$f(t)$ = Percentage of annual installment going for interest charges
$F(t)$ = Percentage of cumulative total payment going for interest charges.

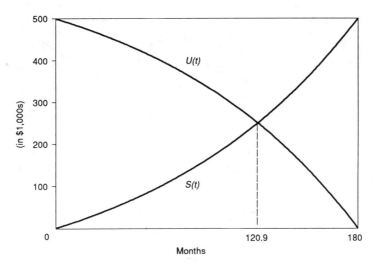

FIGURE 7-11. Accumulation of Equity in Project-Debt Analysis.

the accumulated equity or the cumulative principal payment. For the example, the equity break-even point is 120.9 months (over 10 years). The importance of the equity break-even point is that any equity accumulated after that point represents the amount of ownership or equity that the debtor is entitled to after the unpaid balance on the loan is settled with whatever collateral was placed on the loan. The implication of this is very important and clear in the case of mortgage loans. The equity break-even point can be calculated directly by using the following formula:

$$t^* = \frac{ln[((1 + i)^n + 1)/2]}{ln(1 + i)},$$

Where
ln = the natural log function
n = the number of periods in the life of the loan
i = the interest rate per period.

Figure 7-12 presents a plot of the total loan payment and the cumulative equity with respect to time. The total payment starts from $0.0 at time zero and goes up to $967,147.20 by the end of the last month of the installment payments. Since only $500,000 were borrowed, the total interest payment on the loan is $967,147.20 − $500,000 = $467,147.20. The cumulative principal payment starts at $0.0 at time zero and slowly builds up to $500,001.34, which

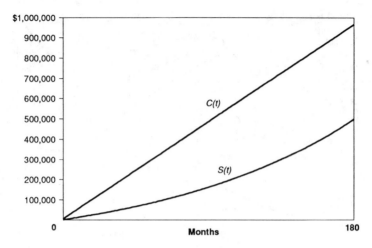

FIGURE 7-12.   Loan Payment versus Cumulative Equity.

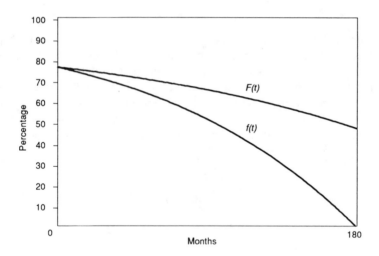

FIGURE 7-13.   Plot of Percentage of Interest Charges.

is the original loan amount. The extra $1.34 is due to round-off error in the calculations.

Figure 7-13 presents a plot of the percentage of interest charge in the monthly payments and the percentage of interest charge in the total payment. The percentage of interest charge in the monthly payments starts at 77.55 percent for the first month and decreases to 0.83 percent for the last month. By comparison, the percentage of interest in the total payment starts also at

77.55 percent for the first month and slowly decreases to 48.30 percent by the time the last payment is made at time 180.

Table 7-1 and Figure 7-13 show that an increasing proportion of the monthly payments goes into the principal payment as the months drag on. If the interest charges are tax deductible, the decreasing values of $f(t)$ means that there would be decreasing tax benefits of the interest charges in the later months of the loan.

7.5.2 Analysis of National Debt
for Industrial Development

A nation in debt is caught in a net. Many developing countries fund their monetary activities through recurring debts. Rising national debts have become a choking problem for both developed and developing economies. Debts that used to amount to millions of dollars have now accumulated to unmanageable billions. Just as ordinary citizens fall prey to easy credit, many nations are falling prey to huge national credits—on a very global scale. Defaults on such huge national debts can easily plunge the global economy into chaos.

Many countries would rather attempt to solve internal problems with external money instead of facing the sources of the problems squarely and deriving a durable solution. Some even finance basic needs, rather than development projects, with external loans. Thus, they use external loans as their primary source of money supply. What happens in most of these cases is that the intended objectives are never achieved despite all the funds expended, and the countries are still left with the huge loan payments. Meanwhile, they go back for more loans in the attempt to again tackle the problems they could not solve in the first round. So, the external debts swell and the internal problems persist.

The cost of serving these loans alone is staggering. As a result, keeping up with the scheduled payments becomes difficult. The slower the payments are made, the larger the debt accumulates. Eventually, the debtor nation goes back to borrow more money to pay the old debt. A never-ending cycle of debt burden is thus created.

A disciplined economy should be able to put a check on its spending, find internal sources for funding development projects, and strive to get higher productivity from the existing limited resources. Many policymakers don't quite understand, and excusably so, all the ramifications of borrowing money. They naively see $1 million borrowed as $1 million to be repaid. In the example that follows, the computational approach presented in the preceding section is applied to a national-debt analysis. Debt-servicing charges (interest charges) are one of the necessary evils of borrowing money. Unfortunately (or sometime fortunately, if we look from the lender's point of view), the properties of interest charges relative to the principal amount are rarely fully understood.

Suppose that a loan of $1,000 million is obtained at an interest rate of 10 percent per year over twenty years. Assuming that the first of the equal end-of-year repayment installments will be made one year from the date the loan is obtained, the total annual payment is calculated to be $117.46 million. A substantial portion of this amount goes into servicing the debt. Using the standard formulas for cash flow and time value of money analysis, the results presented in Table 7-2 are obtained.

It is seen in the table that of the $117.46 million paid at the end of the first year, $100 million go into interest charges, while only $17.46 million go into reducing the principal amount. As another example, of the $117.46 million paid at the end of the tenth year, $76.29 million go into interest charges, while

TABLE 7-2.   National Debt-Servicing Analysis (in millions of dollars)

t	$U(t)$	$A(t)$	$E(t)$	$I(t)$	$C(t)$	$Q(t)$
1	982.54	117.46	17.46	100.00	117.46	100.00
2	963.33	117.46	19.21	98.25	234.92	198.25
3	942.21	117.46	21.13	96.33	352.38	294.59
4	918.97	117.46	23.24	94.22	469.84	388.81
5	893.41	117.46	25.56	91.90	587.30	480.71
6	865.29	117.46	28.12	89.34	704.76	570.05
7	834.36	117.46	30.93	86.53	822.22	656.57
8	800.33	117.46	34.02	83.44	939.68	740.01
9	762.91	117.46	37.43	80.03	1,057.14	820.04
10	721.74	117.46	41.17	76.29	1,174.60	896.33
11	676.45	117.46	45.29	72.17	1,292.06	968.51
12	626.64	117.46	49.81	67.65	1,409.52	1,036.15
13	571.84	117.46	54.80	62.66	1,526.97	1,036.82
14	511.57	117.46	60.28	57.18	1,644.43	1,156.00
15	445.26	117.46	66.30	51.16	1,761.89	1,207.16
16	372.33	117.46	72.93	44.53	1,879.35	1,251.69
17	292.10	117.46	80.23	37.23	1,996.81	1,288.92
18	203.86	117.46	88.25	29.21	2,114.27	1,318.13
19	106.78	117.46	97.07	20.39	2,231.73	1,338.51
20	0.00	117.46	106.78	10.68	2,349.19	1,349.19

$P = \$1,000m$; interest rate $= 10\%$ per year; term of the loan $= 20$.

Table Legend
P = Principal amount
$U(t)$ = Unpaid balance after making t payments
$A(t)$ = Installment payment per year
$C(t)$ = Cumulative total payments after t years
$E(t)$ = Amount of principal paid with payment number t
$I(t)$ = Amount of interest charges paid with payment number t
$Q(t)$ = Cumulative interest charges paid after t years

$41.17 million go for principal payments. Looking at the overall picture, a total payment of $2,349.19 million would have been made by end of 20 years. Of this, $1,349.19 million is for debt servicing, a 57.43-percent penalty.

Table 7-3 presents year-by-year percentages for the interest charges. The 80.22 percent for P_4, for example, indicates that over 80 percent of the payment made at the end of year 4 goes for interest charges. Meanwhile, the q_4 value of 82.75 percent reveals that almost 83 percent of the total payments made over the first four years is solely the cost of borrowing. The interest-charge percentages for the annual payments range from a high of 85.14 percent in the first year to a low of 9.9 percent in year 20. By contrast, the percentages for the charges for cumulative payments range from 85.14 percent down to 57.43 percent over the life of the loan.

Now, if the loan was arranged for thirty years (Tables not shown) rather than twenty years, at the same interest rate of 10 percent per year, the total payments after thirty years would be $3,182.38 million. Of this, $2,182.38 million would be interest charges, at a 68.58-percent cost. Under this alternate arrangement, over 90 percent of each of the payments made in the first six years would be interest charges. Conversely, less than 8 percent of the

	TABLE 7-3.	Analysis of Year-by-Year Interest Charges	
t	$f(t)\%$	$F(t)\%$
1	85.14	85.14
2	83.65	84.39
3	82.01	83.60
4	80.22	82.75
5	78.24	81.85
6	76.06	80.89
7	73.67	79.85
8	71.03	78.75
9	68.14	77.57
10	64.95	76.31
11	61.45	74.96
12	57.59	73.51
13	53.35	71.96
14	48.68	70.30
15	43.55	68.51
16	37.91	66.60
17	31.70	64.55
18	24.87	62.34
19	17.36	59.98
20	9.09	57.43

total payments made over the first six years would go into retiring the loan. In fact, less than 17 percent of the total payments made over the first twenty years would be principal amount—a slow amortization process.

With the availability of accurate data, similar analysis can be easily carried out for any development project loan. Of course, several scenarios are possible for the loan transaction. For example, What happens if some of the annual installment payments, say five, are missed during the loan period? What happens if a country decides, smartly, to pay off the loan early? What happens if the loan needs to be rescheduled for a shorter or longer period? It is hoped managers of industrial development projects will learn how to make use of analyses similar to the ones presented in this section. It is expected that the results of the analyses will be used to educate the public and to enlighten policymakers so that good economic judgment may be developed for managing industrial development projects.

7.5.3 Capital Investment and
Financing Mechanisms

Capital includes not only privately owned production facilities but also public investment. Public investments provide the infrastructure of the economy, such as roads, bridges, water supply, and so on. Other public capital that indirectly supports production and private enterprise include schools, police stations, central financial institution, and postal facilities.

If the physical infrastructures of the economy are lacking, the incentive for private entrepreneurs to invest in production facilities is likely to be lacking also. The government or the community leaders can create the atmosphere for free enterprise by constructing better roads, providing better public safety, facilities, and encouraging ventures that ensure adequate power and water supplies.

The spirit of private enterprise can easily be boosted by government encouragement. A government should facilitate mechanisms for the provision of capital for industrial development projects. As far as investment is concerned, money is not important for itself. It is what can be achieved with it that is important. The avenues for raising capital funds include banks, government loans or grants, business partners, cash reserves, and other financial institutions. The key to the success of the free industrial enterprise system is the availability of capital funds and the availability of sources to invest the funds in ventures that yield products needed by the society.

A clearinghouse of potential goods and services that a new industry can provide may be established by the government. New entrepreneurs interested in providing the goods and services should be encouraged to start suitable enterprises. They should be given technical and financial support to enable them to start their production operations. New product and service ideas may be solicited from the public for the clearinghouse. Some specific ways that funds can be made available for business investments are:

Commercial Loans. Banks should be encouraged to loan money to entrepreneurs, particularly those just starting business. Government guarantees may be provided to make it easier for the enterprise to obtain the needed funds.

Bonds and Stocks. National policies regarding the issuance of bonds and stocks should be expanded and simplified to encourage entrepreneurs to explore those financing options.

Interpersonal Loans. In some communities, there may be individuals with enough personal funds to provide personal loans to aspiring entrepreneurs. But presently, there is no official mechanism that handles the supervision of interpersonal business loans. If a supervisory body exists at a national level, wealthy citizens will be less apprehensive about loaning money to friends and relatives for business purposes. The wealthy citizens can, thus, become a strong source of business capital.

Foreign Investment. Foreign investments can be attracted for local enterprises through government incentives. The incentives may be in terms of attractive zoning permits, foreign exchange permits, or tax breaks.

Investment Banks and Brokers. The operations of investment banks and brokers should be established or strengthened. These companies buy securities from enterprises and resell them to other investors. Proceeds from these investments may serve as a source of business capital.

Mutual Funds. Mutual funds represent collective funds from a group of individuals. The collective funds are often large enough to provide capitals for business investments. Mutual funds may be established by individuals or under the auspices of a government agency. Encouragement and support should be provided for the group to spend the money for business investment purposes.

7.6 EFFECTS OF INFLATION ON PROJECT MANAGEMENT

Inflation can have a significant impact on the way the economic aspects of an industrial development project are handled. Inflation may be defined in economic terms as the increase in the amount of currency in circulation, resulting in a relatively high and sudden fall in its value. To a producer, inflation means a sudden increase in the cost of items that serve as inputs for the production process (equipment, labor, materials, etc). To the retailer, inflation implies an imposed higher cost of finished products. To an ordinary citizen, inflation portends an unbearable escalation of prices of consumer goods. All these views are interrelated.

Inflation involves several related causes. Economists often trace the cause of inflation to the fact that more money is poured into an economy than the economy is worth or capable of supporting. The real wealth of a nation should be in terms of its capability to generate desirable goods and services. Money, unfortunately, is often viewed as the real measure of wealth. A person with $1 million is seen as being wealthy, although that person may have never contributed anything that improves the welfare of humanity. A factory worker, by comparison, may be the key factor in the production of a basic good that the whole society needs. Yet, he or she may be seen as the unwealthy person. Money is, indeed, a misleading measure of wealth—although a convenient one. It seems reasonable, though illogical, that personal wealth should be measured in terms of the efficiency in generating useful products or services.

The amount of money supply, as a measure of a country's wealth, is controlled by the government. With no other choice, governments often feel impelled to create more money or credit to take care of old debts and pay for social programs. When money is generated at a faster rate than the growth of goods and services, it becomes a surplus commodity, and its value (purchasing power) will fall. This means that there will be too much money available to buy only a few goods and services. When the purchasing power of a currency falls, each individual in a product's life cycle has to shed more of the currency in order to obtain the product. Some of the classic concepts of inflation include the following:

1. Increases in producer's costs are passed on to consumers. At each stage of the product's journey from producer to consumer, prices are escalated disproportionately in order to make a good profit. The overall increase, in the product's price is directly proportional to the number of intermediaries it encounters on its way to the consumer. This type of inflation is called cost-driven (or cost-push) inflation.
2. Excessive spending power of consumers forces an upward trend in prices. This high spending power is usually achieved at the expense of savings. The law of supply and demand dictates that the more the demand, the higher the price. This type of inflation is known as demand-driven (or demand-pull) inflation.
3. The impact of international economic forces can induce inflation in a local economy. Trade imbalances and fluctuations in currency values are notable examples of international inflationary factors.
4. Increasing base wages of workers generate more disposable income and, hence, higher demands for goods and services. The high demand, consequently, creates a pull on prices. Coupled with this, employers pass on

the additional wage cost to consumers through higher prices. This type of inflation is, perhaps, the most difficult to solve because wages set by union contracts and prices set by producers almost never fall; at least not permanently. This type of inflation may be referred to as wage-driven (or wage-push) inflation.

5. Easy availability of credit leads consumers to "buy now and pay later" and, thereby, creates another loophole for inflation. This is a dangerous type of inflation because the credit not only pushes prices up but it also leaves consumers with less money later on to pay for the credit. Eventually, many credits become uncollectible debts, which may then drive the economy into recession.

6. Deficit spending by a nation results in an increase in money supply and, thereby, creates less room for each dollar to get around. The popular saying "a dollar does not go far anymore" simply refers to inflation in lay terms.

Inflation affects everyone to some degree. Some effects are immediate and easily perceptible. Other effects are subtly pervasive. Whatever form it takes, inflation has numerous effects, some of which are:

1. Decline is general standard of living. Savings, investments, and disposable income are diminished. People on fixed income are unable to keep up with inflation in terms of their purchasing power. Meanwhile, wage earners' sense of security due to higher incomes is eroded by the double effect of higher tax bracket and lower currency value.

2. Confidence in the leadership and the economy declines. Economic frustration can then lead to corruption, bribery, and other fraudulent practices. Economic rebels may then argue that it is better to be unemployed than to work hard and still not be able to make ends meet. They consequently seek solace in welfare programs, which in turn places a further burden on the economic system.

3. Business decisions are distorted by attempts to cope with inflation. Many of the decisions simply come down to raising prices in order to defray the higher cost caused by inflation.

4. Development projects may be adversely affected by the effects of inflation in terms of cost overruns and poor resource utilization. The level of inflation will determine the severity of the impact on projects.

Inflation can have many faces. The following lists some types of inflation:

Mild Inflation. When inflation is mild (2 to 4 percent) the economy actually prospers. Producers strive to produce at full capacity in order to take advantage of high consumer prices. Private investments tend to be brisk, and more jobs become available. However, the good fortune may only be temporary. Prompted by the prevailing success, employers are tempted to seek larger profits, and workers begin to ask for higher wages. They cite their employer's prosperous business as a reason to bargain for bigger slices of the business profit. So, we end up with a vicious cycle in which the producer asks for higher prices, the unions ask for higher wages, and inflation goes into an upward spiral.

Moderate Inflation. Moderate inflation occurs when prices increase between 5 and 9 percent. Consumers start purchasing more as an edge against inflation. They would rather spend their money now than watch it decline further in purchasing power. The increased market activity only serves to fuel the fury of inflation.

Severe Inflation. Severe inflation is indicated by price escalations of 10 percent or more. Double-digit inflation implies that prices rise much faster than wages do. Debtors tend to be the ones who benefit from this level of inflation because they repay debts with money that is less valuable than the one borrowed.

Hyperinflation. When each price increase signals the increase in wages and costs, which again sends prices further up, the economy has reached a stage of malignant galloping inflation or hyperinflation. Rapid and uncontrollable inflation destroys the economy. The currency becomes economically useless as the government prints it excessively to pay for obligations. The nations that have the greatest need to embark on industrial development projects are the ones that are often faced with hyperinflation.

7.6.1 Flow of Money and Inflation

Money is a convenient medium of exchange. It sets the standard and units in which prices and debts are expressed. The government can effectively control the economy by doing a good job of controlling the flow of money. A limitation in the supply of money is necessary if the money is to retain its value. If money were to be in unlimited supply, people would have so much of it, spend much, and in the process drive prices up. Money would become so abundant that it would become worthless. The society may then resort to the ancient bartering system. The wish to have a central control over money is the reason why the constitutional power over money is vested in the government rather than in private groups.

The government, in order to retain public trust, must properly manage the flow of money. In many emerging economies, a critical mistake that is often made by the government is to attempt to cover up its money-flow mismanagement by printing more money. The government believes that the more money the citizens have at their disposal, the less their discontent. But as can been seen in the case of many developing nations, this approach can only lead to further degradation of the economy.

Controlling the supply of money helps put a rein on inflation and keep the economy manageable. From the viewpoint of government, controlling money implies curtailing spending. In normal economic setting, the availability of money is effected when the central bank of a nation supplies money reserves to commercial banks to support their financial activities. A government's monetary policy (both internal and external) is implemented through the actions of the central bank with the following results:

1. To slow down monetary activities (lower money supply), the central bank makes less reserves available to commercial banks. That means that the banks have to relinquish more of their monetary reserves to the central or federal reserve.
2. Each unit contraction on the currency available to commercial banks translates to a multiple-level contraction in total bank money.
3. The total money contraction at the banking level eventually dictates that credit will become tighter (more costly and in shorter supply) to the public. This immediately raises interest rates.
4. The decreased availability of funds slows down business activities. People generally will defer investment decisions if they have to pay a high interest rate or find it very hard to get loans. Since they have less money to give out, the commercial banks become more conscious of whom they give loans to, how much they give, and for what purpose.
5. The restricted access to money will result in more austere spending patterns by the public. This, in turn, curtails prices and, hence, reduces inflation.

If this sequence of events is carefully diagnosed and proper actions are taken at appropriate times, money supply will be better managed and inflation will be less of a menace. The managing process will have to be iterative. No one action will have a lasting solution. If the economy begins to falter, it may be necessary to boost it again by loosening the control on money. Of course, this is not the whole story of arresting inflation. So many other factors come into play in inflationary effects. The individual factors involved in specific economic situations will have to be identified and treated as well. In the next section, we look at some of these peculiar factors and at how they may be handled to control inflation.

7.7 STRATEGIES FOR COMBATING INFLATION

Effective actions to combat inflation in a developing economy remain very elusive. A combination of actions is usually effective. But sometimes, conflicting effects arise among individual means of control. Measuring the effectiveness of individual actions or a set of actions is an insurmountable task. In addition to controlling the flow of money, the following approaches may be used to combat inflation.

- Price and wage controls to curtail buying power.
- Credit restrictions.
- Raising taxes to extract more from the consumer's purse and, thus, lower purchasing potential.
- Increased supply of goods through higher productivity. The higher the supply, the lower the price.
- Reduction in national spending.
- Reduction in the number of intermediate sellers to avoid price markups.
- Education and awareness programs for producers, sellers, and buyers.

The lack of success in applying these remedies may be attributed to inconsistent usage, impatience in applying them (not enough time allowed for them to take effect), outright misuse, and inattention to other significant factors (concentration on just one remedy). Each remedy has it own pros and cons—and proponents and opponents. The approach of education and awareness programs for producers, sellers, and buyers has not been seriously used in combating inflation. Yet, it could be one of the most effective approaches to curtailing inflation in a developing economy. It is recommended that in the project-management approach to industrial development projects, a major effort should be devoted to educating all the groups that affect or are affected by the project. Education will make each person become better aware of the important role he or she must play in the development effort.

8

Industrial Technology Transfer

Why reinvent the wheel when you can ride the bus.

The concepts of project management can be very helpful in planning for the adoption and implementation of new industrial technology. Because of their many interfaces, industrial technology adoption and implementation are prime candidates for the application of project-planning and -control techniques. Technology managers, engineers, and analysts should make an effort to take advantage of the effectiveness of project-management tools. The various project-management techniques that have been discussed in the preceding chapters can be used for the problem of industrial technology transfer.

In this chapter project-management guidelines are presented within the context of technology adoption and implementation for industrial development and technology management. The Triple C model of *c*ommunication, *c*ooperation, and *c*oordination is applied as an effective tool for ensuring the acceptance of new technology. The importance of new technologies in improving product quality and operational productivity is also discussed. The chapter also outlines the strategies for project planning and control in complex technology-based operations.

8.1 DEFINITION AND CHARACTERISTICS OF TECHNOLOGY

Technology is the ladder of progress. To transfer technology, we must know what constitutes technology. A working definition of technology will enable us to determine how best to transfer it. A basic question that should be asked is: What is technology? Technology can be defined as follows:

> Technology is a combination of physical and nonphysical processes that make use of the latest available knowledge to achieve business, service, or production goals.

Technology is a specialized body of knowledge that can be applied to achieve a mission or purpose. The knowledge concerned could be in the form of methods, processes, techniques, tools, machines, materials, and procedures. Technology design, development, and effective use are driven by effective use of human resources and effective management systems. Technological progress is the result obtained when the provision of technology is used in an effective and efficient manner to improve productivity, reduce waste, improve human satisfaction, and raise the quality of life.

Technology all by itself is useless. However, when the right technology is put to the right application, with an effective supporting management system, it can be very effective in achieving industrialization goals. Technology implementation starts with an idea and ends with a productive industrial process. Technological progress is said to have occurred when the outputs of technology in the form of information, instrument, or knowledge that is used productively and effectively in industrial operations leads to lower production costs, better product quality, and higher levels of output (from the same amount of inputs) and sales. The information and knowledge involved in technological progress include those which improve the performance of management, labor and the total resources expended for a given activity.

Technological progress plays a vital role in improving overall national productivity. Experience in developed countries such as the United States shows that between 1870 and 1957, 90 percent of the rise in real output per man-hour can be attributed to technological progress. Kendrick (1961) stated that when the sources of growth in the United States were decomposed into a number of elements, about 40 percent of the total increase per capita income between 1929 and 1957 was accounted for by technological change. Moore (1983) also stated that industrial or economic growth is dependent on improvements in technical capabilities and on increases in the amount of the conventional factors of capital and labor. Moore noted that technical change is not synonymous with a movement toward the mostly modern capital-intensive process. Changes occur through improvements in the efficiency in use of existing equipment. That is, through learning and through the adaptation of other technologies, some of which may involve different collections of equipment. The challenge to developing countries is how to develop the infrastructures that promote, use, and develop technological knowledge.

Most of the developing nations today face serious challenges that arise not only from the worldwide imbalance of dwindling revenue from industrial products and oil but also from major changes in a world economy that is characterized by competition, imports, and exports of not only oil but also of basic technology, weapon systems, and electronics products. If technology is not given the right attention in all sectors of the national economy, the much-desired industrial development cannot take place. The ability of a nation to complete in the world market will, consequently, be stymied.

The important characteristics or attributes of a new technology may include productivity improvement, improved product quality, production cost savings, flexibility, reliability, and safety. An integrated evaluation must be performed to ensure that a proposed technology is justified both economically and technically. The scope and goals of the proposed technology must be established right from the beginning of the project. This entails the comparison of departmental objectives with overall organizational goals in the following areas, as previously discussed in Chapter 1:

1. *Industrial Marketing Strategy.* This should identify the customers of the proposed technology. It should also address items such as market cost of proposed product, assessment of competition, and market share. Import and export considerations should be a key component of the marketing strategy.
2. *Industry Growth and Long-Range Expectations.* This should address short-range and long-range expectations, future competitiveness and capability, and prevailing size and strength of the industry that will use the proposed technology.
3. *National Benefit.* Any prospective technology must be evaluated in terms of direct and indirect benefits to be generated by the technology. These may include product price versus value, increase in international trade, improved standard of living, cleaner environment, safer workplace, and improved productivity.
4. *Economic Feasibility.* An analysis of how the technology will contribute to profitability should consider past performance of the technology, incremental benefits of the new technology versus conventional technology, and value added by the new technology.
5. *Capital Investment.* Comprehensive economic analysis should play a significant role in the technology-assessment process. This may cover an

evaluation of fixed and sunk costs, cost of obsolescence, maintenance requirements, recurring costs, installation cost, space-requirement cost, capital-substitution potentials, return on investment, tax implications, cost of capital, and other concurrent aspects.

6. *Resource Requirements.* The use of resources (manpower and equipment) in the pretechnology and posttechnology phases of industrialization should be assessed. This may be based on material input–output flows, high value of equipment versus productivity improvement, required inputs for the technology, expected output of the technology, and use of technical and nontechnical personnel.

7. *Technology Stability.* Uncertainty is a reality in technology-adoption efforts. Uncertainty will need to be assessed for the initial investment, return on investment, payback period, public reactions, environmental impact, and volatility of the technology.

8. *National Productivity Improvement.* An analysis of how the technology may contribute to national productivity may be verified by studying industry throughput, efficiency of production processes, use of raw materials, equipment maintenance, absenteeism, learning rate, and design-to-production cycle.

8.2 TECHNOLOGY ASSESSMENT

New industrial and service technologies have been gaining more attention in recent years because of the high rate at which new productivity-improving technologies are being developed. The fast pace of new technologies has created difficult implementation and management problems for many organizations. New technology can be successfully implemented only if it is viewed as a system whose various components must be evaluated within an integrated managerial framework. Such a framework is provided by a project-management approach.

There is a multitude of new technologies that have emerged in recent years. Technologies such as group technology, cellular manufacturing, artificial intelligence, and so on have received much attention in the literature. But much more remains to be done in actual implementation. It is important to consider the peculiar characteristics of a new technology before establishing adoption and implementation strategies. The justification for the adoption of a new technology is usually a combination of several factors rather than a single characteristic of the technology.

The potential of a specific technology to contribute to industrial development goals must be carefully assessed. The technology-assessment process should explicitly address the following questions:

- What is expected from the new technology.

- Where and when the new technology will be used.

- How the new technology is similar to existing technologies.

- How the proposed technology is different from existing technologies.

- Availability of technical personnel to support the new technology.

- Administrative support for the new technology.

- Who, when, and how of using the technology.

The development, transfer, adoption, utilization, and management of technology are problems that are faced in one form or another by business, industry, and government establishments. These problems have attracted the attention of many authors in recent times, including Corsten (1987), Derakhshani (1983), Madu (1988), Benson (1988), Roberson and Weijo (1988), Pandia (1989), Smilor and Gibson (1991), and Keller and Chinta (1990). Some of the specific problems in technology-transfer and -management include:

- Controlling technological change.

- Integrating technology objectives.

- Shortening the technology-transfer time.

- Identifying a suitable target for technology transfer.

- Coordinating the research and implementation interface.

- Formal assessment of current and proposed technologies.

- Developing accurate performance measures for technology.

- Determining the scope or boundary of technology transfer.
- Managing the process of entering or exiting a technology.
- Understanding the specific capability of a chosen technology.
- Estimating the risk and capital requirements of a technology.

Integrated managerial efforts should be directed at solving these problems. A managerial revolution is needed in order to cope with the ongoing technological revolution. The revolution can be effected by modernizing the long-standing and obsolete management culture relating to technology transfer. Some of the managerial functions that will need to be addressed when developing a technology-transfer strategy include:

1. Development of a technology-transfer plan.
2. Assessment of technological risk.
3. Assignment/reassignment of personnel to effect the technology transfer.
4. Establishment of a transfer manager and a technology-transfer office. In many cases, transfer failures occur because no individual has been given the responsibility to ensure its success.
5. Identification and allocation of the resources required for technology transfer.
6. Setting of guidelines for technology transfer. For example,
   Specification of phases (Development, Testing, Transfer, etc.).
   Specification of requirements for interphase coordination.
   Identification of training requirements.
   Establishment and implementation of performance measurement.
7. Identify key factors (both qualitative and quantitative) associated with technology transfer and management.
8. Investigate how the factors interact, and develop the hierarchy of importance of the factors.
9. Formulate a loop system model that considers the forward and backward chains of actions needed effectively to transfer and manage a given technology.
10. Track the outcome of the technology transfer.

Technology development in many industries appears in scattered, narrow, and isolated areas within a few selected fields. This accounts for the fact that technology efforts are rarely coordinated, thereby hampering the benefits of implementing the technology. The optimization of technology use is thus very difficult. To overcome this problem and establish the basis for effective technology transfer and management, an integrated approach must be followed that will be applicable to technology transfer between any two organizations, public or private.

Some nations concentrate on the acquisition of bigger, better, and faster technology. But little attention is given to how to manage and coordinate the operations of the technology once it arrives. When technology fails, it is not necessarily because the technology is deficient. Rather, it is often the communication, cooperation, and coordination functions of technology management that are deficient. Technology encompasses factors and attributes beyond mere hardware and software. Consequently, technology transfer involves more than the physical transfer of hardware and software. Several flaws exist in the present practices involving technology transfer and management. These flaws include:

- *Poor Fit.* The inadequate assessment of the need of the organization receiving the technology. The target of the transfer may not have the capability to properly absorb the technology.
- *Premature Transfer.* This is particularly acute for emerging technologies that are prone to frequent developmental changes.
- *Lack of Focus.* In the attempt to get a bigger share of the market or gain early lead in the technological race, organizations frequently force technology in many incompatible directions.
- *Intractable Implementation Problems.* Once a new technology is in place, it may be difficult to locate sources of problems that have their roots in the technology-transfer phase.
- *Lack of Transfer Precedents.* Very few precedents are available on the management of new technology. Managers are thus often unprepared for their technology-management responsibilities.
- *Unwillingness to Reorganize Priorities.* Unworkable technologies sometimes continue to be recycled needlessly in the attempt to find the "right" usage.
- *Lack of Foresight.* Because of the nonexistence of a technology-transfer model, managers may not have a basis against which they can evaluate future expectations.
- *Insensitivity to External Events.* Some external events that may affect the success of technology transfer are trade barriers, taxes, political changes, etc.
- *Improper Allocation of Resources.* There are usually not enough resources available to allocate to technology alternatives. Thus, a technology-transfer priority must be developed.

The following steps provide a specific guideline for pursuing the implementation of industrial technology.

1. Find a suitable application.
2. Commit to an appropriate technology.
3. Perform economic justification.
4. Secure management support for the chosen technology.
5. Design the technology implementation to be compatible with existing operations.
6. Formulate the project-management approach to be used.
7. Prepare the receiving organization for the technology change.
8. Install the technology.
9. Maintain the technology.
10. Periodically review the performance of the technology based on prevailing goals.

8.3 TECHNOLOGY-TRANSFER MODES

The transfer of technology can be achieved in various forms. Project management provides an effective means of ensuring proper transfer of technology. Three technology-transfer modes are presented here to illustrate basic strategies for getting one technological product from one point (technology source) to another point (technology sink). A conceptual integrated model of the interaction between the technology source and sink is presented in Figure 8-1.

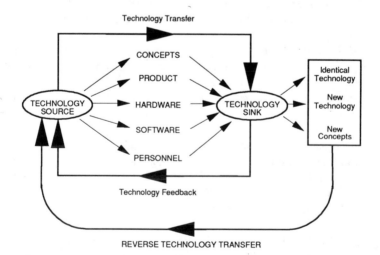

FIGURE 8-1.   Technology-Transfer Modes.

The university-industry interaction model presented in Chapter 1 can be used as an effective mechanism for facilitating technology transfer. Industrial technology application centers may be established to serve as a unified point for linking technology sources with desirous targets. The center will facilitate interactions between business establishments, academic institutions, and government agencies to identify important technology needs. Technology can be transferred in one or a combination of the following strategies:

> - Transfer of complete technological products.
> - Transfer of technology procedures and guidelines.
> - Transfer of technology concepts, theories, and ideas.

1. *Transfer of Complete Technological Products.* In this case, a fully developed product is transferred from a source to a target. Very little product-development effort is carried out at the receiving point. However, information about the operations of the product is fed back to the source so that necessary product enhancements can be pursued. So, the technology recipient generates product information that facilitates further improvement at the technology source. This is the easiest mode of technology transfer and the most tempting. Developing nations are particularly prone to this type of transfer. Care must be exercised to ensure that this type of technology transfer does not degenerate into "machine transfer." It should be recognized that machines alone do not constitute technology.

2. *Transfer of Technology Procedures and Guidelines.* In this technology-transfer mode, procedures (e.g. blueprints) and guidelines are transferred from a source to a target. The technology blueprints are implemented locally to generate the desired services and products. The use of local raw materials and manpower is encouraged for the local production. Under this mode, the implementation of the transferred technology procedures can generate new operating procedures that can be fed back to enhance the original technology. With this symbiotic arrangement, a loop system is created whereby both the transferring and the receiving organizations derive useful benefits.

3. *Transfer of Technology Concepts, Theories, and Ideas* involves the transfer of the basic concepts, theories, and given technology. The transferred elements can then be enha

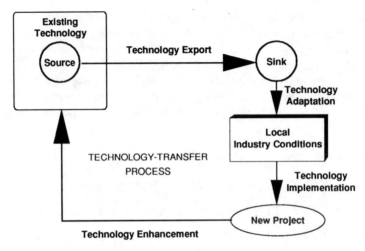

FIGURE 8-2.   Local Adaptation of Technology.

or customized within local constraints to generate new technological products. The local modifications and enhancements have the potential to generate an identical technology, a new related technology, or a new set of technology concepts, theories, and ideas. These derived products may then be transferred back to the original technology source. Figure 8-2 presents a specific cycle for local adaptation and modification of technology. An academic institution is a good potential source for the transfer of technology concepts, theories, and ideas.

It is very important to determine the mode in which technology will be transferred for industrial development purposes. There must be a concerted effort by people to make transferred technology work within local situations. Local innovation, patriotism, dedication, and willingness to adapt technology will be required to make technology transfer successful. It will be difficult for a nation to achieve industrial development through total dependence on transplanted technology. Local adaptation will always be necessary.

8.4 TECHNOLOGY CHANGEOVER STRATEGIES

Any development project will require changing from one form of technology to another. The implementation of a new technology to replace an existing (or a nonexistent) technology can be approached through one of several

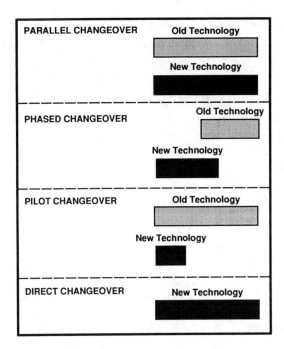

FIGURE 8-3.   Technology Changeover Strategies.

options. Some are more suitable than others for certain types of technologies. The most commonly used technology changeover strategies include:

Parallel Changeover. The existing technology and the new technology operate concurrently until there is confidence that the new technology is satisfactory.

Direct Changeover. The old technology is removed totally and the new technology takes over. This method is recommended only when there is no existing technology or when both technologies cannot be kept operational because of incompatibility or cost considerations.

Phased Changeover. Modules of the new technology are gradually introduced one at a time using either direct or parallel changeover.

Pilot Changeover. The new technology is fully implemented on a pilot basis in a selected department within the organization.

Figure 8-3 shows a graphical representation of the technology changeover options.

8.4.1 Postimplementation Evaluation

The new technology should be evaluated only after it has reached a steady-state performance level. This helps avoid the bias that may be present at the transient stage due to personnel anxiety, lack of experience, or resistance to change. The system should be evaluated for the following:

- Sensitivity to data errors.
- Quality and productivity.
- Use level.
- Response time.
- Effectiveness.

8.5 TECHNOLOGY SYSTEMS INTEGRATION

With the increasing shortages of resources, more emphasis should be placed on the sharing of resources. Technology resource sharing can involve physical equipment, facilities, technical information, ideas, and related items. The integration of technologies facilitates the sharing of resources. Technology integration is a major effort in technology adoption and implementation. Technology integration is required for proper product coordination. Integration facilitates the coordination of diverse technical and managerial efforts to enhance organizational functions, reduce cost, improve productivity, and increase the utilization of resources. Technology integration ensures that all performance goals are satisfied with a minimum of expenditure of time and resources. It may require the adjustment of functions to permit sharing of resources, development of new policies to accommodate product integration, or realignment of managerial responsibilities. It can affect both the hardware and software components of an organization. Important factors in technology integration include:

- Unique characteristics of each component in the integrated technologies.
- Relative priorities of each component in the integrated technologies.
- How the components complement one another.
- Physical and data interfaces between the components.
- Internal and external factors that may influence the integrated technologies.
- How the performance of the integrated system will be measured.

8.6 ROLE OF GOVERNMENT IN TECHNOLOGY TRANSFER

The malignant policies and operating characteristics of some of the governments in underdeveloped countries have contributed to stunted growth of technology in those parts of the world. The governments in most developing countries control the industrial and public sectors of the economy. Either people work for the government or serve as agents or contractors for the government. The few industrial firms that are privately owned depend on government contracts to survive. Consequently, the nature of the government can directly determine the nature of industrial technological progress.

The operating characteristics of most of the governments perpetuate inefficiency, corruption, and bureaucratic bungles. This has led to a decline in labor and capital productivity in the industrial sectors. Using Pareto distribution, it can be estimated that in most government-operated companies there are eight administrative workers for every two production workers. This creates a nonproductive environment that is skewed toward hyperbureaucracy.

The government of a nation pursuing industrial development must formulate and maintain an economic-stabilization policy. The objective should be to minimize the sacrifice of economic growth in the short run while maximizing long-term economic growth. To support industrial technology-transfer efforts, it is essential that a conducive national policy be developed.

More emphasis should be placed on industry diversification, training of the work force, supporting financial structure for emerging firms, and implementing policies that encourage productivity in a competitive economic environment. Appropriate foreign exchange allocation, tax exemptions, bank loans for emerging businesses, and government-guaranteed low-interest loans for potential industrial entrepreneurs are some of the favorable policies that spur growth and development of the industrial sector.

Improper trade and domestic policies have adversely affected industrialization in many countries. Excessive regulations that cause bottlenecks in industrial enterprises are not uncommon. The regulations can take the form of licensing, safety requirements, manufacturing value-added quota requirements, capital contribution by multinational firms, and high domestic-production protection. Although regulations are needed for industrial operations, excessive controls lead to low returns from the industrial sectors. For example, stringent regulations on foreign exchange allocation and control have led to the closure of industrial plants in some countries. The firms that cannot acquire essential raw materials, commodities, tools, and equipment from abroad because foreign exchange restrictions are forced to close and lay off workers.

Price controls for commodities are used very often by developing countries especially when inflation rates for essential items are high. The disadvantages involved in price control of industrial goods include: restrictions of the free competitive power of available goods in relation to demand and supply, encouragement of inefficiency, promotion of dual markets, distortion of cost relationships, and increase in administrative costs involved in producing goods and services.

8.6.1 Example of Successful Technology-Transfer Program

One way that a government can help facilitate industrial technology transfer involves the establishment of a technology-transfer center within the appropriate government agencies. A good example of this approach can be seen in the government-sponsored technology-transfer program by the U.S. National Aeronautics and Space Administration (NASA). In the Space Act of 1958, the U.S. Congress charged NASA with a responsibility to provide for the widest practical and appropriate dissemination of information concerning its activities and the results achieved from those activities. With this technology-transfer responsibility, technology developed in the United States' space program is available for use by the nation's businesses and industry.

In order to accomplish technology transfer to industry, NASA established a *Technology Utilization Program* (TUP) in 1962. The technology-utilization program uses several avenues to disseminate information on NASA technology, including:

1. Complete, clear, and practical documentation is required for new technology developed by NASA and its contractors. These are available to industry through several publications produced by NASA. An example is a monthly publication called *Tech Briefs,* which outlines technology innovations. This is a source of prompt technology information for industry.
2. *Industrial Application Centers* (IACs) were developed to serve as repositories for vast computerized data on technical knowledge. The IACs are located at academic institutions around the country. All the centers have access to a large database containing over 10 million NASA documents. With this database, industry can have access to the latest technological information quickly. The funding for the centers is obtained through joint contributions from several sources including NASA, the sponsoring institutions, and state government subsidies. Thus, the centers can provide their services at a very low fee.
3. NASA operates a Computer Software Management and Information Center (COSMIC) to disseminate computer programs developed through NASA projects. The COSMIC, which is located at North Carolina State University, has a library of thousands of computer programs. The center publishes an annual index of available software.

In addition to the specific mechanisms discussed above, NASA undertakes Application Engineering Projects (AEP). Through these projects,

NASA collaborates with industry to modify aerospace technology for use in industrial applications. To manage the application projects, NASA established a Technology Application Team (TAT), consisting of scientists and engineers from several disciplines. The team interacts with NASA field centers, industry, universities, and government agencies. The major mission of the team interactions is to define important technology needs and identify possible solutions within NASA.

NASA applications engineering projects are usually developed in a five-phase approach with go/no-go decisions made by NASA and industry at the completion of each phase. The five phases are:

1. NASA and the TAT meet with industry associations, manufacturers, university researchers, and public-sector agencies to identify important technology problems that might be solved by aerospace technology.
2. After a problem is selected, it is documented and distributed to the technology utilization officer at each of NASA's field centers. The officer in turn distributes the description of the problem to the appropriate scientists and engineers at the center. Potential solutions are forwarded to the team for review. The solutions are then screened by the problem originator to assess the chances for technical and commercial success.
3. The development of partnerships and a project plan to pursue the implementation of the proposed solution are then pursued. NASA joins forces with private companies and other organizations to develop an applications engineering project. Industry participation is encouraged through a variety of mechanisms such as simple letters of agreement or joint-endeavor contracts. The financial and technical responsibilities of each organization are specified and agreed upon.
4. At this point, NASA's primary role is to provide technical assistance to facilitate the use of the technology. The costs for these projects are usually shared by NASA and the participating companies. The proprietary information provided by the companies and their rights to new discoveries are protected by NASA.
5. The final phase involves the commercialization of the product. With the success of commercialization, the project can have widespread impact. Usually, the final product development, field testing, and marketing are managed by private companies without further involvement from NASA.

Through this well-coordinated, government-sponsored technology-transfer program, NASA has made significant contributions to the U.S. industry. The results of NASA's technology transfer abound in numerous consumer products either in subtle forms or in clearly identifiable forms. Food-preservation techniques constitute one of the areas of NASA's technology transfer that has had a significant positive impact on society.

Other nations can learn from NASA's technology-transfer approach. Wood and EerNisse (1992) present another account of how to accomplish technology transfer from a government agency to private industry. The major problem in developing nations is not the lack of good examples to follow but rather, not being able to operate successfully a program that has proven successful in other nations. It is believed that a project-management approach can help in facilitating success with industrial technology-transfer efforts.

8.6.2 National Strategy

Most of the developing nations depend on technologies transferred from developed nations to support their industrial base, partly because of lack of local research and development, of development funds, and of the skills needed to support such activity. Advanced technology is desired by most industries in developing countries because of its potential to increase output. The adaptability of advanced technology to industries in a developing country is a complex and difficult task. Evidence in most manufacturing firms that operate in developing countries reveal that advanced technology can lead to machine downtime because the local plants do not have the maintenance and repair facilities to support the use of advanced technology.

In some situations, most firms cannot afford the high cost of maintenance associated with the use of foreign technology. One way to solve the transfer-of-technology problem is by establishing *local design centers* for developing nation's industrial sectors that can design and adapt technology for local use. In addition, such centers can also work on adapting fully assembled machinery from developed countries. However, the fertile ground for the introduction of appropriate technology is where people are already organized under a good system of government, production, marketing, and continuing improvement in standard of living. Developing countries must place more emphasis on the production of useful, consumable goods and services.

One useful strategy to ensure the successful transfer of technology is by providing training services that will ensure proper repair and maintenance of technology hardware. It is important that a nation trying to transfer technology have access to a broad-based body of technical information and experience. A plan of technical information sharing between suppliers and users must be ensured.

The transfer of technology also requires reliable liaison between the people who develop the ideas, their agents, and the people who originate the concepts. Technology transfer is only complete when the technology becomes generally accepted in the workplace. Local efforts are needed in tailoring technological solutions to local problems. Technicians and engineers must be trained to assume the role of technology custodians so that implementation and maintenance problems are minimized.

Another strategy for minimizing the technology-transfer problem is to set up central repair shops dedicated to making spare parts and repairing equipment on a timely basis to reduce industrial machine downtime. Improving maintenance and repair centers in developing countries will provide an effective way of assisting emerging firms in developing countries who depend on transferred technology. There should also be a strategy to develop appropriate local technology to support the goals of industrialization. This is important because fully transferred technology may not be fully suitable or compatible with the local product specifications.

For example, many nations have experienced the failure of transferred food-processing technology because the technology was not responsive to the local needs, ingredients, and conditions of food preparation. One way to accomplish the development of local technology is to encourage joint research efforts between academic institutions and industrial firms. The design centers can help in this process. In addition to developing new local technologies, one should calibrate existing technologies for local usage and the higher production level required for industrialization.

The government of developing nations must assume leadership roles in encouraging research and development activities, awarding research grants to universities and private organizations geared toward seeking better ways for developing and adapting technologies for local usage. Effective innovations and productivity improvement cannot happen without adequate public- and private-sector policies. A nation that does not have an effective policy for productivity management and technology advancement will always find itself in a cycle of unstable economy and business crisis. Increases in real product capital, income level, and quality of life are desirable goals that are achievable through effective policies that are executed properly. The following recommendations are offered to encourage industrial growth and technological progress:

1. Encourage a free-enterprise system that believes in and practices fair competition. Discourage protectionism, and remove barriers to allow free trade.
2. Avoid nationalization of assets of companies jointly developed by citizens of developing countries and multinationals. Encourage joint industrial ventures among nations.
3. Both public and private sectors of the economy should encourage and invest in improving national education standards for citizen at various levels.
4. Refrain from dependence on borrowed money and subsidy programs. Create productive enterprise locally that provide essential commodities for local consumptions and exports.
5. Both public and private sectors should invest more on systems and

programs, research and development that generate new breakthroughs in technology and methods for producing food rather than war instruments.

6. The public sector should establish science and technology centers to foster the development of new local technology, productivity-management techniques, and production methodologies.

7. Encourage strong partnership between government, industry, and academic communities in formulating and executing national development programs.

8. Government and financial institutions should provide low-interest loans to entrepreneurs willing to take risks in producing essential goods and services through small-scale industries.

9. Implement a tax structure that is equitable and that provides incentives for individuals and businesses that are working to expand employment opportunities and to increase the final output of the national economy.

10. Refrain from government control of productive enterprises. Such controls only create grounds for fraud and corruption. Excessive regulations should be discouraged.

11. Periodically assess the ratio of administrative workers to production workers and administrative workers to service workers in both private and public sectors. Implement actions to reduce excessive administrative procedures and bureaucratic bottlenecks that impede productivity and technological progress.

12. Encourage organizations and firms to develop and implement strategies, methods, and techniques in a framework of competitive and long-term performance.

13. Trade policy laws and regulations should be developed and enforced in a framework that recognizes fair competition in a global economy.

14. Create a national productivity, science, and technology council to facilitate the implementation of good programs, enhance cooperation between private and public sectors of the economy, redirect the economy toward growth strategies, and encourage education and training of the work force.

15. Implement actions that ensure stable fiscal, monetary, and income policies. Refrain from wage and price control by political means. Let the elements of the free-enterprise system control inflation rate, wages, and income distribution.

16. Encourage moral standards and work ethics so that workers take pride in excellence and foster a value system that encourages pride in consumer products produced locally.

17. Encourage individuals and business to protect full-employment programs, maintain income levels by investing in local ventures rather than exporting capital abroad.

18. Both the public and private sectors of the economy should encourage and invest in retraining of the work force as new technology and techniques are introduced for productive activities.
19. Make use of the expertise of nationals who are professionally based abroad. This is an excellent source of expertise for local technology development.
20. Arrange for annual conferences, seminars, and workshops to exchange ideas between researchers, entrepreneurs, practitioners, and managers with the focus on the processes required for industrial development.

8.7 PROJECT MANAGEMENT AND TECHNOLOGY TRANSFER

Project-management approaches to technology adoption and implementation can help resolve technology conflicts and ensure that compatible technologies are adopted for specific needs. Technology transfer and adoption should be pursued by following the scope of the life cycle of a project. The different steps in technology transfer consist of conceptualization, definition, resource evaluation, implementation, tracking and reporting, control, and phaseout:

Technology Conceptualization. This is the stage at which a need for the proposed technology is identified, defined, and justified. It may be necessary to develop or modify a technology to fit industrialization needs.
Technology Definition. This is the phase at which the purpose of the technology is defined and clarified. A *mission statement* is the major output of this stage. It should specify what the technology-transfer project is expected to achieve. For industrial development projects, a technology strategy should be developed at the national level. The mission statement for each specific project should be based on the national strategy.
Resource Evaluation. Project goals and objectives are accomplished by applying resources to functional requirements. Resources, in the context of project management, are generally made up of people and equipment, which are typically in short supply. The labor and skill levels required to run and maintain an industrial technology should be outlined as a part of the project-planning function.
Project Implementation. This stage involves the operational aspects of initiating the technology project in accordance with specified goals. It may cover a series of functions, including planning, organizing, resource allocation, and scheduling. Research and development should play a crucial role in technology implementation. The early investment commit-

ted to research will later on translate into more successful technology implementation.

Technology Tracking and Reporting. This phase entails the diagnostic process of checking whether or not the results of a technology-transfer project conform to plans and specifications.

Technology Control. In this function, necessary actions are enacted to correct unacceptable deviations from expected performance. Steps must be taken to ensure that a technology is not misused. Contingency plans should be developed for technology catastrophes in case of accidental or deliberate misuse.

Technology Phaseout. This is the termination stage of a technology. Termination of a technology should be executed with as much commitment as the termination of all projects associated with it. Obsolete technologies should be phased out at the appropriate times as new technologies become available. If a technology is not phased out when appropriate, the support for it will wane, and it will be subject to neglect and misuse.

8.8 TECHNOLOGY-PERFORMANCE EVALUATION

Time, cost, and performance form the basis for the operating characteristics of industrial technology. These factors help to determine the basis for technology planning and control. Technology control is the process of reducing the deviation between actual performance and expected performance. To be able to control a technology, we must be able to measure its performance. Typically time (schedule), performance, and cost are measured.

The traditional procedures for measuring progress, evaluating performance, and taking control actions are not adequate for technology management, where events are more dynamic. Some of the causes of technology-control problems are as follows:

Technology Schedule Problems

- Poor precedence relationships.
- Unreliable feasibility study.
- Procrastination of technology adoption.
- Delay of critical activities.

- Poor timing.
- Hasty implementation.
- Technical problems.

Technology Performance Problems
- Inappropriate application.
- Poor quality of hardware.
- Maintenance problems.
- Poor functionality.
- Lack of clear objectives.
- Improper location.
- Lack of training.

Technology Cost Problems
- Inadequate starting budget.
- Effects of inflation.
- Lack of complete economic analysis.
- Poor cost reporting.
- High overhead cost.
- Unreasonable scope.
- High labor cost.

8.8.1 Technology Planning

Technology planning involves establishing the set of actions necessary to achieve the goals of technology. Technology planning is needed to:

- Minimize the effects of technology uncertainties.
- Clarify technology goals and objectives.
- Provide basis for evaluating the progress of technology project.
- Establish measures of technology performance.
- Determine required personnel responsibilities.

Technology Overview
This specifies the goals and scope of the technology and its relevance to the overall mission of the development project. The major milestones, with a description of the significance of each, should be documented. In addition, the organization structure to be used for the project should be established.

Technology Goal
This consists of a detailed description of the overall goal of the proposed technology. A technology goal may be a combination of a series of objectives. Each objective should be detailed with respect to its impact on the project goal. The major actions that will be taken to ensure the achievement of the objectives should also be identified.

Strategic Planning
The overall long-range purposes of the technology and its feasible useful life should be defined. A frequent problem with technology is the extension of useful life well beyond the time of obsolescence. If a technologically feasible life is defined during the planning stage, it will be less traumatic to replace the technology at the appropriate time.

Technology Policy
Technology policy refers to the general guidelines for personnel actions and managerial decision making relating to the adoption and implementation of new technology. The project policy indicates how the project plan will be executed. The chain of command and the network of information flow are governed by the established policy for the project. A lack of policy creates a fertile ground for incoherence in technology implementation because of conflicting interpretations of the project plan.

Technology Procedures
Technology procedures are the detailed methods of complying with established technology policies. A policy, for example, may stipulate that the approval of the project manager must be obtained for all purchases. A

procedure then may specify how the approval should be obtained (e.g., oral or written). A policy without procedures creates an opportunity for misinterpretations.

Technology Resources
The resources (manpower and equipment) required for the adoption and implementation of new technology should be defined. Currently available technology resources should be identified along with resources yet to be acquired. The time frame of availability of each resource should also be specified. Issues such as personnel recruiting and technical training should be addressed early in the project.

Technology Budget
Technology cannot be acquired without adequate budget. Some of the cost aspects that will influence technology budgeting are: first cost, fixed cost, operating cost, maintenance cost, direct/indirect costs, overhead cost, and salvage value.

Operating Characteristics
A specification of the operating characteristics of the technology should be developed. Questions about operating characteristics should include the following:

What inputs will be required by the technology?
What outputs are expected from the technology?
What is the scope of the technology implementation?
How will its performance be measured and evaluated?
Is the infrastructure suitable for the technology's physical configuration?
What maintenance is needed and how will the maintenance be performed?
What infrastructure is required to support the technology?

Cost/Benefit Analysis
The bottom line in any technology implementation is profit, benefit, and/or performance. An analysis of the expenditure required for implementing the technology versus its benefits should be conducted to see if the technology is worthwhile. Can an existing technology satisfy the needs more economically? Even if future needs dictate the acquisition of the technology, economic decisions should still consider prevailing circumstances.

Technology-Performance Measures
Performance standards should be established for any new technolog'
standards provide the yardsticks against which adoption and impl'
tion progress may be compared. In addition, the methods by v

performance will be analyzed should also be defined to avoid ambiguities in tracking and reporting.

Technology Organization
Technology organization involves organizing the technology personnel with respect to required duties, assigned responsibilities, and desired personnel interactions. The organization structure serves as the coordination model for the technology-implementation project.

Technology Work Breakdown Structure
Technology work breakdown structure (TWBS) refers to a logical breakdown of the technology implementation project into major functional clusters. This facilitates a more efficient and logical analysis of the elements and activities involved in the adoption and implementation process. A work breakdown structure (WBS) shows the hierarchy of major tasks required to accomplish project objectives. It permits the implementation of the "divide-and-conquer" concepts. Overall technology planning and control can be improved by using WBS. A large project may be broken down into smaller subprojects that may in turn be broken down into task groups.

Potential Technology Problems
New technologies are prone to new and unknown problems. Contingency plans must be established. Preparation must be made for unexpected problems such as technical failure, software bugs, personnel problems, technological changes, equipment failures, human errors, data deficiency, decision uncertainties, and so on.

Acquisition Process
Technology acquisition deals with the process of procuring and implementing a proposed technology. The acquisition may involve both physical and intangible assets. The acquisition process should normally cover the following analysis:

Hardware. This involves an analysis of the physical component of the technology. Questions that should be asked may concern such factors as size, weight, safety features, space requirement, life span, and ergonomics.

Software. This relates to the analysis of the program code, user interface, and operating characteristics of any computer software needed to support the proposed technology.

Site Selection and Installation. A suitable and accessible location should be found for the physical component of the new technology. The surrounding infrastructure should be such that the function of the technology is facilitated.

8.9 TECHNOLOGY IMPLEMENTATION USING THE TRIPLE C MODEL

The successful execution of technology projects requires a coordinated approach that should utilize conventional project planning and control techniques as well as other management strategies. Intricate organizational and human factors considerations come into play in the implementation of today's complex technologies. The success of projects depends on good levels of communication, cooperation, and coordination. The Triple C model can facilitate a systematic approach to the planning, organizing, scheduling, and control of a technology-transfer project. In the context of technology adoption and implementation, the following functions should be addressed:

- Technology *c*ommunication.
- Technology *c*ooperation.
- Technology *c*oordination.

8.9.1 Technology Communication

Many technologies are just emerging from research laboratories. There are still apprehensions and controversies regarding their potential impacts. Implementing new technology projects may generate concerns both within and outside an organization. A frequent concern is the loss of jobs. Sometimes, there may be uncertainties about the impacts of the proposed technology. Proper communication can help educate all the audience of the project concerning its merits. Informative communication is especially important in cases where cultural aspects may influence the success of technology transfer. The people that will be affected by the project should be informed early about the:

- Need for the technology.

- Direct and indirect benefits of the technology.

- Resources that are available to support the technology.

- Nature, scope, and the expected impact of the technology.

- Expected contributions of individuals involved in the technology.

- Person, group, or organization responsible for the technology.
- Observers, beneficiaries, and proponents of the technology.
- Potential effect of the failure of the project.
- Funding source for the project.

Wide communication is a vital factor in securing support for a technology-transfer project. A concerted effort should be made to inform those who should know. Moreover, the communication channel must be kept open throughout the project life cycle. In addition to in-house communication, external sources should also be consulted as appropriate. A *technology consortium* may be established to facilitate communication with external sources. The consortium will be a link between various organizations about specific technology products and objectives to facilitate the exchange of both technical and managerial ideas.

Figure 8-4 shows an example of a design of a communication-responsibility matrix. A communication-responsibility matrix shows the linking of sources of communication and targets of communication. Cells within the matrix indicate the subject of the desired communication. There should be at least

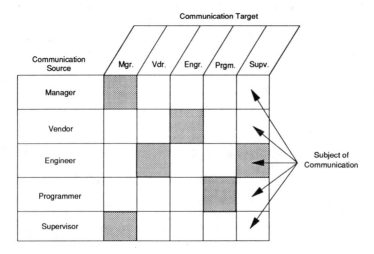

FIGURE 8-4.   Design of a Communication Matrix.

one filled cell in each row and each column of the matrix. This ensures that each individual or department has at least one communication source or target associated with him or her. With a communication-responsibility matrix, a clear understanding of what needs to be communicated to whom can be developed.

8.9.2 Technology Cooperation

Not only must people be informed, their cooperation must also be explicitly sought. Merely saying "yeah" to a project is not enough assurance of full cooperation. In effect, the proposed technology must be sold to management and employees. A structured approach to seeking cooperation should help identify and explain the following items to the project personnel:

- Cooperative efforts are needed to ensure success of the technology.
- Time frame involved in implementing the technology.
- Criticality of cooperation to the technology.
- Organizational benefits of cooperation.
- Implication of lack of cooperation.

Manpower Needs
Manpower needs for new technology implementation are usually difficult to quantify accurately because of the variabilities in application objectives, personnel competence, lack of precedents, and technological constraints. Requests for manpower resources should be realistically based on the practicality of the project situation. This helps secure credibility and support for the effort. The question of personnel training should also be critically analyzed. Many technologies are still at the stage where there is a limited supply of skilled manpower. Thus, organizing a competent and cooperative project group may not be simple.

Equipment Requirement
A list of physical equipment needed to support the technology project should be made. Those already available and those yet to be obtained should be identified. This will aid management in evaluating organizational capability in implementing the proposed technology. Detailed equipment documentation and explanation will contribute significantly in winning the cooperation of management and employees.

Time Requirement
Because of the lack of precedents for new technologies, it is difficult to obtain accurate estimates of project schedule. When seeking the coopera-

tion of those to be involved in the project, it will be prudent to propose conservative schedule estimates. The dynamism of technology can make time estimation very volatile. Setting a precarious terminal date for the project completion may provide the grounds for criticism if the deadline is not met. Time allowances should be made for technology changeover. One strategy is to present time requirements in terms of a series of milestones.

8.9.3 Technology Coordination

Once the communication and cooperation functions have been successfully initiated, the efforts of the project team must be coordinated. Coordination facilitates organization of project efforts. The development of a responsibility chart can be very helpful at this stage. A responsibility chart is a matrix consisting of columns of individual or functional departments and rows of required actions. Cells within the matrix are filled with relationship codes that indicate who is responsible for what. The responsibility chart shown in Figure 8-5 helps avoid overlooking critical functional requirements and responsibilities. The matrix should indicate the following:

- Who is to do what.
- Who is to inform whom of what.

Codes:

R = Responsible
A = Approve
C = Consult
I = Inform
S = Support

Responsibilities	Management	Engineer	Technician	Project Manager	Staff	Plant Manager	Training Dept.
1. Problem Definition						R	
2. Personnel Assignment	C			C		R	
3. Project Initiation				R		A	
4. Technology Prototype	C	R	R	I		S	
5. Full Technology	C	R	R	I		S	
6. Technology Verification	R	R	R	C	I	C	
7. Technology Validation	R	R	R	R	I	C	
8. Technology Integration	R	R	R	R	I	A	
9. Technology Maintenance	R	R	R	C	I	A	
10. Documentation	C	C	C	C	R	A	I

FIGURE 8-5.   Functional Responsibility Chart.

- Whose approval is needed for what.
- Who is responsible for which results.
- What personnel interfaces are involved.
- What support is needed from whom for what functions.

The use of a project-management approach is particularly important when technology is transferred from a developed nation (or organization) to a less developed nation (or organization). In some cases, fully completed technology products cannot be transferred because of the incompatibility of operating conditions and requirements. In some cases, the receiving organization has the means to adapt transferred technology concepts, theories, and ideas to local conditions to generate the desired products. In other cases, the receiving organization has the infrastructure to implement technology procedures and guidelines to obtain the required products at the local level.

In order to reach the overall goal of industrial technology transfer, it is essential that the most suitable technology be identified promptly, transferred under the most conducive terms, and implemented at the receiving organization in the most appropriate manner. Project management offers guidelines and models that can be helpful in achieving these aims.

9

Cultural and Human Resource Issues in Industrial Development

Culture determines the quality of labor, and labor is at the root of culture.

Cultural issues and human resource considerations can have significant impacts on industrial development projects. This chapter addresses these two issues of concern to the industrial project manager. It is through the efforts of labor that many technological achievements have been reached. The cultural aspects of a community will influence the type of human resources available to pursue industrial development projects. Cultural roadblocks to project management constitute the most difficult obstacles to overcome. The guidelines presented in this chapter can help minimize the adverse effects of these obstacles.

9.1 IMPORTANCE OF HUMAN RESOURCES

Human resources make projects successful. Human resources are distinguished from other resources because people can learn, adapt to new project situations, and set goals. Human resources, technology resources, and management resources must coexist to pursue project goals. Figure 9-1 shows the place of human resources in the organization chart of industrial development. People, technology, and good management are essential ingredients for industrial development. The three components must be properly matched to ensure the success of the development efforts. Technology and people must coexist amicably. The increasing prevalence of industrial technology has created major concerns in human resource management.

It is wise to invest in the development of human resources so that they can contribute to industrial development. The converse aspect of Figure 9-1 is that industrial development can facilitate the mechanisms that enable one to obtain better people, better technology, and more effective management.

262

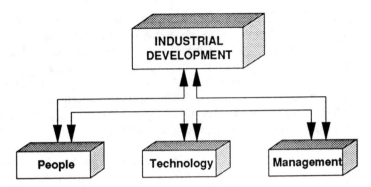

FIGURE 9-1.   Organization Chart of Industrial Development.

Rather than focusing on industrial development, in some nations too many resources are being committed to instruments of destruction under the excuse of war preparedness. However, if the basic needs of the people are not satisfied socially and culturally, the people cannot enthusiastically operate those instruments of war if a war does develop. A positive economic environment will give people the incentive to defend the nation. Industrial development is one way to create such an environment. Even in an era of industrial automation, human resource improvement should still be a major focus in the development project. Using the Triple C model, communication can be used to ensure human resource commitment (cooperation) and active participation (coordination).

A major problem around the world involves a dwindling number of qualified people to do more work. Technical human resources will be needed to develop new technologies to support industrial development projects. Cross-training programs need to be developed to provide the opportunities for workers to cope with the increased responsibilities that they will face.

Although the shortage of educated people exists especially in science, engineering, and technology, developing countries need to focus on effective utilization of the human resources they have available. Often the operating characteristic of both the government and industrial sectors in developing countries underscore the importance of more effective use of all resources, human as well as economic and technical. More focus on training of the work force and on encouraging appropriate use of skills should be done. In some of the developing countries, there are enough capable, qualified, and energetic people around to prove that the inadequacy is not in the people but in the circumstances they have to survive in. Various institutions of learning in developing countries should play a major role in educating the masses on techniques for improving productivity and technological progress.

Perhaps another vital issue that must be addressed is the attitude of some of the people in developing countries toward work. Although some are certainly willing to work hard to improve productivity, many want to buy and sell, and not so many want to make or grow things. In addition, because about 60 to 70 percent of the people employed work for the government or in a government-controlled enterprise, the typical government worker's attitude tends to be take it easy at work, take long lunch breaks, and still have a share of the "national cake." This type of attitude has a negative impact on productivity growth rate. It is important to note that productivity improvement does not start with goods and services or things; it starts with people—their orientation and training, organization and discipline. Better productivity results will demand, among other things, a greater commitment from workers and management to excellence, improvement in innovation, hard work, and above all, a good sense of direction.

Most developing countries do not have enough educated and experienced managers, engineers, and scientists able to plan, organize, and direct development activities effectively. Most development projects, therefore, are supervised by the few experienced managers and professionals who also control all decisions in system change or addition. Because there is an inadequate supply of such professionals, a centralized and authoritarian system of management is enforced to control resources. The lack of indigenous trained professional within the immediate environment also leaves developing countries only with one choice, unlimited use of expatriate professionals, technicians, and managers. There is often no comprehensive strategy in place to train national technicians, professionals, and managers. Moreover, most expatriates take advantage of the situation by limiting skill transfer and keeping the organization centralized and authoritarian. Expatriates should be used as trainers and skill enhancers, not as a permanent source of manpower supply.

9.2 POPULATION AND HUMAN RESOURCES

A large population creates a source of supply of human resources. However, what a modern industrialization project needs is not labor in large numbers, it is a skilled labor force that understands the importance of industrialization and is willing to make commitments and sacrifices to support the project efforts.

In some cultures, there is a subconscious mentality of reproducing poverty. Those with the lowest level of education and living in the highest levels of poverty tend to be the ones who have the largest number of children, themselves engulfed by the cycle of poverty. This segment of the population will have little to contribute to industrialization efforts. Meanwhile, those with high levels of intelligence and wealth are reproducing at an alarmingly decreasing rate. There is a concern that this segment of the population, becoming more and more a minority group, may run itself into extinction. The success of any development effort will rest on the skill of the labor base. Efforts must be made to raise the skill level of those in the backward sections of a population. This can be done through job-training programs, provision of access to education, and social conversion programs.

It is not uncommon to find a high rate of alcoholism in large, densely populated regions. Alcoholism can have a disastrous effect on a nation's economy. This major ill of human resource can be as detrimental as inflation, national debt, industrial mismanagement, and other negative economic factors. To get more productive work out of the human resource, the effects of alcoholism must be reduced. This social ill impairs the judgment and performance of labor—labor that would have, otherwise, been a contributor to industrial development. To combat alcoholism and other negative social habits, management should provide counseling opportunities in the job environment or through professional referrals.

9.3 CLASH OF CULTURES IN PROJECT MANAGEMENT

Industrial development projects require the interaction of people from different cultural backgrounds. A clash of cultures can develop to the extent that project functions may be impaired. Industrial culture must be distinguished from social culture. Industrial culture deals with the business and management processes that are used to support industry operations. What is culturally acceptable may not be legal; what is legal may be a cultural abomination. Industrial culture must be formulated to ensure compatibility. Instituting a sound and receptive industrial culture at the outset of a development project will be much more rewarding than trying to revise the industrial culture after it has clashed with the social culture. Cultural integration may be achieved by the following approaches:

- Identify the prevailing cultural barriers.
- Learn the culture of the project organization.
- Be sensitive to local cultural practices as they may affect labor practices.
- Develope a working knowledge of the local language as much as possible.
- Show a willingness to adapt to the surrogate culture.
- Recognize that productivity may not be a part of the working language in some cultures.

Religion and culture often go hand in hand. Religion played a key role in world development. It is still playing a role today by manifesting itself in the form of cultural influences. The magnitude and sophistication of modern religious strifes could be detrimental to industrial development efforts in some nations. Religious harmony must precede industrial development projects. For example, in religiously segregated communities, the location of a new industry may be a source of dispute as the selection process may be viewed as being religiously motivated by some groups.

9.4 HUMAN RESOURCE MANAGEMENT

Managing human resources involves placing the right people with the right skills in the right jobs in the right work environment. Good human resource management motivates workers to perform better. Both individual and organizational improvement is needed to improve the overall quality of human resources. Management can create a climate for motivation by enriching jobs with the following strategies:

- Specify project goals in unambiguous terms.
- Encourage and reward creativity on the job.
- Eliminate mundane job control-processes.
- Increase accountability and responsibility for project results.
- Define jobs in terms of manageable work packages that help identify lines of responsibility.
- Grant formal authority to make decisions at the task level.
- Create advancement opportunities in each job.
- Give challenging assignments that enable a worker to demonstrate his or her skill.
- Encourage upward (vertical) communication of ideas.
- Provide training and tools needed to get the job done.
- Maintain a stable management team.

Several new management approaches are used to manage human resources in an industrial environment. Some of these approaches are formulated as direct responses to the cultural, social, family, or religious needs of workers. Examples of these approaches are:

- Flextime.
- Religious holidays.
- Half-time employment.

These approaches can offer a combination of advantages. Some of them benefit the employer, and some the workers. The advantages are presented below:

- Low cost.
- Cost savings on personnel benefits.

- Higher employee productivity.
- Less absenteeism.
- Less work stress.
- Better family/domestic situation, which may have positive effects on productivity.

Work force retraining is important for industrialization projects. Continuing education programs should be developed to retrain people who are only qualified to do unskilled work. The retraining will create a ready pool of human resource that can help boost industrial output and competitiveness. Management stability is needed to encourage workers to adapt to the changes of industrial development. If management changes too often, workers may not develop a sense of commitment to the policies of management.

9.4.1 Training and Managing Technical Human Resources

Project goals are achieved through the utilization of resources. The major resource in any organization is manpower, both technical and nontechnical. People are the overriding factor in any project life cycle. Even in automated operations, the role played by whatever few people are involved can be very significant. Such operations invariably require the services of technical people with special managerial and professional needs. The high-tech manager in such situations would need special skills in order to discharge the managerial duties effectively. The manager must have management skills that relate to the following:

- Managing self.
- Being managed.
- Managing others.

Many of the managers who supervise technical people rise to the managerial posts from technical positions. They, consequently, often lack the managerial competence needed for the higher offices. In some cases, technical professionals are promoted to managerial levels and then transferred to administrative posts in functional areas different from their areas of technical competence. The poor managerial performance of these technical managers is not necessarily a reflection of poor managerial competence, but rather an indication of the lack of knowledge of the work elements in their surrogate function. Any technical training without some management exposure is, in effect, an incomplete education. Technical professionals should be trained for the eventualities of their professions.

In the transition from the technical to the management level, an individual's attention would shift from detail to overview, specific to general, and technical to administrative. Since most managerial positions are earned based on qualifications (except in aristocratic and autocratic systems), it is important to train technical professionals for possible administrative jobs. It is the responsibility of the individual and of the training institution to map out career goals and paths and to institute specific education aimed at the realization of those goals. One such path is outlined here:

1. *Technical Professional.* An individual with practical and technical training or experience in a given field, such as industrial engineering. The individual must keep current in his area of specialization through continuing education courses, seminars, conferences, and so on. The mentor program, which is now used in many large organizations, can be effectively used at this stage of the career ladder.
2. *Project Manager.* An individual who is assigned direct responsibility for supervising a given project through the phases of planning, organizing, scheduling, monitoring, and control. The managerial assignment may be limited to just a specific project. At the conclusion of the project, the individual returns to his regular technical duties. However, his performance on the project may help to identify him as a suitable candidate for permanent managerial assignments later on.
3. *Group Manager.* An individual who is assigned direct responsibility for planning, organizing, and directing the activities of a group of people with a specific responsibility; for example, a computer data security advisory committee. This is an ongoing responsibility that may repeatedly require the managerial skills of the individual.
4. *Director.* An individual who oversees a particular function of the organization. For example, a marketing director is responsible for developing and implementing the strategy for getting the organization's products to the right market, at the right time, at the appropriate price, and in the proper quantity. This is a critical responsibility that may directly affect the survival of the organization. Only the individuals who have successfully proven themselves at the earlier career stages get the opportunity to advance to the director's level.
5. *Administrative Manager.* An individual who oversees the administrative functions and staff of the organization. His responsibilities cut across several functional areas. He or she must have proven managerial skills and diversity in previous assignments.

The outline shows just one of the several possible paths that can be charted for technical professionals as they gradually make the transition from the technical ranks to the management level. To function effectively, a manager must acquire nontechnical background in various subjects. Experience, attitude, personality, and training will determine managerial style. Appreciation of the human and professional needs of subordinates will substantially enhance managerial performance. Examples of subject areas in which a manager or an aspiring manager should get training include the following ones:

1. *Project Management.*
- Scheduling and Budgeting: knowledge of project planning, organizing, scheduling, monitoring, and controlling under resource and budget restrictions.
- Supervision: skill in planning, directing, and controlling the activities of subordinates.
- Communication: skill of relating to others both within and outside the organization. This includes written and oral communication skills.

2. *Personal and Personnel Management.*
- Professional Development: leadership roles played by participating in professional societies and peer recognition acquired through professional services.
- Personnel Development: skills needed to foster cooperation and encouragement of staff with respect to success, growth, and career advancement.
- Performance Evaluation: development of techniques for measuring, evaluating, and improving employee performance.
- Time Management: ability to prioritize and delegate activities as appropriate to maximize accomplishments within given time periods.

3. *Operations Management.*
- Marketing: skills useful for winning new business for the organization or preserving existing market shares.
- Negotiating: skills for moderating personnel issues, representing the organization in external negotiations, or administering company policies.
- Estimating and Budgeting: skills needed to develop reasonable cost figures for company activities and the assignment of adequate resources to operations.
- Cash Flow Analysis: appreciation for the time value of money, manipulations of equity and borrowed capitals, stable balance between revenues and expenditures, and maximization of returns on investments.
- Decision Analysis: ability to choose the direction of work by analyzing feasible alternatives.

A technical manager can develop such skills through formal college courses, seminars, workshops, short courses, professional conferences, or in-plant company training. Several companies appreciate these skills and are willing to bear the cost of furnishing their employees with the means of acquiring them. Many of the companies have custom formal courses to teach their employees that they contract out to colleges. This is a unique opportunity for technical professionals to acquire the managerial skills needed to move up the company ladder.

Technical people have special needs. Some of these, unfortunately, are often not recognized by peers, superiors, or subordinates. Inexperienced managers are particularly prone to the mistake of not distinguishing between technical and nontechnical professional needs. In order to perform more effectively, a manager must be administratively adaptive. He or she must understand the unique expectations of technical professionals in terms of professional preservation, professional peers, work content, hierarchy of needs, and the quality of leadership (e.g., the technical competence or background they expect of their managers).

Professional Preservation

Professional preservation refers to the desire of a technical professional to preserve his or her identification with a particular job function. In many situations, preservation is not possible because of a lack of manpower to fill specific job slots. It is common to find people trained in one technical field holding assignments in other fields. An incompatible job function can easily become the basis for insubordination, egotism, and rebellious attitudes. Although in any job environment there will sometimes be a need to work outside one's profession, every effort should be made to match the surrogate profession as closely as possible. This is primarily the responsibility of the human resources manager.

After a personnel team has been selected in the best possible manner, a critical study of the job assignments should be made. Even between two dissimilar professions, there may be specific job functions that are compatible. These should be identified and used in the process of personnel assignment. In fact, the mapping of job functions needed for an operation can serve as the basis for selecting a project team. In order to preserve the professional background of technical workers, job idiosyncrasies must be understood. In most technical training programs, the professional is taught how to operate in the following manners:

1. Make decisions based on the assumption of certainty of information.
2. Develop abstract models to study the problem being addressed.
3. Work on tasks or assignments individually.
4. Quantify outcomes.
5. Pay exacting attention to details.
6. Think autonomously.
7. Generate creative insights to problems.
8. Analyze systems' operatability rather than their profitability.

However, in the business environment, not all of these characteristics are desirable or even possible. For example, many business decisions are made with incomplete data. In many situations, it is unprofitable to expend the time and efforts to seek perfect data. As another example, many operating procedures are guided by company policies rather than by creative choices from employees. An effective manager should be able to spot cases in which a technical employee may be given room to practice his professional training. The job design should be such that the employees can address problems in a manner compatible with their professional training.

Professional Peers
In addition to professionally compatible job functions, technical people like to have other project team members to whom they can relate technically. A project team consisting of members from diversely unrelated technical fields can be a source of miscommunication, imposition, or introversion. The lack of a professional associate on the same project can cause a technical person to exhibit one or more of the following attitudes:

1. Withdraw into a shell and contribute very little to the project by holding back ideas that, it is felt, the other project members cannot appreciate.
2. Exhibit technical snobbery and hold the impression that only he or she has the know-how for certain problems.
3. Straddle the fence on critical issues and develop no strong conviction for project decisions.

Providing an avenue for a technical "buddy system" to operate in an organization can be very instrumental in ensuring congeniality in personnel teams and in facilitating the eventual success of project endeavors. The manager in conjunction with the selection committee (if one is used) must carefully consider the mix of the personnel team on a given project. If it is not possible or desirable to have more than one person from the same technical area, an effort should be made to provide as good a mix as possible. It is undesirable to have several people from the same department taking issues against the views of a lone project member from a rival department. Whether it is realized or not, whether it is admitted or not, there is a keen sense of rivalry among technical fields. Even within the same field, there are subtle rivalries between specific functions. It is important not to let these differences carry over to a project environment.

Work Content
With the advent of new technology, the elements of a project task will need to be designed to take advantage of new developments. Technical profes-

sionals have a sense of achievement relative to their expected job functions. They will not be satisfied with mundane project requirements. They look forward to challenging technical assignments that will bring forth their technical competence. They prefer to claim contribution mostly where technical contribution can be identified. The project manager will need to ensure that the technical people on a project have assignments for which their background is really needed. It will be counterproductive to select a technical professional for a project mainly on the basis of personality. An objective selection and appropriate assignment of tasks will alleviate potential motivational problems that could develop later in the project.

Hierarchy of Needs
Recalling Maslow's hierarchy of needs, one can see that the needs of a technical professional should be more critically analyzed. Being professionals, technical people are more likely to be higher up in the needs hierarchy. Most of their basic necessities for a good life would already have been met. Their prevailing needs will tend to involve esteem and self-actualization. As a result, by serving on a project team, a technical professional may have expectations that cannot usually be quantified in monetary terms. This is in contrast to nontechnical people who may look forward to overtime pay or other monetary gains that may result from being on the project. Technical professionals will generally look forward to one or several of the following opportunities:

1. *Professional Growth and Advancement.* Professional growth is the primary pursuit of most technical people. For example, a computer professional has to be frequently exposed to challenging situations that introduce new technology developments and enable him to keep abreast of his field. Even occasional drifts from the field may lead to the fear of not keeping up and being left behind. The project environment must be reassuring to the technical people in terms of the opportunities for professional growth and for developing new skills and abilities.
2. *Technical Freedom.* Technical freedom, to the extent permissible within the organization, is essential for the full use of a technical background. A technical professional will expect to have the liberty of determining how best the objective of the assignment can be accomplished. One should never impose a work method on a technical professional with the assurance that, "this is the way it has always been done and will continue to be done!" If the worker's creative input to the project effort is not needed, then there is no need to have him or her on the team in the first place.
3. *Respect for Personal Qualities.* Technical people have profound personal

feelings despite the mechanical or abstract nature of their job functions. They will expect to be respected for their personal qualities. In spite of frequently operating in professional isolation, they do engage in interpersonal activities. They want their nontechnical views and ideas to be recognized and evaluated based on merit. They don't want to be viewed as "all technical." An appreciation for their personal qualities gives them the sense of belonging and helps them to become productive members of a project team.

4. *Respect for Professional Qualification.* A professional qualification usually takes several years to achieve and is not likely to be compromised by any technical professional. Technical professionals cherish the attention they receive because of their technical background. They expect certain preferential treatments. They like to make meaningful contributions to the decision process. They take approval of their technical approaches for granted. They believe that they are on a project because they are qualified to be there. The project manager should recognize these situations and avoid the bias of viewing the technical person as being self-conceited.

5. *Increased Recognition.* Increased recognition is expected as a by-product of a project effort. Technical professionals, consciously or subconsciously, view their participation in a project as a means of satisfying one of their higher-level needs. They expect to be praised for the success of their efforts and look forward to being invited for subsequent technical endeavors. They savor hearing the importance of their contribution related to their peers'. Without going to the extreme, the project manager can ensure the realization of the above needs through careful comments.

6. *New and Rewarding Professional Relationship.* New and rewarding professional relationships can serve as a bonus for a project effort. Most technical developments result from joint efforts of people that share closely allied interests. Professional allies are most easily found through project groups. A true technical professional will expect to meet new people with whom he can exchange views, ideas, and information later on. The project atmosphere should, as a result, be designed to be conducive to professional interactions.

Quality of Leadership

The professional background of the project leader should be such that he or she commands the respect of technical subordinates. The leader must be reasonably conversant with the base technologies involved in the project. He must be able to converse intelligently on the terminologies of the project topic and able to convey the project ideas to upper management. If technical credibility is lacking, the technical professionals on the project might view him or her as an ineffective leader. They will consider it impossible to serve under a manager to whom they cannot relate technically.

In addition to technical credibility, the manager must also possess administrative credibility. There are routine administrative matters that are needed to ensure a smooth progress for the project. Technical professionals will prefer to have those administrative issues successfully resolved by the project leader, so that they can concentrate their efforts on the technical aspects. The essential elements of managing a group of technical professionals involve identifying the unique characteristics and needs of the group and then developing the means of satisfying those unique needs.

Recognizing the peculiar characteristics of technical professionals is one of the first steps in simplifying project-management functions. The nature of industrial development projects calls for the involvement of technical human resources. Every manager must appreciate the fact that the cooperation or the lack of cooperation from technical professionals can have a significant effect on the overall management process. The success of a project can be enhanced or impeded by the management style used.

9.5 LABOR RELATIONS

Labor relations determine the level of congeniality of a work environment. Bad labor relations lead to strikes and industrial actions, the crippling effects of which can be felt in terms of declining industrial productivity. Strikes can create unanticipated chain reactions. For example, a strike at a large industrial plant may necessitate the closing of smaller plants that are sources of supplies for the large plant. The overall effect is that total industrial performance will be impeded.

9.5.1 Union-Management Cooperation

Developing nations have serious business problems that stem from the instability of the government and its inability to develop supportive national policies. It is also true that labor-management disputes are very common. Several weeks of strike are not uncommon in most sectors of a developing economy. Generally the root causes of labor-management disputes are as follows:

1. Management likes to assume full responsibility for the overall conduct of the business, including the control of the rights to hire, fire, reward, and punish.

2. Unions distrust management competence and ability to reward effort, share gains in productivity, and guarantee full employment.

To protect its members union leaders set rules and operating guidelines as a form of agreement with the management. These could involve items such as productivity quotas, promotion based on seniority instead of productivity, level of technological improvement that would still guarantee full employment, and fair share of monetary gains.

It has been proved in most successful big businesses in the West that if a good management system is in place in an organization, there will be no need for unions. Successful organizations have done without unions by providing full-employment opportunities, sharing productivity gains with workers, allowing them to participate in decision making, giving them control over their jobs, and using an open-door policy to resolve possible grievances. The following guidelines are recommended for enhancing union-management cooperation:

1. Set up a national arbitration board to ensure fair practices in labor-management relations.
2. Have a minimum-wage policy for jobs at the national level.
3. Encourage labor-management cooperation in goal setting, degree of innovation through workshops and seminars. Union members and management should understand that productivity improvement and technological progress do not always mean layoffs and unemployment.
4. Encourage reward systems that promote and reward workers based on merit.
5. Make sure that cooperation for product improvement and technological progress involves teamwork between managers and nonmanagers. The cooperation should result in formulating goals and objectives, executing plans, and developing methods that improve quality of life for the workers.

9.6 HUMAN RESOURCE PRODUCTIVITY IMPROVEMENT

Several approaches and techniques exist for improving productivity at the various levels of the economy. Each organization or enterprise unit has its own unique problem. The choice of which technique and approach is likely to be successful depends on the type of problem to be resolved and the prevailing circumstances within the organization under analysis. Productivity improvement requires organized use of common sense, tools and techniques constantly to improve work processes, reduce waste, and enhance the use of resources and the overall effectiveness of the organization. Several factors can influence employee-productivity improvement. The workers, their tools, and the work environment must be evaluated as potential avenues for productivity improvement. Some productivity-improvement strategies are:

Employee-Based Productivity-Improvement Approaches

- Training.
- Promotion.
- Job-enrichment programs.
- Education.
- Job rotation.
- Use of monetary incentives.
- Employee consultative arrangements.
- Generous benefits packages.
- Participative decision making.
- Improvement of work environment.
- Unbiased reward and punishment policies.

Task-Based Productivity-Improvement Approaches

- Work-content analysis.
- Methods improvement.
- Task simplification.
- Task prioritization.
- Efficient schedule.

- Work-load balancing.
- Better job design.
- Safety of job.
- Ergonomics.
- Computerization.
- Proper tooling.

Material-Based Productivity-Improvement Approaches
- Material requirements planning.
- Parts evaluation.
- Parts quality control.
- Material durability.
- Material handling systems.
- Material recycling.
- Inventory control.

Product-Based Productivity-Improvement Approaches
- Research and development of product characteristics.
- Product marketing analysis.
- Product value engineering.

- Simplification of product design.
- Product standardization.
- Product diversification.
- Product integration.

Technology-Based Productivity-Improvement Approaches

- Use of robotics.
- Process automation.
- Equipment maintenance.
- Technology transfer and adaptation.
- Parts group technology.
- Energy-efficient processes.
- Computer-aided manufacturing.

9.6.1 Work-Simplification Analysis

Work simplification is the systematic investigation and analysis of planned and existing work systems and methods for the purpose of developing easier, quicker, less fatiguing, and more economic ways of generating high-quality goods and services. Work simplification facilitates workers' tasks, which invariably leads to better performance. Consideration must be given to improving the product or service, raw materials and supplies, the sequence of operations, tools, workplace, equipment, and hand and body motions. Work-simplification analysis helps in defining, analyzing, and documenting work methods.

Techniques such as work measurement and procedure design are used to identify potential areas for cost reduction. Work measurement is a means of determining an equitable relationship between the quantity of work performed and the number of labor hours required for completing that quantity of work. The establishment of measurement is for the purpose of planning, scheduling, and controlling work. The standards developed by work measurement should include standard allowances for rest, delays that occur as part of the job, time for personal needs, and an allowance for personal fatigue.

9.6.2 Incentive Systems

An incentive approach attempts to focus on methods and techniques for motivating individuals and work groups at different organizational levels. Items such as management style, interpersonal relations, employee relations, dismissal procedures, unemployment insurance, job safety, and grievance procedures are reviewed periodically, and enhancement are made to the program in order to increase employee or work group productivity. Some of the views on incentive systems are presented in the sections that follow.

Economic-Incentive Model
The economic-incentive model is based on following views about workers:

1. Workers work only for money.
2. Workers have no self-direction.
3. Workers need leadership.
4. Workers dislike work.
5. Economic incentive is needed to keep workers on the job to perform.

Good salary and financial awards are the two basic ways of implementing the economic-incentive model. The methods of assessing performance for economic-incentive awards include piecework system, simple identifiable tasks, close on-the-job supervision, clear task instructions, and focus on salary administration.

Human Resource Management Incentive Model
The human resource management incentive model is based on the following views about workers:

1. Workers like to work.
2. Workers need a comfortable work environment.
3. There is a need for good leadership.
4. Happy employees will produce more.
5. Happy employees will be committed to the organization.

The approaches to implementing the human resource management incentive model include managerial recognition, good salary, good working conditions, good fringe benefits, and peer recognition. For the model to succeed, the following must be available in the work environment: good management, good organizational policies, fringe benefits, teamwork, and empathetic supervision.

Self-Assessment Incentive Model
The self-assessment incentive model is based on the following views about workers:

1. Workers want meaningful work.
2. Workers possess self-direction to work.
3. Workers have self-control.
4. Workers have creative minds.

The self-assessment model permits each individual to play a significant role in determining job satisfaction. The model allows for personal growth, opportunity to use skill, achievements, recognition, and opportunity to interact with peers and superiors. The supporting environment must include autonomy for workers, flexible supervision, open management system, career policies, goal setting, and design of job content.

Goal-Clarification Model
The goal-clarification model focuses on identifying specific goals and objectives that will improve productivity. Implementing the objectives, tracking performance over time, and providing ongoing assessment of the organization's strengths and weaknesses can help workers set their own goals. Questionnaires and opinion surveys are often used as goal-assessment tools. Techniques such as management by objectives and goal structuring are used during the planning process.

9.6.3 Employee Training and Technical Education

Strong commitment to workers and provision of the required tools, techniques, and training will have a positive impact on workers' productivity. The commitment to training should focus on items such as measurement, planning, evaluation, improvement, feedback mechanisms, resource allocation, information systems, decision-making processes, cultural support systems, performance balance, and process-control techniques. Training is essential because it prepares workers to do their jobs well by building the right knowledge that permits logical actions and decision making.

If the right skills are provided for people, they can develop efficient work habits and positive attitudes that promote cooperation and teamwork. Some approaches to training workers are:

1. Formal education in an academic institution.
2. On-the-job training through hands-on practice.
3. Continuing education short courses.
4. Training videos.
5. Group training seminars.

Management can play a key role in ensuring that the right training is provided by allocating adequate funds for training employees.

Enormous amounts of money are being spent by developing nations on the technical training of their citizens. In addition to government expenditures for education, private citizens spend millions more on self-training. Yet, there is still a shortage of technical manpower in those nations. In some cases, those who have acquired the skills are misplaced in functions where their technical contributions are stymied. In some other cases, training has concentrated on certain areas while other areas have been neglected. Presented below are suggestions for developing and using the technical skills of local workers:

1. Appraise existing categories and levels of local technical skills.
2. Develop a forecast of the skills that would be needed in the future.
3. Assess local and foreign training facilities.
4. Establish vocational training centers.
5. Screen and select candidates for required skill training.
6. Monitor the progress of the trainees.
7. Synchronize the inflow and outflow of trainees with job potentials and national needs.
8. Place trained manpower in relevant technical job functions.
9. Monitor the performance of the technical professionals.
10. Use the feedback of the working technical professionals as inputs for planning future training programs.

Where physical facilities are provided to support the functions of the trained professionals, arrangements should also be made well ahead of time for spare parts to maintain the facilities. In fact, the availability of spare parts should be a required condition for the acquisition of a given piece of equipment or facility.

9.6.4 Technical and Professional Organizations

Technical and professional organizations can be used as an effective mechanism to garner human resource potentials. As a collective body, organizations may be able to have access to policymakers. Thereby, an effective interaction can be developed between the professional and the political systems. Local professionals often have bright ideas on what can be done to achieve economic and technological development. The problem is that these ideas never get a chance to be implemented because they are solitary ideas with no channels to policymakers. For national policymakers to become responsive to the views of professionals, there must be a collective effort by the professional group. The potential activities of a technical or professional organization are to:

1. Encourage the unity of professionals locally and worldwide.
2. Encourage communication and good relationship among professionals, local research institutes, universities, industries, governments, other individuals, and organizations locally and in the rest of the world.
3. Support research and application projects locally and worldwide, either in cooperation with individuals, governments, or private organizations.
4. Exchange technical information among professional peers, other individuals, and organizations.
5. Act as a professional resource center or clearinghouse for professionals in specialized fields such as medicine, engineering, law, social sciences, business, industrial development, music and arts, and so on. The professional activities of all these fields can affect industrial development directly or indirectly.
6. Initiate and support specific professional-development programs to support the needs of developing nations, professionals, other individuals, organizations, and governments.
7. Publish quarterly newsletters to promote communication among professional organizations and local communities.
8. Participate in programs that will eradicate hunger, poverty, and suffering in developing nations.
9. Encourage further education of professional members.
10. Organize conferences, workshops, symposia, and seminars in developing nations and in other parts of the world.

9.7 CRITICAL RESOURCE SCHEDULING

Resource management is a major function in any industrial development project. In a project-management environment, project goals are achieved through the strategic allocation of resources to tasks. Several analytical and graphical tools are available for activity planning, scheduling, and control. Examples are the critical path method (CPM), program evaluation and review technique (PERT), and precedence diagramming method (PDM). But similar tools are not available for resource management.

There is a need for simple tools for resource-allocation planning, scheduling, tracking, and control. In this section, a simple extension of a CPM diagram is presented for resource-management purposes. The extension, called critical resource diagram (CRD), is a graphical tool that brings the well-known advantages of CPM diagram to resource scheduling. The advantages of CRD include simplified resource tracking and control, better job distribution, better information to avoid resource conflicts, and better tools for resource leveling.

9.7.1 Resource-Management Constraints

Resource management is a complex task that is subject to several limiting factors including the following:

- Resource interdependencies.
- Variable levels of resource availability.
- Mutual exclusivity of resources.
- Limitations on resource availability.
- Limitations on resource substitutions.
- Conflicting resource priorities.
- Limitations on partial resource allocation.

These factors invariably affect the criticality of certain resource types. It is logical to expect different resource types to exhibit different levels of criticality in a resource-allocation problem. For example, some resources are very expensive. Some resources entail special skills. Some are in very limited supply. The relative importance of different resource types should be considered when carrying out resource allocation in activity scheduling. The CRD helps in representing resource criticality.

CRD Network Development

Figure 9-2 shows an example of a CRD for a small project requiring six different resource types. Each node identification, *RESj*, refers to a task responsibility for resource type *j*. In a CRD, a node is used to represent each resource unit. The interrelationships between resource units are indicated by arrows. The arrows are referred to as resource-relationship (R-R) arrows. For example, if the job of Resource 1 must precede the job of Resource 2, then an arrow is drawn from the node for Resource 1 to the node for Resource 2. Task durations are included in a CRD to provide further details about resource relationships. Unlike activity diagrams, a resource unit may appear at more than one location in a CRD provided there are no time or task conflicts. Such multiple locations indicate the number of different jobs for which the resource is responsible. This information may be useful for

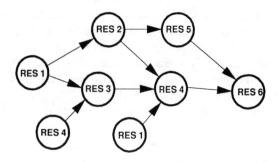

FIGURE 9-2.   Critical Resource Diagram.

task distribution and resource-leveling purposes. In Figure 9-2, Resource Type 1 (RES 1) and Resource Type 4 (RES 4) appear at two different nodes, indicating that each is responsible for two different jobs within the same work scenario.

CRD Computations
The same forward and backward computations used in CPM are applicable to a CRD diagram. However, the interpretation of the critical path may be different since a single resource may appear at multiple nodes. Figure 9-3 presents an illustrative computational analysis of the CRD network in Figure 9-2. Task durations (days) are given below the resource identifications. Earliest and latest times are computed and appended to each resource node in the same manner as in CPM analysis. RES 1, RES 2, RES 5, and RES 6 form the critical resource path. These resources have no slack times with respect to the completion of the given project.

Note that only one of the two tasks of RES 1 is on the critical resource path. Thus, RES 1 has a slack time for performing one job, but it has no slack time for performing the other. None of the two tasks of RES 4 is on the critical resource path. For RES 3, the task duration is specified as zero. Despite this favorable task duration, RES 3 may turn out to be a bottleneck resource. RES 3 may be a senior manager whose task is that of signing a work order. But if he or she is not available to sign at the appropriate time, then the tasks of several other resources may be adversely affected. A major benefit of a CRD is that both senior-level and lower-level resources can be included in the resource-planning network.

CRD Node Classifications
A *bottleneck* resource node is defined as a node at which two or more arrows merge. In Figure 9-3, RES 3, RES 4, and RES 6 have bottleneck resource nodes. The tasks to which bottleneck resources are assigned should be

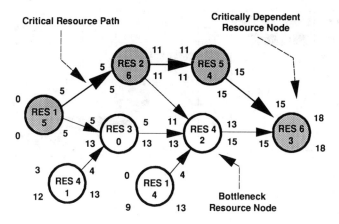

FIGURE 9-3.   Critical Resource Diagram Network Analysis.

expedited in order to avoid delaying dependent resources. A *dependent* resource node is a node whose job depends on the job of the immediately preceding nodes. A *critically dependent* resource node is defined as a node on the critical resource path at which several arrows merge. In Figure 9-3, RES 6 is both a critically dependent resource node as well as a bottleneck resource node. As a scheduling heuristic, it is recommended that activities that require bottleneck resources be scheduled as early as possible. A *burst* resource node is defined as a resource node from which two or more arrows emanate. Like bottleneck resource nodes, burst resource nodes should be expedited since their delay will affect several following resource nodes.

Resource Schedule Chart

The CRD has the advantage that it can be used to model partial assignment of resource units across multiple tasks in single or multiple projects. A companion chart for this purpose is the resource-schedule (RS) chart. Figure 9-4 shows an example of an RS chart based on the earliest times computed in Figure 9-3. A horizontal bar is drawn for each resource unit or resource type. The starting point and the length of each resource bar indicate the interval of work for the resource. Note that the two jobs of RES 1 overlap over a four-day time period. By comparison, the two jobs of RES 4 are separated by a period of six days.

If RES 4 is not to be idle over those six days, "fill-in" tasks must be assigned to it. For resource jobs that overlap, care must be taken to ensure that the resources do not need the same tools (e.g., equipment, computers, lathe, etc.) at the same time. If a resource unit is found to have several jobs overlapping over an extensive period of time, then a task reassignment may

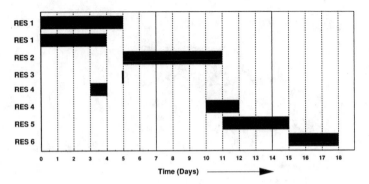

FIGURE 9-4.   Resource Schedule Chart.

be necessary to offer some relief for the resource. The RS chart is useful for a graphical representation of the utilization of resources. Although similar information can be obtained from a conventional resource-loading graph, the RS chart gives a clearer picture of where and when resource commitments overlap. It also shows areas where multiple resources are working concurrently.

CRD and Work Rate Analysis
When resources work concurrently at different work rates, the amount of work accomplished by each may be computed by the procedure for work-rate analysis presented earlier in this chapter. The CRD and the RS chart provide information to identify when, where, and which resources work concurrently.

Example
Suppose that the work rate of RES 1 is such that it can perform a certain task in thirty days. It is desired to add RES 2 to the task so that the completion time of the task could be reduced. The work rate of RES 2 is such that it can perform the same task alone in twenty-two days. If RES 1 has already worked twelve days on the task before RES 2 comes in, find the completion time of the task. Assume that RES 1 starts the task at time zero.

Solution
The amount of work to be done is 1.0 whole unit (i.e., the full task):

The work rate of RES 1 is 1/30 of the task per unit time.
The work rate of RES 2 is 1/22 of the task per unit time.

The amount of work completed by RES 1 in the twelve days it worked alone is $(1/30)(12) = 2/5$ (or 40%) of the required work.

Therefore, the remaining work to be done is 3/5 (or 60 percent) of the full task.

Let T be the time for which both resources work together. The two resources working together to complete the task yield the following table:

Resource Type i	Work Rate, r_i	Time, t_i	Work Done, w_i
RES 1	1/30	T	$T/30$
RES 2	1/22	T	$T/22$
		Total	3/5

That is,

$$T/30 + T/22 = 3/5,$$

which yields $T = 7.62$ days. Thus, the completion time of the task is $(12 + T) = 19.62$ days from time zero. The results of this example are summarized graphically in Figure 9-5. It is assumed that both resources produce identical quality of work and that the respective work rates remain consistent. The respective costs of the different resource types may be incorporated into the work-rate analysis. The CRD and RS chart are simple extensions of very familiar tools. They are simple to use and they convey resource information quickly. They can be used to complement existing resource-management tools. Users can find innovative ways to modify or implement them for specific resource-planning, scheduling, and control purposes. For example,

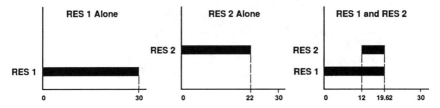

FIGURE 9-5.   Resource Schedule Charts for RES 1 and RES 2.

resource-dependent task durations and resource cost can be incorporated into the CRD and RS procedures to enhance their utility for resource-management decisions.

9.7.2 Resource Loading in Project Management

Resource loading refers to the allocation of resources to work elements in a project network. A resource-loading graph presents a graphical representation of resource allocation over time. Figure 9-6 shows an example of resource-loading graph. A resource-loading graph may be drawn for the different resources types involved in a project.

The graph provides information useful for resource planning and budgeting purposes. A resource-loading graph gives an indication of the demand a project will place on a the available resources. In addition to resource units committed to activities, the graph may also be drawn for other tangible and intangible resources of an organization. For example, a variation of the graph may be used to present information about the depletion rate of the budget available for a project. If drawn for multiple resources, it can help identify potential areas of resource conflicts. For situations where a single resource unit is assigned to multiple tasks, a variation of the resource-loading graph can be developed to show the level of load (responsibilities) assigned to the resource over time. Table 9-1 shows a model of a resource-availability database. The database is essential when planning resource-loading strategies for resource-constrained projects.

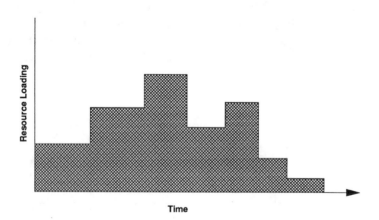

FIGURE 9-6.   Resource-Loading Graph.

TABLE 9-1.   Format for Resource-Availability Database

Resource Type	Brief Description	Special Skills	When Available	Duration of Availability	How Many
Type 1	Technician	Maintenance	8/5/93	Two months	15
Type 2	Programmer	Programming	12/25/93	Indefinite	2
Type 3	Engineer	Design	Immediate	Five years	27
.	.	.	.	.	.
.	.	.	.	.	.
.	.	.	.	.	.
Type $n-1$	Operator	Machining	Always	Indefinite	10
Type n	Industrialist	Financing	9/2/93	Six months	1

9.7.3 Leveling of Resource Allocation

Resource leveling refers to the process of reducing the period-to-period fluctuation in a resource loading graph. If resource fluctuations are beyond acceptable limits, actions are taken to move activities or resources around in order to level out the resource loading graph. For example, it is bad for employee morale and public relations when a company has to hire and lay people off indiscriminately. Proper resource planning will facilitate a reasonably stable level of the work force. Other advantages of resource leveling include simplified resource tracking and control, lower cost of resource management, and improved opportunity for learning. Acceptable resource leveling is typically achieved at the expense of longer project duration or higher project cost. Figure 9-7 shows a somewhat leveled resource loading. When attempting to level resources, it should be noted that:

1. Not all of the resource fluctuations can be eliminated.
2. Resource leveling often leads to an increase in project duration.

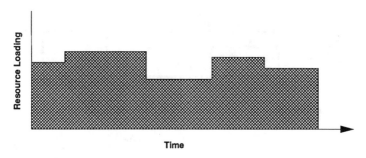

FIGURE 9-7.   Resource-Leveling Graph.

A resource-leveling approach minimizes fluctuations in resource loading by shifting activities within their available slacks. For small networks, resource leveling can be attempted manually through trial-and-error procedures. For large networks, resource leveling is best handled by computer software techniques. Most of the available commercial project-management software packages have resource-leveling capabilities.

9.7.4 Resource-Idleness Analysis

The idleness of critical resources can be analyzed with a resource-idleness graph. A resource-idleness graph is similar to a resource-loading graph except that it is drawn for the number of unallocated resource units over time. The area covered by the resource-idleness graph may be used as a measure of the effectiveness of the scheduling strategy employed for a project. Suppose two scheduling strategies yield the same project duration. Suppose a measure of the resource utilization under each strategy is desired as a means to compare the strategies. Figure 9-8 shows two hypothetical

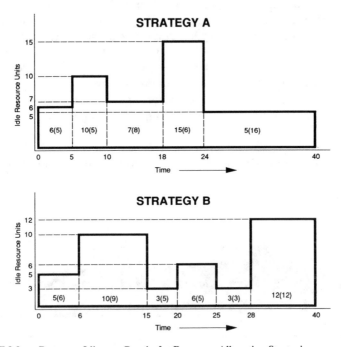

FIGURE 9-8.   Resource-Idleness Graphs for Resource-Allocation Strategies.

resource-idleness graphs for the alternate strategies. The areas are computed as follows:

Area A $= 6(5) + 10(5) + 7(8) + 15(6) + 5(16) = 306$ resource-units time.

Area B $= 5(6) + 10(9) + 3(5) + 6(5) + 3(3) + 12(12)$
$\qquad = 318$ resource-units time

Since Area A is less than Area B, it is concluded that Strategy A is more effective for resource utilization than Strategy B. Similar measures can be developed for multiple resources. However, for multiple resources, the different resource units must all be scaled to dimensionless quantities before computing the areas bounded by the resource-idleness graphs.

9.7.5 Probabilistic Resource Management

In a nondeterministic project environment, probability information can be used to analyze resource-utilization characteristics. Suppose that the level of availability of a resource is probabilistic in nature. For simplicity, we will assume that the level of availability, X, is a continuous variable whose probability density function is defined by $f(x)$. This is true for many resource types such as funds, natural resources, and raw materials. If we are interested in the probability that resource availability will be within a certain range of x_1 and x_2, then the required probability can be computed as:

$$P(x_1 \le X \le x_2) = \int_{x_1}^{x_2} f(x)dx.$$

Similarly, a probability density function can be defined for the use level of a particular resource. If we denote the utilization level by U and its probability density function by $f(u)$, then we can calculate the probability that the utilization will exceed a certain level, u_0, by the following expression:

$$P(U \ge u_0) = \int_{u_0}^{\infty} f(u)du.$$

Example
Suppose a critical resource is leased for a large project. There is a graduated cost associated with using the resource at a certain percentage level, U. The cost is specified as $10,000 per 10-percent increment in utilization level

above 40 percent. A flat cost of $5,000 is charged for use levels below 40 percent. The use intervals and the associated costs are presented below:

$U\ <40\%, \$5,000$
$40\% \le U<50\%, \$10,000$
$50\% \le U<60\%, \$20,000$
$60\% \le U<70\%, \$30,000$
$70\% \le U<80\%, \$40,000$
$80\% \le U<90\%, \$50,000$
$90\% \le U<100\%, \$60,000.$

Thus, a utilization level of 50 percent will cost $20,000, and a level of 49.5 percent will cost $10,000.

Suppose the utilization level is a normally distributed random variable with a mean of 60 percent and a variance of 16 percent squared. Find the expected cost of using this resource.

Solution
The solution procedure involves finding the probability that the use level will fall within each of the specified ranges. The expected-value formula will then be used to compute the expected cost as shown below:

$$E[C] = \sum_k x_k P(x_k),$$

where x_k represents the kth interval of use. The standard deviation of use is 4 percent.

$$P(U<40) = P\left(z \le \frac{40-60}{4}\right) = P(z \le -5) = 0.0$$

$$P(40 \le U<50) = P\left(z<\frac{50-60}{4}\right) - P\left(z \le \frac{40-60}{4}\right)$$
$$= P(z \le -2.5) - P(z \le -5)$$
$$= 0.0062 - 0.0$$
$$= 0.0062$$

$$P(50 \le U<60) = P\left(z<\frac{60-60}{4}\right) - P\left(z \le \frac{50-60}{4}\right)$$
$$= P(z \le 0) - P(z \le -2.5)$$
$$= 0.5000 - 0.0062$$
$$= 0.4938$$

$$P(60 \leq U < 70) = P\left(z < \frac{70 - 60}{4}\right) - P\left(z \leq \frac{60 - 60}{4}\right)$$
$$= P(z \leq 2.5) - P(z \leq 0)$$
$$= 0.9938 - 0.5000$$
$$= 0.4938$$

$$P(70 \leq U < 80) = P\left(z < \frac{80 - 60}{4}\right) - P\left(z \leq \frac{70 - 60}{4}\right)$$
$$= P(z \leq 5) - P(z \leq 2.5)$$
$$= 0.1 - 0.09938$$
$$= 0.0062$$

$$P(80 \leq U < 90) = P\left(z < \frac{90 - 60}{4}\right) - P\left(z \leq \frac{90 - 60}{4}\right)$$
$$= P(z \leq 7.5) - P(z \leq 5)$$
$$= 1.0 - 1.0$$
$$= 0.0$$

$$E(C) = \$5,000(0.0) + \$10,000(0.0062) + \$20,000(0.4938)$$
$$+ \$30,000(0.4938) + \$40,000(0.0062) + \$50,000(0.0)$$
$$= \$25,000.$$

Thus, it can be expected that leasing this critical resource will cost $25,000 in the long run. A decision can be made whether to lease or buy the resource. Resource substitution may also be considered on the basis of the expected cost of leasing.

10

Multinational Industrial Project Management

People are the heart of industry.

This chapter presents an overview of multinational industrial project management. The nature of multinational business, factors that influence multinational projects, a hypothetical case study of the evolution of a multinational industry, and case studies of industrial development projects in Taiwan, Turkey, and Thailand are discussed.

10.1 THE NATURE OF MULTINATIONAL BUSINESS

Multinational business has been viewed by many with suspicion and mixed feelings. Depending on what type of experience a developing nation has had with multinational corporations, there are mixed views about their role and impact on economic growth in developing nations. One school of thought sees multinational businesses as a source for further investment into a growing economy, providing opportunity for higher quality of life, employment, higher wages, growth, and technology transfer. Another school of thought views multinational businesses as an international avenue for economic exploitation, which seeks to drain developing nations of their resources while providing very little in return. Natural resources and cheap labor are often the major considerations for multinational businesses.

There is no wrong or right view. The success of a multinational company will depend on how it conducts and manages its operations and projects around the world. Some developing nations have been criticized for nationalizing huge assets of multinational companies. When trade terms and agreements between multinational firms and host countries are implemented

294

properly, productivity improvement and technological progress can be achieved. The advantages of multinational operations include the following:

1. The expertise of multinational firms in developed countries are transferred to developing countries through management techniques, education, policies, and procedures.
2. The products and services transferred to developing nations provide the basis and sources of technology transfer.
3. Portions of revenues generated from the goods and services are usually reinvested for growth and maintenance of the established firms in the developing countries.
4. Businesses started by multinational companies in developing countries usually provide the basis for local entrepreneurs to start greater ventures in the same product group or related areas.

10.2 PROBLEMS AND ISSUES IN MULTINATIONAL BUSINESS

Industrial development projects require the services of multinational companies. Conversely, multinational businesses need industrial development projects to widen their scope of operations. Thus, mutual understanding and solid business arrangements are essential between host countries and multinational companies. There are several problem areas to review when arranging multinational business operations. These include:

Policies Issues. How major policies are formulated and implemented to guide domestic equity participation, tariffs, foreign exchange control, taxation, labor relations, quotas, and repatriation of earnings. Multinational firms that have performed a thorough analysis of the local operating environment are best able to negotiate with the governments of the host countries for adequate policies that favor industrial growth and business profitability.

Trade Barriers and International Agreements. The various policies governing trading and international operations may be subject to political changes that are sometimes difficult to control. Most developing nations prefer multinational companies to produce their products locally to create employment opportunities for the local work force. Countries that have free trade agreements are usually the best location for multinational investment.

Local Inflation. Inflation in many developing nations is usually higher than in the home countries of many multinational firms. This creates major cost-management problems. To minimize the impact of inflation on cash balance, credit terms, and pricing policy, a thorough analysis of inflationary trend should be performed. This will provide an adequate base for monetary negotiation between the multinational business and the host government.

Balance of Payment. Multinational firms can be faced with the obstacle of currency devaluation resulting from balance-of-payment problems in host countries. Access to foreign currency may also be restricted, and this will limit the ability to acquire essential raw materials, equipment, and tools required to operate in the host country.

Marketing. Multinational companies will discover that product packaging, distribution system, advertising, pricing, product promotion, product design, and manufacturing may need to be tailored to the local conditions and needs of the host country. Marketing could be an expensive task. Enormous product and process design modification are bound to have an impact on product cost, even though there may be advantages in cheap labor, tax relief, and free trade agreements.

Business Management. In most emerging economies, the level of literacy may be very low. A sizeable percentage of the work force may be illiterate or semiliterate. There is a strong possibility of shortage of the adequate business-management skills needed to run day-to-day operations. This is especially acute in the areas of engineering, production, operations management, and other technical areas. Multinational firms have to be willing to invest in education and training of the work force to obtain the right management skills required.

Nationalism. In the attempt to boost economic and industrial welfare, some developing nations have resorted to nationalizing the assets of multinationals. The nationalization is often done through surprise government policies and regulations. To provide a stable industrial environment, what is needed is a fair and equitable trade agreement by multinational companies and host countries. Problems are bound to exist when either the multinational firms or the host governments attempt to dominate in revenue share and other business matters.

Licensing. Licensing is one avenue to generate profits from a market that cannot be served through export. A license can be granted to a foreign firm to produce and market a product. The foreign firm pays royalties to the parent firm. This approach can lead to market restrictions and confusion about the line of authority for product-development operations. It also can create logistic problems involving service, product quality, warranty, pricing, and product promotion.

These are just a few of the potential problems that a multinational company might face. They can impede the project-management functions of multinational companies. The Triple C model of communication, cooperation, and coordination should be implemented to work out mutually beneficial details of multinational operations.

10.3 MULTINATIONAL PRODUCT DISTRIBUTION

The products of a multinational company can be distributed through several channels. Export is a major channel for international product distribution. Export can be accomplished through the following strategies:

1. *Use of Marketing Subsidiary Abroad.* This usually requires a thorough market analysis that would guarantee the necessary product volume to attain maximum sales potential. A marketing subsidiary can be operated by individuals or through joint ventures with the host country.
2. *Use of Well-Established Exporter.* Well-established exporters in most developed countries are usually very efficient. They have seed capital, insurance, and expertise in multinational business. This is a reliable channel for export.
3. *Manufacturer's Representative and Import Centers Abroad.* The manufacturer's representative import centers are good channels if their owners are highly knowledgeable about product availability, marketing, promotion, and distribution systems.

Multinational production can be accomplished through licensing when export mechanisms are not effective. It also can be handled through joint ventures between multinational firms and host governments or individuals. Multinational production can also be done through wholly owned subsidiary, in which case the parent firm owns 100 percent of the overseas facility. In developing countries that require majority local ownership of businesses, production can be arranged with the multinational business having a minority participation.

Operating a multinational business in a developing country may not be easy primarily because of such issues as trade barriers and agreements, lack of political stability, of adequate monetary policy, and of local skilled labor required to run the business effectively. However, enormous opportunities exist in developing nations for new product, expansion of market share for existing product, and the availability of mineral and human resources, including cheap labor. Multinational companies planning to do business in developing nations must be flexible enough to adapt business strategies to conditions that are operative in the host countries. The following is a checklist that can be used for potential industry study by multinational firms considering doing business in a developing nation:

Political, Legal, and Social Considerations
- Government stability.
- Consumer tastes.
- Trade laws and regulation.
- Trends in government policies.
- Consumer behavior.
- Others.

Market structure/Methods/Profitability
- Patterns of successful firms.
- Patterns of unsuccessful firms.
- Market concentration.
- Competition.
- Distribution channels.
- Methods of selling.
- Cost trends.
- Product cycle/profit analysis.
- Market dominance.
- Market forecast.
- Pricing.
- Advertising and promotion channels.
- Profit trends.

- Industry associations.
- Value added by manufacture.
- Inflationary trends.

History of Industry in Operative Environment
- Local technology available.
- Economic stability impact.
- Product limitations.
- Functions of product.
- Technological threats and opportunities.
- Rate of innovation.
- Others.

Investment/Currency Evaluation
- Cost of entry.
- Fixed and working capital requirements.
- Monetary policies and currency strength.
- Stability of local currency.
- Import and export of raw material costs.
- Capital required for maintenance activities.
- Local content costs.
- Others.

Employment/Resource management

- Manpower availability by skill group.

- Labor-management relations.

- Employment levels.

- Labor-capital relationships.

- Raw material availability.

- Others.

10.4 FACTORS AFFECTING MULTINATIONAL PROJECTS

Businesses and projects that cross national boundaries either in concept or essence have characteristics that, if not recognized, can hinder management functions. In multinational projects, individual organizational policies are not enough to govern operations. Factors that normally influence these projects are:

Factors That Affect Multinational Projects

- Health, weather, and environmental considerations.

- Trade agreements.

- National security concerns.

- National productivity level.

- Traditional national allies and adversaries.

- Strategic military positions.

- Territorial laws and regulations.

- Foreign currency exchange rates.

- Time differences.
- Different stages of industrialization.
- Paperwork, permits, and restrictions.
- Poor, slow, or impossible communications links.
- Protection of technological information.
- Different scientific standards of measure.
- National extradition/protection agreements.
- Taxes, duties, and other import/export charges.
- Geographical segregation and restricted access.
- Different labor practices.
- Different governmental and political ideologies.

International communication is one of the most difficult to deal with. The task of international transfer of technology and mutual project support takes on critical dimensions because of differences in the structures, objectives, and interests of the different countries involved. One common communication problem is that information destined for another country may have to pass through several levels of approval before reaching the point of use. The information is subject to all types of distortions and perils in its business journey. The case study presented in the next section illustrates the complexity of managing multinational industrial projects.

10.5 EVOLUTION OF A MULTINATIONAL INDUSTRY: A CASE STUDY

This case study is based on an industrial management essay competition conducted by the Institutional Shareholder Services of Washington, DC (INS, 1987). The case study illustrates the complexity of managing a multinational company that evolved from a simple family-owned business. The problems presented in the case study are typical of what may be faced by any company. Multinational organizations around the world are faced with political, social, and cultural problems similar to those it illustrates.

As one of the essayists put it:

> The business corporation is the cornerstone of a free society. Organizing
> society's resources in a corporate form enables us to combine financial and
> intellectual capital and labor to maximize the return to all parties. The corporate
> form is what makes a free society possible. The accountability of those who
> provide work to those who provide the capital enables us to keep interference
> from the government at a minimum. Resources that would otherwise be spent
> regulating can be allocated elsewhere. The development of the modern
> corporation has been a major factor in improving the quality of life. (INS,
> 1987, p. 1)

Universal Products Corporation

Universal Products Corporation (UP) is a huge industrial manufacturer of
diesels, gas, and steam turbines, electrical goods such as generators and
relays, gardening equipment, household goods, and plastics. In 1986, it was
thirty-sixth on the Fortune 500 list of the largest corporations in America. It
owns a mini-network of six television and radio stations, a restaurant and
hotel chain, and is a haulage contractor. It also runs a small financial-services
subsidiary that offers mortgages to UP employees below market rates that
become more favorable for each five years of employment with UP.

It has facilities in ten states, among them Indiana, Michigan, and Virginia,
and in fourteen countries around the world. About 75 percent of UP's sales
are to private companies or individuals. The remaining 25 percent are
largely performed on contract for the U.S. Department of Defense. UP is the
prime contractor on several important weapon programs. The present chief
executive officer of UP is David Buchanan. A graduate of the University of
Michigan and of Stanford Law School, Mr. Buchanan joined the company in
1965. He was vice-president (finance), then moved to public relations, where
he was vice-president and senior vice-president. He has been chief executive
since 1982.

Historical Background of UP

UP is the descendant of the Southern Indiana Industrial Manufacturing
Corporation. L. M. Zachary, founder of the Southern Indiana Agricultural
Manufacturing Corporation (SI) bought out his principal competitor, the
Machine Tool Company of Detroit, in 1912. Both firms made a variety of
agricultural tools. SI also made steam engines and some early electronic
motors. Machine Tool made light industrial lathes and saws. Zachary was
one of the last of the robber barons, a ruthless industrialist, aggressive and

relentless. If that was not enough to increase business or beat out a competitor, he was willing to be dishonest with competitors and customers. The son of a man who died in his early thirties from occupational disease, Zachary had a firm commitment to his workers' health and safety. He often said that it was in the company's interest to attract and keep good workers and to keep them around long enough to benefit from their expertise.

Zachary died just before World War I, and was succeeded by his nephew, Francis L. Philips. The sudden collapse of farm prices in 1910 had depressed the market for farm tools. Philips redirected the company's resources to the development and manufacture of engines, especially diesel engines. As the United States supplied munitions to the allies in 1914–1917, and after the United States entered the war, SI grew rapidly and changed from a regional toolmaker into a national industrial engine manufacturer. Spurred by Philips's patriotism and moral zeal for the war effort, SI became one of the earliest firms to set up full diesel mass-production lines. It quickly became preeminent in diesel manufacture during the 1920s, and this superiority was reinforced until contacts with German heavy engineering technology were cut off in 1933.

In 1921, SI went public and was listed on the New York Stock Exchange. The Zachary family, however, retained a 40-percent share. The stock market crash and depression hit SI badly. As with other companies serving American agriculture, SI's markets completely evaporated with the drop in farm prices. Francis Philips's sense of personal responsibility for his employees made him determined not to cut any jobs at SI. He paid off his creditors by cutting employees' wages to subsistence levels and by issuing a large amount of preferred stock and senior debt. To compensate employees for their drop in wages, Philips gave each worker shares of common stock in SI based on a formula that took into account the employee's years of service to SI. The increased debt and dilution of his own existing common stock severely diminished Philips's personal fortune. Much was restored, and many employees became millionaires, as the value of their stock increased sixfold by 1950. Philips was an ardent supporter of the New Deal policy of the U.S. government and served as chairman of one of the industrial committees established to coordinate industrial productivity with the development of common standards.

Francis Philips died in 1936. His successor as chief executive was Charles Gregory. Gregory changed Southern Indiana's name to UP Corporation in 1940, to reflect its national and more universal scope. Gregory was the son of immigrants. His first job in the company was to tighten screws on the assembly line. A patriotic individual, Gregory was also a shrewd self-publicist who recognized the importance of maintaining good relations with Washington and the War Department. He built strongly upon Philips's ties with

Washington. World War II more than restored American fortunes and, as in the previous conflict, SI was conspicuously successful in responding to wartime pressures. UP was an important defense contractor, and Gregory hired a large number of ex-officers as consultants to keep it that way. He also established the Philips Award, one of the most prestigious and lucrative research grants in the field of public policy.

UP built on its rapid wartime growth with extensive international expansion, in particular in South America and the Far East. By 1945, it had doubled its prewar size. Charles Gregory stepped down in 1952, and his successor, Robert Elkins, proved to be a poor choice. He set two important goals: diversification of products and consolidation of production. Both proved disastrous. In the early 1960s, under Elkins's direction, UP underwent a period of wild growth, buying TV stations, department stores, and a large hotel and restaurant group. In line with the then-prevailing passion for vertical integration, UP also bought four suppliers of product parts. These acquisitions were paid for by several large issues of UP's own securities.

After the wrenching changes that followed the depression, UP had refinanced most of its outstanding debts during the 1950s. Ten years later, the capital structure of the firm was dramatically altered once again. The new share issuance diluted the substantial holdings of the company's employees, and of the Zachary family.

Although it had initially appeared successful, by the mid-1980s UP's strategy of diversification had failed. The new businesses had little in common, so that attractive economies evaporated. Worse, the firm suffered a failure of industrial purpose. It became unclear what the function of UP was, what businesses it was in, what specifically it stood for. By 1970 the company was making so many products and so many kinds of products, using so many techniques, for so many different markets, under such varying competitive conditions, that it lost its focus in the industries that it knew and for which it had provided industrial leadership. Finally, its competitiveness in even those industries began to decline. Within the company, bureaucracy began to spread. Even the most talented and dedicated employees found the lack of a clearly articulated sense of corporate values and culture and the textbook formulas used to set managerial priorities very unsettling.

Elkins tried to consolidate UP's commercial and military operations, hoping for economies of scale and shorter lines of communication. Unfortunately, he acted without any grasp of the different corporate cultures that existed within UP commercial and government-contracting facilities, and his attempted consolidation resulted in the worst of both worlds. Commercial and military contract employees were kept on dual tracks in the hope of promoting competition between them. Employees on the firm's commercial contracts quickly perceived that they worked harder and were paid less than their peers working on military contracts, because on the military contracts, for which the federal government paid the bills, UP could set higher profit levels. The productivity of employees on the commercial side declined. When wage contracts were renegotiated, UP had little choice but to meet the commercial employees' demands for full parity of work and pay. This began a pattern of granting pay raises unrelated to productivity and of passing the extra costs on to the consumer.

New Vision

In 1960, the key figure of the company's next twenty-five years arrived at UP. His name was David Buchanan. A graduate of the University of Michigan and Stanford Law School, he began work at UP just after he graduated. In 1965, when he was a vice-president in the finance department, he first came to the attention of Elkins's replacement, Robert Diggle. Diggle hired the Boston Consulting Group to prepare a financial and operational survey of UP and assigned Buchanan to act as liaison. Diggle was surprised to find the consulting firm's 200-page report accompanied by an unsolicited 35-page memorandum by Buchanan. It was not only an analysis of UP's current operations, but a manifesto for the future.

Buchanan's analysis began with the assertion that all corporate decisions are driven by managers' calculation of risk. A shoddily made product, for example, could be seen as demonstrating a firm's willingness to tolerate the risk of poor publicity and low sales against the benefit of a higher profit margin. The decision to make a reliable, high-quality product, on the other hand, demonstrated the firm's willingness to invest more up front to gain the benefits of customer loyalty. Buchanan used the example of Zachary's decision to protect employees from occupational health and safety hazards as an early, crude, but essentially correct risk/benefit analysis. A decision to build a new plant versus retrofitting an old one, to bring out a new product versus a change in advertising for the old one, to purchase a supplier versus deploying those resources elsewhere, all were occasions for balancing risks and benefits, and the key question then was the accuracy of the calculations.

The problem, as he identified it, was that all decisions are made on the basis of some kind of cost/benefit or risk/benefit analysis but that most of those analyses were too narrow in scope and too unquantified in calculation. Buchanan recommended more comprehensive central planning and more attention to finding ways to keep costs down, in order to maximize the range of choices.

Routine cost control was normally an ordinary matter of corporate self-discipline. Often, however, what was claimed as cost cutting was, in fact, cost avoidance. The burden would inevitably fall somewhere. It was often less expensive to shift the cost to others. For example, a firm could decide that the cost of installing a new water filter on an effluent pipe was greater than its likely share of any clean-up costs, expressed as taxes, plus any legal liability. Managers' incentives tended to reinforce the habit of cost avoidance. The amortization of the cost of the filter would be a direct charge to earnings, and promotion normally depended on an ability to produce the necessary figures. If the amortization was front-end loaded, so much the worse; the bulk of the charge would fall during the manager's own tenure, paving the way for the promotion of his successor.

Too often, risk/benefit decisions were based on a microanalysis. The bottom line reflects the limitations of the worldview or the accounting system of those doing the calculations. In one instance that Buchanan documented, a division of UP was directed to cut personnel costs. They had simply divided some of the government weapons contracting, which had been confined to one plant, among three plants. Since the work was classified, those plants could no longer use unskilled UP workers as janitors and security guards. They were able to lay off those low-paid employees and contract with outside firms for cleaning crews and security guards with the requisite clearances. The total costs went up, of course (in addition to the extra costs of spreading the contract work among three plants), but those costs were assessed against the Defense Department or the UP umbrella organization, rather than the division. Thus, the division director met his goals and presented the correct bottom line.

Buchanan suggested a broader perspective to provide an alternative to direct cost avoidance. Financial costs arose from two main sources, from the market power of a company's suppliers, creditors, customers, and employees, and from the network of federal and state regulations within which the company operated. If UP could exercise influence over those parties, it could achieve some control over its competitive environment. He listed examples from the histories of the largest companies in America and suggested ways in which UP could do the same. The means he suggested was a strategy he called *indispensabilism.* There were two ways to achieve it. First, UP could concentrate on products that, by quality and originality, gave UP access to a market virtually free from competition. Second, UP could control the various parties that set its costs. The first step for both was to increase UP's influence by making the company a still bigger defense contractor.

Indispensabilism 1: The XM-4 Contract

Buchanan prepared a plan of action, and Diggle told him to go ahead and implement it. Under Buchanan's direction, UP developed a unique fuel-delivery system ideally suited for tanks. UP also began to lobby for the contract to produce the engine, transmission, and exhaust systems of the new M-80 tank in 1966. The company orchestrated a mail campaign to selected congressmen and made large pre-election donations. It used trade organizations, advisory committees, and its long-standing relationship with the Defense Department to gain access to demonstrate its unique capabilities to key decision makers. UP vastly expanded a small plant in Seattle, Washington, because it was in the congressional district of the chairman of the Ways and Means Committee.

UP then formed an informal alliance with the General Engine Corporation. Together, they managed to exploit internal bickering and division at the Pentagon to get the M-80 project shelved in favor of a far larger tank built to small services specification consistent with the designs that they (and other cocontractors) had developed. The new tank would fulfill two, previously thought incompatible, functions, and it would be full of the very latest technology. When the specifications were released by the Department of Defense, they included the requirement for the fuel-delivery system developed by, patented by, and exclusively manufactured by UP.

The new tank, called the XM-4 (the X prefix denoted the experimental model), proved to be disastrous from the very start. Its testing was carried out in great secrecy. The XM-4 broke down frequently in conditions far better than typical battlefield conditions. Its range was much shorter than expected because of its 50-ton weight; but this was irrelevant since its air filters became quickly clogged. At the insistence of a three-star general, its engine had been upgraded from a diesel to a gas turbine, which caused lengthy production delays, and which rendered several standard tank tactics impossible. The new tank's highly sophisticated "shoot on the move" capability requiring a laser range finder and computerized turret-stabilization device worked so badly that testing crews soon requested that an on-off switch be fitted so that the gun could be fired manually, thus giving it a tolerable degree of accuracy. The engine system, particularly the new fuel-delivery system, worked very well. But the tank as a whole was ineffective.

The M-4 proved to be very expensive also. Part of the reason lay in the production delays and constant upgrading of the tank, which caused previously stockpiled spares to become obsolete. There was a more profound reason, however. In order to keep the early cost estimates down for the M-4 (and thus get the contract), UP and General Engine had deliberately produced a vehicle that was cheap to buy rather than cheap to operate. It had used low-quality parts without regard to their durability, or the cost of repairs and replacement. The effects of this decision had been made possible by Defense Department practices. Much of the tank's testing had been deferred, limited, or performed out of sequence, so that problems were not identified early enough.

The contractors succeeded in keeping the facts hidden until the final congressional appropriations investigation. This was done by a combination of several practices: failing to write off the useless spare parts immediately; extrapolating cost basis from the first production run, when the tanks were at their cheapest; by aggregating the hundreds of contracts, all at differing stages of completion, into a huge and largely undifferentiated package, and a host of other shrewd techniques. When the final figures came out, there was an uproar since the total cost of the M-4 program had doubled. By then, the army had invested so much in the tank, politically and financially, that it could not afford to give up on it.

At congressional oversight hearings, the secretary of the army pronounced himself highly satisfied with the results and denounced those who felt that an improved procurement system or overall purchasing strategy might have spent less money to produce a better result. This was supplemented by a further intense lobbying effort on the part of the contractors and by the Defense Department's claim that it simply would not be economical to shelve the program. Too much money had already been sunk into it. These revelations came out during an election year; political expediency demanded an informal agreement by both sides of Congress to drop the matter quickly, and they did so.

Indispensabilism 2: Environmental-Impact Liability

David Buchanan's successful defense initiative led to a transfer from finance to public relations as vice-president. In traditional UP terms, this was thought to be a comedown, but Buchanan actively sought the position, and he made sure that he was able to maintain most of his line authority, while pursuing a second aspect of his strategy. He had argued in his 1965 memo that corporations respond almost mechanistically to changes in the profit-loss equation. Because the goal is to make the greatest possible profit, managers will all but automatically accept whatever projects most improve the bottom line. Factors such as where the projects take place and whom they affect are only considered in so far as they affect profitability, and only then in the limited context of the particular set of costs and profits being matched against each other.

Theoretically, at least two more important constraints existed; the active involvement of the firm's shareholders, and the ebb and flow of public opinion. In practice, the stockholders were less important; most publicly owned companies had thousands of owners, and no single one possessed a stage large enough to justify the expense of a canvass of other owners. In theory, shareholders could ascertain and then remedy fraud or incompetence by gathering support and voting down management at an annual or special meeting. In practice, that process was expensive and uncertain. Shareholders followed the Wall Street rule: vote with management, or sell the stock.

Buchanan argued that the original concept of corporate management's accountability to the owners with a long-term commitment to the firm was out of date. As the ownership of American corporations became more and more widely dispersed, the owners' sense of ownership disappeared altogether. Over time, shareholders came to treat their shares not as property, but as little more than betting slips. Putting money on UP, or any other corporation, came to seem like putting it on a race horse, although the shareholder retained the capacity to sell the stock (and thus end the race) at any time.

The external regulation of business had been set in place partially to replace the functions of active, committed, and powerful shareholders. And public opinion could produce an equally strong regulatory effect, directly and indirectly. Buchanan's motivation for seeking the public relations position was his belief that UP could and should mold public opinion. During the M-4 program and after, Buchanan had learned a lot about developing the means to influence public opinion. In this context, one of the major benefits of UP's diversification had been political. By acquiring a wide range of companies, UP had become powerful in many more Congressional districts than before, allowing it to exercise correspondingly greater leverage on Capitol hill.

Buchanan began by overhauling UP's public relations division. He worked for progress companywide. Internal improvements included better communication between management and employees (a company newsletter with job opportunities at UP, housing and car sale notices, and employee awards, suggestion boxes, with each suggestion personally read and answered by Buchanan himself, frequent brown bag lunches with management for any employees who wanted to attend), skills training and fully competitive salary and bonus schemes, and day care centers for workers' children (Buchanan's cost/benefit analysis showed that it reduced absenteeism, improved productivity, and boosted loyalty and morale).

To improve external relations, Buchanan developed better quality controls, delivery and customer service, and made a policy of patronizing local businesses, involving executives in local politics, and granting leave to employees for community work. Next, UP adopted a mission statement concisely presenting UP's goals and means of achieving them, and that statement was fully and consistently reinforced by its trademarks, slogans, and logos. He established five further areas of corporate involvement to improve public relations: the arts, sports, health, education and research, and the nonprofit sector. UP underwrote an urban redevelopment project in Indianapolis and sponsored important long-term research into advanced supercooling and refrigeration systems at the California Institute of Technology. Its hotel and restaurant chain were depositories for an annual collection of toys for sick and underprivileged children. UP was a major corporate sponsor of the Olympics, and of a travelling exhibit of the works of Andrew Wyeth. UP underwrote a public television series about wildlife.

These ideas were developed over the period 1970–1972. From mid-1973 on, Buchanan assembled a team and began to review UP's existing operations to see if he could make operational or strategic improvements. He quickly ran into trouble at UP's defense manufacturing plant in Newport, Virginia. A proprietary chemical technology had been in use there for twelve years, and UP, like other local manufacturers, used outside contractors to dispose of the highly toxic waste chemicals at a site nearby. Buchanan's staff drew attention to this as potentially highly dangerous. Their suggestions for improvements were met with outright hostility and stalling, however, from senior management and the plant's employees. They could not justify expensive change because they were satisfied that their legal liability was minimal.

In fact, their attorneys advised them that their liability could increase if they acknowledged a problem and failed to take adequate steps to remedy it. After a task force of employees from the plant, from public relation, from the legal staff, and from headquarters was unable to agree on appropriate action, they decided to invite the Environmental Protection Agency (EPA) into the plant. They agreed that they would abide by the agency's recommendations, which would shield the company from legal liability. An EPA inspector came in and found (as hoped) that the facility met or exceeded all applicable standards and issued a formal finding to that effect.

Five years later, however, in February 1979, UP was named as the defendant in a $30-million lawsuit charging the company with gross negligence and malicious conduct. The suit had been filed by five families living near a chemical disposal site that had been used by UP and several other manufacturing firms. The children of the five families had a statistically high outbreak of leukemia, which they claimed had been caused by toxic waste leaking into their water supply. Their allegations were based in part on a five-part investigative story in the local newspaper, the *Tribune*. On discovery, the facts provided, at best, a circumstantial case against UP. Because the company did not appear to have violated any state of federal statues, the plaintiffs had to sue under the common law of torts. Common law placed a very strong burden of proof on the plaintiff to demonstrate cause and effect.

David Buchanan was, by that time, senior vice-president. It was a measure of his personal indispensability that he had achieved this rank while still in charge of UP's public relations. He was responsible for controlling any damage from the lawsuit. He flew to Newport and held an immediate press conference, then stayed up all night working out the legal strategy that would underpin UP's public relations. Temporary headquarters had been set up, and telephone hot lines were installed. UP then revealed that it was suing the *Tribune* for libel and that it had retained an independent panel of experts to report on any contamination and what caused it. The affected towns were supplied with bottled water and other amenities, paid for out of an escrow fund set up against the findings of the panel.

Buchanan and his team devoted a great deal of time and effort to coordinating the national TV and press coverage and working with the EPA to confirm its earlier report. Buchanan also worked hard to placate UP's work force. He wrote a reassuring letter that was immediately sent to stockholders and issued a series of press releases and advertisements explaining the company's position to a wider public. Buchanan's efforts were helped by UP's Maymont Market project, a program of urban redevelopment in the center of Richmond. That program had helped him form good relationships with civic leaders, local labor chiefs, church groups, and the press. This work paid off. Coverage was balanced with some favorable editorials endorsing UP's response.

During the late summer of 1979, there were rumors that Congress, when it reconvened, would thoroughly investigate the contamination. To forestall an adversarial investigation, Buchanan arranged to have the record examined, not by any of the environmental committees, but by the highly conservative Employment and Productivity Subcommittee of the Senate Labor Committee, on the grounds that the issue was not of death from poisoning, but of national competitiveness and the threat to jobs from overstringent regulation. When the committee report came out, it was highly critical of existing federal law and called for Congress to take legislative action. Echoing some of the analysis in Buchanan's 1965 memo, the report concluded that high technology in industry was inevitably risky; how much risk was acceptable to society was, in effect, a political decision. As the maker of that decision and the bearer of ultimate liability, the government should recognize its responsibilities. If a company could not be held harmless after taking care to abide by all applicable law, there was nothing it could rely on.

UP's attitude was sympathetic. Though UP was innocent of culpability, its lawyers were ruthless. Every weapon in the armory of deep-pockets litigation was used in the effort to kill off the lawsuit by exhausting the plaintiff's resources before trial. Attorneys were sent all over the country in search of expert witnesses. Dozens of depositions were taken, in many cases lasting for several days and each requiring the presence of the witness, $200-an-hour opposing counsel, and a stenographer. The records showing what chemicals had been disposed of at the dump were incomplete and of questionable accuracy. Not even the companies who had used the dump were sure of all that had been deposited there over the past thirty years. Two of the companies that had used the dump had gone bankrupt. For these, there were no records at all.

Expert witnesses were brought in from around the world to advise the lawyers on the possible link between chemical exposure and cancer. The medical records of the plaintiff families going back three generations were demanded so that all possible other causes of the leukemia were evaluated. By January 1980 it had become clear that the question of UP's guilt or innocence was, in a sense, irrelevant. The plaintiffs felt toxic tort law was relatively undeveloped and the burdens of proof of common law, unfairly harsh, and that they lacked the legal resources to continue. Without legal grounds for hope, the financial resources of their lawyers (who were working for contingency fees) could not continue the litigation.

The community's dependence on UP as one of the few remaining local industries and the placating effect of the company's quick action in convening the panel of experts and providing bottled water and other amenities made it unlikely that the plaintiffs could find a sympathetic jury willing to reach into the company's deep pockets to pay the parents of the sick children. The plaintiffs accepted a modest settlement contingent on their agreeing in writing that the company's waste-disposal methods were not the cause of any disease.

Indispensabilism 3: The Embargo

In 1981, UP had begun negotiations with a Soviet company to provide turbines and compressors for the natural gas pipeline that the former Soviet Union (USSR) was building. Just before closure of the agreement, however, UP learned that the U.S. government was concerned about the worsening position in Poland, about Europe becoming dependent upon the USSR for energy, and about the Soviet Union acquiring such a large source of foreign exchange. The White House, in fact, might very well prohibit exports of pipeline supplies altogether. UP's response was simple and quick. Reasoning that the ban could only apply to U.S. firms, it quickly had the contracts concluded by its own French subsidiary. As predicted, in January 1982 the U.S. president imposed an embargo on all gas and oil equipment or technology shipments made by American companies in connection with the pipeline.

To UP's dismay, however, this was extended five months later to include all subsidiaries licensed, owned, or controlled by U.S. nationals. The firm quickly joined with Dresser Industries and Creusot-Loire, which had been similarly affected, to contest the embargo. Several other unwitting and entirely innocent English, French, and German firms had also been caught by a provision prohibiting exports licensed by American companies. They joined UP's legal and publicity actions. The affected companies were helped by the outrage expressed by the major European nations at American high-handedness and by a leaked CIA document that showed that the USSR would meet all its gas-delivery commitments in Europe by 1984, on schedule, with or without the ban. Finally, without a face-saving solution, the White House caved in. In a straight face-off between America and its allies; a face-off orchestrated by multinational corporate interests; a pragmatically effective and ideologically determined president had been thwarted on a key issue of foreign policy in a matter of months.

UP in the 1980s

In 1982 UP had made its rapidly expanding industrial products business into a new, autonomous, division. Rather than simply buy new land and build the new facility that would be necessary to house the consolidated headquarters division, UP put the plant out to competitive bid among the states, advertising the jobs and revenue it would produce. Citicorp had done precisely the same thing only a few years earlier with its credit card operation, creating a furious bidding war between the states. In Citicorp's case, South Dakota, not previously thought of as one of the major financial centers of America, had succeeded.

UP's tender proved to be even more competitive than Citicorp's for three reasons: 1982 was a year of elections, recession, and high unemployment. Sixteen governors and representatives of five other states made the trip to UP's headquarters in Indiana to pitch for the new plant. They brought with them a dazzling array of promises, grants, exemptions, subsidies, and discounts. Cheap electricity, housing, job training, mortgages, and other loans; free land, access roads, and daycare for employees' children; and a list of tax holidays and exemptions were among the inducements offered by the states.

UP worked hard to encourage the states to give more away, feeding information to each player and to the press. Finally, UP disclosed that it had been negotiating from the start with several foreign countries. Seduced by the Thatcher government in Great Britain, it had decided to build the new plant in Northern Ireland, just outside conflict-riddled Belfast. The various sweeteners in the offer would save the firm almost $700 million over twenty years; more than enough to offset the political uncertainty of life in Northern Ireland.

UP scheduled a meeting of the Board for January 11, 1988, to address UP's competitive strategy for the next three to five years and to decide capital budgeting accordingly. The Committee was to consider four alternatives: the development of a new range of jet engines, the expansion of UP Finance into a full-fledged mortgage and credit house, an acquisition or divestiture program, and a stock repurchase. Each of UP's senior managers had a great deal at stake in the decision on the future direction of the company, and each person began to lobby extensively for the option that, from idealism or self-interest, or both, he or she supported.

By 1988, David Buchanan had been chief executive for five years. In addition, he had been chairman of UP's board of directors during that time. As was once traditional among major U.S. corporations, all but four of the eighteen directors of UP were members of senior management. The key finance and compensation committees of the board were entirely comprised of insiders; only the audit committee had a majority of independent directors because it was required by the listing standards of the New York Stock Exchange. The four independent directors were selected by Buchanan. One was the trustee for the Zachary family trust, and of the other three, one was a black woman who had been an assistant secretary of Treasury, one was Hispanic, president of a state university, and the last was a woman who had been the first female admiral. Each of the outside directors was paid a large stipend and received numerous other benefits designed to encourage loyalty to UP's management.

Just after the new year, the Clark Equipment Company, a close neighbor of UP in Indiana, was abruptly taken over by Merrion Corp., causing great speculation and great anxiety at UP about its own future, anxiety that was reflected at the budget meeting a week later. The proposal of the finance division was presented first. Their recommendation was to move the company into commercial mortgages, into the aircraft and ship leasing business, and into other investment banking functions. The manufacturing division then presented its recommendation. The manufacture of a new range of highly fuel-efficient jet engines for the military was proposed. The final two proposals, for an acquisition or divestiture, and for a stock buyback, were more contentious, for historical reasons.

UP had recovered completely from its floundering under the direction of Robert Elkins, having sold off most of its irrelevant earlier purchases. The wisdom of an acquisition program, however, remained open to doubt. Like all publicly held firms, UP was in two businesses: its commercial operations and the business of managing its performance in the stock market. Starting in the early 1960s, a large group of UP's top management increasingly viewed its primary consumers not as those who purchased its products but as those who purchased its stock. UP's chief financial officer, John Harrison, was the leader of that group. As a practical matter, UP continuously bought or sold its own stock, either to make money or to send signal to the marketplace. At the January meeting, Harrison supported a more comprehensive stock-purchase program, believing that it would inject some extra vigor into its per-share earnings.

The stock buyback was heatedly debated. Its effects were fairly clear; it would act as a market signal, raising the price of the company's outstanding shares without incurring the tax drawbacks of a one-time payout or increased dividend. It would improve earnings per share, and the repurchased stock would be used to fund managers' stock options. Several of the directors saw a different purpose behind the buyback, however. To them it was merely a paper means of ensuring performance, without any really productive investment in plant or labor. Its true purpose would be to deter takeover by loading up the balance sheet with debt and, thus, making UP less attractive to raiders: possibly, the repurchased shares would be used, with altered warrants, as a poison pill, designed to cripple the company to prevent a suitor from buying it. On this proposal, as with the others, the directors were sharply divided.

The finance committee, which was responsible for presenting all four options to the board, recommended a mixed strategy with the further expansion into defense contracting as its centerpiece. Chief Executive David Buchanan deliberately overrode the finance committee's recommendation. In its place he substituted the first stage of a plan he had designed himself to guarantee UP's power and influence until well into the twenty-first century. He announced that UP would begin a limited repurchase of its stock immediately.

David Buchanan's decision stunned the other directors. To them it was an incomprehensible and almost arbitrary act. In fact, however, Buchanan's plan was the direct, linear result of his general analysis of corporate activity since the mid-1960s and of his corporate gospel of *indispensabilism* and *independence*. These two ideas amounted to a single goal, to be "inside" a society enough to allow indispensability, "outside" enough to avoid any particular penalties, costs, or constraints. The question was, which society? UP was now competing globally, vying for business with other multinational companies that were subject to less restrictive antitrust laws and government regulations. Practically speaking, UP could easily move its legal domicile with huge potential benefits.

It could maintain very strong contacts with the United States, while enjoying the legal protections of a different country altogether, protections that its American competitors would not enjoy. The legal rights would be enshrined in treaties, normally friendship, commerce, and navigation treaties, that each signatory country would be required to observe. Traditionally, the United States' desire to open up new export markets had made it very willing to enter into such treaties, and even in 1987, when its global economic hegemony was seriously threatened by Japan, it continued to give foreigners exceptional latitude to do business within its borders.

David Buchanan had decided to move UP, to "denationalize" it, to free it from American legal regulation. At the same time, he determined to nullify the vestiges of UP's shareholders' capacity to influence the company or hold its management answerable for their actions. More accurately, he would simply transfer ownership to those who could be encouraged not to exercise it. Since the shareholders had no long-term commitment to their ownership, it could be taken away from them without a backlash. Almost half of UP's shareholders were institutions, pension funds, mutual funds, insurance companies, and banks. Their obligation as fiduciaries would predispose them favorably toward any above-market offer. The stock buyback would gain time for Buchanan to enact the rest of his plan. It was, thus, the beginning of UP's final drive for independence, for a kind of power that might prove commercially and economically dominant in the twenty-first century.

David Buchanan believed that UP should make itself indispensable to all the countries with which it traded and directly accountable to none. First, as the global economy changed, the sheer economics of profitability and competition required UP to seek the lowest cost sources of land, labor, and capital worldwide. Of course, as other corporations came to understand this, each firm's income would decline; but there would be a premium to the early comer.

Second, there was virtually nothing a sufficiently determined multinational couldn't do to advance its own interests against those of a single state or nation state. Third, a multinational's chief offensive weapon would be the sovereignty of states itself, which required each to respect another's laws. Some country or other would doubtless be susceptible to UP's influence, while having particularly favorable treaties with the U.S., Europe, South America, and other important places of business for UP. The task, therefore, was simply to find that country.

The Japanese Takeover Attempt

David Buchanan's search for a suitable country was abruptly cut short early in February 1988 when the board of the Mitsuhara Corporation of Osaka, Japan, made a friendly takeover offer for UP. Mitsuhara, a huge conglomerate with interests in electronics, steel, financial services, and houseware products, had recently faltered in its efforts to build a U.S. market for its kitchen appliances because of distribution problems. To surmount this, it had been actively looking to acquire a U.S. company with an extensive network of dealers. It had finally settled on UP. UP had some 1,500 established outlets for its gardening, automotive and hardware products. Its turbines and engines divisions could be vertically integrated into Mitsuhara's own businesses, and UP finance could be invigorated by an infusion of Japanese capital.

February 1988 was an exceptionally favorable time for Mitsuhara to make such an investment. The Japanese macroeconomy had generated huge retained earnings during the late 1970s and 1980s, earnings that probably constituted the largest single pool of investable funds ever accumulated. During the same period, Japanese investors had bought over $50 billion of American Treasury bonds because they assumed that treasuries were riskless and because they tended to offer at least a 3-percent interest rate premium over their Japanese equivalents, enough to offset any currency exposure.

Over time, the same investors, both individual and corporate, increasingly began to examine other opportunities, such as real estate and equities in the USA. They were particularly attracted toward equities for three reasons. First, because their major alternative was becoming steadily less attractive, as the Federal Reserve had steadily cut American interest rates throughout 1985 and 1986, narrowing the differentials between U.S. and Japanese bonds; second, because American companies represented "real" investments, which might offer some hedge against a fall in the value of the dollar in which much of Japan's export-driven profits were denominated. The most important reason, however, was that American companies were, from the Japanese perspective, very cheap. Since 1984 the value of the yen had risen by almost 40 percent against the dollar, making all previously accepted measures of the value of American firms virtually meaningless to the Japanese. In other words, in Mitsuhara's eyes, the cost of a U.S. acquisition was almost irrelevant.

UP received Mitsuhara's all-cash offer with dismay. The bid offered UP's shareholders a clear 30-percent premium over market, and it was contingent upon nothing except the agreement and cooperation of UP's management. Buchanan knew that the easy acceptance he had counted on from the institutions would work just as well for the Japanese offer. Naturally, the merger would involve the loss of some jobs at UP, but Mitsuhara proposed to retrain all relevant employees for new positions at existing pay levels, and, if any wished to leave, it set out a generous compensation scheme as thanks for their work at UP.

As a foreign national, Mitsuhara could not, under U.S. law, own more than 5 percent of a defense contractor. Nonetheless, failure to work out a satisfactory arrangement would not imperil the offer, and UP's defense business would simply be sold off. In an effort to keep UP defense, however, Mitsuhara had worked out an elaborate compromise according to guidelines set out by the recent Presidential Commission on Foreign Ownership, Influence, and Control of U.S. Companies. In effect, it would spin off the division to become an independent company under a supervisory board of U.S. nationals, of whom a majority would be independent directors. Mitsuhara suggested several public figures, including a former secretary of defense, and only one of whom would be from Mitsuhara itself. The Japanese company had received an informal opinion from the State Department that this ownership structure was likely to be accepted.

For David Buchanan, Mitsuhara's bid threatened to snatch away the prizes just as they came within his grasp. He felt personally responsible for the welfare of UP's employees, customers, and suppliers. His feeling that his possession was on the line was shared by other board members. They decided, after much consultation with legal and financial experts, to announce a limited restructuring of UP "to bring out hidden shareholder values." Indeed Buchanan was able to use the threat of takeover to implement the next stage of his strategy. He proposed, and the board quickly agreed, to have UP recapitalized into two classes of common stock with differing votes. Although the recapitalization looked like an anti-takeover amendment, preventing a raider from buying a voting majority and, thus, choosing directors simply by buying a majority of common stock, it was also a way to disenfranchise UP's owners.

The recapitalization was to take the form of a one-time distribution of one share of a new class B stock for every two shares of existing common stock. The class B stock would have ten votes per share, in contrast to UP's existing common (or class A) stock, which had one vote. The transferability of class B stock would be very limited; holders would only be able to sell or give it to certain members of their close families, certain family trusts, or charities, and they would only have six months after issuance in which to do so. B stock could, however, readily be exchanged for A stock, which could then be transferred in the normal ways.

In order to compensate shareholders for the loss of their voting power, UP would raise the dividends payable to holders of class A stock. The proposal would be voted on by stockholders at the annual meeting in April. Easy passage was assured. By not tendering into the stock repurchase, inside shareholders (Zachary family trust, UP's pension, profit sharing, employee stock-ownership plans, and the officers and directors) had increased their relative voting power. Buchanan effectively controlled the votes of the ten largest institutional holders of UP's stock by ensuring that they were also employed as money managers of UP's pension fund. All in all, therefore, he personally controlled nearly 40 percent of the voting power, yet owning less than 1 percent himself.

The Japanese received the news of UP's intended recapitalization impassively. Throughout the negotiations, they had made every effort to accommodate the American firm in a fair and reasonable way. Now, however, they were forced to the belated recognition that there was simply too much intransigence in UP. Far from being a profit-maximizing business run in the interests of its owners, it was, from Mitsuhara's perspective, the private dominion of its managers and directors, whose deeply proprietorial feelings toward the company all but excluded considerations of ownership or efficiency.

In the final analysis, the Japanese realized the impossibility of doing business with UP. They decided to drop their offer. As planned, the recapitalization passed without difficulty. Because none of the inside shareholders exchanged their stock, their relative voting control increased dramatically again. When UP formally withdrew its class B stock from the market in August 1988, David Buchanan had over 50 percent of the voting shares under his effective control. The Zachary family trust had been offshore since the 1960s for tax reasons. Now Buchanan moved all three of UP's employee benefit plans down to the Dutch Antilles. The stage was now set for UP itself to move overseas.

After lengthy consultation with his lawyers, Buchanan settled on Luxembourg. Luxembourg had treaties with the United States and its own European partners in the Far East, which would allow UP to continue to operate exactly as before. The tax advantages of UP's new legal domicile, though limited since UP's tax domicile remained in the United States, were calculated to save the company some $150 million in 1988. Only UP's domicile would change. Its stock, for example, would continue to trade on the New York Stock Exchange, and the company could and would continue to have access to equity capital through the issuance of limited voting stock on the Exchange and, perhaps, in the Euroequity market.

Ironically, however, UP found itself in the same position as Mitsuhara only nine months before, faced by the legal requirement to sell off UP defense. Oddly, Buchanan decided to adopt the Japanese company's solution, setting up a supervisory board and developing a strict code of conduct to prevent undue influence. Despite this, he had confidence that he could continue to control UP's crucial defense subsidiary. With this in mind, in December 1988 UP's chief executive reincorporated UP in the tiny state of Luxembourg.

Important Considerations

The case study account illustrates the complexity of operations and decisions faced by multinational companies. Many of the factors that were presented in this book as being important for project management were addressed in this case study. The role of government and the individual in determining the political and economic influences on a project are illustrated by the events in the case study. Some important considerations for the future of the company are:

- How specific project-management techniques might be used in solving the various problems faced by UP.
- Analysis of the most significant decisions made by UP concerning moving its operations abroad.
- Future composition and actions of the board of directors, shareholders, management, and employees.
- Potential roles of the host government.
- Integration of what is best for the company, the home country, the host country, the shareholders, and the employees.

10.6 INDUSTRIAL QUALITY IMPROVEMENT IN TAIWAN: A CASE STUDY

This case study (Badiru and Chen, 1992) discusses how industrial engineers played direct roles in the transformation of Taiwan from an agricultural economy into an industrial giant. The case study is based on an account from the China Productivity Center (CPC) in Taipei, Taiwan, and the Republic of China (ROC). The case study illustrates how industrial engineering techniques and practices played a key role in the industrialization of Taiwan. Through integrated industrial development programs, the small island of Taiwan has achieved a giant status in the world market. The case of Taiwan is certainly an inspiring lesson for other developing countries with a vision of industrial development.

China Productivity Center

The China Productivity Center (CPC) is the avenue through which most of the techniques for business and industrial productivity and quality improvement have been passed on to Taiwan's small- and large-scale industries. The center, headquartered in Taipei, Taiwan, was established by government statute in 1955. It now has several regional offices around the country. The current state of industrial development in Taiwan is by a careful design dating back to the establishment of the CPC. There is a direct link between the growth of the CPC and the economic development of Taiwan. The center is now 50 percent funded by the government. The other 50 percent of its operating budget was raised entirely through productivity-related services rendered to private industry. It is organized and run as a private non-profit institution.

The primary charter of the CPC is to help to improve business and industrial productivity and quality in Taiwan. It specializes in providing training classes for workers, supervisors, managers, and top executives. Every year, the center invites international experts to give lectures and to conduct seminars on various topics ranging from product design, use of computer software, and joint-venture strategies to project management. The center has enjoyed significant achievements over the past three and a half decades. Of these, the following stand out in terms of direct contribution to industrial development and productivity and quality improvement:

- Establishing *Productivity Magazine* in 1957. The magazine, which was renamed *Strategy Productivity Magazine* in 1990, is dedicated to the dissemination of the latest productivity and quality issues and techniques to local industry.
- Helping to launch the Enterprise Management Development Association in 1963. This association provides business and industrial management strategies to Taiwan's industry.
- Helping to establish the Industrial Engineering Department at Tung Hai University in September 1963. This is one of the earliest full-fledged industrial engineering academic programs.
- Participating in the establishment of the Metals Industry Development Center in 1963.
- Assisting in the establishment of the Chinese Society for Quality Control in 1964.
- Assisting in establishing the ROC Industrial Design Association in 1967.
- Participating in the establishment of the ROC Industrial Safety and Hygiene Association in 1970.
- Establishing the Low-Cost Automation Technology Promotion Department in 1979. This department was later renamed Industrial Automation Promotion Department.
- Launching of a five-year National Productivity Enhancement Program under the auspices of the Ministry of Economic Affairs in 1984.
- Launching of a five-year National Product Quality Enhancement Project under the auspices of the Ministry of Economic Affairs in 1988. In 1990, the average savings from quality improvement projects was U.S. $792,000 per participating company.
- Implementing a three-year Medium and Small Enterprise Technology Acquisition Program in July 1989.

Leadership for Industrialization

The continuing success of the CPC is based on solid leadership and unrelenting effort to improve productivity and quality. The current president of the center is Dr. Casper T. Y. Shih. Dr. Shih was recruited by the government of Taiwan from General Electric in Canada to head the Factory Automation

Task Force in 1983. The automation task force later became an integral part of the CPC. The goal of the task force is to facilitate the injection of automation technology into Taiwan's industry through free consultation, government-subsidized, low-cost loans, and other support services. Prior to going to Canada, Dr. Shih worked in Japan, where he was credited with developing the special welding techniques that were used in the construction of Japan's bullet train railway. So, he came into the productivity-improvement effort with an established industrial reputation. Dr. Shih was the 1991 chairman of the Asia Productivity Organization (APO), which includes Taiwan, Japan, Korea, India, Indonesia, Pakistan, Vietnam, and other Asian countries.

Even though he does not have any formal industrial engineering training (he earned his doctorate in materials science from Tokyo University), Dr. Shih is familiar with and fully appreciates the potential contributions of industrial engineers. He introduced many new concepts and ways of doing things in Taiwan's industry. Some industry leaders call him the "industrial megastar." He admonishes the short-term views of entrepreneurs and advocates long-term strategic plans for productivity and quality improvement. He encourages industry to continue to find better ways of achieving their goals with his proclamation that "winners always have an answer and losers always have an excuse." In his leadership vision, he predicts that by the year 2000, the Pacific Rim will match North America's total GNP and exceed that of Western Europe. He suggests that the "twenty-first century is the Pacific century" and that the countries ringing the Pacific (including Taiwan) will continue to experience tremendous economic growth. He believes that, although the first thirty years of the next century will be dominated by the Japanese, the seventy years that will follow will be dominated by the Chinese in terms of economic activity. A major responsibility of the CPC is to develop and disseminate the strategies needed to achieve and sustain the projected world economic leadership.

Link with Academic Institutions

Industrial engineering played a very significant role in the early success of the CPC. To achieve what Shih and CPC have achieved, a lot of trust was needed on the part of industrial entrepreneurs. As Dr. Shih pointed out, *trust is a prerequisite for innovation.* To get industries to implement his productivity ideas, Shih had to convince them that the techniques could work for them. One of his first approaches as the head of the Factory Automation Task Force was the *strategy of rationalization and conversion.* Prior to 1983, few or none of the basic industrial engineering tools were in regular use in many companies. There were limited quality-control efforts. Consistent production control was nonexistent. Poor plant layout severely limited industrial productivity.

In 1983, Dr. Shih employed scores of industrial engineering students and deployed them strategically to various companies on summer-vacation assignments with specific instructions on how to introduce industrial engineering techniques in the companies. He instructed the industrial engineers to ensure that there were significant gains resulting from the techniques they introduced and to document properly all the benefits achieved. The documented improvements provided the rationalization for the need for new techniques to improve productivity. Once the rationalization was achieved, it was easy to get the companies to convert to industrial engineering approaches. The higher the number of companies that adopt industrial engineering techniques, the better off the overall economic outlook of the nation.

The services of the industrial engineering students were funded by CPC and offered free to the companies as a part of government support for industrial development. The students were supervised and guided by fully qualified industrial engineers. The free service of the students removed whatever initial apprehension the companies might have in hiring them. The techniques included in the students' repertoire were basic industrial engineering tools such as quality control, plant layout, production planning, activity scheduling, and work measurement. The idea was that if the companies had an opportunity to try these techniques, they would become aware of their potential benefits and would, thereafter, embrace the techniques as a part of their regular modes of operation. The approach worked so successfully that most of the companies went on to hire industrial engineers on their regular staff. With the prevailing poor layouts and inefficient practices, the industrial engineering students were able to achieve significant improvements. When other companies that did not even participate in the summer programs saw the gains that were being achieved, they also created industrial engineering positions.

The Policy of Rationalization

Now, industrial engineering is well-known and respected among Taiwanese industries. Once the companies began to trust the efforts of the CPC, they began to avail themselves of the other productivity and quality programs offered by the center. The goal of the strategy is to get companies introduced to a new idea that will benefit them individually and, in turn, benefit the overall economic development of Taiwan. It is believed that the good reputation and goodwill that the CPC enjoys today is due to that initial industrial engineering experiment. It was reported that companies were so impressed by the improvements brought by industrial engineers that they referred to them as *industrial doctors*. Under the guidance of industrial engineers, many companies in Taiwan now routinely adopt Flexible Manufacturing System robotics, Computer-Aided Design and Computer-Aided Manufacturing, Total Quality Management, Statistical Process Control, Automated Process Control, the Taguchi method, PERT/CPM, and expert systems. With minimum investment, many companies were able to increase output. The efforts of industrial engineers helped to prepare companies for the proper attitude toward automation (i.e., rationalization for automation) before actual implementation.

The same strategy of conversion is still in use today. When the CPC brings in an international expert now, the initial consultation and services available are free to the relevant companies. The expert may conduct seminars or study specific industrial problems and offer expert advice. This, at least, gets a new concept or technique introduced to the companies. If the companies like what they see, they will then adopt the idea and be willing to pay consultation fees to the CPC for further help and implementation of the new techniques. It is from such further paid service that the CPC raises the balance of its operating budget.

National Drive for Development

The push for industrial productivity and quality improvement is fully supported by the Taiwanese government through the activities of the Ministry of Economic Affairs. In 1989, after forty years of hard work, Taiwan created a trade quota of U.S. $118 billion. This made Taiwan the world's thirteenth largest trading nation. The economic development of Taiwan is essentially driven by gains in small- and medium-size enterprises. About 95 percent of Taiwan's industry is in the small-scale, privately owned sector. The government has set aside a portion of Taiwan's huge external reserve for construction projects and industrial development. It has been said that behind the postwar reconstruction in Kuwait, Taiwan will have the next largest collection of construction projects within the next few years. The prevailing efforts in industrial development in Taiwan also rival those of any developed country. Joint-venture partners will do well to study the Taiwanese corporate culture and approach to industrial development in order to maximize the potential for success.

Market Globalization

Through the CPC and other similar organizations, several productivity-improvement programs are available to Taiwan's industry. With the available services, small businesses can get help for the financial aspects of their operations, as well as for the technological and managerial aspects. The emerging industrial initiative in Taiwan now is to supplement the prevailing strategy of Original-Equipment Manufacturing (OEM) with Original-Design Manufacturing (ODM) and Original-Brand Manufacturing (OBM). This means that in the near future, products will not only be *made in Taiwan* but also *designed in Taiwan* and *created in Taiwan*. Thus, Taiwanese industry can capture more of the global market for industrial products.

10.7 ECONOMIC DEVELOPMENT PROJECTS IN TURKEY

A few decades ago, Turkey was basically an agricultural economy. With dedicated efforts, the country has been transformed into a nation with a strong industrial base. The successful industrialization has facilitated a stable economic development. Of the several recent development projects that Turkey had embarked on, the GAP Southeastern Anatolia Project has been the biggest. The project has been described as one of the most ambitious regional development projects in the world (Bagis, 1989).

The purpose of the project is to revitalize the Tigris-Euphrates basin by providing irrigation and electricity to the arid and sparsely populated area. The project has spanned a period of over thirty years with an estimated cost of about $25 billion. The Ataturk Dam, the third largest earth-filled dam in the world, is one of the thirteen major integrated projects that make up the GAP. The GAP's irrigation and hydropower schemes are expected to be fully operational by the year 2005. This would irrigate a vast area and facilitate the creation of new farmlands. Turkey's agricultural production will significantly be boosted by the project. The integrated nature of the project provides a strong link to industrial development efforts around the country, thereby creating significant economic development, as illustrated by the chain reaction portrayed below:

Agricultural Development → Industrial Development
→ Economic Development

Private investment, both foreign and domestic, has been actively pursued for the project. Interbank, Turkey's leading corporate bank is the primary sponsor of the project. The management approach used for the project considers human aspects as a key consideration in getting the project done successfully. The planning of the project carefully balances the social structure, economic framework, political, and cultural aspects of the wide-ranging impact of the project. The GAP has been fully supported not only by citizens and investors but also by the government.

The effort committed to transforming the strength of an agricultural base into industrial development without compromising one for the other has helped Turkey to achieve its dual development goals. Turkey is believed to be the largest industrial base between Europe and Asia. At the same time, it is recognized as one of the few food surplus nations in the world. Clearly, sound project-management techniques are being used in managing national projects in Turkey. Other aspiring developing nations should learn from Turkey's example. Bagis (1989) presents a detail account of the GAP project.

Other successful examples of industrial development can be found in the cases of Taiwan, Japan, Thailand, and Korea. Japan provided the infrastructural framework for its industrial development by developing its banking industry first, followed by transportation and communication. After those, assembly plants were developed. This strategy emphasized the fact that capital accumulation is a prerequisite for industrialization. Even after the devastation of World War II, Japan used the same capital accumulation strategy for its economic recovery.

10.8 CONSTRUCTION OF INDUSTRIAL ESTATES IN THAILAND

Chuntaketa (1991) presented an account of how Thailand embarked upon and managed the construction of complete industrial estates to support general industrial development programs. The implementation of the Fifth Five-Year National and Social Development Plan in Thailand began in October 1981. The development of the Eastern Seaboard is one of Thailand's main strategies for development. The plan includes the establishment of industries using natural resources to accelerate the region's urban-industrial development. The construction of industrial estates is a part of Thailand's long-term goal of deconcentrating the population growth in the Bangkok metropolitan region. The industrial development plan emphasizes the development of energy-related and other type of industries.

The development plan was formulated in terms of a master plan and short-term plans with target years from 1987 through 2000. Major industries, as well as minor supporting industries, are planned to be constructed at carefully selected locations. Feasibility studies were conducted to determine which products should be produced at which industrial estates. Formal economic analyses were done for both the short-term plans and the master plan.

Each industrial estate includes industrial plants and completely new towns with all the necessary amenities. In some cases, new seaports and airports are to be constructed for the sole purpose of supporting the industrial estates. These projects were fully supported by the government of Thailand. Cooperation between government and private businesses enabled the projects to be successfully implemented. Formal project-management approaches were used. The completed industrial estates have become home to numerous manufacturing companies from all over the Pacific Rim. Some of the specific approaches used on the industrial development projects are described in the sections that follow.

Overseas Economic Cooperation Fund

To generate financing for the industrial development projects, cooperative economic agreements were made with overseas companies, organizations, and countries. The Overseas Economic Cooperation Fund provided sources for long-term industrial development loans.

Reciprocating Import/Export Arrangements

As a part of the industrial estate development, a reciprocating import-export arrangement was made with foreign countries to ensure that a market will be available for the proposed products of the industrial estates. Industrial liaisons were established with other countries that may become potential customers for the products of the industrial estates.

Buy-In Joint Venture

Under this arrangement, foreign countries that provide low-cost loans or technical expertise to support the industrial development projects will have first priority to export rights from the newly created industrial estates. Initial importation of technical personnel was used to initiate the projects. Training programs were then developed to create the required technical personnel locally.

Cultural Orientation

It was recognized that personal issues would create more problems than the technical issues. Thus, extensive efforts have been made to achieve cultural orientation of the local residents to accept the changes to be caused by the industrial development projects. Changes were introduced in small and strategically planned packages. Thus, the residents were not exposed to changes too quickly. This makes it easier for them to accept the development projects and adapt to the new environment. A center of mobilization for industrial development was established to secure local support for the projects. A major effort of the mobilization program was to encourage people to move to the new estates.

Industrially Ideal Location

The locations for the industrial estates were carefully selected so as to maximize the use of locally available raw materials. The estates were strategically located to take into account the generation and distribution of products. Communication, transportation, and resource supply (water, power, raw material, etc.) were key considerations in the site-selection process. In some cases, new communication, transportation, and water-supply systems were developed to support the proposed industrial operations and urban activities at the industrial estates.

Surrounding Community

The communities surrounding the industrial estates were developed or improved to meet the needs of the estates. New schools were built where necessary. New residential neighborhoods were developed to support the needs of the workers at the industrial estates. Special amenities were built into the neighborhoods to address the specific lifestyles of the proposed work force. The composition of the work force in terms of white-collar and blue-collar workers was also considered in the development of the residential neighborhoods.

Commercial and Business Operations

To provide a complete self-contained estate, commercial and business establishments were encouraged to establish operations near the industrial sites. Thus, the work force would have access to educational services, business activities, shopping centers, banking, and other commercial services. The availability of these facilities made it possible for new residents to settle down quickly. Above all, employment opportunities provided by the industrial estates helped to attract new residents.

Waste Disposal and Environmental Preparedness

New systems were developed to take care of the anticipated increase in garbage, waste-water disposal, and solid-waste disposal. Ecological considerations influenced the design and construction of the disposal systems. The potential impacts on the environment were studied, and contingency plans were put in place. Because the population of the new urban areas depend on the kind and scope of the proposed industrial activities, the impact of the urban development was studied with regard to the changes brought by industrial development.

Management Strategy

The government of Thailand actively participated in the industrial development projects. This has a strong bearing on how the project is managed and implemented. In conventional government operations, it is preferred that one agency take responsibility for the whole development project. Because these are regional development projects, a local or municipal agency would be an appropriate supervising agency. However, local government would have great difficulty in handling a project of such magnitude. In addition, the regional projects are part of a national development project. So, the projects should be managed at the national level. This means that several national government agencies would be involved in the project-management effort as the projects would involve issues that are handled by different government agencies.

One management approach would be to create a totally new agency to supervise the development projects. But this might not be acceptable because the local government agencies might feel left out of their own regional development projects. The approach used was to set up a steering committee consisting of officials from all the relevant government agencies. This steering committee would have power to decide policy and procedures for carrying out the project plans. The broad scope of the steering committee facilitates interface with private business. Thus, working together, the various government agencies would ensure that the goals of the industrial development projects are achieved. As of the time of writing this case study, the construction and settlement of the industrial estates have been well ahead of schedule. This has been credited to good project-management practices.

To achieve project success similar to the ones illustrated in the case studies, management advancement and government commitment are required. These are essential for industrial development in any part of the world. Most of the requirements for industrial development are already available in many developing nations. What is lacking is the management approach to link everything together to provide a cohesive and functional team that can successfully pursue development goals. The project-management approach presented in this book can help to overcome that deficiency and provide new management directions for industrial development efforts.

APPENDIX A

United Nations Information Sources

AGLINET Union List of Serials Food and Agricultural Organization of the United Nations
Department of General Affairs and Information, Library and Documentation Systems Division, Via delle Terme di Caracalla, 00100 Rome, Italy.

Agrarian Research and Intelligence Service
Food and Agriculture Organization of the United Nations, Economic and Social Policy Department, Human Resources, Institutions and Agrarian Reform Division (ESH), Via delle Terme di Caracalla, 00100 Rome, Italy.

Agricultural Information Development
Scheme Economic and Social Commission for Asia and the Pacific, Agriculture Division, United Nations Building, Rajadamnern Avenue, Bangkok 2, Thailand.

AGRIS Data Base
Food and Agriculture Organization of the United Nations, Department of General Affairs and Information, Library and Documentation Systems Division, Via delle Terme di Caracalla, 00100 Rome, Italy.

Asian and Pacific Development Institute Library and Documentation Centre
Economic and Social Commission for Asia and the Pacific, Asian and Pacific Development Institute, P.O. Box 2.136, Sri Ayudhije Road, Bangkok, Thailand.

Audio Materials Library
United Nations, Department of Public Information, Radio and Visual Services Division, One United Nations Plaza, New York, NY 10017.

Bibliography On Transnational Corporations
United Nations, Centre of Transnational Corporations, Information Analysis Division, 605 Third Avenue, New York, NY 10017.

CAFRAD Library and Documentation Centre
United Nations, African Training and Research Centre in Administration for Development (CAFRAD), B.P. 10, Tangier, Morocco.

Cairo Demographic Centre Library
United Nations, Cairo Demographic Centre, 109 Qasr Al-Aini Street, Cairo, Egypt.

Caribbean Information System for Economic and Social Planning
Economic Commission for Latin America, CEPAL office for the Caribbean, Caribbean Documentation Centre, P.O. Box 1113, Room 300, Salvatori Building, Port of Spain, Trinidad and Tobago.

Caribbean Planning Data Base
Economic Commission for Latin America, CEPAL Office for the Caribbean, Caribbean Documentation Centre, P.O. Box 1113, Room 300, Salvatori Building, Port of Spain, Trinidad and Tobago.

Center for Documentation and Information Service
International Labour Office, Inter-American Centre for Research and Documentation on Vocational Training, Casilla de Correo 1761, San Jose 1092, Montevideo, Uruguay.

Central American Centre for Economic and Social Documentation
Economic Commission for Latin America/Central American Higher University Council (CSUCA), Apartada 37, Universidad de Costa Rica, San Jose, Costa Rica.

Central Library and Documentation Branch of the International Labour Office
International Labour Office, Bureau of Information Systems, Central Library and Documentation Branch, 4, Route des Morillons, 1211 Geneva 22, Switzerland.

CEPAL/CSUCA-CEDESC Data Base
Central American Centre for Economic and Social Documentation (CEDESC), Apartada 37, Universidad de Costa Rica, San Jose, Costa Rica.

CLADBIB Data Base
Economic Commission for Latin America, Latin American Centre for Economic and Social Documentation (CLADES), Casilla 179-D, Edificio Naciones Unidas, Avenida Dag Hammarskjold, Santiago, Chile.

CLAPLAN Data Base
Economic Commission for Latin America, Latin American Centre for Economic and Social Documentation (CLADES), Casilla 179-D, Edificio Naciones Unidas, Avenida Dag Hammarskjold, Santiago, Chile.

Comprehensive Information System on Transnational Corporations
United Nations, Information Analysis Division, Centre of Transnational Corporations, 605 Third Avenue, New York, NY 10017.

Computerized Documentation System
United Nations, Educational, Scientific, and Cultural Organization, Division of Library, Archives, and Documentation Services, 7, Place de Fontenoy, 75700 Paris, France.

Corporate Profile System
United Nations Centre on Transnational Corporation, Information Analysis Division, One United Nations Plaza, New York, NY 10017.

Current Research in Family Planning
Economic and Social Commission for Asia and the Pacific, Clearing-house and Information Section, Population Division, United Nations Building, Rajadamnern Avenue, Bangkok 2, Thailand.

Dag Hammarskjold Library
United Nations, Department of Conference Services, One United Nations Plaza, New York, NY 10017.

DARE Data Base
United Nations Educational, Scientific, and Cultural Organization, Social Science Documentation Centre (SSDC), 7, Place de Fontenoy, 75700 Paris, France.

Data Bank
Economic Commission for Africa, Statistics Division, P.O. Box 3001, Africa Hall, Addis Ababa, Ethiopia.

Development Education Exchange Service
Food and Agriculture Organization of the United Nations, Development Department (DD), Via delle Terme di Caracalla, 00100 Rome, Italy.

Development Information System
United Nations, Department of International Economic and Social Affairs, Information Systems Unit, Room DC 594, One United Nations Plaza, New York, NY 10017.

Development Information System Data Base
United Nations, Department of Internaitonal Economic and Social Affairs, Information Systems Unit Room DC 594, One United Nations Plaza, New York, NY 10017.

DOCPAL Data Base
Economic Commission for Latin America, Centro Latinoamericano de Demografia, Casilla 91, Edificio Naciones Unidas, Avenida Dag Hammarskjold, Santiago, Chile.

Documentation and Health Information Office
World Health Organization/Pan American Health Organization, 525 Twenty-Third Street, N.W., Washington, DC 20037.

Documentation Referral Service
World Bank, Records Management Division, Document Acquisition and Control, 1818 H Street, N.W., Washington, DC 20433.

ECA Library
Economic Commission for Africa, P.O. Box 3001, Africa Hall, Addis Ababa, Ethiopia.

ECWA Library
Economic Commission for Western Asia Adninistration, P.O. Box 4656, United Nations Building, Bir Hassan, Beirut, Lebanon.

ESCAP Bibliographic Information Master File
Economic and Social Commission for Asia and the Pacific, Library, United Nations
Building, Rajadamnern Avenue, Bangkok 2, Thailand.

ESCAP Documentation Information System
Economic and Social Commission for Asia and the Pacific, Library, United Nations
Building, Rajadamnern Avenue, Bangkok 2, Thailand.

ESCAP Library
Economic and Social Commission for Asia and the Pacific, United Nations Building,
Rajadamnern Avenue, Bangkok 2, Thailand.

ESCAP Library Library Serials Data Base
Economic and Social Commission for Asia and the Pacific, Library, United Nations
Building, Rajadamnern Avenue, Bangkok 2, Thailand.

External Trade Statistics
United Nations, Department of International Economic and Social Affairs, Statistical Office, One United Nations Plaza, New York, NY 10017

FAO Library Serials Information System
Food and Agriculture Organization of the United Nations, Department of General
Affairs and Information, Library and Documentation Systems Division, Via delle
Terme di Caracalla, 00100 Rome, Italy.

General Industrial Statistics
United Nations, Department of International Economic and Social Affairs, Statistical Office, One United Nations Plaza, New York, NY 10017.

Gross Domestic Product by Kind of Economic Activity
Economic Commission for Latin America, Statistics Division, Casilla 179-D, Edificio
Naciones Unidas, Avenida Dag Hammarskjold, Santiago, Chile.

Group of Experts on Urban and Regional Research
Economic Commission for Europe, Environment and Human Settlements Division,
Palais des Nations, Ch-1211, Geneva 10, 16, Avenue, Jean Trembly, 1209 Geneva 10,
Switzerland.

Habitat Library and Documentation Centre
United Nations, Centre for Human Settlements (HABITAT), Division of Information,
Documentation, and Audio-Visual, P.O. Box 30030, Kenyatta Conference Centre,
Nairobi, Kenya.

Household Surveys Data Bank
Economic Commission for Latin America, Statistics Division, Casilla 179-D, Edificio
Naciones Unidas, Avenida Dag Hammarskjold, Santiago, Chile.

IBE Worldwide Network for Educational Information
United Nations Educational, Scientific, and Cultural Organization, International
Bureau of Education, Documentation, and Information Unit, Palais Wilson, 1211
Geneva 14, Switzerland.

IMF Data Fund System
International Monetary Fund, Bureau of Statistics, 700 19th Street, N.W., Washington, DC 20431.

Industrial and Technological Information Bank
United Nations Industrial Development Organization, Industrial Information Section, P.O. Box 300, Vienna International Center, Wagramer Strasse 5, A-1400 Vienna, Austria.

Industrial Information System Data Base: Industrial Development Abstracts
United Nations Industrial Development Organization, Industrial Information Section, P.O. Box 300, Vienna International Center, Wagramer Strasse 5, A-1400 Vienna, Austria.

Information Services of the Network of Educational Innovation for Development in Africa
United Nations Educational, Scientific, and Cultural Organization, Regional Office for Education in Africa (BREDA), B.P. 3311, 12, Avenue Rome, Dakar, Senegal.

Integrated Statistical Information System
United Nations, Department of International Economic and Social Affairs, Statistical Office, One United Nations Plaza, New York, NY 10017.

International Institute for Population Studies Library
United Nations, International Institute for Population Studies, Govandi Station Road, Deonar-Bombay 4000-88, India.

International Labour Documentation
International Labour Office, Bureau of Information Systems, Central Library and Documentation Branch, 4 route des Morillons, 1211 Geneva 22, Switzerland.

Joint Bank-Fund Library
International Monetary Fund, 700 19th Street, N.W., Wahington, DC 20431.

Joint CEPAL/ILPES Library
Economic Commission for Latin America, Latin American Institute for Economic and Social Planning, Casilla 179-D, Edificio Naciones Unidas, Avenida Dag Hammarskjold, Santiago, Chile.

Joint CEPAL/ILPES Library Bibliographical Information System
Economic Commission for Latin America, Latin American Institute for Economic and Social Planning, Casilla 179-D, Edificio Naciones Unidas, Avenida Dag Hammmarskjold, Santiago, Chile.

Labour Information Record Data Base
International Labour Office, Working Conditions and Environment Department, Social and Labour Bulletin Section, 4 route des Morillons, 1211 Geneva 22, Switzerland.

Latin American Centre for Economic and Social Documentation
Economic Commission for Latin America, Casilla 179-D, Edificio Naciones Unidas, Avenida Dag Hammarskjold, Santiago, Chile.

Latin American Population Documentation System
Economic Commission for Latin America, Centro Latinoamericano de Demografia, Casilla 91, Edificio Naciones Unidas, Avenida Dag Hammarskjold, Santiago, Chile.

Library and Documentation Centre of the UNESCO International Institute for Educational Planning
United Nations Educational, Scientific, and Cultural Organization, International Institute for Educational Planning, 7-9 Rue Eugene Delacroix, 75016 Paris, France.

Library of the UNESCO Regional Office for Science and Technology
United Nations Educational, Scientific, and Cultural Organization, Regional Office for Science and Technology for Latin America and the Caribbean, P.O. Box 3187, Bulevar Artigas 1320, Montevideo, Uruguay.

Library of the UNESCO Regional Office for Science and Technology for Africa
United Nations Educational, Scientific, and Cultural Organization, Regional Office for Science and Technology for Africa, P.O. Box 30592, Bruce House, Standard Street, Nairobi, Kenya.

Macro-Economic Data Bank and Table Processing System
United Nations, Department of International Economic and Social Affairs, Office for Development Research and Policy Analysis, One United Nations Plaza, New York, NY 10017.

Macro-Economic Data Bank and Table Processing System Data Base
United Nations, Department of International Economic and Social Affairs, Office for Development Research and Policy Analysis, One United Nations Plaza, New York, NY 10017.

Population Clearing-House and Information System
Economic and Social Commission for Asia and the Pacific, Clearing-house and Information Section, Population Division, United Nations Building, Rajadamnern Avenue, Bangkok 2, Thailand.

Population Documentation Centre
Food and Agriculture Organization of the United Nations, Economic and Social Policy Department, Human Resources, Institutions and Agrarian Reform Division (ESH), Via delle Terme di Caracalla, 00100 Rome, Italy.

Population Information and Documentation System for Africa
United Nations, Regional Institute for Population Studies, University of Ghana, P.O. Box 96, Legon, Ghana.

Population Information Network
United Nations, Department of International Economic and Social Affairs, Population Division, One United Nations Plaza, New York, NY 10017.

Project Institutional Memory
United Nations Development Programme, Bureau for Programme Policy and Evaluation, One United Nations Plaza, New York, NY 10017.

Project Institutional Memory Data Base
United Nations Development Programme, Bureau for Programme Policy and Evaluation, One United Nations Plaza, New York, NY 10017.

Quarterly Bulletin of Statistics for Asia and the Pacific
Economic and Social Commission for Asia and the Pacific, Statistics Division, United Nations Building, Rajadamnern Avenue, Bangkok 2, Thailand.

Reference Centre of the Population Division
United Nations, Department of International Economic and Social Affairs, Population Division, One United Nations Plaza, New York, NY 10017.

Reference Unit of the Office for Science and Technology
United Nations, Department of International Economic and Social Affairs Division, One United Nations Plaza, New York, NY 10017.

Reference Unit of the Office for Development Research and Policy Analysis
United Nations, Department of International Economic and Social Affairs, Office for Development Research and Policy Analysis, One United Nations Plaza, New York, NY 10017.

Referral Programme of Academic Services Division
United Nations University, Academic Services, 29th Floor, Toho Seimei Building, 15-1 Shibuya 2-chome, Shibuya-ku, Tokyo 150, Japan.

Regional Clearing-House for Population Education
United Nations Educational, Scientific, and Cultural Organization, Regional Office for Education in Asia and Oceania, P.O. Box 1425, Darakarn Building, 920 Sukumvit Road, Bangkok 11, Thailand.

Regional Information System Network for Human Settlements
Economic and Social Commission for Asia and the Pacific, ESCAP/UNIDO Division of Industry, Housing, and Technology, United Nations Building, Rajadamnern Avenue, Bangkok 2, Thailand.

Social and Labour Bulletin Documentation Unit
International Labour Office, Working Conditions and Environment Department, Social and Labour Bulletin Section, 4, Route des Morillons, 1211 Geneva 22, Switzerland.

Social Indicators
The World Bank, Economic Analysis and Projections Department, Economic and Social Data Divison, 1818 H Street, N.W., Washington, DC 20433.

Statistical Indicators for Asia and the Pacific
Economic and Social Commission for Asia and the Pacific, Statistics Division, United Nations Building, Rajadamnern Avenue, Bangkok 2, Thailand.

Statistical Yearbook for Asia and the Pacific
Economic and Social Commission for Asia and the Pacific, Statistics Division, United Nations Building, Rajadamnern Avenue, Bangkok 2, Thailand.

Terminology and Reference Section
Food and Agriculture Organization of the United Nations, Department of General Affairs and Information, Publications Division, Via delle Terme di Caracalla, 00100 Rome, Italy.

Trade Information Service
Economic and Social Commission for Asia and the Pacific, Trade Promotion Centre (TPC), International Trade Division, United Nations Building, Rajadamnern Avenue, Bangkok 2, Thailand.

Training Information Data Base
International Labour Office, Training Department, Documentation, Information and Reports, 4 route des Morillons, 1211 Geneva 22, Switzerland.

UNBIS Data Base
United Nations, Department of Conference Services, Dag Hammmarskjold Library, One United Nations Plaza, New York, NY 10017.

UNCHS-Habitat Film Library
United Nations, Centre for Human Settlements (HABITAT), Division of Information, Documentation, and Audio-Visual, P.O. Box 30030, Kenyatta Conference Centre, Nairobi, Kenya.

UNCRD Library and Documentation Services
United Nations Centre for Regional Development, Marunouchi 2-4-7, Naku-ku, Nagoya 460, Japan.

UNEP Library and Documentation Centre
United Nations Environment Programme, P.O. Box 30552, Nairobi, Kenya.

UNESCAP/Statistics Information System
Economic and Social Commission for Asia and the Pacific, Statistics Division, United Nations Building, Rajadamnern Avenue, Bangkok 2, Thailand.

UNESCO Data Base
United Nations Educational, Scientific, and Cultural Organization, Division of Library, Archives and Documentation Services, 7, Place de Fontenoy, 75700 Paris, France.

UNESCO Statistical Data Bank System
United Nations Educational, Scientific, and Cultural Organization, Office of Statistics, 7, Place de Fontenoy, 75700 Paris, France.

UNITAR Library United Nations Institute for Training and Research
801 United Nations Plaza, New York, NY 10017.

United Nation-Romania Demographic Centre Library
United Nations, Demogrphic Centre, P.O. Box 1-550, 39 Boulevard Ana Ipatescu, 70100 Bucharest, Romania.

United Nations Bibliographic Information System
United Nations, Department of Conference Services, Dag Hammarskjold Library, One United Nations Plaza, New York, NY 10017.

United Nations Fund for Population Activities Library
United Nations Fund for Population Activities, 485 Lexington Avenue, Room 2018, New York, NY 10017.

United Nations Photo Library
United Nations, Deparment of Public Information, Radio and Visual Services Division, One United Nations Plaza, New York, NY 10017.

United Nations University Library
United Nations University, Academic Services, 29th Floor, Toho Seimei Building, 15-1 Shibuya 2-chome, Shibuya-ku, Tokyo 150, Japan.

United Nations Visual Materials Library
United Nations, Department of Public Information, Radio and Visual Services Division, One United Nations Plaza, New York, NY 10017.

UNRISD Library and Documentation Unit
United Nations Research Institute for Social Development, Palais des Nations, Ch-1211 Geneva 10, 16, Avenue Jean Trembley, 1209 Geneva, 10 Switzerland.

WHO South-East Asia Region Health Literature, Library and Information Services Network
World Health Organization, Regional Office for South East Asia (SEARO), SEARO Library, World Health House, Indraprastha Estate, Mahatma Gandhi Road, New Delhi 110002, India.

World Energy Supplies System
United Nations, Department of International Economic and Social Affairs, Statistical Office, One United Nations Plaza, New York, NY 10017.

World Health Statistics Data Base
World Health Organization, Division of Health Statistics, 20 Avenue Appia, 1211 Geneva 27, Switzerland.

World Statistics in Brief
United Nations, Department of International Economic and Social Affairs, Statistical Office, One United Nations Plaza, New York, NY 10017.

World Tables
The World Bank, Economic Analysis and Projections Department, Economic and Social Data Division, 1818 H Street, N.W., Washington, DC 20433.

APPENDIX B

Development-Related Research Institutions

INTERNATIONAL

African Regional Center for Technology
B.P. 2435, Dakar, Senegal.

African Medical and Research Foundation
P.O. Box 30125, Nairobi, Kenya.

African Academy of Sciences
P.O.B. 14798, Nairobi, Kenya.

Afro-Asian Organization for Economic Cooperation
Cairo Chamber of Commerce Building, Midan el-Falsky, Cairo, Egypt.

Asian Association of Development Research and Training Institutes
P.O. Box 2-136, Sri Ayudhya Road, Bangkok, Thailand.

Asian Development Center
11th Floor, Philippines Banking Corporation Building, Anda Circle, Port Area,
    Manila, Philippines.

Asian Institute for Economic Development and Planning
P.O. Box 2-136, Sri Ayudhya Road, Bangkok, Thailand.

Atlantic Institute for International Affairs
120, Rue de Longchamp, 75016 Paris, France.

Caribbean Studies Association
Inter-American University of Puerto Rico, P.O. Box 1293, Hato Rey, Puerto Rico
    00919.

Centre for the Coordination of Social Science Research and Documentation in
    Africa South of the Sahara
B.P. 836, Kinshasa XI, Zaire.

Centre for Studies and Research in International Law and International Relations
The Hague Academy of International Law, Carnegieplein 2, 2517 KJ, The Hague,
   Netherlands.

Club of Rome
Via Giorgione 163, 00147 Rome, Italy.

Committee on Society, Development, and Peace
150, Route de Ferney, 1211 Geneva 20, Switzerland.

Council for Asian Manpower Studies
P.O. Box 127, Quezon City, Philippines.

Council for the Development of Economic and Social Research in Africa
B.P. 3186, Dakar, Senegal.

East African Academy Research Information Centre
Regional Building of East African Community, Ngong Road (rooms 359-60),
   Nairobi, Kenya.

Eastern Regional Organization for Planning and Housing
Central Office: 4a, Ring Road, Indraprastha Estate, New Delhi, India.

Eastern Regional Organization for Public Administration
Rizal Hall, Padre Faura Street, Manila, Philippines.

Economic Development Institute
1818 H Street, N.W., Washington, DC 20433, USA.

European Foundation for Management Development
40, Rue Washington, 1050 Brussels 4, Belgium.

European Institute of Business Administration
Boulevard de Constance, 77305 Fontainebleau, France.

European Institute for Transnational Studies in Group and Organizational
   Development
Viktorgasse 9, 1040 Vienna, Austria.

European Research Group on Management
Predikherenberg 55, 3200 Kessel-Lo, Belgium.

Institute of International Law
82, Avenue de Castel, 1200 Brussels 4, Belgium.

International African Institute
210 High Holborn, London WCIV 7BW, United Kingdom.

International Association for Metropolitan Research and Development
Suite 1200, 130 Bloor Street West, Toronto 5, Canada, Ont M4W 2G8.

International Centre of Research and Information on Public and Cooperative
   Economy
45, Quai de Rome, Liege 7, Belgium.

International Cooperation for Socio-Economic Development
59-61, Rue Adolphe Lacombie, Brussels 4, Belgium.

International Institute of Administrative Sciences
25, Rue de Charité, Brussels 4, Belgium.

International Institute for Labour Studies
154, Rue de Lausanne, Case Postale 6, 1211 Geneva 22, Switzerland.

International Institute for Strategic Studies
18, Adam Street, London WC2N 6AL, United Kingdom.

International Management Development Institute
4, Chemin de Conches, 1200 Geneva 15, Switzerland.

International Science Foundation
2, Rue de Furstenberg, 75006 Paris, France.

International Social Science Council
1, Rue Miollis, 75015 Paris, France.

International Statistical Institute
Prinses Beatrixlaan 428, Voorburg 2270 AZ, Netherlands.

International Training and Research Center for Development
47, Rue de la Glacière, 75013 Paris, France.

Latin American Centre for Economic and Social Documentation
Casilla 179-D, Santiago, Chile.

Organization for Economic Cooperation and Development
Château de la Muette, 2, Rue André Pascal, 75775 Paris Cedex 16, France.

Regional Economic Research and Documentation Center
B.P. 7138, Lome, Togo.

Research Centre on Social and Economic Development in Asia
Institute of Economic Growth, University Enclave, Delhi 7, India.

Society for International Development
1346 Connecticut Avenue, N.W., Washington, DC 20036, USA.

Southeast Asian Social Science Association
Chulalongkorn University, c/o Faculty of Political Science, Bangkok, Thailand.

United Nations Institute for Training and Research
801 United Nations Plaza, New York, NY 10017, USA.

United Nations Research Institute for Social Development
Palais des Nations, 1211 Geneva 25, Switzerland.

AUSTRALIA

Australian Institute of International Affairs
P.O. Box E181, Canberra, ACT 2600.

Institute of Advanced Studies
The Australian National University, P.O. BOX 4,Canberra, ACT 2600.

Strategic and Defense Studies Center
Research School of Pacific Studies, Australian National University, P.O. Box 4,
   Canberra, ACT 2600.

AUSTRIA

Austrian Foundation for Development Research (OFSE)
Turkenstrasse 3, 1090 Vienna, Austria.

Vienna Institute for Development
Karntner Strasse 25, 1010 Vienna, Austria.

BANGLADESH

Bangladesh Institute of Development Studies
Adamjee Court, Motijheel Commercial Area, Dacca 2, Bangladesh.

BELGIUM

Catholic University of Louvain
Center for Economic Studies, Van Evenstraat 2b, 3000 Louvain, Belgium.

Free University of Brussels
Department of Applied Economics, 50, Avenue F-D Roosevelt, Brussels 1050,
   Belgium.

University of Antwerp
Centre for Development Studies, 13 Prinsstratt, 2000 Antwerp, Belgium.

BRAZIL

Brazilian Institute of Economics
Fundacao Getulio Vargas Caixa Postal 4081-zc-05, Rio de Janeiro, Brazil.

Programme of Joint Studies on Latin American Economic Integration
Caixa Postal 740, Rio de Janeiro, Brazil.

BULGARIA

Institute for International Relations and Socialist Integration
Bulgarian Academy of Sciences, Boulevard Pencho Slaveicov, 15, Sofia, Bulgaria.

Scientific Research Centre for Africa and Asia
Academy of Social Science, ul. Gagarin 2, Sofia 13, Bulgaria.

CANADA

Canadian Association of African Studies
Geography Department, Carleton University, Ottawa, Ontario, Canada K1S 5B6.

Canadian Council for International Cooperation
75 Sparks Street, Ottawa 4, Ontario, Canada K1N 7B7.

Canadian Institute of International Affairs
Edgar Tarr House, 31 Wellesley Street East, Toronto 284, Ontario, Canada M5S
   2V9.

Centre for Developing-Asia Studies
McGill University, Montreal, Quebec, Canada H3A 1Y1.

International Association of Science and Technology for Development
P.O. Box 25, Station G, Calgary, Alberta, Canada T3A 2G1.

Institute of International Relations
University of British Columbia, Vancouver 8, British Columbia, Canada V6T 1Z1.

International Development Research Centre
60 Queen Street, P.O. Box 8500, Ottawa, Ontario, Canada K1G 3H9.

Regional Development Research Center
University of Ottawa, Ottawa 2, Ontario, Canada K1N 6N5.

CHILE

Catholic University of Chile
Institute of Economics, Avda. Libertador Bernardo O'Higgins, No. 340, Santiago,
   Chile.

University of Chile
Planning Centre (CEPLA), Avda. Libertador Bernardo O'Higgins, No. 1058,
   Santiago, Chile.

COLOMBIA

University of Antioquia
Economic Research Centre, Apartado Aereo 1226, Medellin, Colombia.

DENMARK

Centre for Development Research
9, NY Kongensgade, 4K-1472 Copenhagen K, Denmark.

Institute for Development Research
V. Volgade 104, DK-1552 Copenhagen, Denmark.

FRANCE

Institute of Economic and Social Development Studies
University of Paris, 58, Boulevard Arago, 75013 Paris, France.

Institute for Economic Research and Development Planning
B.P. 47, 38040 Grenoble Cedex, France.

Institute for Research into the Economics of Production
2 Rue de Rouen, 92000 Nanterre, France.

International Centre of Advanced Mediterranean Agronomic Studies
11 Rue Newton, 75116 Paris, France.

346   Appendices

GERMANY

German Association for East Asian Studies
Rothenbaumchaussee 32, 2 Hamburg 13, Federal Republic of Germany.

International Institute of Management
Wissenschaftszentrum Berlin, Criegstrasse 5-7, Berlin 33, D-1000, Federal Republic
of Germany.

Institute for Development Research and Development Policy
Ruhr-Universität Bochum, 463 Bochum-Querenburg, Pstifach 2148, Federal
Republic of Germany.

GHANA

Institute of African Studies
University of Ghana, P.O. Box 73, Legon, Accra.

HUNGARY

Institute for Economic and Market Research
P.O. Box 133, Budapest 62, Hungary.

Institute for World Economics of the Hungarian Academy of Sciences
P.O. Box 36, Budapest 1531, Hungary.

INDIA

Centre for the Study of Developing Societies
29, Rajput Road, Delhi 6, India.

India Council for Africa
Nyaya Marg, Chankyapuri, New Delhi 21, India.

India International Centre
40 Lodi Estate, New Delhi 110001, India.

Indian Council of World Affairs
Sapru House, Barakhamba Road, New Delhi 110001, India.

Indian Institute of Asian Studies
23/354, Azad Nagar, Jaiprakash Road, Andheri, Bombay 38, India.

Indian School of International Studies
35, Ferozeshah Road, New Delhi 1, India.

Institute of Economic Growth
University of Enclave, Delhi 7, India.

Madras Institute of Development Studies
74 Second Main Road, Gandhinagar Adyar, Madras 20, India.

INDONESIA

National Institute of Economic and Social Research
Leknas, UC, P.O. Box 310, Djakarta, Indonesia.

ISRAEL

Afro-Asian Institute for Cooperative and Labour Studies
P.O. Box 16201, Tel-Aviv 63324, Israel.

David Horowitz Institute for the Research of Developing Countries
Tel-Aviv University, Ramat-Aviv, Tel-Aviv 69978, Israel.

Israeli Institute of International Affairs
P.O. Box 17027, Tel-Aviv 61170, Israel.

JAPAN

Institute of Developing Economies
42 Ichigaya-Hommura-cho, Sinjuku-ku, Tokyo 162, Japan.

Japan Center for Area Development Research
Iino Building, 2-1-1 Uchisaiwai-cho, Chiyoda-Ku, Tokyo, Japan.

KENYA

Institute for Development Studies
University of Nairobi, P.O. Box 30197, Nairobi, Kenya.

KOREA

Industrial Management Research Centre
Yonsei University, Sodaemoon-ku-Seoul, Korea.

Institute of the Middle East and Africa
Rom. 52, Dong-A Building, No. 55, 2nd-ka, Sinmoonro, Congro-ku, Seoul, Korea.

Institute of Overseas Affairs
Hankuk University of Foreign Studies, 270 Rimoon-dong, Seoul, Korea.

MEXICO

Centre for Economic Research and Teaching
Av. Country Club No. 208, Apdo. Postal 13628, Mexico 21, D. F.

NEPAL

Centre for Economic Development and Administration (CEDA)
Tribhuvan University, Kirtipur, P.O. Box 797, Kathmandu, Nepal.

NETHERLANDS

Centre for Development Planning
Erasmus University, Postbus 1738, Rotterdam, 3011 PV, Netherlands.

Centre for Latin American Research and Documentation
Nieuwe Doelenstraat 16, Amsterdam 1000, Netherlands.

Development Research Institute
Hogeschoollaan 225, Tiburg 4400, Netherlands.

Free University, Department of Development Economics
De Boelelaan 1105, Amsterdam 1000, Netherlands.

Institute of Social Studies
Badhuisweg 251, P.O. Box 90733, The Hague 2509 LS, Netherlands.

NEW ZEALAND

New Zealand Institute of Economic Research
26 Kelburn Parade, P.O. Box 3749, Wellington, New Zealand.

New Zealand Institute of International Affairs
P.O. Box 196, Wellington, New Zealand.

NIGERIA

Federal Institute of Industrial Research
Oshodi, PMB 21023 Ikeja, Lagos, Nigeria.

Institute of African Studies
University of Nigeria, Nsukka, Nigeria.

Nigerian Institute of International Affairs
Kofo Abayomi Road, Victoria Island, G.P.O. Box 1727, Lagos, Nigeria.

Nigerian Institute of Social and Economic Research
Private Mail Bag NO. 5, U.I. University of Ibadan, Ibadan, Nigeria.

NORWAY

The Chr. Michelsen Institute (DERAP)
Fantoftvegen 38, 5036 Fantoft, Bergen 5024, Norway.

International Peace Research Institute
Radhusgt 4, Oslo 1, Norway.

Norwegian Agency for International Development (NORAD)
Planning Department, Boks 18142 Oslo Dep., Oslo 1, Norway.

PAKISTAN

Department of International Relations
University of Karachi, Karachi-32, Pakistan.

PHILIPPINES

Asian Center
University of the Philippines, Palma Hall, Diliman D-505, Quezon City, Philippines.

Asian Institute of International Studies
Malcolm Hall, University of the Philippines, Diliman, Quezon City, Philippines.

Institute of Economic Development and Research School of Economics
University of the Philippines, Diliman, Quezon City, Philippines.

POLAND

Centre of African Studies
University of Warsaw, Al. Zwirki i Wigury 93, 02-089 Warsaw, Poland.

Research Institute for Developing Countries
Rakowiecka 24, Warsaw, Poland.

SINGAPORE

Institute of South-East Asian Studies
Campus of University of Singapore, House No. 8, Cluny Road, Singapore 10.

Singapore Institute of Asian Studies
Nanyang University, Jurong Road, Singapore 22.

SRI LANKA

Marga Institute
P.O. Box 601, 61 Isipathana Mawatha, Colombo 5, Sri Lanka.

SUDAN

Institute of African And Asian Studies
Faculty of Arts, University of Khartoum, P.O. Box 321, Khartoum, Sudan.

SWEDEN

Institute for International Economic Studies
Fack S-104 05, Stockholm 50, Sweden.

Stockholm School of Economics, Economic Research Institute
Box 6501, Stockholm 11383, Sweden.

UNITED KINGDOM

Centre of African Studies
University of Edinburgh, Adam Ferguson Building, George Square, Edinburgh 8.

Centre of Latin American Studies (Cambridge)
University of Cambridge, History Faculty Buiding, West Road, Cambridge CB3
    9ES, England.

Centre of Latin American Studies (OXFORD)
Oxford University, St. Antony's College, Oxford OX2 6JF, England.

Center for South-east Asian Studies
Centre of Hull, Hull HU6 7RX, England.

Centre of West African Studies
University of Birmingham, P.O. Box 363, Birmingham B15 2TT, England.

Institute of Development Studies
University of London, 31 Tavistock Square, London WCI, England.

Institute of Latin American Studies (Glasgow)
University of Glasgow, Glasgow G12 8QQ, England.

Institute for the Study of International Organisation
University of Sussex, Stanmer House, Stanmer Park, Brighton BN1 9QA, England.

Royal Institute of International Affairs
Chatham House, St. James' Square, London SW1Y 4LE, England.

UNITED STATES

African Studies Center (Boston)
Boston University, 10 Lenos Street, Brookline MA 02146, USA.

Brookings Institution
1775 Massachusetts Avenue, N.W., Washington, DC 20036, USA.

Center for Asian Studies
Arizona State University, Tempe, AZ 85281, USA.

Center for Comparative Studies in Technological Development and Social Change
University of Minnesota, Minneapolis, MN 55455, USA.

Center for Development Economics
Williams College, Williamston, MA 01267, USA.

Center for International Affairs
Harvard University, 6 Divinity Avenue, Cambridge, MA 02138, USA.

Center for International Studies
Massachusetts Insitute of Technology, Cambridge, MA 02139, USA.

Center of International Studies
Princeton University, 118 Corwin Hall, Princeton, NJ 08540, USA.

Center for Latin American Studies
Arizona State University, Tempe, AZ 85281, USA.

Center for Latin American Studies
University of Florida, Room 319 LAGH, Gainesville, FL 39611, USA.

Center for Research in Economic Development
506 East Liberty Street, Ann Arbor, MI 48108, USA.

Center for Stategic and International Studies
Georgetown University, 1800 K Street, N.W., Washington, DC 20006, USA.

Harvard Institute for International Development
Harvard University, 1737 Cambridge Street, Cambridge MA 02138, USA.

Industrial Research Institute
1550 M Street, NW, Washington, DC 20005, USA.

Institute of Latin American Studies
University of Texas at Austin, S. W. Richardson Hall, Austin, TX 78705, USA.

Institute for World Order
1140 Avenue of the Americas, New York, NY 10036, USA.

Stanford International Development
Education Center, P.O. Box 2329, Stanford, CA 94305, USA.

University Center for International Studies
University of Pittsbourgh, Social Sciences Building, Pittsburgh, PA 15213, USA.

University of Hawaii Centre for Development Studies
Department of Economics, Perteus Hall, 2424 Maile Way, Honolulu, HI 96822, USA.

World Future Society
4916 St. Elmo Avenue, Bethesda Branch, Washington, DC 20014, USA.

URUGUAY

Latin American Centre for Human Economy
Cerrito 475, P.O. Box 998, Montevideo, Uruguay.

VENEZUELA

University of Zulia
Department of Economic Research, Faculty of Economic and Social Sciences, Maracaibo, Venezuela.

YUGOSLAVIA

Institute for Developing Countries
41000 Zagreb, U1. 8 Maja 82, Yugoslavia.

Research Centre for Cooperation with Developing Countries
61 109 Ljubljana, Titova 104 P.O. Box 37, Yugoslavia.

APPENDIX C

International Economic and Industrial Organizations

AACB

(Association of African Central Banks)

The Association of African Central Banks came into existence in December 1969, and the Central Bank of Nigeria was one of the foundation members. The objectives of the Association are:

1. To promote cooperation in the monetary, banking, and financial spheres in Africa.
2. To assist in the formulation of guidelines along which agreements among African countries in the monetary and financial fields shall proceed.
3. To help strengthen all efforts aimed at bringing about and maintaining monetary financial stability in Africa.
4. To examine the effectiveness of international economic and financial institutions in which African countries have an interest and suggest ways of possible improvements.

ADB

(African Development Bank)

The ADB was established in September 1964 under the aegis of the UN Economic Commission for Africa and began operations in July 1966. The office is in Abidjan, Ivory Coast. The bank seeks to contribute to the economic and social development of members either individually or jointly. To this end, it aims at promoting investment of public and private capital in Africa, to use its normal capital resources to make or guarantee loans and investments, and to provide technical assistance in the preparation, financing and implementation of development projects. The bank may grant direct or indirect credits, and it may operate alone or in concert with other financial institutions.

ECA

(Economic Commission for Africa)

Established by the ECOSOC. Headquarters: Addis Ababa, Ethiopa.

353

ECAFE
(Economic Commission for Asia and the Far East)
Established by the ECOSOC. Headquarters: Bangkok, Thailand.

ECE
(Economic Commission for Europe)
Established by the ECOSOC. Members are the United States and European members
of the United Nations. Headquarters: Geneva, Switzerland.

ECLA
(Economic Commission for Latin America)
Established by the ECOSOC. Headquarters: Santiago, Chile.

ECOSOC
(Economic and Social Council)
One of the principal organs of the United Nations that promote economic and social
cooperation and coordinate the work of the specialized agencies.

ECOWAS
(Economic Community of West African States)
Sequel to the adoption of the draft treaty of the proposed Economic Community in
Monrovia, Liberia, in January 1975. Fifteen West African Countries, with a population of some 124 million, signed the agreement establishing the Economic Community of West African States (ECOWAS) in Lagos on May 28, 1975. The community
aims at promoting cooperation and development in all fields of economic activities
and at fostering closer relations among countries in the West African subregion.

ECSC
(European Coal and Steel Community)
Established in 1952 to increase efficiency in coal and steel industries by removing
trade restrictions. The original six members were Belgium, France, West Germany,
Italy, Luxembury, and the Netherlands; Denmark, Ireland, and the United King-
dom joined on January 1, 1973. Headquarters: Luxemburg. (London delegation: 23
Chesham Street SW1 X8NH).

EEC
(European Economic Community)
Established in 1958 by the members of the ECSC to promote economic and political
activities by establishing a customs union (the Common Market) Members: same
as for the ECSC. Headquarters: Brussels, Belgium.

EFTA
(European Free Trade Association)
Established in 1960 to promote economic development and expansion of trade by
progressive reduction of trade restrictions within the area. Original members were
Austria, Denmark, Iceland; from 1970, Norway, Portugal, Sweden, Switzerland,
and the United Kingdom. Finland became associated in 1961. Denmark and the
United Kingdom withdrew on January 1, 1973. Headquarters: Geneva, Switzerland.

EURATOM
(European Atomic Energy Community)
Established in 1958 by the members of the ECSC to coordinate their nuclear, industries and to develop nuclear research. Headquarters: Brussels, Belgium.

FAO
(Food and Agriculture Organization of the United Nations)
Specialized agency established in 1945 to advise on conservation of natural resources and methods of food processing and distribution. 125 members (1973). Headquarters: Rome, Italy.

GATT
(General Agreement on Tariffs and Trade)
Signed in 1947 by twenty-three countries and directed toward the reduction of trade barriers. Eighty contracting parties (1973); sixteen countries have relationship. Headquarters: Geneva, Switzerland.

IAEA
(International Atomic Energy Agency)
Specialized agency established in 1957 to develop the peaceful uses of atomic energy. Headquarters: Vienna, Austria.

IBRD
(International Bank for Reconstruction and Development; the World Bank)
Established in 1946 after the Bretton Woods Conference of 1944. It guides international investment and provides loans, mainly to developing countries. Address: 1818 H Street, N.W., Washington, DC 20433, USA.

ICAO
(International Civil Aviation Organization)
Specialized agency established in April 1947 to promote the safe and orderly development of civil aviation. Headquarters: Montreal, Canada.

ICJ
(International Court of Justice)
All members of the United Nations are parties to the statute of the court (15 judges elected for 9 years), binding themselves to comply with its decisions in cases in which they are involved. Headquarters: The Hague, Netherlands.

IDA
(International Development Association)
Specialized agency affiliated to the IBRD established in 1960 to promote economic development and ease pressures on balance of payments. Address: see IBRD.

IFC
(International Finance Corporation)
Specialized agency affiliated to the IBRD to invest in productive private enterprise in developing countries founded in 1956. Address: see IBRD.

ILO
(International Labour Organization)
Established in 1919 and now a specialized agency aiming at improving working conditions. Headquarters: Geneva, Switzeland.

IMCO
(Inter-governmental Maritime Consultative Organization)
Specialized agency established in 1959 to promote cooperation on international maritime questions. Seventy-four members. One associate (1973). Headquarters: 101 Piccadilly, London WIV OAE, Great Britain.

IMF
(International Monetary Fund)
Specialized agency established in 1945 with the IBRD after the Bretton Woods Conference. It promotes foreign exchange stability to stimulate world trade and operates as a central banker. Address: 19th and H Streets, N.W. Washington, DC 20431, USA.

ITU
(International Telecommunication Union)
Formed in 1932 and now a specialized agency. Headquarters: Geneva, Switzerland.

NATO
(North Atlantic Treaty Organization)
Founded by twelve countries in 1949 to unite efforts for collective defense. Headquarters: Brussels, Belgium.

OAU
(Organization of African Unity)
The OAU was born on May 25, 1963, in Addis Ababa, Ethiopia, following the formal signing of its charter by thirty independent African heads of state. The principles and objectives of the Organization are:
  1. To promote the unity and solidarity of African States.
  2. To coordinate and intensify their cooperation and efforts to achieve a better life for the people of Africa.
  3. To defend their sovereignty, their territorial integrity, and their independence.
  4. To eradicate all forms of colonialism from Africa.
  5. To promote international cooperation, with due regard to the charter of the United Nations and the Universal Declaration of Human Rights.

OECD
(Organization for Economic Cooperation and Development)
Established in 1961 as a successor of the EEC (European Economic Cooperation). Nineteen European members, Australia, Canada, Japan, and United States. Headquarters: Paris, France.

SEATO
(South-East Asia Collective Defense Treaty Organization)
Established in 1955 by eight members. Headquarters: Bangkok, Thailand.

UN
(United Nations)
Established on October 24, 1945. Its principal components are:
1. General Assembly of all members, normally meeting once a year.
2. Security Council of members.
3. Economic and Social Council.
4. Trusteeship Council.
5. International Court of Justice.
6. Secretariat Membership.
Headquarters: New York, USA (London information centre: 14-15 Stratford Place, WIN 9AF).

UNCTAD
(United Nations Conference on Trade and Development)
Established in 1964 to promote international trade. Headquarters: Geneva, Switzerland.

UNDP
(United Nations Development Programme)
Established in 1965 to raise the standard of living in developing countries. Headquarters: New York, USA.

UNESCO
(United Nations Educational, Scientific, and Cultural Organization)
Specialized agency established in 1946; it developed from the International Institute of Intellectual Cooperation that existed under the League of Nations. Headquarters: Paris, France.

UNIDO
(United Nations Industrial Development Organization)
Established in 1965 to promote industry in developing countries. Headquarters: Vienna, Austria.

UPU
(Universal Postal Union)
Specialized agency established in 1875 to unite members in a single postal territory. Headquarters: Berne, Switzerland.

WACH
(West African Clearing House)
At the fifth regular meeting of the West African Sub-Regional Committee of the Association of African Central Banks (AACB) held in Lagos on March 13 and 15, 1975, the governors initialed the Articles of Agreement establishing the West African Clearing House. The clearing arrangement is aimed at facilitating trade and payment among member countries. The clearing house formally commenced business at the 12 centers on July 1, 1976. Headquarters: Freetown, Sierra-Leone.

WHO
(World Health Organization)
Specialized agency established in 1948 to raise standards of health. Headquarters: Geneva, Switzerland.

APPENDIX D

Glossary of International Business Terms

Abrogate   To abolish or declare void by formal authoritative measures.

Acceleration Clause   A condition in a loan or mortgage that makes the whole of the outstanding balance due in the event of failure by the debtor to maintain regular payments.

Acceptance Supra Protest   When a bill of exchange is protested and then accepted by another party to save the name of the drawer. Also called acceptance for honor.

Accommodation Note   A document signed by an individual who is prepared to act as a guarantor on behalf of a person whose credit is doubtful.

Acknowledgment   A formal notice to the sender of goods or money informing him that they have been received.

Advice Note   Usually notes sent by railways for freight companies to inform firms that their consignments have arrived and are awaiting collection.

Airway Bill   An air transport term for the document made out on behalf of the shipper as evidence of the contract of carriage. Also also called air consignment note.

Annual Return   Document that must show the names of persons who have ceased to be owners since the last return, a statement showing the sales and profits of the business for the year and a statement of the assets and capital of the business at the end of the year. It is open for inspection by any person.

Appropriation Account   The account of a business that shows how the profits are to be allocated.

Articles of Association   The document containing the conditions of regulations for the conduct of the internal affairs of a company.

Assets   Items of value whose value arises not from any intrinsic worth but from their ability to earn revenue.

Assets (current)   Those assets which form part of a company's trading cycle (e.g., stocks, raw materials, etc.).

Assets (fixed)   Those assets which enable a company to carry out its operations. They form the basic production facilities of a company (e.g., land, factories, offices, machinery, etc.). Most are tangible, but some are intangible, for example, patents.

Average Costs   The total production expenses (including minimum profit) divided by the number of commodities produced.

Balance Sheet   A statement produced periodically, normally at the end of the financial year, showing an organization's assets and liabilities, expressed either as totals or as balances if a two-way flow has occurred.

Balloon Note   A promissory note that necessitates small repayments during the early period of a loan and larger repayments toward the latter period.

Bill of Exchange   Defined officially as "an unconditional order in writing addressed by one person to another, signed by the person giving it, requiring the person to whom it is addressed to pay on demand, or at a fixed or determinable future time, a certain sum in money to, or to the order of a specified person, or to the bearer" (Bills of Exchange Act, 1882), a bill of exchange is essentially a post-dated cheque, drawn by a supplier in his own favor to be signed by a company.

Bill of Lading   A bill of lading serves three purposes: (1) when signed by the ship-owners, it acknowledges the safe receipt of the goods on board ship; (2) it constitutes the contract between shipowner and shipper and states to what extent the shipowners can be held responsible for safe carriage of the goods; (3) it is also the document of title, and the holder is entitled to demand delivery of the merchandise on producing it.

Blanket Insurance   Insurance cover that relates to a range of goods or property that may vary at different periods of time.

Bridging Loan   A short-term advance by a bank to a customer pending the receipt by him of funds from another source (e.g., when a person buying a new house has to wait for the old house to be sold).

Buffer Stock   A quantity of raw material retained in store to safeguard against unexpected shortages due to delivery delays or sudden upsurge in demand.

C.I.F. (cost insurance freight)   Agreement whereby the seller undertakes to arrange to supply goods, pay the freight charges, and insure them until they reach the destination, for a quoted price.

Cambist   A dealer who exchanges foreign currency or who negotiates transactions in bills of exchange.

Ceiling Prices   The maximum prices that are permitted when price-control legislation is in effect.

Certificate   A written declaration of the truth about a specific matter.

Condition   A term in a contract that must be a statement fact. Failure to fulfill allows the other party to repudiate.

Consignee   The party to whom goods are being sent.

Consignor   The sender of a consignment of goods.

Continuation Clause   A marine insurance clause covering situations where a ship is still at sea when its insurance runs out. The insurer agrees to cover risks at a pro rata rate of premium.

Contract   A legally enforceable agreement between two or more persons. It normally takes the form of one person's promise to do something in consideration of the other's agreeing to do, or suffer to do something in return.

Copyright   The exclusive right legally granted to the author to make and control copies of a book or other artistic work.

Debentures   Loans to a company as opposed to shares in it, as a form of investment. The holders have no say in the company policy or in the election of directors; they are, however, entitled to interest on their loans before profits are distributed. If the company fails to make these payments, debenture holders would be entitled to sell the business in order to obtain their due interest and loan repayment.

Debit Notes   Notes sent to customers to inform them that their accounts in the seller's ledger has been charged with a stated sum, and the reason for this. Debit notes are used to adjust undercharges, as credit notes are used to adjust overcharges.

Depreciation   A term for the amount by which the usefulness of a fixed asset has diminished.

Dividend   A proportion of company profits paid to shareholders at regular intervals.

Dividend Warrant   A check in payment of a dividend, issued by a company to shareholder.

Down Market   A term used to describe goods aimed at the lower quality end of the market.

Dry Goods   A collective term for clothing, hardware, and related merchandise as distinct from grocery items.

Duty   A tax levied on goods as a means of producing revenue for the country.

Ejectment   A legal action for the recovery of the possession of property.

Elastic Demand   Market condition in which a small change in price results in a large change in demand.

Endorsement   A signature written on the back of a document or a bill of exchange so that it is transferred to a third party.

Endowment Fund   A fund from which the interest may be spent but the capital sum must be maintained.

Escalator Clause   A condition in a contract that allows for increases in price under certain specific circumstances.

Estimate   An approximate assessment of the price of goods or services given in advance by those who wish to undertake their supply.

Executed Contract   A contract where one party has performed all that is required of him to fulfill his obligations.

Exemption Clause   A clause, often in a sale of goods contract, excluding the supplier from any claims as to the condition of the goods.

Extended Coverage   An additional clause in an insurance policy that provides cover against risks in addition to those stated in the basic policy.

F.A.S. ("free alongside ship")   Indicates that the quoted price includes all costs up to bringing the goods alongside the vessel. The importer must then pay for goods to be taken on board and all freight and insurance charges.

F.O.B. ("free on board")   Indicates that the cost quoted includes all expenses up to and including the loading of the goods on the vessel at a specified port.

Fixed Charge   Unavoidable overheads such as interest payments, depreciation and rent, which cannot be related to the level of business activity of an organization.

Fixed Costs   Overhead costs that do not vary with the volume of production (e.g., rent).

Free from Particular Average   A marine insurance term meaning that the insurers are not responsible for anything other than total loss and general average loss.

Free of all Average   A term for policies where the insurer takes no responsibility for general average loss and will pay only on total loss.

Free Trade   International trade unrestricted by import and export quotas, tariffs, and other controls that impede the free movement of goods between countries.

Freight Absorption   The practice of a seller of goods of not charging the purchaser for costs incurred in the transport of goods.

Fundamental Disequilibrium   The constant discrepancy between the official exchange rate of the currency of a country and purchasing power of that currency.

General Average   A marine insurance term for a loss deliberately incurred in order to avoid a danger (e.g., when cargo is thrown overboard to prevent a ship from sinking). In such instances, the loss is apportioned between the shipowners and the cargo owners.

General Tariff   A standard rate of duty applied to an unparted commodity irrespective of the country of its origin.

Going Long   The practice in the commodity markets of buying first and then selling, in the hope of a rising price trend (opposite of going short).

Going Short   The commodity market term for selling before purchasing, with a view to profiting by a fall in prices (opposite of going long).

Gross Weight   The combined weight of goods and packaging.

Groundage   A charge levied by some port authorities for permitting vessels to anchor there.

Guarantee   An agreement to be responsible for the debt, default, or miscarriage of another person.

Guarantor   A person who makes or gives a guarantee.

Harbor Dues   A payment made for use of port facilities.

Hard Sell   A marketing term denoting a vigorous sales campaign, a procedure adopted when selling is difficult.

Hedging   Protecting an investment against loss caused by fluctuations in the market. This is usually achieved by offsetting the cost of a present purchase against a purchase of the same commodity or security in the future.

Holder   The person who has possession of a negotiable instrument.

Holding Company   A company formed for the express purpose of exercising financial control over a number of operating companies by buying up all or the majority of their shares.

Impost   Another name for a tax, especially levied on imports.

Indemnity   An agreement whereby one person agrees to make good any loss suffered by a party to contract to which he or she himself is a stranger. The most common contracts of indemnity are insurance contracts.

Indenture   A form of agreement drawn up for the sale of bonds or debentures.

Instrumental Capital   All capital equipment used in the production of goods.

Interest Warrant   A document sent to shareholders that entitles them to the payment of interest on stock.

Invoice   A document issued by a vendor of goods stating the nature of those goods, the name of the debtor and sum due.

Jettison   A marine insurance term meaning to throw goods overboard for a good and sufficient reason (e.g., in order to lighten ship in time of danger).

Job Costing   The allocation of all costs to a specific contract for a particular customer.

Judgment Note   A legal document acknowledging the existence of a debt.

Keelage   The payment made by a shipowner when a ship enters and remains in port.

Kickback   Illegal payment made to obtain a contract or favor.

Kiting   Taking advantage of the check clearing system by drawing checks on deposits that are already committed, assuming that the delay in clearing the check will allow time to replenish the account.

Landed Terms   A quotation for the sale and carriage of goods by sea that includes all costs up until the goods are actually landed.

Lay Days   A specified number of days allocated for the unloading and loading of a ship, commencing with arrival in port.

Lease   A contract specifying the terms, of time and cost, of possessing and using a property.

Lessee   The person to whom a lease is granted.

Letter of Credit   A document issued by a bank that entitles the bearer to draw money on the bank's account. Often used for overseas transactions.

Leverage   The ratio between the debts of the business and the owner's capital.

Limited Liability   A company that at law is a separate entity quite apart from the people who own it (i.e., and only the company can be sued). It follows that the liability of the shareholders of such a company is limited to the amount of capital they have invested in it.

Limited Partner   A limited partner cannot take part in the running of the business, his liability is limited to the amount he has invested.

Liquidated Damages   The amount calculated as recompense if a contract is not fulfilled.

Liquidation   This is effectively the bankruptcy of a company. There are two forms of liquidation: voluntary and compulsory. When a company is wound up, assets are realized and debts paid as far as possible. If any monies remain these are distributed to the owners of the company according to their respective rights.

Marginal Costing   Calculating the production costs excluding all fixed costs and overheads that do not alter with the volume of production.

Marked Check   A check that is guaranteed by the bank on which it is drawn.

Merger   The combination of two or more companies to form one new company.

Monopoly   Any firm that produces such a high proportion of the total output of a commodity that it can influence price by regulating supply.

Monopsony   A market situation where there is only one major purchaser of goods or services.

Mortgage Debenture   A fixed-interest security the commonest of which is a mortgage debenture. This is usually secured on the most saleable assets of the company (e.g., head office, land, etc.).

Notice   A period of time granted by law to employees who have been made redundant or dismissed during which they must continue to be employed at their original jobs or alternatively who must be given wages if dismissed immediately.

Not Negotiable   The cancellation of the free transferability of a negotiable instrument, usually by writing the phrase on the face of the document.

Objective Value   The value in exchange or the market value of a product. A product can have value to the owner without being of value to anyone else.

Oligopsony   A market situation where there are only a few purchasers of certain goods or services so that each purchaser is in a position to influence the price paid.

Open Check   A check that is uncrossed and can therefore be cashed over the counter without first being paid into an account.

Ordinary Shares   Customary form of equity investment in a company on a par value. Ordinary shareholders have no guaranteed claim on profits, but they receive dividends from profits on the recommendation of directors and may vote at the election of those directors.

Original Bill   A bill of exchange sold before it has been endorsed.

Pari Passu   In equal proportions.

Partnership   A relationship that exists between two or more people to carry on a business in common with a view to profit.

Patent   A license taken out by an inventor to protect an invention from unauthorized use by other persons.

Power of Attorney   A form of instrument authorizing the holder to act on behalf of another (e.g., to sign deeds). This is often used when the principal is in a different country.

Preference Shares   Shares that, as opposed to ordinary shares, carry a fixed rate of dividend payable as a first charge out of profits.

Primage   A freight charge paid in order to ensure that care is taken when loading or unloading goods.

Prime Costs   Costs that vary with output, as opposed to fixed costs that are standing charges that do not change with increase or decrease of output.

Pro Forma Invoice   A preliminary invoice stating the value of goods and notifying the recipient that they have been dispatched. It is not a demand for money and might for instance accompany goods sent off on approval.

Prohibited Risk   Risk that is not insurable because it is too great for the insurance company to accept.

Promissory Note   A document containing a promise to pay a certain sum of money at a fixed time. It can become a negotiable instrument.

Proof of Loss   The written document required by an insurance company as proof that a loss has taken place.

Pro Rata   In proportion to a total sum.

Proviso   A condition in a document or contract.

Qualification Shares   Shares that a director of a company is obliged to own if he or she is to be recognized as a director.

Quick Ratio   The relationship between current assets and current liabilities. This should indicate if a business can pay its liabilities quickly in cash.

Quorum   The number of persons who must be present at a meeting in order that it may officially take place.

Quota   A limit set on the entry of goods or persons into a country.

Quotation   A definition in writing of the price, terms, and conditions of a potential contract.

Rally   An improvement in the market price of shares or commodities after a decline.

Rate of Exchange   The rate at which one currency will exchange for another.

Ratification   The formal confirmation of an agreement applied especially in the law relating to agents.

Realization   Conversion of assets into cash.

Receiving Order   The first stage in bankruptcy proceedings. It is a court order that brings the property of a debtor under the protection of the court until the bankruptcy proceedings have been concluded.

Redraft   A new bill of exchange that is drawn up when a bill is dishonored. It incorporates the additional charges involved in the dishonor.

Remittance   Money in any form sent from one person to another.

Repudiation   Formal refusal to pay a debt by the debtor.

Rights Issue   With a rights issue of ordinary shares, new shares are offered to the holders of existing ordinary shares in proportion to their existing holdings. The right is a preemptive choice of purchase of the new shares.

Risk   A situation in which the outcomes of a decision can be estimated and each outcome can be estimated to have a probability of occurring. This is to be distinguished from an uncertainty situation when the outcomes can be estimated but the probability of each outcome occurring is unknown, and a situation of complete uncertainty, when neither outcomes nor probabilities can be estimated.

Royalty   A regular payment made for the use of land for mining, or the use of a patent or trademark, or the right to publish and sell copyrighted material.

Scab   A worker who refuses to cooperate with the unions in a strike.

Scrip Issue   Free shares issued to shareholders in order to reduce reserves.

Search Warrant   A legal document that authorizes a person to enter private property or open packages in the pursuit of stolen goods.

Security   Something given or guaranteed by a borrower as safeguard for a loan. The term is not applied to shares, but to debentures and similar loan stock and to negotiable instruments.

Severable Contracts   This phrase often occurs in contracts for the sale of goods particularly where the goods are to be delivered in installments. It is possible, but not necessary, to treat separate installments as separate contracts.

Sight Bill   A bill that becomes payable as soon as it is presented.

Sleeper   A security or business that has not been active but is believed to be potentially valuable.

Spot Price   Current market price.

Stale Check   Check that has been unpaid or not presented for a considerable time.

Stamp Duty   A tax applied to legal documents.

Subpoena   A legal writ that compels a person to appear in court.

Sunk Cost   A fixed overhead of a business such as buildings, roads, special machines.

Surtax   Extra tax paid usually on incomes over a certain level.

Tare   The weight of the package or container in which goods are held.

Time Bill   Bill of Exchange with a fixed date of payment.

Title Deeds   The documents that act as proof of ownership of property.

Toll   A charge made for the use of a dock, motorway, bridge, tunnel, and so on.

Trademark   An identifying mark that distinguishes the product of one firm from another in the same field.

Turnover   An accountancy term for gross takings or total sales before any deductions are made.

Underwriting   The term that describes the commitment on the part of a collection of investing institutions or issuing houses to take up shares at the issue prices if other investors fail to do so in exchange for a fixed fee of between 1 percent and 3 percent of the issue.

Undue Influence   A form of moral pressure. A contract will not be enforced by a court if it can be shown that the defendant was in a position that prevented him or her from forming a free and unfettered judgment. Undue influence will not be presumed unless certain relations (e.g. parental or confidential) exist between the parties.

Unrealized Profits   Profits that exist but have not yet been turned into cash.

Unsecured Loan   A type of fixed-interest security not secured to any assets by the deed covering the loan. There is still a right to realize the assets of the company should it not comply with the conditions laid down in the deed.

Upset Price   The minimum price that a seller will accept for his or her property.

Venture Capital   High-risk investment (e.g., shares bought in a new business).

Vertical Integration   The linking-up of a number of business concerns, each operating at a different stage in the same industry. This is opposed to horizontal integration, the linking-up of a number of firms at the same stage.

Vested Interest   Interest now, as opposed to interest anticipated. Property is said to vest when the absolute owner is finally established, and his interest is in no way capable of being terminated by anyone but himself.

Visa   An endorsement on a passport that permits a person to travel in a particular country where entry restrictions are in force.

Visible Items of Trade   Physical imports and exports excluding the invisibles such as insurance, freight and bank charges, etc.

Voidable Contract   A contract that can be declared void on the basis of insanity, minority or incompetency of one of the parties to it.

Warranty   A statement of fact in a contract, either express or implied. If it is unfulfilled, the injured party cannot repudiate the contract but may be able to claim damages. The difference between a warranty and a condition is that a condition is fundamental to a contract, whereas a warranty is not.

Wasting Asset   An accounting term for assets that are used up gradually in producing goods. It is generally applied to fixed assets, but is perhaps better applied to assets that are exhausted after a certain period of time (e.g., quarries, mines, etc.).

Without Recourse   A phrase used to protect the seller of a bill of exchange in the event that the bill is unpaid when due.

Working Assets   Those assets that can readily be turned into cash, such as raw materials, semifinished goods, debts, and so on.

Working Capital   A term for that part of a company's capital that is continually circulating. The figure is calculated by deducting current liabilities from current assets.

Work in Progress   The value of work commenced but not yet completed (e.g., in a manufacturing business, partly finished goods; in a contracting business, uncompleted contracts).

Writ   A court order.

Write Down   An accountancy expression describing the process of reducing the book value of an asset.

Write-off   An accountancy term denoting a debt that cannot be collected and is therefore written off against profits. It is also more generally applied to any property that has been damaged and cannot be repaired.

Bibliography

Adebayo, Adedeji, and Timothy M. Shaw, eds. *Economic Crisis in Africa: African Perspective on Development Problems and Potentials.* Lynne Rienner Publishers, Boulder, CO., 1985.

Agmon, Tamir. *Political Economy and Risk in World Financial Markets.* Lexington Books, Lexington, MA, 1985.

Akande, Agboola. "Potential Problems in Introducing the Concept of 'Contracting Out' (Privatization) in Developing Nations." Working Paper, Department of Public Administration, University of Oklahoma, Norman, 1987.

Akande, Olayinka. "Science and Technology Policy: Speaking Truth with Power and the Need for a New Direction." *The Financial Newsline,* Lagos, Nigeria, Vol. 1, No. 1, 1987, pp. 32-34.

Akao, Y., and T. Asaka, eds. *Quality Function Deployment.* Productivity, Inc., Cambridge, MA, 1990.

Arinze, Bay, and F. Y. Partovi. "A Knowledge-Based Decision Support System for Project Management." *Computers & Operations Research,* Vol. 19, No. 5, 1992, pp. 321-334.

Arndt, H. W. *Economic Development: The History of an Idea.* The University of Chicago Press, Chicago, IL, 1987.

Assad, A. A., and E. A. Wasil. "Project Management Using A Microcomputer." *Computers and Operations Research,* Vol. 13, No. 2/3, 1986, pp. 231-260.

Atta, Jacob K. *A Macroeconomic Model of a Developing Economy: Ghana,* University Press of America. Washington, D.C., 1981.

Badiru, Adedeji B. "Communication, Cooperation, Coordination: The Triple C of Project Management." In *Proceedings of 1987 IIE Spring Conference,* Washington, D.C., May 1987, pp. 401-404.

―――. *Expert Systems Applications in Engineering and Manufacturing.* Prentice-Hall, Englewood Cliffs, NJ, 1992.

————. "A Management Guide to Automation Cost Justification." *Industrial Engineering,* Vol. 22, No. 2, Feb. 1990a, pp. 26-30.

————. *Project Management in Manufacturing and High Technology Operations.* John Wiley & Sons, NY, 1988.

————. *Project Management Tools for Engineering and Management Professionals.* Industrial Engineering and Management Press, Norcross, GA, 1991.

Badiru, Adedeji B., and Jacob Jen-Gwo Chen. "IEs Help Transform Industrial Productivity and Quality in Taiwan." *Industrial Engineering,* Vol 24, No. 6, June 1992, pp. 53-55.

Badiru, Adedeji B. "A Systems Approach to Total Quality Management." *Industrial Engineering,* Vol. 22, No. 3, March 1990b, pp. 33-36.

————. "Training IEs for a Management Role." *Industrial Engineering,* Vol. 19, No. 12, December 1987, pp. 18-23.

Badiru, Adedeji B., and Gary E. Whitehouse. *Computer Tools, Models, and Techniques for Project Management.* TAB Books, Blue Ridge Summit, PA, 1989.

Bagis, Ali Ihsan. *G.A.P.: Southeastern Anatolia Project — The Cradle of Civilization Regenerated.* InterBank, Instanbul, Turkey, 1989.

Barker, C. E., et. al. *African Industrialisation.* Gower Publishing Company, Brookfield, VT, 1986.

Bedworth, David D. *Industrial Systems: Planning, Analysis, and Control.* The Ronald Press, NY, 1973.

Bedworth, D. D., and James E. Bailey. *Integrated Production Control Systems: Management, Analysis, Design.* John Wiley & Sons, NY, 1982.

Bell, Colin E. "Maintaining Project Networks in Automated Artificial Intelligence Planning." *Management Science,* Vol. 35, No. 10, 1989, pp. 1192-1214.

Benson, Summer. "How National Security Considerations Affect Technology Transfer." *Journal of Technology Transfer,* Vol. 13, No. 1, Fall 1988, pp. 34-41.

Bent, James A., and Albert Thumann. *Project Management for Engineering and Construction.* The Fairmont Press, Lilburn, GA, 1989.

Berg, Robert J., and Jennifer S. Whitaker, eds. *Strategies for African Development,* University of California Press, Berkeley, CA, 1986.

Bergen, S. A. *R&D Management: Managing Projects and New Products.* Basil Blackwell, Cambridge, MA, 1990.

Bey, Roger B., Robert H. Doersch, and James H. Patterson. "The Net Present Value Criterion: Its Impact on Project Scheduling." *Project Management Quarterly,* June 1981, pp. 223-233.

Bidanda, Bopaya. "Techniques to Assess Project Feasibility." *Project Management Journal,* Vol 20, No. 2, June 1989, pp. 5-10.

Boctor, Fayez F. "Some Efficient Multi-Heuristic Procedures for Resource-Constrained Project Scheduling." *European Journal of Operational Research,* Vol. 49, 1990, pp. 3-13.

Brand, J. D., W. L. Meyer, and L. R. Shaffer. "The Resource Scheduling Method for Construction." *Civil Engineering Studies Report,* No. 5, University of Illinois, Urbana, 1964.

Browne, Jimmie, J. Harhen, and J. Shivnan. *Production Management Systems: A CIM Perspective.* Addison-Wesley, Reading, MA, 1988.

Bussey, Lynn E., and Ted G. Eschenbach. *The Economic Analysis of Industrial Projects,* 2d ed. Prentice-Hall, Englewood Cliffs, NJ, 1992.

Canada, John R., and William G. Sullivan. *Economic and Multiattribute Evaluation of Advanced Manufacturing Systems.* Prentice-Hall, Englewood Cliffs, NJ, 1989.

Chapman, C. B., D. F. Cooper, and M. J. Page. *Management for Engineers.* John Wiley & Sons, NY, 1987.

Chase, Richard B., and Nicholas J. Aquilano. *Production Operations Management,* rev. ed. Richard D. Irwin, NY, 1977.

Chuntaketa, Prateeb. "Planning and Development of Industrial Cities." Public Lecture, College of Architecture, University of Oklahoma, Norman, October 4, 1991.

Clayton, E., and F. Petry, eds. *Monitoring Systems for Agricultural and Rural Development Projects.* Food and Agriculture Organization of the United Nations, Rome, 1981.

Cleland, David I. *Project Management: Strategic Design and Implementation.* TAB Professional and Reference Books, NY, 1990.

———. "Strategic Issues in Project Management." *Project Management Journal,* Vol. 20, No. 1, March 1989, pp. 31-39.

———, eds. *Project Management Handbook.* Van Nostrand Reinhold, NY, 1983.

———. *Systems Analysis and Project Management,* 3d ed. McGraw-Hill, NY, 1983.

Cleland, David I., and Dundar F. Kocaoglu. *Engineering Management.* McGraw-Hill, NY, 1981.

Cohen, William A. *High-Tech Management.* John Wiley & Sons, NY, 1986.

Cooper, Dale, and Chris Chapman. *Risk Analysis for Large Projects: Models, Methods, and Cases.* John Wiley & Sons, NY, 1987.

Corsten, Hans. "Technology Transfer from Universities to Small and Medium-sized Enterprises—An Empirical Survey from the Standpoint of Such Enterprises." *Technovation,* Vol. 6, No. 1, April 1987, pp. 57-68.

Davies, C., A. Demb, and R. Espejo. *Organization for Project Management.* John Wiley & Sons, NY, 1979.

Davis, Edward W., ed. *Project Management: Techniques, Applications, and Managerial Issues,* 2d ed. Industrial Engineering and Management Press, Norcross, GA, 1983.

Derakhshani, S. "Factors Affecting Success in International Transfers of Technology: A Synthesis and a Test of a New Contingency Model." *Developing Economies,* Vol. 21, 1983, pp. 27-45.

Dhillon, B. S. *Engineering Management: Concepts, Procedures, and Models.* Technomic Publishing, Lancaster, PA, 1987.

Dinsmore, Paul C. *Human Factors in Project Management,* rev. ed. American Management Association, NY, 1990.

Doersch, R. H., and J. H. Patterson. "Scheduling a Project to Maximize Its Present Value: A Zero-One Programming Approach." *Management Science,* Vol. 23, No. 8, 1977, pp. 882-889.

Drexl, Andreas. "Scheduling of Project Networks by Job Assignment." *Management Science,* Vol. 37, No. 12, 1991, pp. 1590-1602.

Drigani, Fulvio. *Computerized Project Control.* Marcel Dekker, NY, 1989.

Du Bois, Peter C. "Togo to Go Private." *Barron's,* Jan. 26, 1987.

Dumbleton, J. H. *Management of High-Technology Research and Development.* Elsevier, NY, 1986.

East, E. William, and Jeffrey G. Kirby. *A Guide to Computerized Project Scheduling.* Van Nostrand Reinhold, NY, 1989.

Elmaghraby, Salah E. *Activity Networks: Project Planning and Control by Network Models.* John Wiley & Sons, NY, 1977.

———. "Project Bidding Under Deterministic and Probabilistic Activity Durations." *European Journal of Operational Research,* Vol. 49, 1990, pp. 14–34.

Elmaghraby, Salah E., and Willy S. Herroelen. "The Scheduling of Activities to Maximize the Net Present Value of Projects." *European Journal of Operational Research,* Vol. 49, 1990, pp. 35–49.

Fabrycky, Wolter J., and B. S. Blanchard. *Life-Cycle Cost and Economic Analysis.* Prentice-Hall, Englewood Cliffs, NJ, 1991.

Farid, Foad, and R. Kangari. "A Knowledge-Based System for Selecting Project Management Microsoftware Packages." *Project Management Journal,* Vol. 22, No. 3, 1991, pp. 55–61.

Finger, Nachum. *The Impact of Government Subsidies on Industrial Management: The Israeli Experience.* Praeger, NY, 1971.

Fisk, Donald, Kiesling Herbert, and Muller Thomas. *Private Provision of Public Services: An Overview.* The Urban Institute, Washington, D.C., 1987.

Fitzgerald, E. V. *Public Sector Investment Planning for Developing Countries.* Holmes and Meier, NY, 1978.

Fleischer, G. A. *Engineering Economy: Capital Allocation Theory.* Brooks/Cole, Monterey, CA, 1984.

Food and Agricultural Organization. *Regional Food Plan For Africa.* Food and Agriculture Organization of the United Nations, Rome, Italy, 1978.

Frame, J. Davidson. *Managing Projects in Organizations.* Jossey-Bass, San Francisco, 1987.

Gharajedagtii, Jamshid. A Prologue to National Development Planning. Greenwood Press, NY, 1986.

Gessner, Robert A. *Manufacturing Information Systems: Implementation Planning.* John Wiley & Sons, NY, 1984.

Ghosh, Pradip K., ed. *Developing Africa: A Modernization Perspective.* Greenwood Press, Westport, CT, 1984.

Gibson, John E. *Modern Management of the High-Technology Enterprise.* Prentice-Hall, Englewood Cliffs, NJ, 1990.

Gilbreath, Robert D. *Winning at Project Management: What Works, What Fails, and Why.* John Wiley & Sons, NY, 1986.

Glasser, Alan. *Research and Development Management.* Prentice-Hall, Englewood Cliffs, NJ, 1982.

Golden, Bruce L., Edward A. Wasil, and Patrick T. Harker, eds. *The Analytic Hierarchy Process: Applications and Studies.* Springer-Verlag, NY, 1989.

Gonen, Turan. *Engineering Economy for Engineering Managers with Computer Applications.* John Wiley & Sons, NY, 1990.

Gordon, Theodore J., and Olaf Helmer. "Report on a Long-Range Forecasting Study." Rand Corporation, NY, Paper 2982, Sept. 1964.

Graham, Robert J. *Project Management: Combining Technical and Behavioral Approaches for Effective Implementation.* Van Nostrand Reinhold, NY, 1985.

Grant, Eugene L., W. G. Ireson, and R. S. Leavenworth. *Principles of Engineering Economy,* 7th ed. John Wiley & Sons, NY, 1982.

Hajek, Victor G. *Management of Engineering Projects.* McGraw-Hill, NY, 1977.

———. *Project Engineering: Profitable Technical Program Management.* McGraw Hill, 1965.

Hanrahan, John D. *Government by Contract.* Norton, NY, 1983.

———. *Government for Sale.* American Federation of State, County, and Municipal Employees, 1625 L Street, NW, Washington, D.C. 20063, 1977.

Harrison, F. L. *Advanced Project Management,* 2d ed. John Wiley & Sons, NY, 1985.

Hatry, Harry P. *A Review of Private Approaches for Delivery of Public Services.* The Urban Institute Press, Washington, D.C., 1983.

Herzberg, Frederick. *Work and the Nature of Man.* World Publishing, Cleveland, OH, 1960.

Hicks, Philip E. *Introduction to Industrial Engineering and Management Science.* McGraw-Hill, NY, 1977.

Hoelscher, H. E. "Managing in an Unmanageable World." *Engineering Management International,* Vol. 4, 1987, pp. 151-154.

Hoffman, Thomas R. *Production Management and Manufacturing Systems.* Wadsworth Publishing, Belmont, CA, 1967.

House, Ruth Sizemore. *The Human Side of Project Management.* Addison-Wesley, Reading, MA, 1988.

Hribar, John P. "Development of an Engineering Manager." *Journal of Management in Engineering,* Vol. 1, 1985, pp. 36-41.

Humphreys, Kenneth K., ed. *Project and Cost Engineer's Handbook,* 2d ed. Marcel Dekker, NY, 1984.

Hutcheson, John M. "Developing Countries—A Challenge to Project Managers." *Project Management Journal,* March 1984, pp. 77-85.

Institutional Shareholder Services, Inc. "Face the Corporate Challenge: Essay Competition." INS, Washington, D.C., 1987.

International Labour Office. *Employment Effects of Multinational Enterprises in Developing Countries.* ILO, Geneva, 1981.

Izuchukwu, John I. "Shortening the Critical Path." *Mechanical Engineering,* February 1990, pp. 59-60.

Jelen, Frederic C., and James H. Black. *Cost and Optimization Engineering.* McGraw-Hill, NY, 1983.

Jennett, Eric. "Guidelines for Successful Project Management." *Chemical Engineering,* July 1973, pp. 70-82.

Johnson, James R. "Advanced Project Control." *Journal of Systems Management,* Vol. 28, No. 5, May 1977, pp. 24-27.

Johnson, L. A., and D. C. Montgomery. *Operations Research in Production, Scheduling, and Inventory Control.* John Wiley & Sons, NY, 1974.

Johnson, R. A., F. E. Kast, and J. A. Rosenzweig. *The Theory and Management of Systems,* 2d ed. McGraw-Hill, NY, 1967.

Juran, J. M. *Juran on Planning for Quality.* The Free Press, NY, 1988.

Juran, J. M., and Frank M. Gryna, Jr. *Quality Planning and Analysis,* 2d, ed. McGraw-Hill, NY, 1980.

Keeney, R. L., and H. Raiffa. *Decisions with Multiple Objectives; Preferences and Value Trade-offs.* John Wiley & Sons, NY, 1976.

Keller, Robert T. "Project Group Performance in Research and Development Organizations." *Academy of Management Proceedings,* San Diego, CA, Aug. 11-14, 1985, pp. 315-318.

Keller, Robert T., and Ravi R. Chinta. "International Technology Transfer: Strategies for Success." *The Executive,* Vol. 4, No. 2, May 1990, pp. 4-11.

Kelley, Albert J., ed. *New Dimensions of Project Management.* Lexington Books, MA, 1982.

Kelley, James E. "Critical Path Planning and Scheduling: Mathematical Basis." *Operations Research,* Vol. 9, No. 3, 1961, pp. 296-320.

Kendrick, J. W. *Productivity Trends in the United States.* National Bureau of Economic Research, Princeton University Press, 1961.

Kerridge, Arthur E., and Charles H. Vervalin, eds. *Engineering and Construction Project Management.* Gulf Publishing Company, Houston, TX, 1986.

Kerzner, Harold. *Project Management: A Systems Approach to Planning, Scheduling, and Controlling,* 3d ed. Van Nostrand Reinhold, NY, 1989.

———. *Project Management Operating Guidelines: Directives, Procedures, and Forms.* Van Nostrand Reinhold, NY, 1986.

Kezsbom, Deborah S., Donald L. Schilling, and Katherine A. Edward, *Dynamic Project Management: A Practical Guide for Managers and Engineers.* John Wiley & Sons, NY, 1989.

Khorramshahgol, Reza, H. Azani, and Y. Gousty. "An Integrated Approach to Project Evaluation and Selection." *IEEE Transactions on Engineering Management,* Vol. 35, No. 4, 1988, pp. 265-270.

Kimmons, Robert L. *Project Management Basics: A Step-by-Step Approach.* Marcel Dekker, NY, 1990.

Kimmons, Robert L., and James H. Loweree. *Project Management: A Reference for Professionals.* Marcel Dekker, NY, 1989.

Koenig, Michael H. "Management Guide to Resource Scheduling." *Journal of Systems Management,* Vol. 29, January 1978, pp. 24-29.

Kolderie, Ted. "Currents and Soundings: The Two Different Concepts of Privatization." *Public Administration Review,* July/August, 1986.

Kondonassis, A. J., et al. *Major Issues in Global Development.* Continuing Education and Public Service, University of Oklahoma, Norman, OK, 1991.

Koontz, Harold, and Cyril O'Donnel. *Principles of Management,* 2d ed. McGraw-Hill, NY, 1959.

Koopmans, Tjalling C., ed. *Activity Analysis of Production and Allocation.* John Wiley & Sons, NY, 1951.

Kume, Hitoshi. *Statistical Methods for Quality Improvement.* Quality Resources, White Plains, NY, 1987.

Lapin, L. *Statistics for Modern Business Decisions,* 2d ed. Harcourt Brace Jovanovich, NY, 1978.

Lawrence, Kenneth D., and S. H. Zanakis. *Production Planning and Scheduling: Mathematical Programming Applications*. Industrial Engineering and Management Press, Norcross, GA, 1984.

Lee, Sang M., and H. B. Eom. "A Multi-Criteria Approach to Formulating International Project-Financing Strategies." *Journal of Operational Research Society*, Vol. 40, No. 6, 1989, pp. 519-528.

Levine, Harvey A. *Project Management Using Microcomputers*. McGraw-Hill, NY, 1986.

Liao, W. M. "Effects of Learning on Resource Allocation Decisions." *Decision Sciences*, Vol. 10, 1979, pp. 116-125.

Liberatore, Matthew J. "An Extension of the Analytic Hierarchy Process for Industrial R&D Project Selection and Resource Allocation." *IEEE Transactions of Engineering Management*, Vol. EM34, No. 1, 1987, pp. 12-18.

Lighthall, Frederick F. "Launching the Space Shuttle *Challenger:* Disciplinary Deficiencies in the Analysis of Engineering Data." *IEEE Transactions on Engineering Management*, Vol. 38, No. 1, 1991, pp. 63-74.

Lillrank, Paul, and Noriaki Kano. *Continuous Improvement: Quality Control Circles in Japanese Industry*. Center for Japanese Studies, The University of Michigan, Ann Arbor, MI, 1989.

Lin, Ching-Yuan. *Developing Countries in a Turbulent World: Patterns of Adjustment since the Oil Crisis*. Praeger, NY, 1981.

Love, Sydney F. *Achieving Problem Free Project Management*. John Wiley & Sons, NY, 1989.

Machina, M. J. "Decision-Making in the Presence of Risk." *Science*, Vol. 236, May 1987, pp. 537-543.

Mackie, Dan. *Engineering Management of Capital Projects: A Practical Guide*. McGraw-Hill Ryerson, Toronto, Canada, 1984.

Madu, Christian N. "An Economic Decision Model for Technology Transfer." *Engineering Management International*, Vol. 5, No. 1, 1988, pp. 53-62.

Main, Jeremy. "When Public Services Go Private." *Fortune*, May 27, 1985.

Malcomb, D. G., J. H. Roseboom, C. E. Clark, and W. Fazar. "Application of a Technique for Research and Development Program Evaluation." *Operations Research*, Vol. 7, No. 5, 1959, pp. 646-699.

Malstrom, Eric M. *What Every Engineer Should Know about Manufacturing Cost Estimating*. Marcel Dekker, NY, 1981.

Maslow, Abraham H. "A Theory of Human Motivation." *Psychological Review*, Vol. 1, 1943, pp. 370-396.

McDavid, James C. "The Canadian Experience with Privatizing Residential Solid Waste Collection Services." *Public Administration Review*, September-October, 1985.

McEntee, Gerald W. "The Case against Privatization." *American City & County*, Jan. 1987.

McGregor, D. *The Human Side of Enterprise*, McGraw-Hill, NY, 1960.

Melcher, Bonita H., and Harold Kerzner. *Strategic Planning Development and Implementation*. TAB Professional and Reference Books, Blue Ridge Summit, PA, 1988.

Meredith, Jack R., ed. *Justifying New Manufacturing Technology.* Industrial Engineering and Management Press, Norcross, GA, 1986.

Meredith, Jack R., and Samuel L. Mantel, Jr. *Project Management: A Managerial Approach,* 2d ed. John Wiley & Sons, NY, 1989.

Meredith, Jack R., and Nallan C. Suresh. "Justification Techniques for Advanced Manufacturing Technologies." *International Journal of Production Research,* September-October 1986.

Merino, Donald N. "Developing Economic and Noneconomic Models Incentives to Select among Technical Alternatives." *The Engineering Economist,* Vol. 34, No. 4, Summer 1989, pp. 275-290.

Michaels, Jack V., and William P. Wood, *Design to Cost.* John Wiley & Sons, NY, 1989.

Miller, David M., and J. W. Schmidt. *Industrial Engineering and Operations Research.* John Wiley & Sons, NY, 1984.

Miller, Jule A. *From Idea to Profit: Managing Advanced Manufacturing Technology.* Van Nostrand Reinhold, NY, 1986.

Mizuno, Shigeru, ed. *Management for Quality Improvement.* Quality Resources, White Plains, NY, 1988.

Moder, Joseph J., Cecil R. Phillips, and Edward W. Davis. *Project Management with CPM, PERT, and Precedence Diagramming,* 3d ed. Van Nostrand Reinhold, NY, 1983.

Moffat, Donald W. *Handbook of Manufacturing and Production Management Formulas, Charts, and Tables.* Prentice-Hall, Englewood Cliffs, NJ, 1987.

Monden, Yasuhiro, R. Shibakawa, S. Takayanagi, and T. Nagao. *Innovations in Management: The Japanese Corporation.* Industrial Engineering and Management Press, Norcross, GA, 1985.

Moore, F. T. "Technological Change and Industrial Development, Issues, and Opportunities." World Bank Paper No. 613, Washington, D.C., 1983.

Moore, Laurence J., B. W. Taylor, III, E. R. Clayton, and Sang M. Lee. "Analysis of a Multi-Criteria Project Crashing Model." *AIIE Transactions,* June 1978, pp. 163-169.

Mueller, Frederick W. *Integrated Cost and Schedule Control for Construction Projects.* Van Nostrand Reinhold, NY, 1986.

Mustafa, Mohammad A., and Jamal F. Al-Bahar. "Project Risk Assessment Using the Analytic Hierarchy Process." *IEEE Transactions of Engineering Management,* Vol. 38, No. 1, 1991, pp. 46-52.

Mustafa, Mohammed A., and E. Lile Murphree. "A Multicriteria Decision-Support Approach for Project Compression." *Project Management Journal,* Vol. 20, No. 2, June 1989, pp. 29-34.

Navon, Ronie. "Financial Planning in a Project-Oriented Industry." *Project Management Journal,* Vol. 21, No. 1, 1990, pp. 43-48.

Nelson, C. A. "A Scoring Model for Flexible Manufacturing Systems Project Selection." *European Journal of Operations Research,* Vol. 24, No. 3, 1986, pp. 346-359.

Newman, Karin. *The Selling of British Telecom.* St. Martin's Press, NY, 1986.

Newman, William H., E. K. Warren, and A. R. McGill. *The Process of Management: Strategy, Action, Results,* Prentice-Hall, Englewood Cliffs, NJ, 1987.

Noori, Hamid. *Managing the Dynamics of New Technology: Issues in Manufacturing Management.* Prentice-Hall, Englewood Cliffs, NJ, 1990.

Noori, Hamid, and R. W. Radford. *Readings and Cases in the Management of New Technology: An Operations Perspective, Prentice-Hall.* Englewood Cliffs, NJ, 1990.

O'Brien, James J. *CPM in Construction Management,* 3d ed. McGraw-Hill, NY, 1984.

Obradovitch, M. M., and S. E. Stephanou. *Project Management: Risks and Productivity.* Daniel Spencer, Malibu, CA, 1990.

Olayiwola, Peter O. *Petroleum and Structural Change in a Developing Country: The Case of Nigeria.* Praeger, NY, 1987.

Onwuka, Ralph I., and Olajide Aluko. *The Future of Africa and the New International Economic Order.* St. Martin's Press, NY, 1986.

Oral, M., O. Kettani, and P. Lang. "A Methodology for Collective Evaluation and Selection of Industrial R&D Projects." *Management Science,* Vol. 37, No. 7, 1991, pp. 871-885.

Orczyk, Joseph J., and Luh-Maan Chang. "Parametric Regression Model for Project Scheduling." *Project Management Journal,* Vol. 22, No. 4, 1991, pp. 41-47.

Ostwald, Phillip F. *Cost Estimating for Engineering and Management.* Prentice-Hall, Englewood Cliffs, NJ, 1974.

Pandia, Rajeev M. "Transfer of Technology: Techniques for Chemical and Pharmaceutical Projects." *Project Management Journal,* Vol. 20, No. 3, Sept 1989, pp. 39-45.

Park, Chan S., and Gunter P. Sharp-Bette. *Advanced Engineering Economics.* John Wiley & Sons, NY, 1990.

Park, Chan S., and Young K. Son. "An Economic Evaluation Model for Advanced Manufacturing Systems." *The Engineering Economist,* Vol. 34, No. 1, Fall 1988, pp. 1-26.

Pegels, Carl C. "Start Up or Learning Curves—Some New Approaches." *Decision Sciences,* Vol. 7, No. 4, Oct. 1976, pp. 705-713.

Phillips, Don T., and A. Garcia-Diaz. *Fundamentals of Network Analysis.* Prentice-Hall, Englewood Cliffs, NJ, 1981.

Pienar, A., et al. "An Evaluation Model for Quantifying System Value." *IIE Transactions,* Vol. 18, No. 1, March 1986, pp. 10-15.

Pitts, Carl E. "For Project Managers: An Inquiry into the Delicate Art and Science of Influencing Others." *Project Management Journal,* Vol. 21, No. 1, 1990, pp. 21-23, 42.

Quinn, James Brian. "Managing Innovation: Controlled Chaos." *Harvard Business Review,* May-June, 1985, pp. 73-84.

Ravindran, A., Don T. Phillips, and James J. Solberg. *Operations Research: Principles and Practice,* 2d ed. John Wiley & Sons, NY, 1987.

Render, Barry, and Ralph M. Stair, Jr. *Quantitative Analysis for Management,* 3d ed. Allyn and Bacon, Needham, MA, 1988.

Renninger, John P. *Multinational Cooperation for Development in West Africa.* Pergamon Press, NY, 1979.

Roberson, Bruce F., and R. O. Weijo. "Using Market Research to Convert Federal

Technology into Marketable Products." *Journal of Technology Transfer,* Vol. 13, No. 1, Fall 1988, pp. 27-33.

Roman, Daniel D. *Managing Projects: A Systems Approach.* Elsevier, NY, 1986.

Rosenau, Milton D., Jr. *Project Management for Engineers.* Lifetime Learning Publications, Belmont, CA, 1984.

———. *Successful Project Management.* Lifetime Learning Publications, Belmont, CA, 1981.

Rothkopf, Michael H. "Scheduling with Random Service Times." *Management Science,* Vol. 12, No. 9, 1966, pp. 707-713.

Ruskin, Arnold M., and W. Eugene Estes. *What Every Engineer Should Know about Project Management.* Marcel Dekker, NY, 1982.

Saaty, Thomas L. *The Analytic Hierarchy Process.* McGraw-Hill, NY, 1980.

Samaras, Thomas T., and Kim Yensuang. *Computerized Project Management Techniques for Manufacturing and Construction Industries.* Prentice-Hall, Englewood Cliffs, NJ. 1979.

Saunders, Robert J., et. al. *Telecommunications and Economic Development.* World Bank Publication, Johns Hopkins University Press, Baltimore, MD, 1983.

Savas, E. S. "Intracity Competition between Public and Private Service Delivery." *Public Administration Review,* January–February 1981.

———. *Privatizing the Public Sector.* Chatman House, Totowa, NJ, 1982.

———. "Public vs. Private Refuse Collection: A Critical Review of the Evidence." *The Journal of Urban Analysis,* Vol. 6, 1979.

Schneider, Kenneth C., and C. R. Byers. *Quantitative Management: A Self-Teaching Guide.* John Wiley & Sons, NY, 1979.

Schultz, R. L., D. P. Slevin, and J. K. Pinto. "Strategy and Tactics in a Process Model of Project Implementation." *Interfaces,* May-June 1987.

Schwartz, S. L., and I. Vertinsky. "Multi-Attribute Investment Decisions: A Study of R&D Project Selection." *Management Science,* Vol. 24, 1977, pp. 285-301.

Shtub, A. "Scheduling of Programs with Repetitive Projects." *Project Management Journal,* Vol. 22, No. 4, 1991, pp. 49-53.

Silverman, Melvin. *The Art of Managing Technical Projects.* Prentice-Hall, Englewood Cliffs, NY, 1987.

———. *Project Management: A Short Course for Professionals,* 2d ed. John Wiley & Sons, NY, 1988.

Simon, H. A. *The New Science of Management Decision,* rev. ed. Prentice-Hall, Englewood Cliffs, NJ, 1977.

Smilor, Raymond W., and David V. Gibson. "Technology Transfer in Multi-Organizational Environments: The Case of R&D Consortia." *IEEE Transactions on Engineering Management,* Vol. 38, No. 1, February 1991, pp. 3-13.

Smith, David E. *Quantitative Business Analysis.* John Wiley & Sons, NY, 1977.

Somasundaram, S., and Adedeji B. Badiru. "Project Management for Successful Implementation of Continous Quality Improvement." *International Journal of Project Management,* Vol. 10, No. 2, May 1992, pp. 89-101.

Spinner, M. *Elements of Project Management: Plan, Schedule, and Control.* Prentice-Hall, Englewood Cliffs, NJ, 1981.

Sprague, J. C., and J. D. Whittaker. *Economic Analysis for Engineers and Managers.* Prentice-Hall, Englewood Cliffs, NJ, 1986.

Stark, Robert M., and Robery H. Mayer, Jr. *Quantitative Construction Management: Uses of Linear Optimization.* John Wiley & Sons, NY, 1983.

Stefani, Raymond T. "Optimal Control of a Developing Nation's Economy." *IEEE Transactions on Systems, Man, and Cybernetics,* Vol. SMC-13, No. 6, Nov.-Dec. 1983, pp. 1076-1089.

Stephanou, S. E., and M. M. Obradovitch. *Project Management: System Developments and Productivity.* Daniel Spencer, Malibu, CA, 1985.

Stevens, G. T., Jr. *Economic and Financial Analysis of Capital Investments.* John Wiley & Sons, NY, 1979.

Stuckenbruck, Linn C., ed. *The Implementation of Project Management: The Professional's Handbook.* Addison-Wesley, Reading, MA, 1981.

———. "The Matrix Organization." *Project Management Quarterly,* September 1979, Vol. 5, No. 3, pp. 21-33.

Swalm, Ralph O., and J. L. Lopez-Leautaud. *Engineering Economic Analysis: A Future Wealth Approach.* John Wiley & Sons, NY, 1984.

Taguchi, Genichi. *Introduction to Quality Engineering: Designing Quality into Products and Processes.* Quality Resources, White Plains, NY, 1986.

Taylor, Frederick, W. *Scientific Management.* Harper & Row Publishers, NY, 1911.

Tees, David W., and Wilkes, Stanley E., Jr. *The Private Connection: A Texas City Official's Guide for Contracting with the Private Sector.* Institute of Urban Studies, University of Texas, Arlington, 1982.

Thomas, D. Babatunde. *Importing Technology into Africa: Foreign Investment and the Supply of Technological Innovations.* Praeger, NY, 1976.

Toelle, Richard A., and J. Witherspoon. "From 'Managing the Critical Path' to 'Managing Critical Activities.'" *Project Management Journal,* Vol. 21, No. 4, 1990, pp. 33-36.

Troxler, Joel W., and Leland Blank. "A Comprehensive Methodology for Manufacturing System Evaluation and Comparison." *Journal of Manufacturing Systems,* Vol. 8, No. 3, 1989, pp. 176-183.

Tsubakitani, Shigeru, and Richard F. Deckro. "A Heuristic for Multi-Project Scheduling with Limited Resources in the Housing Industry." *European Journal of Operational Research,* Vol. 49, 1990, pp. 80-91.

Tushman, Michael L. and W. L. Moore, ed. *Readings in the Management of Innovation.* Ballinger, Cambridge, MA, 1988.

United Nations. "World Economy Forecast for 1988." United Nations, NY, 1988.

United Nations. *Cooperation between Latin America and Africa in the Field of External Trade.* United Nations, NY, 1982.

U.S. Department of Energy. *Cost & Schedule Control Systems: Criteria for Contract Performance Measurement: Work Breakdown Structure Guide.* U.S. Department of Energy, Office of Project and Facilities Management, Washington, D.C., 1981.

U.S. Government Printing Office. *International Economic Report of the President 1977.* GPO, Washington, D.C., 1977.

Pommerehne, Werner W., and Bruno S. Frey. "Public versus Private Production

Efficiency in Switzerland: A Theoretical and Empirical Comparison." *Urban Affairs Annual Review,* Vol. 12, 1977, pp 35-46.

Weseman, Edward H. *Contracting for City Services.* Innovations Press, PA, 1981.

Wiest, Jerome D., and F. K. Levy. *A Management Guide to PERT/CPM with GERT/PDM/DCPM and Other Networks,* 2d ed. Prentice-Hall, Englewood Cliffs, NJ, 1977.

Willborn, Walter. *Quality Management System: A Planning and Auditing Guide.* Industrial Press, NY, 1989.

Wit, Jan De, and Willy Herroelen. "An Evaluation of Microcomputer-Based Software Packages for Project Management." *European Journal of Operational Research,* Vol. 49, 1990, pp. 102-139.

Wood, O. Lew, and Errol P. EerNisse. "Technology Transfer to the Private Sector from a Federal Laboratory." *IEEE Engineering Management Review,* Vol. 20, No. 1, 1992, pp. 23-28.

World Bank. *Accelerated Development in Sub-Saharan Africa.* Agenda for Action, The World Bank, Washington, D.C., 1981, pp. 45-52.

――――. *World Development Report 1987.* Oxford University Press, Oxford, England, 1987.

――――. *World Development Report 1989.* Oxford University Press, Oxford, England, 1989.

Yunus, Nordin B., D. L. Babcock, and C. O. Benjamin. "Development of a Knowledge-Based Schedule Planning System." *Project Management Journal,* Vol. 21, No. 4, 1990, pp. 39-45.

Index